The Educator's Guide to
Mental Health Issues in the Classroom

The Educator's Guide to
Mental Health Issues in the Classroom

edited by

Frank M. Kline, Ph.D.
Seattle Pacific University
Seattle, Washington

and

Larry B. Silver, M.D.
Georgetown University Medical Center
Washington, D.C.

·P A U L·H·
BROOKES
PUBLISHING Cº ®

Baltimore • London • Sydney

Paul H. Brookes Publishing Co.
Post Office Box 10624
Baltimore, Maryland 21285-0624

www.brookespublishing.com

Typeset by International Graphic Services, Inc., Newtown, Pennsylvania.
Manufactured in the United States of America by
Sheridan Books, Fredericksburg, Virginia.

The information provided in this book is in no way meant to substitute for a medical
or mental health practitioner's advice or expert opinion. Readers should consult a
health or mental health professional if they are interested in more information. This
book is sold without warranties of any kind, express or implied, and the publisher
and authors disclaim any liability, loss, or damage caused by the contents of this
book.

Appendix B (Medications), which appears on pages 369–378, is in no way meant to
substitute for a physician's advice or expert opinion. Some medications listed in
Appendix B have not been officially approved for use with pediatric populations. A
medical professional may still prescribe such a medication if he or she believes that it
is suitable for a certain child or adolescent. Readers should consult a medical
practitioner if they are interested in more information.

Portions of Chapters 2, 4, 5, and 14 and Appendix B previously appeared in the
companion book *The Educator's Guide to Medical Issues in the Classroom* (Paul H.
Brookes Publishing Co., 2001) and are used by permission.

The stories in this book are based on the authors' experiences. Some of the vignettes
represent actual people and circumstances. In these cases, individuals' names and
identifying details have been changed to protect their identities. Other vignettes are
composite or fictional accounts that do not represent the lives or experiences of
specific individuals, and no implications should be inferred.

Library of Congress Cataloging-in-Publication Data
The educator's guide to mental health issues in the classroom / edited by Frank M.
Kline and Larry B. Silver.
      p.   cm.
   Includes bibliographical references and index.
   ISBN 1-55766-670-9 (pbk.)
   1. Students—Mental health—Handbooks, manuals, etc. 2. Mentally ill
children—Education—Handbooks, manuals, etc. I. Kline, Frank M. II. Silver, Larry B.
LB3430.E38 2004
371.7'13—dc22   2004043606

British Library Cataloguing in Publication data are available from the British Library.

Contents

About the Editors

Frank M. Kline, Ph.D., is Professor and Associate Dean and Director of Teacher Education at Seattle Pacific University in Washington State. He has served at Seattle Pacific University for a number of years in a variety of positions, all related to the preparation of educators. Prior to his positions at Seattle Pacific University, Dr. Kline was Assistant Professor of Special Education at Wichita State University in Kansas. Dr. Kline obtained his doctoral degree from The University of Kansas, where he was a research assistant at the Institute for Research in Learning Disabilities. Dr. Kline has also taught students with learning disabilities at the elementary and secondary levels.

Dr. Kline's research interests include collaboration between professional communities. He has written about and surveyed the actual and potential relationships among school personnel, physicians, and mental health workers. Dr. Kline has also written extensively on a number of topics related to educational systems change, learning disabilities, and overall special education issues.

Dr. Kline is an active member of the Learning Disabilities Association of America. He serves on the organization's Conference Program Committee and Professional Advisory Board and is co-editor of its publication *Learning Disabilities: A Multidisciplinary Journal.* In addition, Dr. Kline was co-editor of *The Educator's Guide to Medical Issues in the Classroom* (Paul H. Brookes Publishing Co., 2001).

Larry B. Silver, M.D., is a child and adolescent psychiatrist in private practice in the Washington, D.C., area. He is Clinical Professor of Psychiatry at Georgetown University Medical Center, Washington, D.C. Prior to his current work, Dr. Silver was Acting Director and Deputy Director of the National Institute of Mental Health. Previously, he was Professor of Psychiatry, Professor of Pediatrics, and Chief of the Division of Child and Adolescent Psychiatry at Robert Wood Johnson Medical School in New Jersey.

For more than 30 years, Dr. Silver's research, clinical, and teaching interests have focused on the psychological, social, and family impacts of a group of related, neurologically based disorders: learning disabilities, language disabilities, sensory integration dysfunction, and attention-deficit/hyperactivity disorder. Among his more than 150 publications are the books *The Misunderstood Child: Understanding and Coping with Your Child's Learning Disabilities, Third Edition* (Times Books, 1998), *Attention-Deficit Hyperactivity Disorder: A Clinical Guide to Diagnosis and Treatment for Health and Mental Health Professionals, Third Edition* (American Psychiatric Publishing, 2004), and *Dr. Larry Silver's Advice to Parents on Attention Deficit Hyperactivity Disorder, Second Edition* (Times Books, 1999). Dr. Silver also was co-editor of *The Educator's Guide to Medical Issues in the Classroom* (Paul H. Brookes Publishing Co., 2001).

Dr. Silver is an active member of the Learning Disabilities Association of America, serving as President of the organization. In 1992, he received the Learning

Disabilities Association Award, the organization's highest award, for outstanding leadership in the field of learning disabilities. In 1996, he received the American Academy of Child and Adolescent Psychiatry's Berman Lifetime Achievement Award for his contributions to the study and treatment of learning disabilities.

About the Contributors

Rochelle Caplan, M.D., is Professor of Psychiatry in the Department of Psychiatry and Biobehavioral Sciences at University of California, Los Angeles (UCLA). She also directs UCLA's Pediatric Neuropsychiatry Program and Childhood Psychosis Clinic. In addition, Dr. Caplan is a member of UCLA's Mental Retardation Research Center and Pediatric Epilepsy Surgery Group.

Connie Kundahl Craig, M.N., Ph.D., is in private practice, serving children, adolescents, and families in Bellevue, Washington. Dr. Craig has devoted a great deal of her professional career to the educational challenges for youth and their families. Her clinical and research interests within these groups include depression, obsessive-compulsive disorder, and anxiety disorders.

Elisa Gagnon, M.S., has worked with children with autism and Asperger syndrome for 15 years. She is the author of *Power Cards: Using Special Interests to Motivate Children and Youth with Asperger Syndrome and Autism* (Autism Asperger Publishing Co., 2001) and *This Is Asperger Syndrome* (Autism Asperger Publishing Co., 1999). Ms. Gagnon works for Blue Valley Public Schools in Overland Park, Kansas, as a student service consultant.

Rosa A. Hagin, Ph.D., ABBP, is Research Professor of Psychology in the Department of Psychiatry at the New York University School of Medicine, is a fellow of the American Psychological Association, and holds the diplomate of the American Board of Professional Psychology. As a psychologist, Dr. Hagin's major work has been devoted to research, training, and clinical services for children and adults with a wide spectrum of learning disorders.

Anne Hammond-Meyer is a doctoral student in clinical psychology at Seattle Pacific University. She has a wealth of experience in working with women of size.

Cher N. Igelman, Ph.D., is Assistant Professor of School Counseling and Psychology at Seattle Pacific University. She is a licensed professional clinical counselor in Ohio and has clinical experience in the areas of diagnosis and treatment of mental health disorders, clinical supervision, school counseling, multicultural issues, substance abuse, and domestic violence.

Janine Jones, Ph.D., is a licensed clinical psychologist, nationally certified school psychologist, and a licensed marriage and family therapist. She earned a master's degree in marriage, family, and child counseling from the University of Southern California and a doctoral degree in school psychology from the University of Texas at Austin. Dr. Jones's full-time private practice, For A Child, serves children, adolescents, and their families in Seattle, Washington.

Kathleen Lehman, Ph.D., is a licensed psychologist and a nationally certified school psychologist with an educational background in counseling/clinical and school psychology. Dr. Lehman has worked with children and families in residential treatment, group care, foster care, outpatient clinic, community mental health, and school system settings. She is affiliated with the Center on Human Development and Disability and the Fetal Alcohol Syndrome Diagnostic and Prevention Network, both at the University of Washington in Seattle.

Don MacDonald, Ph.D., is Professor of Marriage and Family Therapy in the School of Psychology, Family, and Community at Seattle Pacific University. He teaches in the doctoral program in clinical psychology, the master's degree program in marriage and family therapy, and the bachelor's degree program in psychology. In addition to what his three children have taught him about working with young people, Dr. MacDonald's preparation and experiences as an elementary school teacher, high school counselor, college counselor, teacher educator, and community agency therapist have been invaluable.

Ginger MacDonald, Ph.D., is Professor and Director of the Education Program at the University of Washington in Tacoma. Dr. MacDonald is a former high school English teacher, community mental health counselor, and chair of school counseling and psychology programs. And, yes, she and Don MacDonald are married.

Sherry A. Moyer, B.S., is the former Executive Director of the Asperger Syndrome Coalition of the U.S. and the mother of a teenager with Asperger syndrome. Ms. Moyer currently provides therapeutic support in classroom settings to students with autism spectrum disorders; is the co-editor of *The MAPP,* an international newsletter about Asperger syndrome and other pervasive developmental disorders; and is a member of the professional advisory board of the Learning Disabilities Association of America.

Brenda Smith Myles, Ph.D., is Associate Professor of Special Education at The University of Kansas in Lawrence, where she co-directs a graduate program in Asperger syndrome and autism. She has written numerous articles and books on Asperger syndrome and autism, including *Asperger Syndrome and Adolescence: Practical Solutions for School Success* (co-authored with Diane Adreon; Autism Asperger Publishing Co., 2001), which won the Autism Society of America's Outstanding Literary Work of the Year for 2002, and *Asperger Syndrome and Difficult Moments: Practical Solutions for Tantrums, Rage, and Meltdowns* (co-authored with Jack Southwick; Autism Asperger Publishing Co., 2001). Dr. Myles is on the executive boards of several organizations, including the Organization for Autism Research and MAAP Services for the Autism Spectrum. She is also the editor of *Intervention in School and Clinic,* the journal with the third largest readership in the special education field.

Rick Ostrander, Ed.D., is Chief of Neuropsychology and Assistant Professor of Psychiatry at The Johns Hopkins University in Baltimore. His clinical and research interests include learning disabilities, childhood depression, and externalizing disorders.

Tamara Buker Parrott, B.A., has 10 years work experience in a variety of clinical and research settings. She is in the fourth year of her doctoral studies at Seattle

Pacific University. Ms. Parrott works in the Friends and Family Lab at Seattle Pacific University with Dr. Beverly J. Wilson, investigating family dynamics and peer relationships of elementary students around the Seattle area.

Katherine S. Quie, M.S., Ph.D., is a pediatric clinical psychologist at Fraser Child and Family Center in Minneapolis, Minnesota. In 2002, she earned a doctoral degree in clinical psychology from Seattle Pacific University, and she completed a postdoctoral fellowship in pediatric neuropsychology at Children's Hospital and Regional Medical Center in Seattle in 2003. Dr. Quie's research interests are related to the impact of marital and parenting factors on children's social and emotional development. She is also a co-investigator on a study about childhood cancer and the impact of father involvement on coping and perception of illness.

Scott Shiebler, M.S.W., Ph.D., is a senior staff member at the University of Washington Student Counseling Center in Seattle. Dr. Shiebler's work has brought him to public school and university settings, providing clinical services, training, and research in the areas of children, youth, and families. His specific clinical research interests include emotional, behavioral, and learning problems, in addition to masked depression in men.

Deborah R. Simkin, M.D., was a high school teacher for 10 years before going to medical school. She is Clinical Assistant Professor at Florida State University's College of Medicine in Tallahassee and is in private practice in Destin, Florida. Dr. Simkin also is Co-chair of the American Academy of Child and Adolescent Psychiatry's Adolescent Substance Abuse Committee and is the American Academy of Child and Adolescent Psychiatry's liaison to the American Academy of Pediatrics' Committee on Substance Abuse. In addition, she is an advisor to the National Task Force on Juvenile Justice. Dr. Simkin trained in child and adolescent psychiatry at McLean Hospital in Belmont, Massachusetts, and at Massachusetts General Hospital in Boston. She is board certified in adult, child, and adolescent and addiction psychiatry.

Christopher A. Sink, Ph.D., NCC, LMHC, is Professor of School Counseling and Chair of School Counseling and Psychology at Seattle Pacific University. He is the former editor of *Professional School Counseling* (the scholarly journal of the American School Counselor Association) and continues to serve on the journal's editorial board. For many years, Dr. Sink was also an associate editor for the refereed publication *National Association for Laboratory Schools Journal.* Dr. Sink previously served as a secondary and community college counselor. He received two distinguished service awards by state counseling organizations for his work on fostering comprehensive school counseling programs in Washington State. Publishing extensively in the areas of school counseling and educational psychology, his research and teaching interests focus on the role of school counselors in preventing school violence; promoting citizenship and moral education; developing systemic approaches to educational restructuring, including comprehensive school counseling programs; and the school-based communitarian movement. Dr. Sink works and consults with school districts across the United States as a comprehensive school counseling program developer and evaluator.

John Thoburn, Ph.D., is Associate Professor of Graduate Psychology at Seattle Pacific University. Dr. Thoburn is a licensed psychologist in Washington State and is board certified in family psychology.

Melissa L. Trautman, M.S., is a special education teacher for children with autism in the Blue Valley School District in Overland Park, Kansas.

Beverly J. Wilson, Ph.D., is Associate Professor in the Department of Graduate Psychology at Seattle Pacific University. In 1994, she earned a doctoral degree in developmental psychology at the University of Washington in Seattle. She has been at Seattle Pacific University since 1998. Her research investigates factors related to children's social and emotional competence, especially individual child differences such as physiological functioning and attention processes, as well as family factors.

Acknowledgments

In this era of specialization, a work of this scope is beyond the skill set of any one author. Without the expertise and knowledge of the contributors, this book would not exist. We thank and acknowledge their dedication to education and their wish to help teachers understand and educate students with mental health issues. We also recognize their scholarship and the excellent quality of their chapters.

Dedicated to general education classroom teachers
who are charged with serving ALL students!

The Educator's Guide to
Mental Health Issues in the Classroom

Mental Health Issues in Schools

Frank M. Kline

Schools have a mandate to serve all children; consequently, schools see more and more children with significant disabilities. Many of those children have mental health issues. Having a greater number of students with various disabilities, particularly mental health issues, means that schools are being challenged to provide appropriate educational opportunities.

Educators do not have a background in mental health, and mental health workers do not have a background in education. Section I of this book, therefore, seeks to provide basic background information to educators about mental health issues. Chapter 1 explores the need for such knowledge. It details the increasing numbers of students with mental health problems who are served in schools. It also points to potential uses for this book and provides an overview of its organizational structure.

Chapter 2 focuses on how mental health workers view brain–mind emotional interactions. Taking an historical approach, Chapter 2 explores the development of the professional opinion on the brain, mind, and emotional areas of human life.

Chapter 3 explains the various types of mental health workers. The chapter provides both the commonalities and contrasts among the different types of mental health workers, featuring clear descriptions of the strengths and capacities of each type of professional.

Chapters 1, 2, and 3 provide the background information and focus for *The Educator's Guide to Mental Health Issues in the Classroom*. The rest of the book takes on a larger meaning in light of the rationale provided by Chapter 1; the explanation of brain, mind, and emotional interactions laid out in Chapter 2; and the descriptions of various mental health professionals found in Chapter 3.

1

Introduction

Frank M. Kline

· ·

Chapter Concepts

- The rationale for this book
- Potential uses for this book
- The organization of this book

Growing numbers of students have significant mental health issues. A report from the Center for Mental Health in Schools suggests that in some schools, 75%–85% of students do not come to class ready and able to work. The report also suggests that 40%–50% of students will not be able to fulfill their educational potential. Although mental health issues are not the sole cause of these findings, they contribute significantly. The Bazelon Center for Mental Health Law conducted a study for Medicaid and found that approximately 5%–7% of students with no other disabilities received mental health services (Koyanagi, 1999). In addition, this study noted that an average of 20% of students have an emotional, behavioral, or mental health problem and that 70%–80% of these students can be classified as having serious emotional disturbances. A key point in this study is that only 5%–7% of these individuals are receiving mental health services; furthermore, their schools do not classify them as having disabilities, so they are not eligible for special education services. These statistics are important because they show that mental health issues are pervasive among all students, not just those in special education classes.

For students who are identified as having a disability and do receive special education services, the multidisciplinary teams who make identification and write individualized education programs (IEPs), as well as the teachers who serve these students, are turning to community resources outside of the school systems. Multidisciplinary teams are required by the mandates of the Individuals with Disabilities Education Act (IDEA) of 1990 (PL 101-476) and its amendments to consider outside evaluation results. Increasingly, mental health services are provided in school-based or school-linked services. There is still, however, significant opportunity and need for individual educators and mental health professionals to work together. Progressively more educators are finding themselves engaged in professional conversations with mental health professionals and in interpreting the ubiquitous paperwork generated by both the educational and mental health bureaucracies as part of their ongoing responsibilities. Mental health professionals have much to offer both general and special educators. Their view of a student's life provides a complementary perspective on the student's abilities.

The increase in school violence is another reason why *The Educator's Guide to Mental Health Issues in the Classroom* is important. The Center for School Mental Health Assistance at the University of Maryland School of Medicine found a steady increase in research on violence in society since the early 1980s (Acosta, Albus, Reynolds, Spriggs, & Weist, 2001). Furthermore, this research focuses on assessment of the violence rather than on prevention. Youth are exposed to increasing amounts of all types of violence, including physical and sexual abuse, domestic violence, community violence, gang warfare, juvenile delinquency, and dating violence. This exposure results in significant psychological effects, such as increased depression, posttraumatic stress disorder, aggression, memory problems, social withdrawal, and difficulties concentrating. Thus, much of the increase in violence stems from mental health problems but also causes significant mental health problems. That is, many of the manifestations of mental health problems include violence. At the same time, exposure to violence, especially over a period of time, can result in mental health problems. This situation creates a downward spiral of increasing violence. Although this situation is general to society as a whole, it is also manifested in schools.

Partially resulting from increased school violence and the recognition of increased mental health problems in schools, more school-based mental health service delivery models are being developed. This requires work with outside agencies, which adds significantly to both a school's capacity for service and the expectations of school personnel to assist in the provision of mental health services.

School-based and school-linked programs have been developed for purposes of early intervention, crisis intervention and prevention, and treatment of the increasing mental health problems seen among school-age children. In addition, schools are being seen as institutions through which positive social and emotional development can be fostered. There is evidence that schools may be the primary source of mental health assistance for students. As early as 1995, reports surfaced regarding schools as important places of mental health care for students. As many as three quarters of the students who have received mental health services have received them through their schools. For many, this was the only source of mental health care (Burns et al., 1995).

Therefore, this book is important because students' mental health needs are increasing. Students with mental health needs who are identified as being eligible for special education will undoubtedly bring their mental health files with them and occasionally will bring the mental health professional as well. Furthermore, the growing awareness of violence in schools indicates the need for additional expertise in mental health issues—not only to prevent violence but also to deal with the results of violence. Finally, interagency agreements between schools and various community agencies that provide mental health services have increased. This book, which is designed to assist educators in understanding and working with and through the mental health community, can assist educators in understanding the context, vocabulary, concepts, and treatment plans commonly used by mental health professionals. Careful and clear presentation of complex understandings from mental health professionals as well as discussion of the implications of mental health issues in educational settings help prepare educators for a collaborative experience with mental health professionals.

USES OF THIS BOOK

The general purpose of *The Educator's Guide to Mental Health Issues in the Classroom* is to help educators learn to work with mental health professionals. It accomplishes this aim by providing information about professions, vocabulary, and concepts of the mental health community. Increasing educators' familiarity with this information will allow more effective communication with mental health workers.

In addition, there are some specific uses for this book in academic environments. It will serve well as a supplementary text to various classes for training special education teachers. This text relates to classes about behavioral disorders or serious emotional disturbances. In addition, it could be used in an introductory class. Significant mental health issues are often secondary disabilities that result from late diagnoses, mistreatment, or other educational problems resulting in repeated failure. Other classes that may profit from using this text include any course for educators that has a mental health component.

Beyond its preservice use, this book will be useful to educators serving students who have mental health issues. This includes virtually all teachers and school administrators, as well as school counselors, nurses, social workers, and psychologists. In addition to being a primary source of information, the book is designed to serve as a reference.

ORGANIZATION OF THE BOOK

The Educator's Guide to Mental Health Issues in the Classroom is divided into five sections. Section I shares basic information about the context of mental health services. Chapter 2 provides basic information about presuppositions of the mental health community regarding interactions among the brain, the mind, and emotions. Chapter 3 includes information about the structure of the mental health community, detailing the training and duties of various types of mental health professionals.

Sections II–IV provide specific information about specific mental health issues. Section II covers biologically based disorders, including attention-deficit/hyperactivity disorder (Chapter 4), autism and pervasive developmental disorders (Chapter 5), Asperger syndrome (Chapter 6), and psychotic disorders (Chapter 7). Section III addresses four biologically based and/or psychologically based disorders: substance abuse (Chapter 8), eating disorders (Chapter 9), anxiety disorders (Chapter 10), and mood disorders (Chapter 11). Section IV focuses on behavioral disorders through chapters about peer disorders (Chapter 12), adjustment disorders (Chapter 13), and oppositional defiant and conduct disorders (Chapter 14). Each chapter in Sections II–IV describes the characteristics of, assessment of, and common treatment or interventions for the specific mental health issue. The chapters also give suggestions for addressing these types of mental health issues at school.

Section V provides information about collaboration among mental health workers, educators, and families. Chapter 15 gives educators basic information about collaborative efforts with mental health professionals. Chapter 16 suggests ways to work with families and describes patterns of family development typical to families with children who have significant impairments. Because the family is the key to successful treatment, such information is useful for teachers working with families whose children have mental health problems.

The appendixes at the end of *The Educator's Guide to Mental Health Issues in the Classroom* are references regarding mental health issues in school. Appendix A provides the common diagnostic criteria for the mental health issues covered in Sections II–IV. Appendix B includes information on medications, along with suggestions on how to find regular updates on information about medications. Appendix C lists various professional and support organizations that are relevant to the topics discussed in this book.

The Educator's Guide to Mental Health Issues in the Classroom is designed to assist educators in collaborating with mental health workers. Research shows the need for such collaboration. Furthermore, there is evidence that such collaborative efforts are increasing. This book provides basic information about professions in the mental health field, specific types of mental health issues found in schools, and methods and conditions necessary for collaboration among educators, mental health professionals, and families.

REFERENCES

Acosta, O.M., Albus, K.E., Reynolds, M.W., Spriggs, D., & Weist, M.W. (2001). Assessing the status of research on violence-related problems among youth. *Journal of Clinical Child Psychology, 30,* 152–160.

Burns, B.J., Costello, E.J., Angold, A., Tweed, D., Strangl, D., Farmer, E., & Erkanli, A. (1995). Children's mental health service use across service sectors. *Health Affairs, 14,* 147–159.

Individuals with Disabilities Education Act (IDEA) of 1990, PL 101-476, 20 U.S.C. §§ 1440 *et seq.*

Koyanagi, C. (1999). *Making sense of Medicaid for children with serious emotional disturbance.* Washington, DC: Bazelon Center for Mental Health Law.

2

Brain–Mind Emotional Interactions in the Classroom

Larry B. Silver

• •

Chapter Concepts

- An understanding of the brain and the mind and how they interrelate
- A frame of reference for understanding the topics covered in this book

The learning process takes place in the brain. Thus, anything that influences the functioning of the brain will affect learning. The brain is unique in that it has a biological function (i.e., "the brain") and a behavioral function (i.e., "the mind"), which are interwoven. Changes in the brain result in changes in behavior, and changes in behavior might change brain functioning. The classroom is one of the key places where these brain–mind interactions are played out. Therefore, it is essential that educators understand these relationships. This chapter provides the background material needed to understand and apply the information in this book to teaching in the general education classroom.

OBSERVATION AND UNDERSTANDING OF BEHAVIOR

Observation and understanding of behavior have changed over time and continue to change. New knowledge requires rethinking of once-established concepts. Research since the mid-1970s has greatly influenced the understanding of brain–mind interactions. Although research on the structure and anatomy of the brain began centuries ago, knowledge of the physiology or functioning of the brain had to wait until modern research technology provided the necessary research tools.

Theological Model

The first formal model proposed to explain deviations from typical behavior was based in theology. In 1487, the *Malleus Maleficarum* [The Witches' Hammer] was published by two monks, Sprenger and Kramer, at the request of the Pope (discussed in Alexander & Selesnick, 1966, pp. 67–69). This document presents the devil as an explanation for inappropriate or bizarre behavior that had no other apparent explanation. This concept of understanding individuals who would be diagnosed as mentally ill by current standards predominated thinking for more than 400 years. Treatment was provided by theologians and was based on confronting and removing the influence of the devil. Exorcism and burning at the stake were not uncommon treatments. Although this concept is no longer accepted as a model for understanding mental illness, its influence remains in daily language. For example, phrases such as "This child has the devil in him," "The devil made me do it," and "I'm going to beat the devil out of you" are still common.

Intrapsychic Model

Freud was one of the first people to attempt to relate mental illness to the brain (Jones, 1953). In 1895, Freud reported that the brain was the site of mental illness. He was a physician; thus, he called the individual with this condition a *patient*. He believed that treatment was within the scope of medicine. In an effort to communicate what he observed, he developed a psychological model for studying interactions within the brain. His psychology was called an *intrapsychic model,* meaning that all problems occur within what he called the *psychic apparatus* of the brain. Freud stated that behavior does not just happen and may not be caused by outside influences. Yet, all behavior is meaningful. Freud introduced the concept of the *unconscious* to explain why it is not always possible for an individual to understand the reasons for his or her behavior. According to Freud, some feelings and thoughts influence behaviors, but these associated feelings and thoughts are not always consciously available to the individual. He referred to these hidden feelings and thoughts as *unconscious*.

Freud believed that it is necessary to understand the psychological functioning of the mind. He described internal drives within the brain that led to the desire to do certain behaviors, and he called the psychic apparatus for these drives the *id*. Also within the brain are value systems that define what one should do. Freud named the psychic apparatus for these concepts the *superego*. Finally, the mind has to integrate the demands of the id with the values of the superego, taking into account the realities of the outside world. Freud gave the name *ego* to the psychic apparatus for this executive function.

Psychoanalytic theory focuses on the interactions among these psychic systems, the outside world, and behaviors. The use of these concepts to understand behavior is called *psychoanalytic theory*, and the application of this theory to treat disorders is called *psychoanalysis* or *psychoanalytically oriented psychotherapy*. The goal of psychoanalytically oriented psychotherapy is to help the individual understand his or her concerns and conflicts and to assist in the development of coping methods. The therapist observes and learns of the interactions between the individual's internal thinking processes (i.e., basic wishes and needs, conscience or value system), and his or her ability to assess the realities of the outside world. A primary focus of this therapy is to identify the areas of conflict between these processes (which take the form of defense mechanisms) and to strengthen or build more appropriate defenses or coping skills.

Behavioral Model

Psychologists such as Pavlov, Thorndike, Watson, Skinner, and Hall began to question the importance of the intrapsychic model (Alexander & Selesnick, 1966). These researchers still viewed the brain as the site for behaviors, behavioral problems, and mental illness. Nonetheless, they considered the need to understand what happens within the brain (based on psychoanalytic theory) less important than understanding how the individual responded to specific inputs from the environment. Their focus was on understanding stimuli that are received and the resulting responses; thus, the *stimulus–response model* of behavior was developed. Treatments that evolved from this research include—among others—classical and operant conditioning, modeling, and cognitive behavioral therapy.

Behavioral observations are used to clarify that a child has learned inappropriate or unacceptable behaviors through reinforcement. Intervention targets decreasing unacceptable behavioral responses and increasing acceptable responses through manipulation of antecedent or consequent events. In addition to the individual's participation, this therapy might involve anyone in contact with the child, including teachers, administrators, peers, parents, and other family members. Observable behaviors are addressed. For example, the behavior of anxiety is addressed directly through the observable manifestations. The individual is taught specific behavioral techniques, including relaxation methods, to better control the manifestations that he or she observes.

Cognitive behavioral therapy is an extension of behavioral concepts. In this therapy model, feelings, thoughts, and actions—instead of observable behaviors—are the focus of intervention. Often, an individual is unable to observe and understand the influence that feelings, thoughts, and actions have on each other. Interventions focus on helping one become more aware of the relationships among feelings, thoughts, and actions as well as learning how to gain better control over inappropriate interpretations or interactions.

Interpersonal Model

In the 1950s, another model for observing behavior was developed. The importance of the brain remained, but the focus shifted to understanding behaviors based on the interactions between individuals. How does one relate to others, and what responses are created in others? Harry Stack Sullivan was one of the early writers on the interpersonal model (Alexander & Selesnick, 1966, pp. 365–367). Within this model, assessment focuses on the interactions between the individual and parents or other significant adults (e.g., teachers) and between the individual and siblings or significant peers. Does the child or adolescent repeat the same patterns of interacting with each adult or peer? How did the individual learn to interact in this way? Interpersonal theory focuses on models for understanding these issues.

Interpersonal problems might be treated by recreating life situations within a group. Group therapy focuses on observing and commenting on styles of interacting. New approaches and strategies are taught and tested. Role playing and practicing more appropriate interactions lead to generalizations in real-life situations.

Systems Model

The systems model, perhaps the newest model for understanding behavior, began to be conceptualized in the 1950s. The concept was first described by Stanton and Schwartz (1954). A *system* is defined as a group of people with common boundaries, functions, and expected behaviors. The most critical system is the family system, in which there are clear boundaries. The expected behaviors for each member are established. Because the system is closed and has boundaries, any change by one member of the system will affect the other members of the system. This model is different from previous models in that it focuses on the system and not on the individual. Deviant or disruptive behaviors are seen as reflective of the interactions within the system. In this model, there are no patients. The system is the concern. The person being evaluated is called the *identified patient.* Children and adolescents learn patterns of behavior within the family that allow the family to function. They may carry these behaviors into other systems, such as with peers or in school, where such behaviors may not be functional.

Family therapy addresses the child or adolescent whose problems reflect difficulties within the family. The stresses within the family are assessed and addressed. These stresses might be related to marital problems, difficulties experienced by one of the parents, problems with another child in the family, problems experienced by the identified patient, or poor parenting skills. Family therapy focuses on establishing a healthier equilibrium within the family, thereby freeing up the identified patient to try different behaviors in other systems (e.g., in school, with peers).

Biological Model

With increasing knowledge of the brain and brain functioning, it is possible to understand that many behaviors reflect structural, physiological, or chemical difficulties within the brain. Some disabilities are explained by alterations or malfunctions in the basic structures of specific systems in the brain (i.e., "faulty wiring"). Other disabilities may be the result of deficiencies of specific chemicals (e.g., neurotransmitters) within the brain. Understanding genetic influences on brain development also helps explain certain problems. The relatively new understanding that environment stimuli (e.g., speaking to an infant, engaging an infant in play) influence brain development adds another perspective in explaining brain development.

The biological model has resulted in a better understanding of many emotional disorders. It also has led to improved interventions and medications used to treat disorders such as anxiety, depression, anger control, and obsessive-compulsive disorder (OCD). Increased knowledge of the neurological dysfunctions caused by altered or faulty wiring within the cortex has led to better understanding of reading disorders, written language disorders, and other learning disabilities.

The Biopsychosocial Model

At the beginning of the 21st century, it is clear that each of the previously mentioned models is helpful in understanding specific behavioral problems and psychiatric disorders. Behavior is understood by studying the brain and brain functioning, as well as by studying the mind and mind functioning. It is this total view that helps one interpret behaviors and determine how best to address atypical behaviors. Clinical interventions are often multimodal, involving more than one approach to treatment. Such interventions might include engaging in individual psychoanalytically oriented psychotherapy, behavioral therapy, group therapy, and/or family therapy along with using appropriate medications, addressing school or community issues, and helping the individual handle problems with information-processing difficulties. The goal is to understand and to treat the total individual in his or her total environment.

This book is based on the biopsychosocial model for understanding students in the general education classroom. The information in this book will help the educator understand the brain–mind interactions that are observed and experienced within the general education environment.

ROAD MAP FOR UNDERSTANDING BRAIN–MIND INTERACTIONS FROM THE PERSPECTIVE OF THE BRAIN

If something affects the brain, the result might involve more than one part of the brain. Thus, it is not uncommon to find that children and adolescents might have more than one difficulty to address. For example, many children who have attention-deficit/hyperactivity disorder (ADHD) also have learning disabilities. This association demonstrates a continuum of neurologically based disorders. In approximately 50% of children and adolescents who have such neurologically based disorders, there is a familial pattern. That is, there appears to be a genetic pattern, and it is not unusual to find that a parent, sibling, or extended family member has the same disorder.

A full understanding of this impact does not yet exist. It appears that something influences the early development of the brain. In approximately 50% of individuals who have a neurologically based disorder, this appears to be directed by the genetic code instructing the brain to develop differently—hence, the observed familial pattern. At the beginning of the 21st century, only early information is available as to the cause for the other 50%.

Before further explaining this continuum, it is important to understand that the brain is immature at birth. Every nerve cell (neuron) that one has during a lifetime is present at birth. Growth after birth occurs by changes in these nerve cells. Areas of the brain may expand by branching and connecting with others. Other areas might decrease in size. These growth phases are called *maturational spurts.* This growth takes place throughout childhood and adolescence and into early adulthood. Each maturational spurt is analogous to someone going to a computer store and buying a software package. Once the software installed, the computer can do things it could not do before. So, too, with each activation of new areas within the brain, the brain can do things it could not do before. As each new area activates, there are two possibilities. It may be that the wires in this area were not affected initially and are wired "normally." Thus, when this area of the brain begins to work, the individual suddenly can do things that were difficult before. It is also possible that when this area of the brain begins to work, it will be apparent that this area is wired differently. There will be difficulties, but until this area begins to work, there is no way of knowing whether the brain's growth spurt would result in typical functioning. New problems may arise as new brain functions are required.

This process is the reason why a child may struggle with and then suddenly master something that was difficult before. It is great to be the teacher working with such a child at this time, as the child suddenly makes significant progress.

This is also the reason why, over time, a child may improve in one area only to have another area of difficulty become apparent. This continuum of neurologically based disorders is first explained in the ensuing discussion on problems related to the cortex of the brain. A discussion on problems in other areas of the brain follows.

Cortically Based Problems

The cortex, or thinking part of the brain, has many functions. Four basic functions are explored for the purposes of this discussion: 1) language skills, 2) muscle (motor) skills, 3) thinking (cognitive) skills, and 4) organization/planning (executive function) skills. In reality, these areas interact and overlap; however, it is easier to begin understanding them by considering each separately. Any or all of these areas might be wired differently.

If the area of the person's brain that is wired differently relates to language functioning, then the person has a language disability. The first clue may be a delay in language development, such as when a child does not speak or speaks with a limited vocabulary by 2–3 years of age. Some children may still have such difficulties by 4–5 years of age. If a speech-language pathologist works with the child, then it might be possible to speed up the development of language. This improvement may result in the parents sighing with relief; however, by 4–5 years of age, another problem might become apparent. For example, the child may have difficulty with processing and understanding what is being said (i.e., a receptive language disability) or with organizing thoughts, finding the right words, and speaking in a fluid and clear way (i.e., an expressive language disability). Early in elementary grades, another problem might become apparent. The first task in reading is language based. A child must recognize each unit of sound, or phoneme, and connect it to the correct unit of symbol, or grapheme. There are 44 phonemes in the English language. Each letter has a sound, vowels have a short and a long sound, and certain combinations (e.g., *sh, th, ch*) have their own sounds. There are 36 characters in the English language (i.e., the letters *a* through *z* and the numbers 0 through 9). To learn to read, a child must learn to break this code by learning which sounds go with which symbols and by sounding out words. Many children with a history of delay in language development and who later show receptive and expressive language problems have difficulties learning to read. Spelling is the reverse process. One must start with the language in the brain and connect it with the right grapheme by writing on the page. Children who have difficulty "getting language in" often have difficulty "getting language out." Thus, many children with reading problems because of a language disability also have problems with spelling.

If the area of the brain that is wired differently relates to the use of muscles, the child or adolescent has a motor disability. For some individuals, the primary problems relate to gross motor skills, or the ability to coordinate and use teams of large muscles, resulting in difficulty with activities such as running, jumping, skipping, or climbing. Others might have difficulty with fine motor skills, or coordinating and using teams of small muscles, resulting in difficulties with buttoning, zipping, tying, coloring, using scissors, using eating utensils, and writing. Still others might have a broader pattern of motor problems called sensory integration (SI) dysfunction. With SI dysfunction, in addition to difficulties with gross and/or fine motor planning functions, children may have difficulty interpreting information coming from nerve endings in the skin. They might be very sensitive to touch or the feeling of their clothes, or they may misread temperature or pain. They also may have difficulty processing information from their vestibular system, which is located in the inner ear and indicates where the body is in relation to gravity. Problems result with movement or position in space. Which of these many possible motor problems is present depends on the areas of the cortex involved.

If the area of the cortex that is wired differently relates to cognition, or processing information, the individual has a learning disability. Again, this division of the cortex is in some ways artificial, as more than one area of the brain is involved when a learning disability is present. The person with a learning disability might also have a language disability and/or SI dysfunction. This individual will have difficulty processing information, possibly resulting in difficulties mastering basic skills (e.g., reading, writing, math) or might involve higher-level functions (e.g., sequencing, abstraction, organization, memory).

The most recent evolutionary addition to the cortex is the sophisticated area in the front of the cortex that acts like the chief executive officer in a company. This area carries out what is called *executive function*. It orchestrates behaviors. This is the area that assesses a task or problem, decides how to tackle or solve the task, coordinates the necessary activities or functions, continually makes any needed mid-course changes or corrections, and eventually reaches a successful conclusion in a timely way. When this area of an individual's brain is wired differently, the person has difficulty with organizational planning and developing a strategy for successfully carrying out tasks.

Other Brain-Based Problems

Many functions of the brain are carried out by a network of interrelated systems, each communicating with the other to organize and execute specific tasks. One such system might be called the area of *vigilance*. This is the area of the brain that allows animals and humans to be hunters. To be a hunter, one needs the ability to sit very still so that the prey is not scared away, track the prey and not be distracted by any background activities, and strike just at the right time. Imagine a frog sitting on a lily pad, waiting to catch a fly. Not a muscle moves or the fly will leave. The frog's eyes track the fly without losing sight. At just the right moment, the frog's tongue comes out and catches the fly. Some children and adolescents have problems with the wiring in the area of vigilance. As a result they might be hyperactive, distractible, and/or impulsive—thereby exhibiting symptoms of ADHD.

Thus far, this brain-based road map demonstrates how some children have a learning disability. Others might have a language disability or SI dysfunction.

Still others might have ADHD. A student may have one, two, three, or all four of these problems. This child does not have multiple disorders. He or she has multiple manifestations of the initial underlying problem that resulted in areas of the brain being wired differently.

Modulating Disorders

Beginning in the 1980s, dramatic new methods for studying the brain began to provide explanations for other areas of difficulty. Another network of interrelated systems allows modulation of specific functions. This network maintains emotional equilibrium, helping one avoid extremes. Many functions need to be modulated. If any specific area is involved, a problem modulating this specific function results. The specific modulating problem often is present and can be noted by the early months of life or by early childhood.

Some individuals have difficulty modulating anxiety. They have an early history of being high-strung or anxious. Over the years the focus of the anxiety may change, but the central theme is a high level of anxiety. For example, a child might be afraid to go to sleep alone. Later, he or she might have a fear of being in part of the house alone or a fear of robbers. Another child might be afraid of bees or a natural disaster. If the anxiety becomes significant enough to cause emotional discomfort, the child has an anxiety disorder. He or she might have so much difficulty regulating anxiety that the level gets high enough to trigger a physical (i.e., fight-or-flight) response. During panic attacks, an individual's heart may pound, or he or she may break out into a sweat or feel weak. A person who has repeated panic attacks has what is called *panic disorder*.

Another modulating problem relates to anger. A child or adolescent with this disorder has been particularly irritable and angry since early childhood and has always had tantrums. As the child grows, he or she shows a specific clinical problem with regulating anger called *intermittent explosive disorder.* Thus, when the child gets angry, he or she does not simply have a tantrum or pout or slam doors. The child has a short fuse, exploding so quickly that the cause of the anger is not often apparent. Once this individual passes his or her threshold, he or she loses it and has what parents often call a "meltdown." The person may yell, scream, curse, hit, throw, and/or threaten others. The individual acts irrationally and does not respond to reason. Sometimes the child's thinking seems paranoid, as he or she might say people are trying to hurt him or her. The episode can last 5–15 minutes or more and ends almost as abruptly as it started. Once finished, the child may be tired and want to rest or sleep. He or she usually does not want to discuss what happened and seems confused about the behavior. Later comments might suggest feelings of remorse. Children with this problem behave in a Dr. Jekyll/Mr. Hyde manner.

Other children or adolescents might have difficulty modulating mood. They seem to be unhappy or sad much of their life. Some will develop a depressive disorder. A few children or adolescents may show difficulty modulating not only depression but also the reverse state, showing excessive excitement or manic behaviors. These individuals also might have difficulty regulating anger and vacillate between being pleasant and irritable or even explosively angry. The disorder involving such mood swings is called *bipolar disorder* (formerly called *manic-depressive disorder*).

Another modulating disorder, OCD, relates to the ability to regulate thoughts and behaviors. Some individuals have difficulty controlling their thoughts and experience the need to rethink a thought or thought pattern. These intrusive thoughts are called *obsessions*. Others might have difficulty regulating behaviors. They become anxious and feel the need to do certain things to relieve the anxiety. They know their actions are silly, but they cannot stop. They might need to touch things a certain way or number of times. They might need to check and recheck things (e.g., whether the front door is locked, whether the stove is off). They might need to perform certain patterns or rituals, or they might need to hoard or save things. Another pattern that might be seen is nail biting; picking at cuticles, sores, and scabs; or twisting and pulling out hair, eyelashes, or eyebrows.

One additional area of difficulty with modulation often found within this continuum is related to regulating certain patterns of motor functions. Individuals with this problem experience motor tics, or clusters of muscles contracting. Others might have the need to express certain sounds or words in the form of vocal tics. These individuals have a tic disorder. A specific form of a tic disorder that has a strong familial pattern and involves both motor and vocal tics is called *Tourette syndrome*.

The Clinical Picture

The brain is a fascinating part of the body that has many functions. If something affects the brain early in development, areas of the brain will develop differently. The difficulties that develop depend on which areas of the brain are involved. It is not unusual for individuals to have one or more of these disorders. They are comorbid, meaning that clinically, they often occur together.

In sum, this continuum of neurologically based disorders includes the following:

1. Cortical problems
   - Language disabilities
   - Motor disabilities
   - SI dysfunction
   - Learning disabilities
   - Executive function disorders
2. ADHD
3. Modulating disorders
   - Anxiety disorders
   - Anger-regulation disorders

- Mood disorders

- OCD

- Tic disorders

ROAD MAP FOR UNDERSTANDING BRAIN–MIND
INTERACTIONS FROM THE PERSPECTIVE OF THE MIND

In general, the behavior of a child or adolescent with a neurologically based modulating disorder is chronic and pervasive. That is, it lasts over a significant period of time and manifests in almost all areas of the person's life. The brain has been with the individual all of his or her life; thus, the behavioral pattern is chronic. In addition, the brain is always with the individual; thus, the behavioral pattern is pervasive. Such behaviors differ from those that suggest that an individual is under stress. Stress-induced behaviors start at a certain time or occur only in certain situations. For example, the behaviors do not arise until a child's parents separate, or they occur in school but not at home.

When a child or adolescent experiences change or stress, he or she often feels anxiety or sadness. For example, many students feel anxious when they graduate from elementary school and move on to middle school. They may also feel sad about leaving the safe and known world of elementary school. Such reactions are normal. When a child or adolescent experiences increased or prolonged stress, however, he or she will experience increasing levels of anxiety and/or depression. _It is important to realize that behavior is a message, not a diagnosis._ The observed behavior demonstrates how an individual is handling the anxiety and/or depression caused by stress. It does not tell or explain what is causing the stress. It is essential to find out whether the stress is the result of family dysfunction, abuse, peer or community problems, academic difficulties, or any of numerous other possibilities. Only with this knowledge is a comprehensive intervention strategy possible. Coping methods may include internalizing stress, externalizing stress, somatizing stress, or using other approaches to cope with stress.

Internalizing Stress

Some children become very aware of their problems and feel anxiety, depression, or both. These feelings are seen in school and at home. The cause may be apparent, such as a recent divorce or death of a family member. For some children, however, the cause may need to be ascertained.

Anxiety A student might focus his or her anxiety on school, showing a fear of going to school (i.e., school avoidance) or a fear of doing schoolwork. This anxiety might expand into generalized anxiety disorder. For example, the child might be afraid to ride on the school bus. The child may become so upset when doing homework that he or she will not start or will become upset as soon as difficulty with the work is encountered. It is possible that the student will become fearful in the classroom. He or she may become unavailable for learning by withdrawing from any potentially frustrating or uncertain situations—either by becoming upset and resisting work or by pulling back and becoming passive.

Depression Some children experience stress by keeping their sadness inside and becoming depressed. The symptoms of depression in older children and adolescents may be similar to those in adults: sadness, crying, difficulty sleeping, loss of appetite, or irritability. Younger children might only express their sadness by being irritable and aggressive. Some children and adolescents may become self-destructive, speak of life as not being worth living, or mention wanting to commit suicide. The following two vignettes exemplify depression in an adolescent and a child, respectively.

David, an 11-year-old with learning disabilities and a long history of academic failures, describes himself as a troublemaker. He often says he is stupid or that he cannot learn anything. He gets mad at himself when he makes mistakes. His parents describe him as an unhappy child who gets no pleasure from anything.

• •

Bobby, age 8, is very intelligent; however, because no one identified his learning disabilities early, he failed often. In fact, he is currently starting second grade for the second time. When asked how he reacts in school when he cannot do his work, Bobby replied, "When I was younger I got mad. I used to scribble on my paper and be angry. School was no fun. Now, I get scared all of the time that the teacher will be mad with me or that I won't know how to do the work. I get so worried that I can't pay attention."

• •

Externalizing Stress

Some children and adolescents find it too difficult to cope with the discomfort and pain of stress. In addition, the resulting anxiety and depression add to the stress. They decide not to cope with the stress but, instead, to get rid of it. They externalize the anxiety and depression by projecting all of their problems onto others and accepting no responsibility for their problems. Suddenly, their behavioral or academic problems are because this kid did this and that kid did that. They get into fights and insist that the fights are due to someone else's behavior. "Don't blame me! He started it," is a common refrain.

By projecting all of the blame onto others, a child does not have to accept responsibility for his or her problems. Thus, a student who externalizes stress does not seem anxious or depressed. However, parents, teachers, and adults who care about this student may feel anxious and depressed. Because these children do not accept responsibility for their behaviors, they do not see a need for help.

Disruptive Behavior Disorders   According to the text revision of the *Diagnostic and Statistical Manual for Mental Disorders, Fourth Edition* (DSM-IV-TR; American Psychiatric Association, 2000), children and adolescents receive diagnoses based on the extent of their externalizing behaviors. An individual who externalizes stress primarily within the family by challenging rules and becoming oppositional and defiant has an oppositional defiant disorder (ODD). If the individual's behaviors expand beyond the family—leading to problems with other authority figures (e.g., teachers, principals, police officers) and resulting in challenging school and society rules, fighting, and stealing—then the individual has conduct disorder (CD). It is important to understand that a diagnosis of ODD or CD describes how the student is coping but does not identify the cause of the stress.

Somatizing Stress

A child or adolescent may focus his or her anxiety and depression onto bodily functions. A child might develop stomachaches, lower abdominal cramps, headaches, diarrhea, or frequent urination or bowel movements. These complaints might occur only on school-day mornings or just before a test. A child might need to leave class to go to the school nurse or to go home. As with any physical symptom, the discomfort is real. The pain goes away when the child is allowed to be in a situation that avoids the stress. For a child with an academic difficulty, staying home from school often relieves the stress, and the symptom goes away. The following examples demonstrate somatic symptoms of stress.

Seven-year-old Katie said, "Sometimes I get into trouble because I forgot to do what the teacher said or I erase too much. The teacher yells at me, and I get scared. Then my stomach starts to hurt and I have to go to the nurse."

. . . .

Eight-year-old Franklin woke up each school day with severe stomach cramps and vomiting. His mother kept him home from school, and the pains usually disappeared by noon. A complete medical workup found Franklin perfectly healthy. He must have guessed why he was taken to a child psychiatrist. His first words to the psychiatrist were, "I know my stomach trouble is because I'm afraid of school. Only, it really does hurt—no kidding!"

. . . .

Other children may explain their anxiety by focusing on their increasing awareness that something must be wrong with them. They hear parents or teachers talking about them. They may have been to several professionals for evaluations. They begin to express their worries through hypochondria. "My back hurts," "My head aches," or "My knee feels funny." Sometimes this concern with their body extends into a general concern with body image or body damage. At times these complaints become a complete rationalization for failure: "I can't help it if I made a mistake. My arm hurts today."

Adolescents might somatize their stress through eating disorders such as anorexia and bulimia. These disorders can be very serious and are addressed in Chapter 9.

Other Approaches to Coping with Stress

Some children or adolescents may express their stress in the way that they interact with others or influence their environment. Their behaviors reflect these problems.

Clowning Behavior Some children cope with their stress by becoming the class clown. This behavior is often found in students with academic difficulties. Clowning behavior serves several functions. It can be a way of controlling feelings of inadequacy by covering up feelings of worthlessness and depression. By playing the clown, a child seems to be saying, "They call me a clown, but that's only because I choose to be one. I really can turn it off if I want to, but it's too much fun this way." If the child succeeds in this behavior, he or she disrupts the lesson plan or is told to leave the group, thus avoiding the academic work and potential failure. Clowning behavior may win a certain measure of peer acceptance. Suddenly, the child everyone teased as being dumb becomes the class hero because of what he or she does. As a result, clowning behaviors are reinforced.

Anger-Handling Styles One indirect style of expressing difficulty with feelings is passive-aggressive behavior. The child's behavior is not actively aggressive, yet the child seems to make everyone angry with him or her. The student might dawdle in class, making the teacher angry. Or he or she might be so cooperative and helpful that it actually angers others.

Other children might be passive-dependent. Initially, a child avoids unpleasant feelings by staying out of the situations that cause such feelings. He or she avoids taking initiative for anything and minimizes getting involved in activities. A truly helpless child arouses sympathy in adults; however, passive-dependent behaviors often make people angry because the helplessness appears to be deliberate and contrived.

THE MIND, THE BRAIN, AND EDUCATION

Teaching takes place in the classroom. Learning takes place in the brain. Anything that affects brain function may also affect learning and behavior. In addition, anything that creates stress within a student might influence behavior and availability for learning.

The goal of teaching is to facilitate learning, and anything that affects learning or a student's availability for learning will affect teaching. The teacher, then, may become part of the breakdown in learning that results from such difficulties. Yet, the classroom is the exciting laboratory in which the brain and mind interact in a positive way, resulting in positive growth and development. Thus, the general education classroom teacher is also the best person to recognize evidence of problems, to recommend that necessary evaluations are completed, to provide essential information in the diagnostic process, and to participate in the treatment plan.

REFERENCES

Alexander, F.G., & Selesnick, S.T. (1966). *The history of psychiatry.* New York: HarperCollins Publishers.

American Psychiatric Association. (2000). *Diagnostic and statistical manual of mental disorders* (4th ed., text rev.). Washington, DC: Author.

Jones, E. (1953). *The life and works of Sigmund Freud: Vol. I.* New York: Basic Books.

Stanton, A.H., & Schwartz, M.S. (1954). *The mental hospital.* New York: Basic Books.

3

Structure of the
Mental Health Profession

Larry B. Silver

• •

Chapter Concepts

- Groups of mental health professionals with which general education teachers interact
- General types of clinical interventions provided by mental health professionals
- Systems of diagnostic categories used by mental health professionals

Gaining a general understanding of the mental health field helps educators communicate and, in turn, collaborate more effectively with mental health professionals. To that end, this chapter provides information about various mental health professions. In addition, it gives an overview of intervention and diagnostic concepts that are common in the field.

TYPES OF MENTAL HEALTH PROFESSIONALS

Several types of professionals provide mental health services to children and adolescents—psychiatrists, psychologists, social workers, psychiatric nurses, and mental health counselors. These professionals might be in private practice, part of a mental health organization, or part of a public school system. All mental health professionals share a core of common knowledge and skills in diagnosis and treatment, but each group also has unique areas of expertise. Each requires different levels of training and certification. Therefore, it is perfectly acceptable to ask any mental health worker about his or her experiences and skills.

Before proceeding, it is important to note that not all mental health professionals, even if fully qualified within their discipline, are equally competent to work with children and adolescents. Not all can conduct psychological testing or prescribe medication. Not all are familiar with school systems or the special issues that school systems face. Those with specialized training with this age group are the most qualified.

Psychiatrist

A psychiatrist is a medical doctor (a physician). A general psychiatrist has completed medical school and the training required to become a general physician. He or she also completes 4–5 additional years of specialized training in psychiatry. Most of this training focuses on working with adults; however, part of the training includes experiences working with children and adolescents. A child and adolescent psychiatrist has completed the medical education and psychiatry training required to become a general psychiatrist as well as 2 additional years of training in child and adolescent psychiatry.

Because of their medical training, general psychiatrists and child and adolescent psychiatrists are familiar with the biological and the psychological aspects of diagnosis and treatment. Among all mental health professionals, only psychiatrists can prescribe medication and admit patients to the hospital. (There are a few exceptions; in some states, psychologists with additional training can prescribe medication.) All psychiatrists are trained in psychopharmacological treatments as well as in individual therapy. Many are also trained in group and/or family therapy. Because of their additional 2 years of specialized training, child and adolescent psychiatrists may be the most qualified to assess and treat individuals with a mixture of neurological, psychological, and social problems.

Psychologist

A psychologist usually has a doctoral degree, which is a requirement for practice in most states. This degree, which may be a Ph.D. or a Psy.D., is typically in clinical, counseling, school, or developmental psychology. The doctoral-level psychologist has completed 4–6 or more years of training beyond college, including a year-long internship to receive special clinical training. In some cases, a psychologist may practice with a master's degree. The master's-level psychologist has completed a 2-year graduate program beyond college.

Most psychologists have special training and skills in administering psychological and educational testing. Because training can occur in so many areas and numerous types of internships are available, psychologists have differing skills with particular age groups or approaches to therapy. Thus, the depth and variety of training in working with children or adolescents may vary. Because training and clinical experiences tend to differ for each psychologist, it is appropriate to clarify a psychologist's area of special interest.

Social Worker

A social worker has completed college plus a 2-year master's degree program in a graduate school of social work. (Some colleges offer a bachelor's degree in social work; however, individuals who only have a bachelor's degree cannot become clinically certified as described in the following passage.) Following the completion of a master's in social work (M.S.W.) degree, an individual must work under supervision for several years before becoming eligible to take the necessary clinical certifying examination. If the candidate completes the required hours of clinical supervision and passes this examination, he or she becomes a licensed clinical social worker (L.C.S.W.).

A social worker is not necessarily experienced in working with children and adolescents. The individual's diagnostic and treatment skills in working with children and adolescents depend on his or her experiences during the 2 years of supervised work, in other work situations, or through specific courses. Thus, having an L.C.S.W. certification does not clarify the age groups or types of therapy in which an individual has expertise.

Psychiatric Nurse

A psychiatric nurse may have completed a training program for a certificate as a registered nurse or may have obtained a bachelor's degree in nursing. Many psychiatric nurses also have a 2-year master's degree in psychiatric or mental health nursing. To be certified as a clinical specialist in psychiatric nursing, an individual must have a master's degree or a doctoral degree in psychiatric or mental health nursing or an acceptable equivalent. In addition, the candidate must pass a national certifying examination.

Psychiatric nurses with graduate school training have knowledge and skills comparable to those of other mental health professionals with a similar level of training. As most earn a nursing degree before getting the master's degree in mental health nursing, their focus may be based on their training in nursing and in a medical setting. Many psychiatric nurses focus on family therapy. However, many are also skilled in the forms of psychotherapy. As with social workers, having a clinical certification does not clarify areas of expertise. Skill levels are based on each individual's specific type of training and experience.

Mental Health Counselor

A mental health counselor's training is somewhat difficult to define. Doing so will become easier as the profession's national organization, the American Mental Health Counselors Association, has greater impact on the requirements for credentialing. Many mental health counselors have completed a 2-year graduate degree in counseling, then several years of supervised work experience. Following this training, candidates take a clinical certifying examination. If they pass, they are certified as mental health counselors.

It should be noted that the licensing laws in some states permit individuals with little to very little training and experience to identify themselves as counselors. Furthermore, some states do not offer a license to practice as a mental health counselor, even for individuals who are clinically certified by the National Board for Certified Counselors and Affiliates. Thus, the level of expertise and the specific level of training in working with children and adolescents must be clarified for each mental health counselor.

MENTAL HEALTH INTERVENTIONS

A biopsychosocial model is one of the more useful tools for understanding behavior (see Chapter 2). Understanding that *behavior is a message, not a diagnosis* is critical to assessing the needs of a child or adolescent. Behavior is a clue that, along with other observations and evidence, leads to a diagnosis. Diagnosis leads to a treatment plan and to treatment interventions based on the experiences of others with similar diagnoses. Thus, it is important that a competent clinician or a team of clinicians conducts the diagnostic process. The types of interventions used will be based on the diagnosis or diagnoses. These interventions might focus on the individual, the family, or the individual in a group setting, taking the form of medication, individual therapy, group therapy, and/or family therapy. Within each type of therapy, there are several approaches to consider. It is important that the mental health professional conducting the evaluation select the most appropriate intervention(s). In many cases, several models of therapy are used at the same time; this approach that is referred to as *multimodal therapy.*

It is always important to determine whether the presenting emotional, social, or family problems are the *cause* of the difficulties seen at school or whether the presenting emotional, social, or family problems are a *consequence* of the difficulties seen at school. That is, are the child's emotional problems causing behavioral problems in school, or does the child have unidentified—and, thus, untreated—

problems (e.g., learning disabilities)? If there are unidentified problems, the behavior seen at school may be a result of the child's feelings of frustration and failure rather than the root cause.

It is critical to clarify whether the observed problems are primary or secondary. If the emotional, social, or family problems are the result of an underlying problem, such as a learning disability, interventions focused on the behaviors will not be successful until the underlying problems are addressed. Treating the secondary problems without treating the underlying cause will not improve performance or behavior. For instance, if a child has a poor self-image because of academic frustration and failure, psychotherapy will not improve his or her self-image until the proper special education services are provided.

Occasionally, the type or mode of therapy may need to change over time. For example, if the family is in crisis, it may be necessary to do family therapy first. Once the family is more stable, the underlying reasons for the family dysfunction might become clear and other treatment approaches might be used. The following subsections provide brief descriptions of five common approaches to therapy: psychoanalytic psychotherapy, behavioral therapy, group therapy, family therapy, and psychopharmacology.

Psychoanalytic Psychotherapy

The goal of psychoanalytically oriented psychotherapy is to help a child or adolescent better understand his or her concerns and conflicts and address these problems or develop better coping methods. It is essential to understand developmentally appropriate behaviors for children and adolescents when assessing whether the behaviors in question are age appropriate, normally occur at an earlier age, or are precocious. This evaluation is done by working with the individual and with his or her parents. For younger children, play materials are used as a vehicle for facilitating communication. During the evaluation, the professional observes the interactions among the child's

- Internal thinking processes (*ego*)
- Basic needs and wishes (*id*)
- Conscience or value system (*superego*)
- Ability to assess the realities of the outside word and shape behaviors based on the preceding three areas of input

The clinician explores the relative strengths of each process, the coping skills (or *defense mechanisms*) available to handle conflicts among these processes, and whether the conflicts and strategies are age appropriate and successful.

Behavioral Therapy

Behavioral observations and other observational data are used to clarify which behaviors are inappropriate or unacceptable and how they have been reinforced.

Behavioral therapists consider the presenting problems a reflection of learned patterns of behavior by the individual or his or her parents. Behavioral therapy is initiated to change these behaviors. Different approaches may be used to help the child use more acceptable responses and to decrease the frequency of unacceptable behaviors. This therapy might be conducted with the individual only, with the individual and his or her parents, or as part of work with the entire family.

One form of behavioral therapy might be directed toward helping the individual control anxiety. He or she might be taught specific behavioral techniques, such as relaxation therapy, to stay calm or to better control frustration.

Feelings, thoughts, and actions can all be conceived of as behaviors. If a child or adolescent is not able to see the influence one of these three experiences has on the others, cognitive behavioral therapy might be used. Its goal is to help the individual become more aware of the relationships among his or her feelings, thoughts, and actions. The individual learns how to become more aware of inappropriate or negative feelings, thoughts, or behaviors; to gain better control over them; and to substitute more positive responses.

Group Therapy

If the child or adolescent has difficulty interacting successfully with peers, group therapy might be considered. In the therapeutic group setting, patterns of behaviors and interactions are observed and noted. New approaches and strategies are then taught and practiced. Role playing and practice might be used to teach more acceptable styles of interaction.

Some children and adolescents have difficulty reading body language. They miss visual and auditory clues (e.g., facial expression, tone of voice) that suggest their behaviors are annoying another person. The social skills group is a special form of group therapy that addresses this situation. There are many types of social skill groups; in general, however, these groups focus on a series of steps. The first step is helping group members become aware of how their behaviors might bother others. This step is critical because some children have limited awareness of their social skills difficulties. They might deny their problems or blame others. The second step is teaching group members alternative strategies for dealing with their feelings and thoughts. The third step is helping group members practice these better social skills until the skills become natural. The goal is for these new social abilities to generalize to other situations.

Family Therapy

If assessment of the child or adolescent indicates that the difficulties reflect family functioning, then family therapy might be used. Sometimes, family therapy starts by working with parents. Marital issues may be addressed or a mutually agreed-on model of parenting and disciplining might have to be discussed, developed, and implemented before all members of the family participate in therapy.

The focus might be behavioral, helping the parents to regain control and teaching the child that he or she can be safe even if not in control. Or therapy might focus on family communication or interactions. With family therapy, the goal is to help all family members find ways to make the family happier, safer, and more positive. As behaviors change within the family, behaviors change outside the family.

Psychopharmacology

Medication is often an essential part of treating behavioral or emotional problems. Medication might be prescribed to address anxiety, depression, or anger control difficulties, whether resulting from situational or psychological issues or from a deficiency of a specific neurotransmitter in the brain (e.g., as with ADHD, bipolar disorder, and OCD). Medication should not be used in isolation. Education, counseling, and other interventions are needed as well. The use of specific medications for particular mental health issues is discussed throughout this book.

DIAGNOSTIC CATEGORIES

The purpose of any diagnostic manual is to establish specific criteria for each diagnosis and provide uniformity in what is meant by each disorder. A look at the World Health Organization (WI IO) illustrates how diagnostic criteria are developed. WHO is made up of representatives from each member nation of the United Nations. One of WHO's goals is to establish common definitions for all medical disorders, with specific criteria for diagnosing each. Doing so allows worldwide uniformity in diagnosing diseases and the collection of uniform data on each disease. These guidelines are developed and finalized by committees of medical professionals from each member nation, and the member nations must follow the agreed-on definitions. The guidelines document, called the *International Statistical Classification of Diseases and Related Health Problems,* is in its tenth edition (ICD-10; WHO, 2003).

When a new edition of the ICD is published, each nation must modify its own classification system to conform. In the United States, the American Medical Association (AMA) performs this task. The final product is published in the United States as the *International Classification of Diseases, Clinically Modified* (ICD-CM). In creating the ICD-CM, however, the AMA assigns specialty areas of the ICD to specific organizations, which revise and update the U.S. classification system. The American Psychiatric Association (APA) is assigned the parts of the ICD that relate to mental illness. This part of the ICD-CM is published separately for mental health professionals as the *Diagnostic and Statistical Manual of Mental Disorders* (DSM). Slight text revisions were made to the DSM's fourth edition, resulting in the DSM-IV-TR (APA, 2000). In the United States, the DSM-IV-TR is the official publication used for establishing mental health diagnoses. Therefore, the diagnostic categories and criteria discussed throughout *The Educator's Guide to Mental Health Issues in the Classroom* are based on the DSM-IV-TR.

CONCLUSION

The rising need for mental health services in schools means that professionals from the education and mental health fields must work together. Educators can increase the effectiveness of this collaboration by becoming familiar with duties and training of various types of mental health professionals. Furthermore, learning about mental health interventions and diagnostic criteria helps educators understand the types of services that their students may receive from mental health workers.

REFERENCES

American Psychiatric Association. (2000). *Diagnostic and statistical manual of mental disorders* (4th ed., text rev.). Washington, DC: Author.

World Health Organization. (2003). *International Statistical Classification of Diseases and Related Health Problems* (10th ed.). Retrieved August 21, 2003, from http://www.who.int/whosis/icd10

SECTION II

Biologically Based Disorders

Larry B. Silver

Advancements in biological research have created a basic science relating to mental health disorders. Specific disorders are now understood to result from structural ("faulty wiring") and/or neurochemical (neurotransmitter) problems. Future research may introduce yet other possible explanations of brain disorders.

After more than 20 years of study, attention-deficit/hyperactivity disorder (ADHD) became the first neurotransmitter deficiency disorder to be recognized. This knowledge has led to improved treatments and a better understanding of the need for multimodal treatment approaches. This disorder is detailed in Chapter 4.

Although intensive, ongoing research about other mental health disorders exists, it has not yet provided an understanding of the causes of pervasive developmental disorders (PDDs) or psychotic disorders. As of 2004, research suggests that these disorders might be the result of faulty wiring within the cortex and between the cortex and other areas of the brain. Without a fuller understanding, however, diagnostic criteria are less than exact, and clinical treatment approaches are more symptom related. On that note, Chapter 5 explores autism and other severe PDDs, and Chapter 6 details Asperger syndrome, a specific type of PDD. Chapter 7 focuses on psychotic disorders.

The biologically based disorders explored in Section II have a major impact on the individual, his or her family, and society. School systems are increasingly expected to provide an education, plus other needed services, within the general education system. Thus, this section shares important information with general education teachers. Educators need to understand these disorders, which affect behavior and learning in the classroom. It is equally important for educators to understand the interventions that mental health workers provide for the disorders and how to collaborate with these professionals.

4

Attention-Deficit/ Hyperactivity Disorder

Larry B. Silver

• •

Chapter Concepts

- Definition of attention-deficit/hyperactivity disorder (ADHD) and its component parts of hyperactivity, inattention, and impulsivity

- Criteria and process used to make a diagnosis of ADHD

- Common treatment regimens for ADHD in relation to the individual and his or her family and school

- Suggested roles for general education teachers, including roles involving possible accommodations

School is the work of children and adolescents. Thus, anything that interferes with mastery and success in school will cause stress for the student and his or her family. Attention-deficit/hyperactivity disorder (ADHD) can cause academic and school difficulties. ADHD can also lead to emotional or behavioral problems, difficulty with peer relationships, and problems within the family. Unrecognized and untreated, this disorder will interfere greatly with all aspects of the child's or adolescent's life.

By the time a family brings a child to a health or mental health professional because of academic or school difficulties, there are often multiple problems. Each must be identified and addressed. Emotional, social, and family issues may be the most apparent. Parents and teachers might report that the child or adolescent cannot sit still or is easily distracted and unable to stay on task. Lack of success in learning academic or study skills may also be described. These problems may be an indirect or a direct result of ADHD or may be secondary to another disorder frequently associated with ADHD, such as a learning disability. *Therefore, teachers, parents, and professionals must look beyond the most obvious problems to what might be causing these problems.* This important point is illustrated by the following example.

John was 7 years old and in the first grade when his parents took him to a child psychiatrist (the author of this chapter). John was constantly in trouble at school and at home, and he had no friends. John's parents said that their son spent an extra year in preschool and 2 years in kindergarten because of his "immaturity." I reviewed the teachers' reports for these 4 years and found many references to John's inability to sit still or pay attention. These behaviors were the examples that teachers used to say he was immature. I also spoke with John's first-grade teacher. She described him as restless, saying he was often out of his seat. She said that he never paid attention to her and never completed his work. John's mother said that when she helped John with his homework, she had to remind him to pay attention. He would get up and sit down. She said, "The way I learn is not the way he learns."

When specifically asked, John's parents said that he had always been hyperactive, distractible, and impulsive. His impulsivity caused problems at home. He constantly interrupted others, he fought with his sister, and he did "wild" things. For example, John would climb on the roof or climb up on chairs to get things, or he would see something he wanted and dash for it, often bumping into things. From helping him with his homework, his parents realized that he could not decode, let alone understand, what he read. He held his pencil in an awkward way and still could not form all of his letters. He did not know his number facts, nor could he count to 20.

During his sessions with me, John was fidgety and easily distracted by any sound, as well as by the pictures in the office. It was difficult for him to stay on task when talking or when playing. His choice of play activities and style of interacting were appropriate for his age. When I spoke of school, though, he became sad. He felt he was dumb and not as good as the other children in his class. He had had difficulty with early first-grade reading, writing, and math tasks.

I called John's teacher again. She agreed that John's skills were poor, especially for someone already a year older than the other first graders. She insisted that his difficulties were due to his immaturity. "If his parents made him act his age," the teacher stated, "John would do so much better."

I diagnosed John as having ADHD and prescribed methylphenidate (Ritalin). At a dose of 5 milligrams (mg) three times per day, there was a dramatic improvement in John's behavior. He became less active, was better able to stay on task, and became more reflective rather than impulsive. His teacher said the change was remarkable and that "he is such a different child." The teacher insisted that the change was due to the psychotherapy sessions and had difficulty accepting the ADHD diagnosis. She admitted, however, that she had never heard of ADHD. John's parents also reported a major change. He was now calm and pleasant at home. He stopped fighting with his sister and was able to do his homework. He was able to sit and play by himself, and he played much better with the children in the neighborhood.

A full psychological and educational evaluation revealed learning disabilities that clearly affected John's academic ability. His parents learned to be assertive with his school system. They had John identified as having a learning disability so that he would receive the necessary services.

Counseling was started with John's parents. As they better understood their son's problems, they were able to modify their parenting behaviors. Brief therapy was started with John. Over time, as he better understood his problems and why he was taking medicine and getting special tutoring, he became happier and more pleasant. His behavioral problems at school and at home stopped. He related better to children his age and began to make friends.

• •

If John's behaviors had been seen only as those of an oppositional child and he was treated accordingly, progress would not have been made. Furthermore, such a diagnosis would have added support to the school staff's consistent misunderstanding of John's behaviors. Progress was made with the correct diagnoses and interventions, including recognizing that John's emotional, social, and family problems were a *result* of his ADHD and his learning disabilities and not the *cause* of his problems in school and at home.

John's case illustrates the major problems facing parents of a child or adolescent with ADHD. The diagnosis is often missed. Emotional, social, and family problems are seen as the cause of the behavioral and academic difficulties and not as the consequence of the behavioral and academic difficulties. Often, the focus of treatment in school, as well as that offered by mental health professionals, is treating the behaviors without attempting to identify possible causes of the behaviors.

At the beginning of the 21st century, it is becoming increasingly possible to be more precise when diagnosing and treating ADHD. It is essential that general education teachers know as much as health and mental health professionals know about ADHD and its diagnostic criteria and treatment. Thus, this chapter reviews in detail the information that is known by health and mental health professionals. This information will help teachers work with these professionals as well as with families of children who have ADHD.

WHAT IS ATTENTION-DEFICIT/HYPERACTIVITY DISORDER?

ADHD is a neurologically based disorder. It is usually apparent by 6 years of age, although it may be recognized at an earlier age. It is estimated to be present in approximately 1%–3% of school-age children. About 50% appear to "grow out of it" by puberty; the other 50% continue to have ADHD in adolescence and, most likely, adulthood. ADHD is manifested by hyperactivity, inattention (i.e., distractibility), and/or impulsivity. Individuals with this disorder might have one, two, or all three of these behaviors, but they need not have all three to receive a diagnosis of ADHD. These three characteristics are examined next.

Hyperactivity

The term *hyperactivity* can be misleading. Some children with ADHD literally run around in circles or up and down the hall. Most children with ADHD, however, display fidgety, squirmy behaviors. Some part of their body is in motion—often purposeless motion. They tap their fingers or play with their pencil. They may be sitting, but their legs are swinging, or they may be twisting or squirming in their chair. They might sit with one knee on the floor or rock in the chair. Some children appear to be verbally hyperactive, talking constantly. As children move toward adolescence, this obvious high activity level may become less apparent. Nonetheless, individuals with ADHD tend to remain fidgety, especially regarding their hands. They might stand or pace when they are doing their homework.

Inattention

Prior to the 1994 change in the diagnostic criteria reflected in the *Diagnostic and Statistical Manual of Mental Disorders, Fourth Edition* (DSM-IV; American Psychiatric Association, 1994), the term *distractibility* was used as a component of ADHD. The terms *inattention* and *distractibility* are similar. Individuals with ADHD may be inattentive because they are distracted. As a result, they have short attention spans and difficulty staying on task. The most frequent problem that children and early adolescents with ADHD encounter is blocking out unimportant stimuli in their environment. They are distracted by auditory and/or visual stimuli. If the person has auditory distractibility, he or she hears and responds to sounds that most people tune out. The teacher might notice that other students ignore someone tapping a pencil, whispering, or walking in the hallway, but this child must turn and listen. If someone is talking in another room or dribbling a basketball on the playground, this student looks up and notices. At home, he or she might react to minor sounds, such as a floorboard creaking, the dog's wagging tail thumping the floor, outside traffic, or someone on the telephone. If a person has visual distractibility, she or he might pay attention to the design on a rug, a picture, or a poster. This student may not return from an errand if he or she sees something on the way and begins to play with it, then sees something else and is off again. Outside, this child notices birds flying, clouds going by, and trees moving and may not focus on the appropriate activity.

Another form of inattention or distractibility might be noticed in adolescence or adulthood. Some individuals with ADHD have difficulty blocking out their internal thoughts in order to focus on the task at hand. Individuals with internal distractibility often comment that they have two or more thoughts going on at the same time. Some may jump from thought to thought. They appear to be daydreaming or drifting. They may be talking to someone and suddenly realize that their mind wandered and they were not paying attention. It is clear that they are not avoiding something stressful because this drifting occurs everywhere, even when relaxed and with friends. Other people who have ADHD with internal distractibility note that when their minds jump to another thought, they then make a comment based on this thought. In turn, conversation partners comment that these people were not talking about the topic at hand. Still others with internal distractibility find that their minds jump to another thought and they have to respond to this thought. Then, they jump to another thought and must respond. They go through periods of jumping from one activity or task to another, so their lives may be full of incomplete or unfinished activities.

Some children and adolescents with auditory or visual distractibility appear able to attend to certain tasks for long periods of time. One questions whether someone who can, for example, spend hours watching television or playing a video game is truly distractible. Yet, these are tasks that the individual finds enjoyable and highly motivating. To attend to such activities, the person learns to hyperfocus. As a result, the individual often appears to be in a trance, and his or her concentration can only be broken if one touches or shakes the child or stands between the child and the activity. Some adolescents with auditory distractibility seem to study best with music playing in the background. One might ask, "How can a person who does his or her homework with music in the background be distractible?" In this case, the music is like white noise. This steady sound blocks out all of the small distracting sounds (e.g., people talking, a telephone ringing).

Young children with auditory and visual distractibility may also display sensory overload when in busy, noisy environments (e.g., a shopping mall, a birthday party, a circus). They become irritable and upset and complain about the noise. They may hold their ears and want to leave the particular environment.

Impulsivity

An individual with impulsivity appears unable to reflect before he or she talks or acts. This person does not learn from experience, as he or she cannot delay action long enough to recall past experience and consequences. The student may call out an answer without raising his or her hand or interrupt the teacher while he or she is working with another student. At home, this child or adolescent might interrupt parents when they are on the telephone or talking to someone else. Older individuals may say something before thinking and hurt someone's feelings.

Actions may be impulsive as well. For instance, children with impulsivity may get upset and push or hit others, or they may want something and grab for it. These children act quickly and, for example, may run into the street or run away from their parents in a busy shopping center. Adolescents may use poor judgment in their actions. Adults might buy something without thinking about whether they can afford it or quit a job before having another one. People with ADHD of all ages may be seen as having poor judgment or being accident prone.

DIAGNOSING ATTENTION-DEFICIT/HYPERACTIVITY DISORDER

The official guidelines that physicians and mental health professionals use to diagnose ADHD are found in the DSM-IV-TR. (See Appendix A at the end of the book for the criteria used in the DSM-IV-TR to establish a diagnosis.) The DSM-IV-TR lists three types of ADHD (see Table 4.1); the clinician must clarify which type the individual has.

Although ADHD is defined by the presence of hyperactivity and/or inattention and/or impulsivity, it is difficult to establish a diagnosis because there are many reasons for these three behaviors. Anxiety is the most frequent cause of hyperactivity, distractibility, and/or impulsivity in children, adolescents, and adults. When one is anxious, he or she cannot sit still or pay attention. This person might be irritable and snap at people. The second most frequent cause for these behaviors in any age group is depression. Like adults, children might be restless and unable to stay focused when they are depressed. The third most common cause of these behaviors is a neurologically based processing disorder, such as a learning, language, or motor disability. The child or adolescent with a learning disability may not finish classwork, have difficulty doing homework, or appear not to be listening because of an underlying learning disability, not ADHD. The child or adolescent with obsessive-compulsive disorder might be so preoccupied with intrusive thoughts that he or she cannot attend to a task. In fact, the least

Table 4.1.   Three types of attention-deficit/hyperactivity disorder (ADHD)

Attention-Deficit/Hyperactivity Disorder, Combined Type
If both Criteria A1 and A2 are met for the past 6 months
Attention-Deficit/Hyperactivity Disorder, Predominantly Inattentive Type
If Criterion A1 is met but Criterion A2 is not met for the past 6 months
Attention-Deficit/Hyperactivity Disorder, Predominantly Hyperactive-Impulsive Type
If Criterion A2 is met but Criterion A1 is not met for the past 6 months

For information on Criteria A1 and A2, refer to the diagnostic criteria for ADHD that appear in Appendix A at the end of this book.

From American Psychiatric Association. (2000). *Diagnostic and statistical manual of mental disorders* (4th ed., text rev., p. 93). Washington, DC: Author; reprinted by permission.

common cause of hyperactivity, distractibility, and/or impulsivity in any age group is ADHD.

At the beginning of the 21st century, the only approach available for diagnosing ADHD is the use of clinical history. If the observed behaviors *started at a certain time or occur in certain situations*, anxiety, depression, or a different neurologically based disorder must be considered. For example, reviewing the history of a child first described as hyperactive and impulsive in third grade might reveal that his or her parents separated during the summer before or that a favorite grandparent died. A student who is only inattentive/distractible in a reading group but is very attentive during class discussion probably does not have ADHD. Being distracted when doing homework but at no other time at home does not suggest ADHD.

ADHD is present from birth. Thus, the behaviors are both *chronic and pervasive*. A child is born with the disorder and, as the child's brain remains with him or her throughout life, the behaviors are seen year after year. This brain is with the child or adolescent every minute of every day; therefore, the behaviors occur all day.

The history of an individual with ADHD is chronic. A mother might say that her child was very active in utero or has been active all of his or her life: "He started walking at 10 months of age, and at 10 months and 1 minute, my life became impossible." Another mother might go to a school conference for her daughter, who is in third grade. The teacher comments that the child does not stay in her seat or pay attention. The mother says, "Her second-grade teacher complained about the same thing. Her first-grade and kindergarten teachers also complained. She was kicked out of nursery school because she would not sit at circle time and pay attention." Adults with ADHD describe their problems as being present at least since adolescence or childhood. With some effort, the clinician can usually find evidence to support the chronic nature of the problems.

The problems must also be pervasive to signify ADHD. For instance, a child's morning teachers complain about his or her behaviors, as do the lunchroom monitor and the afternoon teachers. These behaviors are not just school problems, however; they interfere with friends, family life, and after-school activities. The tutor complains. The piano teacher complains. The soccer coach complains. Sunday school teachers complain.

Perhaps the reason that some children and adolescents are misdiagnosed as having ADHD is that clinicians are unaware of this differential diagnostic issue and do not use the appropriate diagnostic approach. To illustrate, a teacher tells the parent that a student cannot sit still and pay attention. This parent goes to the family doctor and repeats these concerns. The family doctor immediately concludes ADHD and prescribes medication. Yet, would a doctor immediately conclude that a child with a lack of energy, listlessness, and pale inner eyelid linings be treated for anemia? No, the doctor would first carry out the necessary tests, including blood studies. The same approach must be taken when determining a diagnosis for children or adolescents who are hyperactive, inattentive, or impulsive. This information is only the starting point of the diagnostic process.

It is necessary to collect the other essential information before making the diagnosis. It is important to emphasize that not all children who are hyperactive, inattentive/distractible, and/or impulsive have ADHD. As noted previously, ADHD is the least common cause of these behaviors.

To make the diagnosis, then, the following steps must be taken:

1. Confirm the presence of DSM-IV-TR criteria to establish the presence of one or more of the three behaviors that are characteristic of ADHD.

2. Show through the clinical history that these behaviors have been present throughout life—that is, they are chronic.

3. Show through the clinical history that these behaviors are present in two or more life settings—that is, they are pervasive.

Obtaining Information on Behavior

It is difficult for clinicians to observe the characteristic behaviors in the office. The typical general practice physician or pediatrician sees a child for 5–7 minutes per visit. A child may have learned to be very alert in this medical office environment to avoid being stuck, gagged, or poked. Thus, he or she may be quiet and very attentive. If the office is that of a general psychiatrist, child and adolescent psychiatrist, or other mental health professional, the room is likely to be quiet and the interaction one to one. It is important to understand that if hyperactivity, distractibility, and/or impulsivity are not seen in the clinician's office, it cannot be concluded that these behaviors do not exist.

The best source of observational data is real-life situations, such as the classroom. It is uncommon, however, for a clinician to visit the child's school or to observe the child at play. Professionals must learn from parents, teachers, tutors, and other adults who interact with the child or adolescent and who can describe what he or she is like in structured and unstructured situations. Each can describe whether the behaviors exist all of the time or only during certain activities or tasks. It becomes critical, then, that behavioral descriptions are obtained from teachers. Teachers can complete rating scales and other informational forms and send them to the professional for evaluation. These tools are described next. Clinicians may also use computer-based tests for making diagnoses.

Rating Scales   Rating scales are commonly used to assess children's behaviors (reviewed in Barkley, 1998, pp. 278–280). Behavior rating scales might be completed by parents, teachers, and/or the child or adolescent being evaluated. Then results are analyzed and compared with established norms, allowing important information to be obtained in an efficient way. These findings provide a baseline for comparison if any changes in behavior occur.

Many clinicians find rating scales useful as part of the diagnostic process. Conners' Rating Scales–Revised (CRS-R; Conners, 1997), which are completed by parents and teachers, are very popular. Other behavioral rating scales are in use, and new rating sheets are being developed constantly. Some clinicians have devised their own rating scales, and some school systems use standard rating scales that have been modified to fit the needs of the school.

Using the results to make a diagnosis is difficult. Although results can clarify whether the individual is hyperactive, inattentive/distractible, or impulsive, they do not clarify the cause of these behaviors because the scales are two-dimensional. The results are reported as a behavior or behavior cluster that is present (or not present) at a significant level. More significant information can be learned through conversations with a child or adolescent and his or her parents and teacher(s). A teacher might say that the child is hyperactive and inattentive, and the rating scale would be marked accordingly. Through discussion with the teacher, for instance, the clinician may learn that these behaviors are only present during certain activities, occurred after something happened at home, or are more evident when a child whose parents are divorced spends time with a particular parent. A clinician can also gain more from the teacher's affect, such as how upset he or she is about the child's behaviors. A teacher's saying, "The student is so disruptive that I can't teach my class!" tells a clinician more than a check for impulsive behavior on a rating scale does. This process might take more time, but it is worth it.

Computer-Based Tests   Several computer-based tests have been developed to assess a child's or adolescent's ability for sustained attention. The results suggest whether the individual has difficulty sustaining attention or shows evidence of impulsivity. The Continuous Performance Test (CPT; reviewed in Barkley, 1998, pp. 302–304) and the Test of Variables of Attention (TOVA; Greenberg, 1990) are the most frequently used computer-based tools. In each test, vigilance is assessed by having the child respond to an auditory or visual stimulus with the press of a button. The stimulus is usually a series of signals, and the individual must respond to a specific sequence of these signals. For example, the child is asked to respond when a certain stimulus appears or when the same symbol appears consecutively. The tasks are monotonous and require constant attention. The speed or complexity of the task can be increased. Children or adolescents with ADHD perform more poorly than children who do not have ADHD. They might make more errors of omission (by missing signals) and errors of commission (by pressing the button in error). Errors of omission are reflective of inattention. Errors of commission are reflective of impulsivity.

Clinicians cannot, however, diagnose ADHD solely on the results of these computer-based assessment tools. The results should be used only as part of the diagnostic process. The results might also provide an excellent baseline for later use when assessing the impact of medication on these behaviors.

INDIVIDUAL AND FAMILY-FOCUSED TREATMENT

The treatment of ADHD must involve many factors, including individual and family education, individual and family counseling, appropriate behavioral management programs, and appropriate medications. Each approach requires working closely with the child's school. Medications and nonmedication interventions, as well as the role of the general education teacher, are further examined in the following discussions.

Medications

ADHD is caused by a deficiency of a specific neurotransmitter, norepinephrine, in a series of interrelated brain circuits that are responsible for maintaining vigilance (reviewed in Barkely, 1998, pp. 164–185; see also Chapter 2). The goal of using medication to treat ADHD is to increase the level of this neurotransmitter at the nerve interfaces in the areas of the brain involved (Silver, 1999). Two different mechanisms can accomplish this increase. (Think of a lake without enough water in it. The level of water in the lake could be increased one of two ways. The first would be to pour more water into the lake. The second way would be to build a dam: No more water is flowing into the lake, but the water flows out more slowly and the water level will go up.)

One mechanism for increasing the level of this neurotransmitter is to produce more of it. Stimulants (Group One medications) appear to work by stimulating the nerve endings to produce more norepinephrine. The second mechanism decreases the breakdown (or metabolism) of the neurotransmitter, thus causing what is produced to remain longer. The relative amount of the neurotransmitter then goes up. Tricyclic antidepressants and other medications (Group Two medications) appear to work in this way, resulting in an increase in the amount at the nerve interface.

Each Group One and Group Two medication has a generic or chemical name and a trade name. The medications used to treat ADHD are listed in Table 4.2, with the generic name first and the trade name in parentheses. It is common practice to start with one of the Group One medications. If this medication or another one in this group is not successful or if side effects prevent continuation of the medication, then a medication from Group Two is tried.

There are several medications within each group. It is important for educators to have an understanding of Group One and Group Two medications. Because methylphenidate (e.g., Ritalin) is the most frequently used Group One medication

Table 4.2. Medications used to treat attention-deficit/hyperactivity disorder (ADHD)

Group One medications	Methylphenidate (Ritalin, Metadate, Concerta)
	Dextroamphetamine (Dexedrine, DextroStat)
	Dextroamphetamine and levoamphetamine (Adderall)
	Dexmethylphenidate (Focalin)
Group Two medications	Imipramine (Tofranil)
	Desipramine (Norpramin)
	Nortriptyline (Pamelor)
	Bupropion (Wellbutrin)
	Clonidine (Catapres)
	Guanfacine (Tenex)
	Atomoxetine (Strattera)

and imipramine (Tofranil) is the most frequently used Group Two medication, these two medications are discussed in greater depth as representatives of their respective categories. Clonidine (Catapres), a medication sometimes used with certain Group One and Group Two medications, is also discussed.

Group One Medications Before discussing the details of Group One medications, it is helpful to know the different release mechanisms used and, thus, the length of time that each medication lasts. Each medication is available in the standard tablet form that starts to work 45–60 minutes after it is taken and lasts approximately 4 hours. Most also are available in longer-acting tablets. These tablets are designed to release approximately half of the medication initially and the other half 4 hours later. Therefore, these longer-acting tablets start to work in the same amount of time but last approximately 8 hours. These longer-acting tablets are packaged in a way that does not allow them to be crushed or cut in half. (This is important because all of the medication is released at once if the longer-acting tablets are crushed or cut.)

Many of the longer-acting medications are also available in a different 8-hour form: The medication is inside a capsule in the form of small pellets. As the capsule dissolves, the pellets are released. Each pellet is designed to be absorbed at a certain time. Thus, unlike the longer-acting tablet that releases about half of the dose at once and half 4 hours later, these capsules slowly release a steady flow of the medication over 8 hours. These capsules also start to work 45–60 minutes after they are taken and last 8 hours. The capsules can be opened and the pellets sprinkled over food, thereby making ingestion easier for young children who cannot swallow pills.

The newest release mechanism involves a pump-like system. The medication is inside a capsule. The top third of this capsule is filled with the medication. The bottom two thirds are filled with a sponge. There is a very small hole at the top of the capsule. As the sponge absorbs fluid, it expands, thus pushing the medication out of the tiny hole. This release mechanism is designed to last for 10–12 hours. For the medication to start working quickly (i.e., before the sponge can absorb enough fluid to expand), a small amount of the medication is designed to be released immediately from the surface of the capsule.

As noted, all of these release mechanisms start to work in 45–60 minutes. Depending on the release mechanism, the medication effect may be experienced over 4 hours, 8 hours, or 10–12 hours. It is also possible that each release mechanism might not last as long as the time noted.

The numbers used by the manufactures to represent the dose of a specific medication may be confusing. Thus, it is important for educators to understand this system as well. For the short-acting (4-hour) tablets, the number represents the amount of medication in the tablet. For example, a 5-mg tablet of methylphenidate holds 5 mg of the medication. For the 8-hour long-acting tablets, the number represents the total amount of medication in the tablet. For example, a tablet that releases approximately 5 mg of the medication immediately and 5 mg 4 hours later is identified as 10 mg. It is important to remember that the number represents the total amount of medication in the pill or capsule. A long-acting *tablet* identified as 20 mg does not release 20 mg over the 8 hours. Approximately 10 mg is released initially and approximately 10 mg is released after 4 hours. The long-acting *capsules,* however, do identify the amount released. Thus, a long-acting 20 mg capsule does slowly release about the equivalent of 20 mg over the 8 hours. The amount of medication listed for the new pump system release mechanism must identify the full amount of medication in the system. For example, if the capsule is to slowly release 10 mg over 12 hours, it must hold 30 mg of medication. However, an additional 6 mg is designed to be released immediately to start the effect. Thus, a capsule designed to release 10 mg steadily over 12 hours is identified as 36 mg.

It is important for educators to understand these release mechanisms and the amount noted for each dose. Table 4.3 lists all of the different dosages and forms of Group One medications available at the time of publication (also see Appendix B at the end of this book). An extended discussion of methylphenidate illustrates the use of Group One medications. Most of what is described about this medication is true about the other drugs in this group.

Methylphenidate   When methylphenidate is prescribed for a student, three questions must be addressed to establish the best dosage and treatment plan. Each question requires feedback from parents and teachers. First, what dose does the child or adolescent need? The dose needed is not based on age or body

Table 4.3.   Information on Group One medications

Generic medication name	Dosages for brand name versions of the medication
Methylphenidate	4-hour tablets Ritalin 5, 10, and 20 milligram (mg)

	8-hour tablets
	    Ritalin SR 20
	    Metadate ER 10 and 20 mg

	8-hour capsules
	    Ritalin LA 20, 30, 40, and 60 mg
	    Metadate CD 20 mg

	12-hour capsules Concerta 18, 27, 36, and 54 mg

Dextroamphetamine	4-hour tablets
	    Dexedrine 5 mg
	    DextroStat 5 and 10 mg

	8-hour capsules Dexedrine Spansules 5, 10, and 15 mg
Dextroamphetamine and levoamphetamine	4-hour tablets Adderall 5, 7.5, 10, 12.5, 15, 20, and 30 mg
	8-hour capsules Adderall XR 5, 10, 15, 20, 25, and 30 mg
Dexmethylphenidate	4-hour tablets Focalin 2.5, 5, and 10 mg

weight but on how quickly the individual metabolizes the medication. Thus, some children may need 5 mg per dose and others may need 10 mg, 15 mg, or 20 mg per dose to get the necessary effect. Second, how often should the medication be taken? For some individuals, methylphenidate short-acting tablets last 4 hours. For others, the tablets last 3–5 hours. The 12-hour capsule may only last 10 hours. Duration must be determined to decide how frequently the individual should take medication. The student should be on medication whenever the hyperactivity, distractibility, and/or impulsivity interfere(s) with her or his success in life. For some people, medication is only needed for school or homework. For many, however, the medication is needed all day, every day.

Clinical knowledge about managing a child's or adolescent's medication continues to grow. Some physicians may not have updated information regarding the need to determine dose, timing of dose, or time of coverage. As a result, some physicians may do things differently than what is described in this chapter. For example, some may not prescribe a dose greater than 10 mg. Others may insist that the individual not take medication during afternoons, weekends, holidays, and summer school breaks. These actions can result in difficulties at home, with peers, and in various activities.

Side effects seen when using methylphenidate, in decreasing frequency of occurrence, include loss of appetite, difficulty falling asleep at night, headaches, and stomachaches. A very uncommon side effect is development of motor tics. Two particular side effects suggest that an individual's dose is too high: emotional fragility—becoming more angry or irritable—and becoming too focused, thus appearing to be "spacey" or having a flattened personality. Side effects must be addressed; a child or adolescent should not have to live with them. It is important for the classroom teacher to share information with the physician either directly, when permission is given, or through the parents so that changes can be made.

Group Two Medications Imipramine is discussed next to describe the tricyclic antidepressant medications within Group Two. Most of what is explained about this medication is true of the other tricyclic antidepressants. Later, other Group Two medications are noted.

Imipramine Imipramine is long acting. It is taken in the morning and at night, and approximately a week is required for the medication to take effect. Like methylphenidate, the dose cannot be predicted; it must be adjusted until maximum benefits are noted.

The main side effect of imipramine is fatigue. Unusual side effects are constipation, dry mouth, or blurred vision. If any of these side effects occur, they must be addressed. In addition, a disadvantage of imipramine is that it usually decreases hyperactivity and distractibility but might not decrease impulsivity. Therefore, a second medication might have to be added to address impulsivity. This second medication might be methylphenidate, used at a lower dose than when initially tried, or it might be clonidine or guanafacine (Tenex).

Clonidine and Guanafacine Clonidine is used to treat high blood pressure in adults. At lower doses, it may decrease the impulsivity associated with ADHD.

Thus, it is used when imipramine or another Group Two medication does not help impulsivity. The main side effect is fatigue to the point that a student might fall asleep in class. Because of its sedating effect, clonidine might be used at night to help students taking a Group One medication fall sleep when the medication causes a sleep disturbance. Guanafacine works in the same way as clonidine; however, it is less sedating.

Other Medications   Atomoxetine (Strattera), released in the United States in January 2003, is advertised as a nonstimulant medication that works as well as the stimulant medications. It is a selective norepinephrine reuptake inhibitor. Its structure, time to take effect, length of action, and side effects appear to be more similar to those of selective serotonin reuptake inhibitors (SSRIs) than any of the medications discussed in this chapter. It is taken each morning, and the dosage is based on body weight in kilograms (kg), ranging from 0.5 mg/kg to 1.2 mg/kg. A further discussion of this medication is not feasible because at the time that this book was written, the medication was new and collective clinical experience from practitioners was not available.

Nonmedication Interventions for Families

Once the use of medication decreases the behaviors associated with ADHD, it is important to assess which challenges remain. Family life might continue to be difficult. Parents might continue to disagree on discipline. The impact of having ADHD for years before medication was started might have resulted in problems with the child, with one or both parents, or within the whole family. The specific form of clinical intervention depends on the problems identified.

TREATMENT IN SCHOOLS

When planning the placement, curriculum, and classroom strategies needed for a student with ADHD, two important factors must be considered. Each factor influences the program that is developed. The first factor is whether the student also has a learning disability. Because 30%–50% of students with ADHD also have a learning disability, it is essential to clarify this. The second factor is whether the student is on a successful medication regimen.

If the student has a learning disability, then these processing problems must be addressed through appropriate special education services as well as accommodations provided within the general education classroom. Some students with ADHD may not have learning disabilities but have difficulty with specific skills, or they may be behind their peers in certain knowledge areas because they were not available for learning during the school years before the diagnosis was made and treatment was started. For such students, efforts must be made to fill in the gaps and help them catch up to grade level.

If the student is on a successful medication regimen, few adjustments will be needed in the classroom or in teaching style. The teacher will need to understand the medication, its effects and side effects, and how and when to communicate with the child's physician. If the student is not on medication or is on a poorly managed medication regimen, the hyperactivity, distractibility, and/or impulsivity must be addressed. If the ADHD behaviors make the student unavailable for learning or make the classroom environment such that other students cannot learn, it may be appropriate to consider identifying him or her under the Individual with Disabilities Education Act (IDEA) of 1990 (PL 101-476) guidelines. In this way, the student could receive special education services, through which the behaviors may be better addressed than in the general education classroom.

The public school system can recognize and provide service for a student with ADHD under education law (IDEA) or under civil law (Section 504 of the Rehabilitation Act of 1973 [PL 93-112]). Part B of IDEA defines the categories of disability recognized for special education by the U.S. Department of Education. ADHD is not identified as a separate disability. Thus, in 1991 the U.S. Department of Education issued a memorandum that clarified how students with ADHD could be eligible for special education services under IDEA. If the student with ADHD also has a learning disability, he or she can obtain special services through the "Learning Disability" category. If the student has a significant emotional disorder, he or she can receive services under the "Seriously Emotionally Disturbed" category. Or if the student does not meet the criteria for either of these two disabilities, he or she can be identified under the "Other Health Impaired" category. Having any of these three classifications will make a student with ADHD eligible for special education services.

This same U.S. Department of Education memorandum clarifies that students with ADHD can also be served under Section 504 of the Rehabilitation Act of 1973 if their condition is severe enough to be considered a handicap. In this law, a disorder is considered a handicap if it "substantially limits a major life activity," such as learning. Therefore, under Section 504, children and adolescents with ADHD may be eligible for accommodations and possibly for services in the general education classroom to meet their educational needs. Many students with ADHD may not qualify for services using a school district's discrepancy model for determining who has learning disabilities and, thus, not be eligible for services. However, these students could meet the criteria to receive services under Section 504. Eligible students under Section 504, like students receiving services under IDEA, are entitled to reasonable accommodations in order to benefit from the educational process. The necessary accommodations for academic success are to be made for the entire school program, including the teacher within the general education classroom.

Role of the General Educator

It is not possible to provide a "cookbook" or a list of things to do in the classroom. Each student is different, and each needs a specially designed approach. It is important to ascertain which of the many ADHD behaviors a specific student has and to accommodate for his or her specific needs. The list of possible behaviors includes the following:

1. Hyperactivity (i.e., fidgety or squirming behaviors)

2. Inattention (i.e., distractibility)

   • Auditory distractibility

   • Visual distractibility

   • Internal distractibility

3. Impulsivity

   • Does not stop to think before speaking

   • Does not stop to think before acting

In addition to addressing the specific behaviors, it is important to determine the student's level of academic performance. If knowledge or skills that should have been learned in an earlier grade are weak or absent because the student was not treated and, thus, not available for learning at that time, these areas will need to be addressed. Often, once the student is diagnosed as having ADHD and is treated with medication, he or she is able to catch up in these areas.

Working successfully in the general education classroom with students who have ADHD requires a competent teacher who has a positive attitude toward inclusion. In addition, the teacher must have the ability to collaborate as part of an interdisciplinary team and have knowledge of behavioral management techniques. General education teachers who work well with students who have special needs are generally fair, firm, warm, and responsive. They have patience and a sense of humor and are able to establish a rapport with students. Specific accommodations that may assist a student with ADHD follow.

Accommodations for Hyperactivity Hyperactivity is a challenging behavior in the classroom. Students who are hyperactive have difficulty sitting in their seats for prolonged periods. They may get up to sharpen their pencils or go to the bathroom frequently. They fidget with pencils, pens, or paper clips, appearing never to be calm and relaxed. The need for physical movement and activity must be taken into account when planning classroom accommodations. Simply telling the child or adolescent to stop her or his disruptive, hyperactive behaviors will not work. The student needs ways to channel this excessive activity into acceptable behaviors. Examples follow:

• Allow movement in the classroom that is directed and not disruptive.

• Allow standing during seat work.

• Give opportunities for activity by permitting specific actions (e.g., running an errand, cleaning the board, organizing materials).

• Use teaching activities that encourage active responding (e.g., talking, moving, working at the board).

• Encourage diary writing, notetaking, painting, and other meaningful work-related activities.

- Consider seating the student with ADHD near the teacher. If the student begins to engage in disruptive behaviors, the teacher can quickly remind him or her of what is happening. Perhaps the teacher and the student could develop a hand signal that says, "You are too hyper. Relax." Other hand signals might be used for distractibility or impulsivity. Because the student may not be aware of his or her behavior, this signal might be what he or she needs to stop.

The other students must be informed of why this student is permitted to do some things that are not permissible for the rest of the class.

Accommodations for Inattention/Distractibility Some students with ADHD have short attention spans and frequently do not complete assignments. There are some accommodations that help with all forms of distractibility and others that are more appropriate for a specific type of distractibility (i.e., auditory, visual, or internal). General accommodations to prolong concentration on a task include the following:

- Shorten the task.

- Break one task into smaller parts to be completed at different times.

- Give two tasks, and require the student to complete the less preferred task first.

- Assign fewer problems (e.g., spelling words, math problems).

- For rote tasks, set up more short, spaced practice sessions rather than fewer but longer and more concentrated sessions.

- Use hand signals to remind the student that he or she is distracted and needs to refocus.

Auditory Distractibility In addition to the previously listed accommodations, a student with auditory distractibility should work in the quietest place in the classroom—away from doors, windows, air conditioners, and high-traffic areas. It might be helpful to allow the student to go to the library or to another quiet place for certain assignments or tests.

Visual Distractibility In addition to the general interventions for distractibility, a student who has visual distractibility needs the opportunity to work in the least visually active part of the classroom—away from doors, windows, traffic, posters, and pictures. Placing a cubicle on a student's desk may help. He or she might be asked to work in a corner facing the wall. If this is done, the student and the others in the class need to understand that this is not a punishment. It is possible that a student with visual distractibility will work best by sitting in the front row. This will decrease much of the visual distraction caused by the other students. (Do not use this idea for a student with auditory distractibility. He or she will continually turn around to look at the activity or noise behind him or her.) Try to keep the student's desktop free of clutter. If only the task to be done is visible, the student is less likely to be distracted.

Internal Distractibility A specific accommodation for being distracted by one's own thoughts is placing the student's desk near the teacher's desk. When the student appears to be daydreaming, a gentle touch or word from the teacher can get his or her attention. Once the student looks at the teacher, the teacher can use a hand signal to remind the student to refocus.

Accommodations for Students Who Are Impulsive Students who are impulsive commonly interrupt or call out answers without raising their hands or waiting to be called on. They might make inappropriate comments or hurt others' feelings because they do not think before speaking. Students with impulsivity might act before they think—resulting in pushing, yelling, or hitting—or they might turn to do something so fast that they bump into other students or knock things over. Some may rush through assignments and tests, putting down the first thought or answer that enters their head. Younger children may have difficulty learning to wait (e.g., for their turn to do something, for a toy, for attention).

Behavioral approaches for helping a student become aware of his or her impulsivity should be combined with accommodations in teaching style and activities and with teaching the student techniques for delaying responses or actions. It might be helpful to consult with a school psychologist, a school counselor, or other mental health professional when designing specific strategies for helping students who are impulsive.

Accommodations for helping a student learn to wait include the following:

- Teach substitute verbal or motor responses to use while waiting.

- Instruct the child on how to continue with easier parts of tasks while waiting for the teacher's help for the more difficult parts.

- Allow this student to doodle or play with clay, paper clips, or other items while waiting or listening to instructions.

- Let the child participate in setting the pace for activities when possible.

Accommodations for assisting a student who calls out or interrupts include the following:

- Suggest and reinforce alternative ways for getting attention (e.g., being a line leader, being the person who passes out papers).

- Teach the child to recognize pauses in conversations so that he or she can learn when to speak and how to hold on to ideas while listening for these pauses.

- Let the child know about upcoming transitions or difficult times or tasks for which he or she will need extra control.

- Teach and practice social routines (e.g., saying "hello," "goodbye," and "please").

CONCLUSION

Most children and adolescents with ADHD can learn in the general education classroom. Some have significant learning disabilities or significant emotional disturbances and may need supplemental services within the classroom or place-ment in a special education program. Some students with ADHD may not be on medication. Their hyperactivity, inattention, and/or impulsivity result in their being unavailable for learning in the general education classroom or disrupting the classroom so that other students are not able to learn. These students may need a special education placement, not necessarily because of ADHD but because the ADHD is not being treated.

Students with ADHD do not want to be hyperactive, inattentive, and/or impulsive. They do not want to be "bad" or to get into trouble. They want to learn. By providing the appropriate accommodations in the classroom as well as with the curriculum and teaching strategies, a child or adolescent with ADHD can be a happy, productive, successful student in the general education classroom.

REFERENCES

American Psychiatric Association. (1994). *Diagnostic and statistical manual of mental disorders* (4th ed.). Washington, DC: Author.

American Psychiatric Association. (2000). *Diagnostic and statistical manual of mental disorders* (4th ed., text rev.). Washington, DC: Author.

Barkley, R.A. (1998). *Attention-deficit hyperactivity disorder: A handbook for diagnosis and treatment* (2nd ed.). New York: The Guilford Press.

Conners, C.K. (1997). *Conners' Rating Scales–Revised (CRS-R).* North Tonawanda, NY: Multi-Health Systems.

Education for All Handicapped Children Act of 1975, PL 94-142, 20 U.S.C. §§ 1400 *et seq.*

Greenberg, L. (1990). *Test of Variables of Attention.* Minneapolis, MN: Attention Technology Systems.

Individuals with Disabilities Education Act (IDEA) of 1990, PL 101-476, 20 U.S.C. §§ 1400 *et seq.*

Rehabilitation Act of 1973, PL 93-112, 29 U.S.C. §§ 701 *et seq.*

Silver, L.B. (1999). *Attention-deficit/hyperactivity disorder: A clinical guide to diagnosis and treatment for health and mental health professionals* (2nd ed.). Washington, DC: American Psychiatric Publishing.

RECOMMENDED READINGS

Lerner, J.W., Lowenthal, B., & Lerner, S.R. (1995). *Attention deficit disorders: Assessment and Teaching.* Pacific Grove, CA: Brooks/Cole Publishing Co.
    This is an excellent handbook for the general education classroom teacher. It contains a great deal of information and practical suggestions.

Silver, L.B. (1999). *Dr. Larry Silver's advice to parents on attention deficit hyperactivity disorder* (2nd ed.). New York: Times Books.
    This book is written for parents but would be equally helpful for classroom teachers. Details on diagnoses and nonmedication therapies are discussed. Specific information is provided on each medication used, including how dosage is established and side effects.

5

Autism and Other Severe Pervasive Developmental Disorders

Rosa A. Hagin

• •

Chapter Concepts

- Definitions and diagnostic terminology that describe pervasive developmental disorders
- Changes that have occurred in the estimated incidence of these disorders
- Diagnostic and etiological issues in the field of autistic disorders
- Subgroups of autistic disorders
- The importance of educational interventions for these disorders
- The importance and contributions of parent organizations for autistic disorders

Individuals with autism and severe pervasive developmental disorders (PDDs) share fundamental impairments in three areas of human activity: social responsiveness and interaction, verbal and nonverbal communication, and behavioral flexibility. Their developmental delays become apparent early, usually by 3–5 years of age. Although the degree of impairment may vary in its expression among individual children, these disorders are severe and the prognosis is not optimistic. Children with PDDs are qualitatively different from their age-mates in a variety of ways. Their basic personality disturbances are manifested in distortions and delays in their emotional relationships with adults and other children, their comprehension and use of language, their cognitive functioning, their acquisition of self-help skills, and their responses to sensory stimuli.

DIAGNOSTIC TERMINOLOGY

Nomenclature (the diagnostic names by which the disorders are identified) can be confusing. Various terms appear in the professional literature, more often reflecting the writer's professional orientation than illuminating the nature of the condition. Many terms have been used: atypical development, symbiotic psychosis, childhood psychosis, Kanner's syndrome, childhood schizophrenia, developmental deviate, and semantic pragmatic syndrome. These variations in terminology have had a negative effect for several reasons. First of all, some terms imply specific causative factors that have not been validated by continued research. For example, some children with autism have been diagnosed as having childhood schizophrenia, yet longitudinal follow-up has not found that autism results in adult schizophrenia. Furthermore, differences in terminology can make it difficult to arrive at generalizations across research sites, a particular problem in the case of low-incidence disorders such as these. Thus, some researchers made broad generalizations on the basis of samples whose limited size made them vulnerable to biases in the selection of subjects. Finally, the vague descriptions of diagnostic criteria have made it difficult to confirm the findings of a given investigation by comparing the findings with the results of other investigations.

The American Psychiatric Association (APA) has published numerous editions of the *Diagnostic and Statistical Manual of Mental Disorders*. The increasing precision of the diagnostic criteria in these manuals has helped to correct some of these difficulties with nomenclature. Table 5.1 shows the evolution of terms as more information on PDDs became available and accepted by greater numbers of diagnosticians.

As Table 5.1 illustrates, some early diagnostic labels have dropped out of usage entirely; others appeared in later years as increased research permitted more precise descriptions. Hence, the DSM-IV (APA, 1994) recognized and described variations in the spectrum of autistic disorders, which contrast with the original single diagnosis of infantile autism used in the DSM-III (APA, 1980). The adjective *infantile* was dropped when it became apparent that the disorder continued throughout life.

Table 5.1. Nomenclature for pervasive developmental disorders according to different editions of the American Psychiatric Association's *Diagnostic and Statistical Manual of Mental Disorders* (DSM)

DSM 1952	DSM-II 1968	DSM-III 1980	DSM-III-R 1987	DSM-IV 1994; DSM-IV-TR 2000
Schizophrenic Reaction: Childhood Type	Schizophrenia: Childhood Type			
		Infantile Autism	Autistic Disorder	Autistic Disorder
		Childhood Onset: Pervasive Developmental Disorder	Pervasive Developmental Disorder—Not Otherwise Specified	Pervasive Developmental Disorder—Not Otherwise Specified
				Rett's Disorder
				Childhood Disintegrative Disorder
				Asperger's Disorder

From Kline, F.M., Silver, L.B., & Russell, S.C. (Eds.). (2001). *The educator's guide to medical issues in the classroom* (p. 161). Baltimore: Paul H. Brookes Publishing Co.; adapted by permission.

Provision has also been made for variations in degrees of impairment. Thus, individuals who have only some of the characteristics of PDD can be described as having the disorder "not otherwise specified" (NOS). Yet, as more specific subtypes have been identified, more specific subgroups have been recognized.

CHANGES IN ESTIMATES OF INCIDENCE

PDDs are relatively rare. Past incidence estimates suggested approximately 4–5 individuals with PDD among 10,000 people (Kabot, Masi, & Segal, 2003; Rapin, 2002). Yet, later reports have suggested that this may be an underestimate. For example, Croen, Grether, Hoophate, and Silver (2002) reported an incidence estimate of 11 per 10,000 births in eight successive birth cohorts in California from 1987 to 1994. They concluded that the increase was not influenced by maternal age, race, ethnicity, maternal education, or gender of the children. This same investigation also reported that the incidence of mental retardation fell from 28.8 to 19.5 in the same cohorts, causing the writers to attribute the changes to improvement in methods of diagnosis. An Australian study also reported increased incidence of PDDs. Baker (2002) compared clinic referrals for 1991 and 1997 and found a 200% increase in the number of milder cases, despite a 5% drop in the number of referrals. However, Wing and Potter (2002) reviewed these reports and concluded that there were many reasons for the increased number of cases reported: 1) changes in diagnostic criteria, 2) differences in methodology, 3) growing awareness of and knowledge about PDDs among parents and professionals, and 4) the development of specialist services for children with PDDs.

They also explored possible environmental causes—including measles, mumps, and rubella—and found that scientific investigation confirmed none of these possible causes. Conversely, they found increasing evidence that complex genetic factors play a major role in etiology. Their final conclusion was that the reported rise in incidence may result from increasing awareness and recognition of the range of autistic disorders; whether there has been a rise in incidence remains an open question.

CORE SYMPTOMS OF AUTISM

Autism, a disorder characterized by lack of social responsiveness, lack of communication skills, and impoverished ideation, is now understood to be biological and neurological in origin. Although originally considered emotional in origin (Kanner, 1944), accumulated research and clinical evidence has pointed toward a neurobiological explanation. Data available from technical developments (particularly the techniques of magnetic resonance imaging and positron emission tomography) and about documented brain abnormalities, such as significant differences in the size of the cerebellum and in the numbers of Purkinje cells (certain neurons), suggest a biological basis. Genetic studies have revealed autistic patterns among the members of some families. Furthermore, follow-up studies have revealed that at least 25% of individuals diagnosed with autism developed seizure disorders, which also are neurological in origin, as adults (De Meyer et al., 1973; Gilberg & Coleman, 1992; Rapin, 2002). These trends point to the need for research that can refine the nature of these neurobiological factors. Appendix A at the end of the book provides the DSM-IV-TR diagnostic criteria for autism. Some specific symptoms that characterize autism are examined in the following subsections.

Impaired Responsiveness

Children with autism seem to tune out the world to such a degree that many parents have their children examined for deafness. Wing (1988) postulated a triad of impaired social recognition, social communication, and social understanding. Unlike most typically developing 6- to 8-month-olds, children with autism do not learn to anticipate being picked up and cuddled by caregivers. They do not learn to respond when their names are called. They do not show distress when a caregiver departs or are not comforted by the caregiver's return. They have a tendency to look through people or to use them as objects. For example, they will use the caregiver's hand as a tool to get for them a toy that may be out of reach.

This aloofness and lack of reactivity places a heavy burden on the parent–child relationship. Among typically developing children, the parent–child bond is strengthened by the child's response to parents' language or efforts in spontaneous play. When a child with autism fails to recognize and respond in some manner to these playful actions, his or her parents may become discouraged from initiating further interaction. Parents who continue to encourage interactions with their children who have autism are to be admired considering the limited reinforcement that they usually receive from their children.

Delays and Deviations in Language Development

The development of communicative language is usually delayed in children with autism, and 50% of them never possess functional speech (Schwartz & Johnson, 1985). Those who do develop language may use it atypically. They may demonstrate echolalia, repeating sentences said to them. They may reverse pronouns, confusing, for example, *me* and *you.* Some of them learn to use gestures. Therefore, some intervention programs have experimented with the use of sign language. The language of some individuals with autism may lack the logic and pragmatic give-and-take of typical conversations yet may contain interesting metaphoric language. One child used advertising slogans that were comically relevant to the situations in which she found herself. For example, when leaving a clinical conference during which her case was presented, she commented, "Smile, you're on *Candid Camera.*" When a visiting psychiatrist asked, "How are you today?" she replied, "Only your hairdresser knows for sure."

Inconsistent Sensory Awareness

For people with autism, sounds like ringing telephones and school bells may be terrifyingly loud. Their hypersensitivity to touch may make dressing or wearing clothes with rough textures very painful. The pat on the shoulder that many teachers use to reassure students or a hug from a relative can set off waves of fear in children who have autism. Children with autism may also use senses peculiarly in exploratory activity. For example, they might examine a toy by licking it with their tongues rather than using distal senses, such as vision.

Many children with autism tend to engage in tantrum behavior. Some researchers attribute this to the unstable sensory world that children with autism experience (Cohen, 1998). This instability probably produces the difficulties the children experience in adapting to change and, hence, their insistence on consistency in their physical environments. Changes such as rearranged furniture can constitute an intrusion into their private worlds. The repetitive questioning that may be an annoyance to caregivers may be an attempt by children with autism to understand the sensory disorganization that they experience.

Preoccupation with Circular Movement

Children with autism are often preoccupied with spinning movements, such as those produced by electric fans, record players, and wheeled toys. These children may also appear to be preoccupied with their own movement in space, whirling, rocking, waving their hands in the air, and flicking light switches.

Uneven Cognitive Functioning

Although some children with autism are found to have mental retardation, they do not present the "flat" profile associated with mental retardation syndromes. Children with autism may have scattered areas of strength, such as musical abilities, proficiency in mathematical computation, drawing, and rote memory

~~for isolated facts. It is estimated that approximately 20% of people with autism earn average or above average scores on clinical evaluations of intelligence.~~ However, it is important to look beyond the numerical scores earned on intelligence tests. Because of the associated difficulties in communication and interpersonal relationships that people with autism experience, test results should be considered carefully—both quantitatively and qualitatively.

Restriction of Interests

Using stereotyped movements and patterns for organizing activities is another characteristic of children with autism. Many children with autism have a limited interest in the general environment but have consuming (even obsessive) interests in specific topics, such as train or bus schedules, television commercials, or numerals.

One must remember that not all people with autism display all of these characteristics. Furthermore, follow-up studies (Kabot et al., 2003) report that the disorder may change with age and intervention. Nonetheless, most studies confirm the persistence of autistic characteristics throughout an individual's life. The following vignette demonstrates some of these characteristics.

Michael was 4 years old when he was referred to a therapeutic nursery for children with special needs because of his lack of speech and his hyperactivity. Staff at the referring clinic believed that he had severe brain damage. From his medical history, this possibility had to be considered. He was the third child of Rh-incompatible parents. The pregnancy was normal, and Michael weighed 6 pounds, 7 ounces at birth. At 1 month of age, however, Michael's hemoglobin levels fell and he developed congestive heart failure. He was given a transfusion with packed red blood cells. No further neonatal difficulties occurred. In spite of the tumultuous events of his first month of life, the classic neurological examination and electroencephalogram findings were within normal limits. Yet, Michael displayed atypical symptoms in affect, interpersonal relationships, and language.

When Michael came to the nursery, he was small in stature, with pale translucent skin, full cheeks, and a pouting expression. He appeared to see no one. He wandered aimlessly about the room, paying no heed to verbal, visual, or tactile attempts to reach him. At the chalkboard, Michael grasped the chalk in his left hand with an awkward palmar grip and began to write a sequence of well-formed numerals and letters. He tolerated no interference while doing this.

Michael's parents reported that he developed typically, except he did not speak until he was 2¹/₂ years old. At that age, however, he could recite the alphabet and count to 100. At age 3, he began to spell words using his blocks. By age 4, Michael could read and spell several hundred words. Spontaneous language was limited, but he would occasionally manage to clearly articulate television commercials. He did not respond to words spoken to him.

There were other symptoms as well. Michael's parents reported that he would not go to bed until midnight. Sometimes, he came to the nursery in his pajamas. At *other times, he insisted on wearing his shoes to bed. He also could not tolerate anything being broken, not even soap bubbles.*

Michael's behavior and abilities demonstrated that he had high-functioning autism. In the nursery, initial contact was made with Michael by writing descriptions of his activities (e.g., "Michael eats a cookie"). Then, directions were written (e.g., "Draw a house"). Sometimes when Michael engaged in his number compulsion, his therapist would write "No numbers," and Michael would comply. Michael began to read the communications aloud. Sometimes, he was unwilling to write, so magnetic letters and a board were used. Michael started to pick up thoughts and elaborate on them in his writing, increasingly using sentences of greater complexity. There were also vocal productions, but they could only be followed with difficulty, if at all.

After his transition from the therapeutic nursery, the program's director followed Michael's progress. Michael's family moved out of state, and he was placed in a special education class for children with mild impairments. Correspondence with the family until Michael was 12 years old indicated that Michael was adjusting well to the school environment, although his achievement was sometimes erratic. Some of the obsessive behavior continued, but there were no seizures or other symptoms of neurological problems.

• •

The preceding vignette represents an optimistic outcome for a child with autism. A number of positive indicators were present: his high level of abilities, strong family support, early diagnosis, and appropriate intervention. Two important prognostic signs were his language before age 5 years and the absence of gross neurological findings.

Not all children with autism have such favorable outcomes. De Meyer et al. (1973) reported outcomes for 85 boys and 35 girls seen 7 years after the completion of intervention. Few used language spontaneously except to meet immediate needs. Some were echolalic, all were loners, and a large proportion functioned at levels commensurate with mental retardation. In addition, seizures were reported in approximately 25% of the children.

ETIOLOGY AND DIAGNOSIS

Since 1980, there has been greater specificity in the use of the term *autism*. Originally used as an adjective to describe the aloof behavior seen in these children, it became a diagnostic term used to describe all PDDs.

Kanner (1944) used the term for children who tend to look through people and lack responsiveness to others. He attributed this lack of responsiveness to "refrigerator parenting" (i.e., coldness) that stifled typical personality development. Although Kanner's contribution to the recognition of autism as a distinct disorder should be recognized, his tendency to blame parents for emotional frigidity represented a detour in the path toward understanding the disorder. Blaming "overintellectual" parents and attributing the inability of the children to form relationships was part of the strongly psychoanalytic temper of the times during the years in which Kanner worked. The presumption followed that the most effective treatment for autism was to treat the relationship between parents and children. This was the treatment of choice for many years until finally, in 1975, a task force appointed by the National Institute of Mental Health concluded that insight-based psychotherapy was an ineffective treatment approach for autism.

Other investigators had begun accumulating data that pointed to a developmental-biological etiology. Signs of central nervous system dysfunction were reported in studies in the United Kingdom by Rutter (1978). Bender (1952) and colleagues at Bellevue Hospital in New York City described the physiological and developmental characteristics in motility, homeostasis, body image, and muscle tone that were reflected in the psychological behavior associated with autism. Rimland (1964), a psychologist and the father of a child with autism, summarized the accumulating data as supporting a developmental-neuropsychological etiology for autism. His work and the continuing studies at the Autism Research Institute in San Diego, which he founded, provide a clearinghouse for information that is available to researchers and parents.

Although the etiology of autism still is not completely understood, accumulating evidence verifies that the disorder is a developmental disability, not a psychosis (Gilberg & Coleman, 1992). Most investigators conceptualize autism as a spectrum of disorders based on genetic susceptibility and triggered by unidentified pre- or postnatal factors. The genetic conditions are not Mendelian (i.e., inherited by the genetic principles described by Gregor Mendel) in character and are more likely to be the partial deletion of certain chromosomes that produce atypical behavior and development. These patterns have been determined from the family pedigrees of individuals with autism. (Family pedigrees are charts for determining genetic inheritance of certain diseases and disorders.) Not all family members display the disorder because precipitating factors affect individuals with genetic predisposition for autism. A broad range of precipitating factors is the focus of investigation. In studies of the histories of children with autism, Gilberg and Coleman (1992) found two statistically significant factors: 1) unusual amounts of exposure to chemicals and 2) maternal hypothyroidism, caused by autoimmune disease or possibly increased maternal age. Randall and Parker (1999) found that viral illnesses may be involved, suggesting that there is increased risk of autism after exposure to rubella during the first trimester of development. Kabot et al. (2003) cited investigations that implicate neurotransmitters, abnormalities in the limbic system of the brain, and defects involving the sixth and fifteenth chromosomes. However, the relationships between these neurobiological factors and the characteristic behaviors of autism are not yet clearly understood.

Some individuals claim that a deficit in theory of mind—or the ability to attribute mental states to oneself and others—is the core cause of the behaviors associated with autism (Baron-Cohen, 1989; Frith, 1989). Using the understanding of autism as a triad of impairments in communication, imagination, and socialization, this theory proposes that communication impairments arise from a problem with the semantics of mental states, imagination impairments arise from a problem in attributing mental states that are contrary to reality, and social impairments arise from an inability to understand the way that mental states affect behavior. As a result of this deficiency, this theory proposes that individuals with autism do not understand social situations and, thus, how to interact appropriately. Yirmiya, Erel, Shaked, and Solomonica-Levi (1998) performed three meta-analyses that compared the theory of mind abilities of individuals with autism, individuals with mental retardation, and typically developing individuals. Results indicated that those with autism and those with mental retardation had impaired abilities with theory of mind tasks and that the etiology associated with mental retardation was an important moderating variable in the analyses. This study concluded that theory of mind could not be regarded as a core explanation of autism because this impairment was not shown to be unique to autism.

The symptoms of autism make accurate assessment with conventional clinical measures difficult. For this reason, increased emphasis has been placed on developing methods for systematic observation of behavior and developmental history. Numerous checklists, inventories, and structured interviews have been created. However, practitioners in the field advise caution in the use of any assessment. They note that the identification of a single indicator, or even a cluster of indicators, does not warrant a diagnosis of autism. A more prudent course is for the professional to follow the child's development and to maintain contact with the family through the provision of long-term observation and preventive services.

Although the final definition of autism's etiology remains open to the results of ongoing research, current information suggests that the most plausible explanation involves a biological trait, genetic in origin, that renders a developing child vulnerable to insult early in life. This insult is physiological, possibly related to the conditions of uterine life or to chemical agents in the environment. In turn, the trauma produces autism as a behavioral response in the genetically vulnerable child.

The Need for Diagnosis

Although many etiological questions remain, conducting early, comprehensive, multidisciplinary, and ongoing evaluations can make important contributions to management of children with PDDs. Assessments of cognition can provide significant predictive clues to guide ongoing planning. They may also uncover special abilities that can play a role in adult vocational adjustment. Data on baseline functioning can be most useful for evaluating change and dispelling myths about "miracle cures" that appear from time to time, in both popular and professional literature. Finally, early comprehensive testing is necessary to verify the diagnosis and to ensure access to educational programs for the child and support services for the family.

Some parents report that the quality of diagnostic services is not always helpful. A clinician who expects children to respond on demand may find that this is not the case with children who have PDDs. Rigid approaches often result in empty reports that lecture parents and conclude the child is "untestable." A more useful approach to diagnosis is to structure the process as an ongoing, flexible activity that involves the child and his or her family.

Elements of Diagnosis

Before an evaluation is undertaken by a team of clinicians, including those in the disciplines of education, psychology, social work, and medicine, it is necessary to consider the purposes of diagnosis. What value will it have for the child and his or her family? It should not be arranged merely to provide data for a research project. The process of making a diagnosis can be painful for the family in that it recounts the child's history. The questions raised in this encounter with the parents might include the following:

• What are the child's current areas of weakness?

• What strengths are shown?

• What progress has been made?

• What are the next steps?

• What alternatives exist?

• How is the child's behavior managed at home, at school, and in the community?

The problems defined in this initial encounter can become the structure for the diagnostic process. The steps of the diagnostic process are as follows:

1. Collect family history data, the results of previous evaluations, and the child's medical history.

2. Get the parents' firsthand view of the child's typical day, areas of weakness, and interests, as well as of management issues.

3. With the parents, complete a questionnaire for autism (e.g., Autism Behavior Checklist [Krug, Arick, & Almond, 1993], Autism Diagnostic Interview–Revised [Lord, Rutter, & Le Couteur, 1994], Autism Diagnostic Observation Schedule [Lord, Rutter, Goode, et al., 1989], Pervasive Developmental Disorder Screening Test [Kabot et al., 2003]).

4. To the extent possible, administer measures of cognition, educational achievement, and verbal and nonverbal communication skills.

5. Conduct a play observation of the child in a natural setting such as school, clinic playroom, or home.

6. Integrate the information and data obtained from multiple sources and observers, then hold a conference to discuss this material with the family and other professionals involved in the child's care. In addition to sharing evaluation results, this conference should be used to plan the next steps in diagnosis and intervention.

This model is for an ideal diagnostic process; in reality, the parts of it available to children and their families depend on the availability of resources. Testing children suspected of having PDDs requires patience and flexibility. Examiners must make intelligent selections among existing instruments. Instructions may need to be given through gestures and pictures. Examiners should be willing to depart from regular test procedures, testing the limits through the use of graded cues. Such departures should be recorded for use in future evaluations. Insofar as possible, data concerning the child's ability to cope with measures of cognition, educational achievement, and communication skills should be obtained by observations in natural environments. Rather than the traditional techniques for personality assessment, observation of the child in natural settings would probably produce more useful data.

The planning conference is essential to the effectiveness of the diagnostic process. It should not be conducted with the purpose of examiners "informing" each other and the child's parents but, rather, in a cooperative spirit of sharing information among concerned individuals. Many examiners have much to learn from listening to parents. The brief periods of observation in connection with the diagnostic process are little more than sound bites. Parents have knowledge of their children in situations that cannot be observed in even the richest clinical settings.

Subgroups within the Autism Spectrum

Bishop (1989) cogently pointed out the differences in diagnostic terms used by professionals. For example, a child demonstrating the behaviors associated with a PDD may be diagnosed by a psychologist as being "autistic, with language problems, poor socialization, and lacking emotional warmth" (p. 107). A neurologist might describe the same child's problems as resulting from developmental aphasia. A child psychiatrist might term the problem as Asperger syndrome and observe that the child's insensitivity to others results in their rejecting him or her. The speech-language pathologist might use the term *semantic pragmatic disorder* to describe the child's condition, whereas a pediatrician might conclude that the child has pervasive developmental disorder-not otherwise specified (PDD-NOS). Each person according to his or her own discipline!

Bishop (1989) suggested that clinicians abandon rigid categories and recognize the core symptoms that shade into the milder forms of PDDs. Although language delays and deviations are often the symptoms that are recognized most prominently, the social and behavioral impairments cannot be considered secondary to language impairment. A child with autism does not need to learn how to speak but how to use language to communicate socially. Nonetheless, there are some subtypes within the general category of PDDs which have been recognized for distinguishing characteristics.

Rett's Disorder and Childhood Disintegrative Disorder Rett's disorder (per DSM terminology; also called Rett syndrome) and childhood disintegrative disorder are seen infrequently by mental health professionals because the problems involved usually cause the family to seek mental retardation programs and pediatric neurology services. Although Rett's disorder shares many characteristics with other PDDs, two diagnostic criteria differentiate it: 1) deceleration of growth in head circumference between the ages of 5 and 48 months and 2) apparently typical development for the first 5 months of life, followed by a loss of previously acquired motor, social, and prelanguage skills.

Childhood disintegrative disorder also represents a loss of previously acquired skills, but its course is more gradual than that of Rett's disorder. With childhood disintegrative disorder, typical development may continue for as long as 2 years, as indicated by age-appropriate language, interpersonal relationships, play, and adaptive behaviors. The DSM-IV-TR criteria for this diagnosis require atypical cognitive functioning and a loss (before age 10 years) of previously acquired skills in the areas of self-help, gross and fine motor control, and socialization.

Asperger's Disorder   Asperger's disorder (per DSM terminology; also called Asperger syndrome) is sometimes considered a milder subtype of autism because the two disorders have many characteristics in common. Although people with Asperger's disorder have the familiar triad of problems in social relationships, social communication, and social understanding, there are identifiable differences. Individuals with Asperger's disorder demonstrate relatively typical behavior in casual contact, but they tend to seem aloof and sometimes have long-winded conversations on obscure topics that may be of interest only to themselves. In addition, they may have motor "clumsiness" and a lack of common sense.

Children with Asperger's disorder differ from those with other PDDs in that their cognitive functioning is often average or above average. In addition, they usually have typical language development, although their word choices may be limited and their voice quality may be stilted, flat, and expressionless. They fail to master the give-and-take of the pragmatics of conversation as well. Although individuals with Asperger's disorder sometimes show an interest in making friends, their restricted interests make them seem eccentric, often rendering them the focus of teasing by other children. They may be good students—in fact, some become "perpetual students" who continue to study for the sake of studying rather than to pursue specific career goals.

Asperger's disorder has a more optimistic outcome than many other PDDs. Clinicians continue to discuss whether Asperger's disorder is part of the autistic spectrum or a separate disorder (Eisenmajer et al., 1996; Freeman, Cronin, & Candela, 2002). See Chapter 6 for more detailed information.

Pervasive Developmental Disorder-Not Otherwise Specified   Clinicians use the term *pervasive developmental disorder-not otherwise specified (PDD-NOS)* for children who, at an early age, possess some but not all of the characteristics of autism. It may be applied to young children who developed typically through 2 or 3 years of age and seem to have more general impairments in social interaction and communication skills. They do not meet all of the criteria for either autism or Asperger's disorder, and they tend to be "flat" in terms of cognitive functioning, with little evidence of specific interests or preoccupations. They may have relatively high levels of academic functioning, but these are often the result of intensive tutoring rather than motivation on the child's part. The skills learned are not usually integrated in a productive manner; rather, they remain isolated splinter skills. Children with PDD-NOS have an immature level of socialization that often results in their being teased by schoolmates. The next vignette illustrates the school placement problems of children with PDD-NOS.

Eleven-year-old Matthew's parents requested a psychological study to assist with determining his school placement. Matthew had been assigned to a class for children with moderately severe learning disabilities like his own, but many of his classmates had conduct disorders. Matthew soon bore the brunt of their aggressive behavior. When he was transferred to a classroom for children with mild learning disabilities, he was not teased but was unable to keep up with the academic requirements.

The developmental history provided by Matthew's mother indicated that he was born at 8 months' gestational age and weighed 7 pounds at birth. She said that there were no real concerns about his early health and development, except that he had chronic ear infections. By 5 months of age, he was sitting up, chattering, and doing all that was expected. He had some favorite foods and was taking steps toward walking, such as pulling himself up and holding on to the bars of his crib. At times, Matthew's mother noticed that he seemed not to hear her when she spoke to him and did not always respond to his name. She suspected a hearing loss, but Matthew's hearing was found to be normal at age 3 years. A change in development came when Matthew's mother was hospitalized briefly and he was left in the care of others. After that, both language and social development slowed down.

On the Wechsler Intelligence Scale for Children, Third Edition (Wechsler, 1991), Matthew earned a Full Scale IQ score of 59, with a Verbal score of 58 and a Performance score of 66. These scores are within the same range as those obtained 4 years earlier, although there was some increase in the Performance score. Matthew scored high points in the present record on subtests that measured speed and accuracy in a code-like task. Items dealing with social judgment and school achievement (e.g., arithmetic problem solving, vocabulary) were more difficult for Matthew. Individual achievement tests placed word recognition and word attack scores at high third-grade level. These scores probably resulted from 2 years of intensive tutoring arranged by his parents because of their concerns about his school placement. Unfortunately, these skills were not integrated in the process of reading text. Matthew's score for reading comprehension was at a low second-grade level, as was his score for spelling. Mathematics scores for calculation and applied problems placed him at the beginning first-grade level. Matthew could count, read numerals, and point out quantities as asked. He could read a thermometer and tell time to the hour, but he could not use coins to make change for simple purchases.

Fine motor control had improved since Matthew's previous evaluation. He was able to copy all of the figures of the Bender Visual Motor Gestalt Test (Bender, 1942), but they were disorganized and spread over two pages. There was perseveration in *his drawings of the serial figures; Matthew stopped drawing only when the edge of the paper was reached. On recall, he was able to draw three of the nine figures. Matthew was unable to draw a clock to indicate time because he did not know the symbolic relationships of the clock's hands and numerals. In addition, he was able to say the names of the days of the week and the months in sequence, but he could not locate elements within these sequences. Finally, he was unable to correctly identify his right and left.*

Matthew did not have much to say about his schooling. He stated that his present class was better because there was not so much fighting. He said that he liked working with his tutor, but it was not possible to elicit information about his relationship with any classmates or neighborhood peers. Other than saying that he watched television, Matthew could not describe how he spent his time after school.

INTERVENTION

The tantrums, destructive behavior, noncompliance, and self-injury exhibited by children with PDDs can make it difficult to include them in general social and educational settings. Rapin, a national figure in the field of child psychiatry and neurology, pointed out that medication cannot cure autism because, in most cases, "the brain has undergone atypical cellular development dating from the earliest embryonic stages" (2002, p. 303). According to Rapin, the goal is to alleviate troublesome symptoms so that a child with autism can profit from intensive targeted education. This statement places a tremendous responsibility on educators who administer and implement educational services for individuals with PDDs. Although educational intervention presents hopeful alternatives, it must be remembered that such intervention is not a cure. That is, children's symptoms may lessen or even change positively, but most individuals will continue to display some symptoms throughout their lives.

Wide-ranging interventions have been considered and recommended, and some have even been tested in controlled experimental programs. Many types of insight-based psychotherapy have been tried, but long-term results have not been impressive. Behavioral approaches have had varied results. Hewett (1965) used positive reinforcement to develop language use and to modify social skills. Lovaas (1987) has used intensive behavior modification approaches to improve interpersonal skills and to extinguish self-injurious behaviors. His approach has advocates and critics because it requires an extended intervention period (as long as 40 hours per week of one-to-one treatment) and both positive and aversive reinforcement. Other approaches include the use of megavitamins, dietary restrictions, sensory integration methods to reduce tactile defensiveness, and auditory integration techniques to reduce sensitivity to some sound frequencies. All approaches have some advocates, but it is generally believed that no single approach is effective in all cases.

Although results have not been dramatic, educational programs have been found useful in improving the quality of life of many people with PDDs. Most authorities recommend educational programs with the following components: communication therapy, social skills development, treatment for sensory impairment, and modification of behavior.

The goal of intervention for individuals with autism is to help them become fully functioning members of society. Many intervention projects are so focused on providing services, however, that they cannot allocate the time and structure for research and evaluation. Some researchers view this with concern. For example, Kabot et al. (2003) observed that the lack of evaluation research results in families and professionals making decisions on the basis of limited information. Most authorities agree that intervention plans must consider all options available, evaluate results regularly, and make adjustments in terms of the long-term goals. Freeman (1997, p. 649) suggested some basic questions to ask before adopting any intervention or placement:

- Will the treatment harm the child?

- Is the treatment developmentally appropriate for the child?

- Has the treatment been validated scientifically?

- How will the treatment be integrated into the child and the family's current intervention program?

- How will the child's progress toward desired outcomes be evaluated?

- Is there a back-up plan?

- Are there less restrictive or better researched options?

Such considerations are useful in planning for individuals, although hard data on program results, especially long-term effects, are scant. Nonetheless, some general trends that support educational intervention have been observed. For example, a generation ago, a high proportion of the people with PDDs were placed in institutions. Appropriate individualized services and programs have since made it possible for individuals with severe disabilities to learn skills for developing to their fullest potential at home, in day-treatment programs, and in group homes.

Principles of Educational Management

Some long-standing projects have reported results that make them useful models in guiding future programs. Schopler and Mesibov (1995) have worked for many years in the TEACCH (Treatment and Education of Autistic and related Communications handicapped Children) program on a statewide basis in North Carolina. The program goals have been to increase skill levels and to provide an environment in which effective accommodations can be provided for people with PDDs. Maintenance work with parents and supported work programs have ensured smoother transitions to adult life by program participants. Some hard data on long-term results, including modest IQ gains, have resulted.

Harris and Handleman (1994) conducted an intervention program at Douglas Developmental Disability Center of Rutgers University in New Jersey. Program goals were to narrow the gap between language skills and IQ scores through intensive behavior modification techniques, reciprocal play, and strengthening interpersonal relationships. Harris and Handleman found that even 1 year of such preschool intervention could narrow the language and cognitive functioning gaps between children with autism and their typically developing peers. The meticulous data collection at the Douglas Developmental Disability Center has provided excellent information on the natural history of the disorder.

Klin (1996) wrote in detail concerning intervention strategies with children with Asperger's disorder and other PDDs. He emphasized the need for initial transdisciplinary assessment by clinical specialists as a foundation for educational planning. These data, according to Klin, should be formulated into a report of assets and weaknesses to avoid the "unwarranted assumptions" that grow from stigmatizing labels. He believed that these children need direct instruction in how to

- Interpret the behavior of others

- Monitor their own social interactions

- Maintain interpersonal relationships by using eye contact, gaze, and gestures

- Understand the pragmatics of language

Klin (1996) described numerous teaching strategies that he has found to be useful for helping children with PDDs. Content should move from parts to the whole when rote skills are being taught. Some help with problem solving should be given in the classroom so that the children can learn to recognize and address potentially troublesome social situations. Teaching must provide opportunities for generalization to daily life—a transition that may be lacking in some behavioral modification programs, which teach isolated skills and do not ensure their application within the repertoire of real-life skills. Emphasis should also be placed on self-evaluation so that adaptive behavior skills encourage the highest level of self-sufficiency possible.

Klin (1996) included vocational education as part of this intervention program for older students. He also considered work with parents as an integral part of the intervention process. To provide effective education for their children, parents need to know about the range of available services and the quality of available programs. They also need to learn advocacy skills for dealing with special education planning teams in schools.

Grandin's (1991) first-person account provided striking insights about the education of people with autism. She recalled her frustration as a young child in being unable to express herself. She commented, "I understood but could not get the words out" (p. 1). She said that she communicated with a scream to express her discomfort when, for instance, her mother tried to put a hat on her head.

This example illustrates the confusing nature of hypersensitivity to touch often associated with autism.

Grandin (1991) described her thinking processes as visual, with little verbal mediation. She said that even as an adult, she is confused by long verbal strings of directions, complicated plots in novels, and sequences of calculation in algebra. In contrast, she described having excellent spatial skills.

Specific educational suggestions can be derived from Grandin's descriptions of her early education. Her early years were rigidly organized, with nursery school at 2¹/₂ years of age, daily speech therapy, and the services of a nanny who played games with Grandin and her sister for 3–4 hours each day. She said, "I was not allowed to tune out. My brain was kept connected to the world" (1991, p. 3). She provided numerous suggestions for educating children with autism, some of which are simply effective teaching methods for any child:

- Avoid long verbal strings.
- Use concrete visual methods to teach numbers.
- Protect children from loud sounds; whisper to them.
- Use padded, weighted vests to help control fidgeting.
- Avoid perceptual overload.
- Use realistic pictures or photographs because children with autism cannot integrate line drawings into complete pictures.

Parent Organizations

As with many other disorders, parents in self-help organizations can help one another enormously by providing support, information, and advocacy regarding PDDs. This may be accomplished through meetings, newsletters, journals, and Internet communications. For example, an Internet chat room organized by Wobus (1996) relayed some cogent advice to parents who have recently discovered that their children have autism. Some of this advice is summarized here:

- Seek intervention early.
- Start talking to other parents; for example, join the local chapter of the Autism Society of America.
- Remember that diagnostic testing is often the route to services through public schools, but make sure that the examiner is experienced in the assessment of children with autism.
- Watch out for groups that claim to know "the cure."
- Watch out for anyone who claims that autism is your fault.
- Look for someone who will write a detailed report of the child's intervention needs as determined by assessment, not someone who is married to a specific program.
- Read the popular and professional literature about autism.

CONCLUSION

Individuals with PDDs have fundamental impairments in social responsiveness, communication, and ideation. These disorders vary in degree and specific symptoms and can represent severe impairments with guarded outcomes. Although autism was once believed to reflect a family's emotional problems, most researchers at the beginning of the 21st century consider PDDs neurodevelopmental in origin. The unexplained increase in the number of children with PDD diagnoses has caused some authorities to express concern. Yet, others dismiss it as a reflection of increased knowledge on the part of parents and clinicians.

Although some common core symptoms link disorders on the autism spectrum, the DSM-IV-TR differentiates them in terms of age of onset, levels and quality of cognitive and language functioning, and outcomes. Some symptoms persist throughout life, and there are no cures for PDDs. Nevertheless, parent groups—in providing support, information, and advocacy skills—have made important contributions to the welfare of children with PDDs. Furthermore, early and intensive intervention can reduce some symptoms and enable people with PDDs to enjoy more inclusive lives.

REFERENCES

American Psychiatric Association. (1952). *Diagnostic and statistical manual of mental disorders.* Washington, DC: Author.

American Psychiatric Association. (1968). *Diagnostic and statistical manual of mental disorders* (2nd ed.). Washington, DC: Author.

American Psychiatric Association. (1980). *Diagnostic and statistical manual of mental disorders* (3rd ed.). Washington, DC: Author.

American Psychiatric Association. (1987). *Diagnostic and statistical manual of mental disorders* (3rd ed., rev.). Washington, DC: Author.

American Psychiatric Association. (1994). *Diagnostic and statistical manual of mental disorders* (4th ed.). Washington, DC: Author.

American Psychiatric Association. (2000). *Diagnostic and statistical manual of mental disorders* (4th ed., text rev.). Washington, DC: Author.

Baker, H.C. (2002). A comparison of autism spectrum disorder referrals: 1997 and 1989. *Journal of Autism and Developmental Disabilities, 32,* 121–125.

Baron-Cohen, S. (1989). The autistic child's theory of mind: A case of specific developmental delay. *Journal of Child Psychology and Psychiatry, 30,* 285–297.

Bender, L. (1942). *Bender Visual Motor Gestalt Test.* New York: American Orthopsychiatric Association.

Bender, L. (1952). *Child psychiatric techniques.* Springfield, IL: Charles C Thomas.

Bishop, D.V.M. (1989). Autism, Asperger's syndrome, and semantic pragmatic disorder: Where are the boundaries? *British Journal of Disorders of Communication, 24,* 107–201.

Cohen, S. (1998). *Targeting autism.* Berkeley: University of California Press.

Croen, L., Grethen, J., Hoophate, J., & Silver, S. (2002). Changing prevalence of autism. *Journal of Autism and Developmental Disorders, 32,* 207–217.

De Meyer, M.K., Barton, S., De Meyer, W.E., Norton, J.A., Allen, J., & Steele, R. (1973). Prognosis in autism: A follow-up study. *Journal of Autism and Childhood Schizophrenia, 3,* 199–246.

Eisenmajer, R., Prior, M., Leekam, S., Wing, L., Gould, J., Welham, M., & Ong, B. (1996). Comparison of clinical symptoms in autism and Asperger's disorder. *Journal of the American Academy of Child and Adolescent Psychiatry, 35*(11), 1523–1531.

Freeman, B.J. (1997). Guidelines for evaluating intervention programs for children with autism. *Journal of Autism and Developmental Disorders, 27,* 641–651.

Freeman, B.J., Cronin, R., & Candela, P. (2002). Asperger syndrome or autistic disorder? *Focus on Autism and Other Developmental Disorders, 17*(3), 145–149.

Frith, U. (1989). *Autism: Exploring the enigma.* Malden, MA: Blackwell Publishers.

Gilberg, C., & Coleman, M. (1992). *The biology of the autistic syndromes.* New York: MacKeith Press.

Grandin, T. (1991). Overcoming autism: A first-person account. *Harvard Mental Health Newsletter, 3,* 1–4.

Harris, S.L., & Handleman, E. (1994). *Preschool education for children with autism.* Austin, TX: PRO-ED.

Hewitt, F. (1965). Teaching speech to autistic children through operant conditioning. *American Journal of Orthopsychiatry, 35,* 927–936.

Kabot, S., Masi, E., & Segal, M. (2003). Advances in the diagnosis and treatment of autism spectrum disorders. *Professional Psychology: Research and Practice, 34*(1), 26–33.

Kanner, L. (1944). Early infantile autism. *Journal of Pediatrics, 25,* 211–217.

Klin, A. (1996). *Asperger's syndrome: Guidelines for treatment and intervention.* Pittsburgh: Learning Disabilities Association of America.

Krug, D., Arick, J., & Almond, P. (1993). *Autism Screening Instrument for Educational Planning, Second Edition* (ASIEP-2). Austin, TX: PRO-ED.

Lord, D., Rutter, M., Goode, S., Heernsbergen, J., Mawhood, L., & Schopler, E. (1989). Autism diagnostic observation schedule: A standardized observation of communicative and social behavior. *Journal of Autism and Developmental Disorders, 19,* 185–212.

Lord, C., Rutter, M., & Le Couteur, A. (1994). Autism Diagnostic Interview–Revised: A revised version of a diagnostic interview for caregivers of individuals with possible pervasive developmental disorders. *Journal of Autism and Developmental Disorders, 24,* 659–685.

Lovaas, O.I. (1987). Behavior treatment and normal education and intellectual functioning in young autistic children. *Journal of Consulting and Clinical Psychology, 55,* 3–9.

National Institute of Mental Health Research Task Force. (1975). *Research in the service of mental health.* Bethesda, MD: Author.

Randall, P., & Parker, J. (1999). *Supporting the families of children with autism.* New York: John Wiley & Sons.

Rapin, I. (2002). The autistic spectrum disorders. *The New England Journal of Medicine, 347*(5), 302–303.

Rimland, B. (1964). *Infantile autism: The syndrome and its implications for a neural theory of behavior.* New York: Appleton-Century-Crofts.

Rutter, M. (1978). Diagnosis and definition of childhood autism. *Journal of Autism and Developmental Disorders, 8,* 135–161.

Schopler, E., & Mesibov, G.B. (1995). *Learning and cognition in autism.* New York: Kluwer Academic/Plenum Publishers.

Schwartz, S., & Johnson, J.H. (1985). *Psychopathology of childhood.* New York: Pergamon Press.

Wechsler, D. (1991). *Wechsler Intelligence Scale for Children, Third Edition.* San Antonio, TX: The Psychological Corp.

Wing, L. (1988). The continuum of autistic characteristics. In E. Schopler & G.B. Mesibov (Eds.), *Diagnosis and assessment in autism* (pp. 91–110). New York: Kluwer Academic/Plenum Publishers.

Wing, L., & Potter, D. (2002). The epidemiology of autistic spectrum disorders: Is prevalence rising? *Mental Retardation & Developmental Disorders, 8*(3), 151–161.

Wobus, J. (1996). Advice to parents who discover their child is autistic. *Autism Resources.* Retrieved August 12, 2003, from http://www.autism-resources.com/advice-to-parents.html

Yirmiya, N., Erel, O., Shaked, M., & Solomonica-Levi, D. (1998). Meta-analyses comparing theory of mind abilities of individuals with autism, individuals with mental retardation, and normally developing individuals. *Psychological Bulletin, 124*(3), 293–307.

6

Asperger Syndrome

**Brenda Smith Myles, Elisa Gagnon,
Sherry A. Moyer, and Melissa L. Trautman**

* *

Chapter Concepts

- Definition of Asperger syndrome and its associated characteristics
- The criteria and process used to make a diagnosis of Asperger syndrome
- Common treatment regimens for families, educators, and individuals with Asperger syndrome
- Suggested roles for general and special educators in the treatment of Asperger syndrome
- Accommodations that enhance school success for students with Asperger syndrome

Picture for a moment being plucked from comfortable, familiar surroundings, dropped into the center of the most foreign culture imaginable, and told to find your way home. Correctly navigating social customs, expressions, body language, and tone of voice would all be important factors to a successful journey. This is what individuals with Asperger syndrome (AS) must do every day, even in what should be the comfort of their home. It is assumed that these skills come naturally to everyone; however, people with AS are forced to think continually about what should happen next. The following vignette provides an illustrative introduction to AS.

Fifteen-year-old Jon has a diagnosis of AS and is a sophomore at a suburban public high school. He has an obsessive interest in Godzilla and frequently attempts to dominate conversations by discussing this topic. His classmates have always considered him odd and, despite his desire to have friends, he has been unable to fit in with any group.

Jon lives with his parents and younger sibling in an upper middle-class neighborhood. His father is an engineer and a highly focused individual who takes his role as family breadwinner very seriously. He works long hours and has limited involvement with his family. Jon's mother is his primary caregiver. Her persistence was instrumental in finding a correct diagnosis for Jon's condition, and she has been very involved in obtaining services for him. She seems as obsessed with AS as Jon is with Godzilla.

Day-to-day life in the household is predictable and structured. Even the family meals follow a definite structure, with predictable meals being served each evening. For example, Monday is spaghetti night, and roast beef is always served on Sunday. Any change in routine produces anxiety in Jon and his family. In fact, Jon's 12-year-old sister demonstrates similar traits, including expressing a high degree of anxiety, an obsessive need for cleanliness, and a lack of friends. Jon's mother appears unaware of this and describes her daughter as "pretty and popular."

A parent interview revealed that Jon's birth was uneventful. Jon's mother was 30 when he was born, and she eagerly anticipated the role of full-time wife and mother. She pursued her new role with as much passion as she had previously shown for her job as an accountant for a major corporation.

Developmentally, Jon appeared to progress typically. During his infant and toddler years, he was even described as a "perfect" child by more than one person. He ate, never attempted to climb out of his crib, and would spend hours looking at books or playing with his shape sorter. He was content to entertain himself and showed no interest in other children during weekly playgroups. He displayed signs of being very intelligent, talked early, and demonstrated great interest in numbers and letters. Because his parents had no typically developing child for comparison, they were unconcerned when Jon insisted on wearing the same clothes each day, always carried his toy monsters with him, or became outraged by any change of routine.

When Jon was 4 years old, his preschool teacher expressed concern that Jon was unable to put on his shoes or dress himself. Jon's mother made an appointment with a developmental pediatrician at the nearby university medical center. The examining doctor found that Jon was nearly 2 years behind his peers in gross motor and daily living skills, so an appointment was scheduled for a multidisciplinary team screening. This evaluation revealed that Jon demonstrated many characteristics commonly associated with a pervasive developmental disorder.

Jon's kindergarten year was a disaster. Despite his above-average intelligence, Jon refused to participate in a variety of activities, including fingerpainting, circle time, and coloring. He was clumsy, could not catch a ball, and would not join the other children in the classroom's play centers. He wandered aimlessly around the classroom and constantly interrupted adults and classmates with long narratives about monsters.

At age 6, Jon received a diagnosis of AS from a clinical psychologist. Jon's mother pursued the diagnosis after reading an article about the disorder. She began attempting to educate the local school district about her son's special needs. She discovered that most educators had little or no information about AS and became frustrated at what she perceived as refusal to provide her son what he needed to progress in school.

In elementary school, Jon was seldom invited to anyone's house and was never invited to a classmate's birthday party. He had difficulty transferring social rules between settings and had to learn each set of rules in isolation. For example, the rule "no kicking in school" did not translate to "no kicking on the playground" for him until he was directly taught the new connection. He continued his interest in monsters, but by sixth grade, he had narrowed his interest to Godzilla. He spent hours watching Godzilla videotapes and looking through his collection of Godzilla comic books. His long dialogues about the monster were annoying to everyone, including his family, and his obsession led to his being the butt of classmates' jokes. He did not understand teasing and was often the victim of cruel schoolyard pranks.

Middle school proved no better. Dealing with seven teachers was nearly impossible for Jon, and he began to have "meltdowns" (severe tantrums) several times per month. These meltdowns consisted of yelling, crying, and running away from adults. The teachers believed that these meltdowns happened for no reason and insisted that Jon needed to learn to live in the real world and accept the consequences of his actions. Jon refused to use his locker and carried a 35-pound backpack all day. He interrupted others in class, ate lunch alone, and frequently refused to go to school. Monthly meetings were set up to review Jon's individualized education program (IEP), and his teachers slowly began to understand Jon's unique needs.

Once appropriate interventions were in place, Jon began to be more comfortable in a school environment. For Jon, these interventions included having a home base, visual supports, and individual time with a school counselor to work on social skills. He continues to make progress in high school and appears to be increasingly comfortable with himself as a unique individual.

CHARACTERISTICS OF ASPERGER SYNDROME

In 1944, Hans Asperger, a Viennese pediatrician, wrote extensively about a group of children who exhibited social differences despite having average cognitive and speech development. His writings went unrecognized, however, until Wing (1981) published a paper about Asperger's work in relation to her work with 35 individuals 5–35 years of age. Recognition of AS was further advanced when the American Psychiatric Association (APA) added AS to its list of pervasive developmental disorders identified in the *Diagnostic and Statistical Manual of Mental Disorders, Fourth Edition* (DSM-IV; APA, 1994). Interest in the syndrome that now bears Asperger's name has continued to grow; as of 2003, AS is recognized as a relatively common developmental disability with profound impact.

Despite this recognition, little is known about the disorder. For example, researchers and practitioners continue to debate whether AS is an independent diagnostic category or an autism spectrum disorder (Klin, Volkmar, & Sparrow, 2000). There is no debate, however, that increasing numbers of individuals have AS (Fombonne & Tidmarch, 2003). Although the text revision of the *Diagnostic and Statistical Manual of Mental Disorders, Fourth Edition* (DSM-IV-TR; APA, 2000), declined to identify a prevalence rate for AS, researchers such as Kadesjo, Gillberg, and Hagberg (1999) have estimated that as many as 48.4 per 10,000 children could have the syndrome.

Social and Emotional Characteristics of the Syndrome

AS is thought to be primarily a social disorder (Myles & Adreon, 2001; Myles & Simpson, 2003; Paul, 2003). Despite a desire to interact with others, children and adolescents with AS lack knowledge of and skills for initiating and responding in various social situations. They also demonstrate an inability to understand the thoughts or beliefs of others. Children and youth with AS are typically considered socially awkward, egocentric, and inflexible. In addition, they have difficulty understanding nonverbal social cues and interpreting facial expressions, postures, gestures, and tone of voice in social contexts (Koning & McGill-Evans, 2001). Therefore, even when children and adolescents with AS actively seek interactions with others, their lack of understanding about the rules of social behavior—including eye contact, proximity to others, gestures, and posture—causes social isolation (Myles & Southwick, 1999).

Although lack of social awareness is a hallmark of AS, many students with AS acknowledge that they are different from their peers. Thus, difficulties with self-esteem and self-concept are common among individuals with AS (Barnhill & Myles, 2001). These problems are particularly significant during adolescence and young adulthood (Myles & Adreon, 2001). Even when self-esteem problems are apparent to others, however, children and youth with AS may deny their existence and even be unaware of them (Barnhill et al., 2000).

Children and youth with AS often experience emotional and behavioral problems related to their social deficits. Moreover, these challenges frequently involve feelings of stress, loss of control, or inability to predict outcomes (Myles & South-wick, 1999). Thus, students with AS typically have behavioral problems connected to their inability to function in a world they consider unpredictable and threaten-ing. In addition, many individuals with AS acquire learned helplessness and experience depression that is often related to social failures.

learned helpless

Restricted Range of Interests

Individuals with AS often have a restricted range of interests or obsessions (APA, 2000; Gagnon, 2001). No pattern has been found in the special interests of children and youth with AS; the interests appear to be diverse and may encompass subjects such as geology, astronomy, mechanics, numbers, or fabrics. Special interests may be similar to those enjoyed by peers without disabilities, but individuals with AS often choose one topic to the exclusion of all others or possess an exhaustive knowledge of the topic that is inconsistent with that of their neurotypical peers.

Intellectual and Academic Characteristics

Although the DSM-IV-TR lists typical cognitive functioning as a diagnostic crite-rion, little is known about the cognitive abilities of students diagnosed with AS. One of the few studies conducted in this area found that the average intelligence quotient (IQ) of children and youth with AS was 100, with 22% demonstrating superior to very superior IQ scores (Barnhill, Hagiwara, Myles, & Simpson, 2000).

Students with AS frequently experience significant academic problems in reading, math, and written expression. Moreover, they often have difficulty gener-alizing knowledge and skills. With suitable support, however, most students with AS are able to succeed in school, and a number of them are able to attend college and enjoy a variety of successful careers. In particular, students with AS generally have difficulty comprehending abstract materials (e.g., idioms, metaphors), under-standing inferentially based materials, and applying skills and knowledge to solve problems. Strengths among children and youth with AS tend to be in comprehension of factual material (Church, Alisanki, & Amanullah, 2000; Gris-wold, Barnhill, Myles, Hagiwara, & Simpson, 2002).

Sensory and Motor Characteristics

Children and youth with AS experience sensory integration challenges across all sensory areas. In fact, the sensory issues seen in children and youth with AS are pervasive and resemble those of individuals with autism (Rinner, 2000). However, children and youth with AS are apt to demonstrate more disruptive behaviors when they encounter sensory problems (Dunn, Myles, & Orr, 2002).

Wing (1981) and others (Dunn et al., 2002; Ghaziuddin & Butler, 1998; Myles, Cook, Rinner, Robbins, & Miller, 2000) observed that children with AS tend to have poor motor skills along with coordination and balance problems. These issues significantly affect sports, social skills, writing, art, and industrial arts (Myles et al., 2000).

Comorbidity Issues

Comorbidity refers to the presence of two (or more) disorders. Research on AS comorbidity issues is in its infancy. Limited evidence suggests that AS is similar to autism in that "comorbidity is often the rule rather than the exception" (Ghaziuddin, 2002, p. 139). Attention-deficit/hyperactivity disorder (ADHD) and depression are the two most common psychiatric conditions that may occur in individuals with AS. Other coexisting psychiatric conditions include mood disorders, schizophrenia, obsessive compulsive disorder, and tic disorders (Ghaziuddin, 2002). According to Raja and Azzoni (2001) and Ghaziuddin (2002), as many as 40% of individuals with AS may have these conditions. Medical conditions—such as seizure disorders, chromosome abnormalities, and sleep disorders—although less common than psychiatric disorders, are also evidenced in children and youth with AS (Ghaziuddin, 2002).

DIAGNOSING ASPERGER SYNDROME

Because no biological markers exist for diagnosing AS, medical professionals rely on the identification of behavioral indicators found in the DSM-IV-TR. As shown in Appendix A at the end of the book, these diagnostic criteria include 1) impairments in social interaction; 2) restricted repetitive and stereotyped patterns of behavior, interests, and activities; and 3) impairment in social, occupational, or other important areas of functioning. Individuals with AS must also have average IQ scores, demonstrate age appropriate self-help and adaptive skills, and experience no delay in language onset (APA, 2000).

Several methods exist by which to identify AS:

- Diagnostic tests

- Interviews with caregivers (Filipek et al., 1999; Plotts & Webber, 2001–2002)

- Observations in multiple settings

- Assessment of skills, behavior, and other previously identified areas of challenge (Charak & Stella, 2001–2002; Plotts & Webber, 2001–2002)

The following subsections describe each aforementioned method. In addition to identifying core characteristics of AS, these methods can be used to identify comorbid conditions that are common in individuals with AS (Filipek et al., 1999; Ghaziuddin, 2002).

Diagnostic Tests

As of 2004, AS is a medical diagnosis that is rendered by a medical professional based on his or her clinical judgment from a variety of sources, including the completion of assessments that directly measure student performance or obtain parent perceptions and observations of behaviors. Because AS is a relatively new diagnosis, not appearing in the DSM until the fourth edition in 1994, few screening instruments exist.

The Asperger Syndrome Diagnostic Scale (ASDS; Myles, Bock, & Simpson, 2000) was developed specifically to differentiate children and youth with AS from those with other disabilities (i.e., ADHD, autism, emotional and behavioral disorders, learning disabilities). The norm-referenced measure contains 50 items and can be completed in 10–15 minutes by caregivers, educators, or others who know the child well. It has good reliability and validity, and normative procedures found that the ASDS was able to correctly classify subjects with AS with 85% accuracy (Charak & Stella, 2001–2002).

The Autism Diagnostic Interview–Revised (ADI-R; Lord, Rutter, & LeCouteur, 1994) is a comprehensive interview protocol to be used with caregivers whose children might have autism spectrum disorder (Plotts & Webber, 2001–2002). Despite good reliability and validity, this instrument is used by a limited number of clinicians because of its lengthy administration time (i.e., approximately 1 hour) and requirements for specific training and validation procedures. The ADI-R can lead to a diagnosis of autism spectrum disorder in general rather than a diagnosis of AS. It is, however, considered a part of the gold standard research protocol (Filipek et al., 1999).

Ehlers, Gillberg, and Wing (1999) developed the Autism Spectrum Screening Questionnaire (ASSQ) to assess symptoms indicative of AS and other high-functioning autism spectrum disorders. The authors noted that the ASSQ was designed to detect a "wider range of symptoms and more subtle social impairments than the DSM-IV . . . criteria for Asperger Syndrome" (p. 137). Ehlers and colleagues cautioned that this 27-item survey is not to be used to make a diagnosis but, rather, to determine whether further assessment is needed for high-functioning autism spectrum disorders (Ehlers et al., 1999).

Interviews with Caregivers

Procuring a thorough familial and developmental history as well as parental perceptions of a child's behaviors can be important in diagnosing AS. Obtaining a family history is critical because incidences of autism, anxiety disorders, fragile X syndrome, and tuberous sclerosis increase in families of children with autism spectrum disorders, including AS (Fombonne, Bolton, Prior, Jordan, & Rutter, 1997). Interviewers can obtain a child's physical, language/communication, social, behavioral, and educational profile by using a diagnostic protocol that directly addresses the behaviors and skills present in individuals with AS or by using a semistructured format (i.e., one without a specific protocol) (Plotts & Webber, 2001–2002). Semistructured interviews can be valuable, but, as noted by Plotts & Webber, "the utility and validity of the information gathered from the interview is largely dependent upon the interviewer's skills and knowledge" (2001–2002, p. 25). Filipek et al. (1999) identified a series of parental concerns that are red flags for children with autism spectrum disorders, as well as a set of questions regarding socialization, communication, and behavior that can serve as interview items. Plotts and Webber (2001–2002) asserted that the interview framework developed by Sattler (1998) is appropriate for children and youth with autism spectrum disorders, including AS. Sattler's interview is comprehensive and quite lengthy, with 353 questions focusing on 16 areas of functioning, including 1) peer interactions, 2) affective responses, 3) communication ability, 4) use of senses and responses to the environment, 5) a need for sameness, and 6) play and amusements.

The Autism Diagnostic Observation Schedule (ADOS; Lord, Rutter, DiLavore, & Risi, 2001) is a semistructured observational assessment designed to identify individuals with autism spectrum disorders. The ADOS has four modules, two of which are designed to be administered to individuals who are higher functioning (Module 3: Fluent Speech–Child/Adolescent; Module 4: Fluent Speech–Adolescent/Adult). Approximately 30–45 minutes are required to complete this tool. Although reliability and validity are considered good, the ADOS does not specifically lead to an AS classification (Charak & Stella, 2001–2002). Considered the gold standard among autism research protocols, this instrument is not widely used in clinical practices in the United States because of time constraints (Filipek et al., 1999).

Observations in Multiple Settings

The social interactions of a child with AS may differ across individuals (e.g., adult versus child interactions), across varying environmental structures (e.g., a structured game versus an unstructured play sequence), or when specific sensory stimuli are present (e.g., loud noises for a child who experiences auditory sensitivity). Thus, observation of the child at home, in school, and in the community can yield invaluable information. Most often, however, this diagnostic option is not viable for medical professionals with time limitations.

Assessment of Skills, Behavior, and Other Previously Identified Areas of Challenge

Individuals with AS experience myriad challenges that exceed the criteria identified by the DSM-IV-TR (APA, 2000). Thus, a comprehensive assessment of a child or youth with AS is mandatory. Specifically, the following areas should be assessed:

- Problem and adaptive behaviors (Barnhill et al., 2000)

- Academic subjects, including reading (Myles et al., 2002), mathematics (Griswold et al., 2002), and written expression (Myles, Huggins, Rome, Hagiwara, & Barnhill, 2003)

- Problem solving (Griswold et al., 2002)

- Sensory integration (Dunn et al., 2002)

A comprehensive discussion of the aforementioned assessment protocol is beyond the scope of this chapter. Readers interested in further information should refer to Myles, Adreon, and Stella (2003).

ESTABLISHING A CORRECT
DIAGNOSIS AND FAMILY-FOCUSED INTERVENTION

Interventions performed only at school or at home are less successful than a comprehensive intervention plan that is implemented in all of the child's environments. Consistent communication between family members and professionals is essential, and the program should allow for the child's changing needs as he or she matures. AS is a developmental disability that is pervasive in nature, so family members and professionals must learn to recognize its dynamic nature. By definition, a *syndrome* is a collection of related symptoms or characteristics that can vary slightly in each person, and its presenting characteristics will change across an individual's life span.

Regardless of who initially suspects a diagnosis of AS—whether family members, school personnel, or health care providers—it is likely that the other parties involved have seen the child's areas of challenge or dysfunction. Once all stakeholders have been notified of the potential or definitive diagnosis of AS, all involved with the child must meet and assess the situation. This is the first step toward creating a proper intervention program.

The following example illustrates a family whose child has not yet received a formal diagnosis, thereby providing a more complete and realistic profile of a typical family's experience:

A parent e-mailed an organization that disseminates information about AS. He believed that his child had AS. However, the child's physician had only tested the child for ADHD. This person requested diagnostic criteria to give his child's doctor, whom the man believed would consider a diagnosis of AS if presented with the correct information. This parent concluded by expressing gratitude for any information that might address the difficulties that his child was experiencing.

• •

An immediate item of interest in this story is the pediatrician's testing the child for ADHD. ADHD is a common initial misdiagnosis because of its similarities with AS in executive function skill deficits, including organizational skills, impulse control, and the ability to generalize information. The parent's decision to search the Internet for information represents many families' situations as well. This also holds true for teachers and other school personnel who, frustrated by a student's classroom difficulties, turn to the Internet for additional information. In fact, this approach is the first step toward an accurate diagnosis in a large number of cases. Furthermore, the parent's request for guidance and expression of emotion demonstrate a common progression of events for family members who have discovered that they need a way to approach physicians for additional support and guidance. It is important to note that parents typically experience a wide range of emotions while navigating the time between first noticing their child's difficulties and getting an accurate diagnosis. The guilt and frustration of feeling inadequate or unsuccessful in their role as parents often strips them of their sense of self-esteem and competence in other areas of their life.

On average, children with AS receive 4.5 misdiagnoses prior to receiving a correct diagnosis (Myles, Simpson, & Becker, 1994–1995). In the best situation, a knowledgeable professional will quickly recognize the disorder, but the reality is often years of inappropriate interventions that only aggravate the child's symptoms and the family's problems.

If school staff members first suggest AS as a possibility, they should approach a child's family knowing that stress levels are probably quite high. An objective presentation of the indications for further evaluation, along with recommendations for the type of professional appropriate for conducting such assessment, would be most helpful at this point. Asking the following questions during the assessment phase helps establish fitting interventions:

1. *How old is the child?* This is helpful for developmental purposes because children with AS typically display social or emotional behaviors that are much younger than their chronological age.

2. *What problem behavior(s) prompted someone to seek help for the child?* Every individual with AS presents with a slightly different list of dominating characteristics.

3. *In which environment does the child have the most difficulty? At home, at school, or both?* Sometimes, the problems are not present in both environments, but this should not deter the family from continuing to explore the issues at hand. For families in crisis because of their child's behavior, prioritization of problem areas and viable solutions offers the best chance for everyone to gain a sense of control and success. Once the primary concerns are addressed, there is plenty of time to move to the less troubling issues.

4. *Has intervention been tried yet? If so, therapies, medications, or both?* If the parents previously sought help but the child received inaccurate diagnoses or interventions, it is unlikely that they have seen meaningful positive change in their child's behaviors or well-being. Knowing the previous history, though, helps establish more reliable patterns of behavior and likely solutions.

5. *How well does the family handle the challenging behaviors? Are family members willing to acknowledge that the problem exists or that it might be AS?* No parent ever expects to face the overwhelming nature of a developmental disability, so denial is a common—but potentially dangerous—parental coping mechanism.

6. *If the parents acknowledge the situation, do they agree on the root causes of the challenging behaviors and on possible treatments or interventions?* The answer to this question is extremely important regarding ideas on how to proceed.

7. *What is the child's total environment like?* It is often necessary to get a picture of the child's surroundings and degree of success in navigating daily life. This requires conducting a functional behavioral assessment, which is designed to

comprehensively evaluate the child's total environment and to identify areas that could be modified to improve the likelihood of future success.

Strategies for Intervention

The primary goal of intervention is for the child and family to learn to manage AS more than it manages them. With proper supports, families should eventually find that the effects of AS no longer consume their lives. In general, the following process can be used when formal intervention is indicated, regardless of who takes the lead intervention role or which of the ensuing strategies is used:

1. Assess the situation as thoroughly and accurately as possible.

2. Stabilize the child *and* the family. Initiate whatever treatment is required for them to regain some control over the environment.

3. Become educated on all of the issues and interventions surrounding the disorder.

4. Create a long-term treatment plan and stick with it. Most of these issues do not remediate themselves or go away over night.

5. Be flexible enough to reassess the process and start over. Try, try again!

Assessment Phase: Observe and Document Behavioral Triggers A functional behavioral assessment can determine the environmental triggers that cause challenging behaviors, frustration, or meltdowns in children with AS. Some people think that children with AS are simply having a tantrum or are extremely manipulative. In reality, most of children with AS do not have enough flexibility in their thought processes to entertain such ambiguities. They view situations in black-or-white terms.

For a child with AS, behaviors generally occur because he or she does not know how to respond to a situation. Because of information processing problems, a buildup of emotions, and/or executive function deficits, the child responds emotionally—before a logical solution can be selected. This is important to note when consulting with medical or educational professionals (e.g., occupational therapists, speech-language pathologists). The professionals chosen for consultation must understand that behavioral change requires modification of the child's environment to minimize behavioral triggers; otherwise, the behaviors may actually worsen over time (O'Neill et al., 1997).

Stabilization Phase: Take Immediate Steps to Reduce Anxiety at Home and School Sometimes it is necessary to retreat from complicated interventions and revert to a simplified lifestyle until a crisis subsides. If a child with AS is in crisis mode, the ability to regain control of poorly modulated emotions is impaired—if not completely exhausted—by anxiety. It truly is a situation in which rest and relaxation is all that should occur until the child can process a cognitively based conversation regarding his or her difficulties. A reduction in all scheduled activities—including school—is necessary for at least a few days; up to 2 weeks may be required in more dire cases. The best advice at this point is to provide a safe environment and demand as little as possible from the child until he or she regains emotional stability and is ready to tolerate a more demanding schedule.

Education Phase: Get the Right Kind of Professional Help   Obtaining the right kind of professional help is critical, but finding such help is not necessarily obvious. Thus, the following subsections act as a brief guide to certain types of help.

Psychiatrists, Psychologists, and Social Workers   Psychiatrists can make the actual diagnosis of AS and prescribe medications for comorbid conditions. If medication is required, they will continue to monitor it, but psychiatrists generally do not provide the type of therapy that ameliorates AS issues. Because of theory of mind deficits (i.e., an inability to appropriately assess other people's thoughts and motivations), traditional psychoanalysis based on feelings is not helpful for individuals with AS (Pope, 1993).

Psychologists can also make the initial diagnosis of AS but cannot prescribe medication that may aid behavioral interventions. However, psychologists are a very good choice for providing cognitively based behavioral therapy, which is effective for issues associated with problem solving, relationships, and negative emotions. Social workers can provide similar services and crisis or anger management techniques. Insurance companies tend to prefer social workers because their rates are lower.

Medication   Unfortunately, irresponsible and sensational media coverage has made the use of medications with children controversial. In very small doses, however, certain types of medication have proven to be effective when used in combination with behavioral intervention. No medication is available specifically for the treatment of AS, although treating comorbid symptoms such as anxiety, depression, or obsessive-compulsive disorder is an effective practice. It is also anecdotally reported that the standardized doses for these comorbid disorders are generally too high for individuals with autism spectrum disorders. The same medications can be used but are more effective in much smaller dosages.

Speech-Language Pathologists   Speech-language pathologists are excellent resources when children require assistance in pragmatics (the functional use of language) and semantics (the distinction between literal meaning and insinuation). Difficulties in these two areas often cause miscommunication. Frustration often ensues, leading to all kinds of behavioral problems.

Social Skills Training   Social skills training is a necessity because social skills deficits are pervasive among individuals who have received a diagnosis of AS. Numerous social skills techniques are available, but no conclusive research exists on the efficacy of one program over another. Myles and Southwick (1999) developed one such effective social skills training method. Using direct instruction, the program elements include rationale, presentation, modeling, verification, evaluation, and generalization. Thus, this method offers 1) an explanation of why a certain skill or behavior is necessary, 2) an active or multimodal presentation of the skill, 3) modeling of the desired behaviors and close interaction with the child,

4) evaluation of the child's performances with thorough explanations, and 5) discussion of opportunities for using the same skill in other situations.

Occupational Therapists   Occupational therapy usually is essential because studies have shown that more than 50% of children with AS also have sensory integration processing deficits (Myles et al., 2000). Sensory integration problems affect basic human sensory experiences, causing oversensitivity to the taste or texture of foods, oversensitivity to the feel of clothing, an inability to tolerate bright lights or large crowds, and a tremendous sensitivity to smells that most people never notice. Obviously, occupational therapy is a first line of defense for many families just to make daily living tolerable for their children with AS.

Long-Term Goals: Include the Rest of the Family   Involving the rest of the family is very important for both the stabilization and long-term phases of the intervention process. Neither will be completed successfully until the effect of the person's behavior on other members of the household has been addressed. Siblings may be embarrassed by their brother or sister's awkward behaviors. At other times, siblings feel neglected by their parents, who must care for the more immediate needs of the family member with AS.

Parents may feel trapped, having to reconcile their own feelings while providing support and guidance for their family. They also must come to an agreement on the best intervention method for the child with AS, and that agreement typically does not come easily. As if those issues were not enough, parents must navigate through a sea of documentation and bills.

A long-term plan and reassessment of intervention steps are possible only after control has been regained and all family members' emotions have calmed enough for constructive participation. Statements made about emotions, the child's behavioral motivations, and others' behavioral motivations may be unreliable when made during the heat of the moment. There is no rule of thumb for which step is right or how much time is needed to see measurable results. Flexibility is crucial to successful efforts, as is the consistency with which stakeholders carry out their daily activities.

Following the general guidelines in this section and tailoring them to fit the specific needs of each child and family is the best approach. It may take several months or even years of intervention for the child and family to consistently reach the primary goal of managing AS more than it manages them.

It is important to remember that the family members, educators, and professionals working with them can only make the best use of the resources available to them at any given time. If these do not work, stakeholders should be comfortable making changes and deviating from the culturally accepted norm (e.g., home-schooling, placement in a more restrictive setting, reducing homework). It is particularly important to determine the actual feelings of the individual with AS and to involve him or her in every step of the process. Ultimately, family members and educators will find more success if they help the child learn to recognize his or her own feelings and to express his or her needs effectively. Doing so lays a solid foundation for independent living skills in adulthood. Adults with AS who are more able to express themselves often share that they could function well and be happy if just a few modifications were made to their environments.

SCHOOL-BASED INTERVENTIONS

Children and adolescents with AS typically participate in general education classrooms with support from a special educator or consultant. Because of their complex academic and social needs, individuals with AS may require numerous modifications or accommodations for school success. As the following subsection explains, these are often provided via an IEP or a 504 plan.

Legislation to Meet Mental Health and Academic Needs

The first law recognizing children with disabilities was the Education for All Handicapped Children Act of 1975 (PL 94-142). More than 20 years later, it was amended and renamed the Individuals with Disabilities Education Act (IDEA) Amendments of 1997 (PL 105-17). AS is not recognized as a specific disability category under IDEA guidelines, however, so children with AS are often served under the diagnostic labels of "autism," "behavior disorders," or "learning disabilities."

Section 504 of the Rehabilitation Act of 1973 (PL 93-112) provides services and accommodations for students with disabilities who do not qualify under IDEA. Section 504 defines a disability as a limitation or impairment that substantially limits the following activities: caring for oneself, doing manual tasks, walking, seeing, hearing, speaking, breathing, working, and learning. A student's 504 plan includes accommodations for learning in general education classes. Many students with AS are served under Section 504 and have 504 plans that address their specific academic, social, behavioral, and vocational needs.

Role of Educators

Students with AS present many social, behavioral, and academic challenges in the classroom. General and special educators are responsible for making accommodations and modifications so that students with AS can succeed and be comfortable in their environment. Communication and collaboration among special education teachers, general education teachers, and other members of the student's multidisciplinary team (e.g., speech-language pathologists) are crucial for the student's success. Without consistency among his or her teachers, a student with AS may exhibit inappropriate behaviors in certain environments and not meet his or her academic potential. To reduce inappropriate behaviors, stress, and anxiety—as well as to increase academic skills—appropriate accommodations must be made.

Environmental Supports

A variety of interventions and supports are effective for students with AS. Providing such interventions and supports gives students the structure, routine, and predictability that they need to be successful. Modifications that are addressed in the following subsections are home base, priming, visual supports, and academic modifications.

Home Base   Home base is a positive behavioral support that provides a safe area for a student with AS. Because of high levels of stress and anxiety (Barnhill & Myles, 2001), the student may need to calm him- or herself at home base—away from the overstimulation of the classroom. The purpose of home base is to provide the student with a safe place to plan or review the day's events; escape the stress of the classroom; prevent a meltdown; or regain control if rage is evident or a tantrum or meltdown has occurred (Myles & Adreon, 2001). A variety of places can serve as a home base, such as a resource room, the counselor's office, or another classroom. The home base may include materials that an occupational therapist has identified for reducing stress (e.g., mini trampoline, stress ball, weighted blanket). Teachers also should schedule specific times in the student's day for him or her to stop at the home base. This allows school personnel to develop a consistent relationship with the student. Home base should not be used as a place for time-out or punishment.

Priming   Priming is another example of an environmental modification for students with AS. Wilde, Koegel, and Koegel (1992) created priming to familiarize students with academic material prior to its use in school, bring predictability to new tasks by reducing stress and anxiety, and increase the students' success. Priming can occur at school or at home and involves presenting the student with class materials, books, worksheets, schedules, or activities for his or her review. A typical priming session lasts 10–15 minutes and is held in a relaxing environment with a teacher or parent who is patient and encouraging. Using priming on a daily basis with a student with AS can help reduce the stress of new activities. It often occurs the evening or morning before the materials are to be used or the activities are to occur. The following vignette illustrates priming.

Kim, age 10, is a student with AS who participates in the general education classroom. Her science teacher is about to begin teaching a unit on the human body. During the priming session, the teacher describes what is going to happen during the unit, providing Kim with an opportunity to look at the relevant chapter in the textbook and the accompanying worksheets. In addition, the teacher concretely describes the class activities and rules and responsibilities for student use of the unit materials. Kim is given time to ask questions about the schedule or any activities about which she feels anxious. This session reduces the unpredictability of a new unit, which helps Kim participate more successfully in science class.

• •

Visual Supports   Students with AS often think concretely, which makes verbal instructions difficult to process. Visual supports help students make transitions from one class to another, complete multistep tasks, and follow rules and routines (Savner & Myles, 2000). Visual schedules, Task Cards (Savner & Myles, 2000), and a Travel Card (Carpenter, 2001) can help students with AS understand content and carry out assignments.

Visual Schedules   Visual schedules are used to help students reduce stress and anxiety by providing predictability. They can be handwritten or created by using photographs or line drawings. Posting the schedule in an assigned place or on a student's notebook makes it accessible throughout the day. According to Moore (2002), a visual schedule should also include a phrase that lets the student know that sometimes schedules change (e.g., "Things change once in a while"). Including this phrase on the schedule will help reduce inappropriate behavior, anxiety, or stress due to scheduling changes or surprises. Figure 6.1 is an example of a written schedule for a 12-year-old student with AS.

Task Cards   Task Cards help students with AS by providing a visual reminder of content, directions, or routines needed to complete a task. Usually the size of a business card, the Task Card uses simple, concise language to outline the steps a student must follow. Uses for Task Cards include outlining the steps to a classroom center activity or the typical routine in a specific class.

Travel Card   Another visual support, the Travel Card, is designed to increase productive behavior in adolescents with AS across environments, facilitate collaboration between teachers, increase awareness among teachers of the goals for the student, and improve home–school communication (Carpenter, 2001; Jones & Jones, 1995). The Travel Card includes the student's objectives, the student's classes, space to record the results of the objectives, and a place to tally the results. There is also a space for teachers to add comments.

Tom's Schedule

8:30 A.M.	Arrival
8:35 A.M.	Homeroom
9:15 A.M.	Math class
10:15 A.M.	Language arts class
11:15 A.M.	Lunch
12:00 P.M.	Free time in homeroom
12:30 P.M.	Science class
1:30 P.M.	Social studies class
2:30 P.M.	End of the school day

Things change once in a while.

Figure 6.1.   Sample visual schedule.

Both the student and the teacher who tracks the outcomes have responsibilities with a Travel Card. The student carries the card at all times, asks teachers to complete the card, and returns the card to the teacher in charge. The teacher must provide the student with a new card daily, collect the card at the end of the day, communicate with the student's parents and other teachers about the card, and help monitor the student's target behaviors. Figure 6.2 is a sample Travel Card.

Travel Card

Student's name: _Marla_   Date: _April 7, 2004_

Use this key to answer the questions that follow:

    + Yes   X No   N/A Not Applicable

	Followed class rules	Participated in class	Completed in-class assignments	Turned in homework	Teacher's initials
Reading	+	+	+	+	TY
Science	+	+	+	+	JK
History	+	X	+	X	PA
Study skills	+	N/A	+	+	TY
Choir	X	+	N/A	N/A	WL
Spanish	+	+	+	+	CE

Bonus points

   +   Arrived at homeroom on time

   X   Brought assignment book to homeroom

Total

  19   +

   4   X

   3   N/A

Comments and suggestions

Marla dosen't seem to like our current history unit, but she needs to participate more in class—even if it is to ask questions about the unit's homework assignments that she says she doesn't understand. —PA

Figure 6.2. Sample Travel Card. (From Carpenter, L.B. [2001]. Travel Card. In B.S. Myles & D. Adreon, *Asperger syndrome and adolescence: Practical solutions for school success* [p. 93]. Shawnee Mission, KS: Autism Asperger Publishing Company; adapted by permission.)

Academic Modifications　To make learning less stressful for a student with AS, accommodations can be made to the presentation of concepts, the environment, classroom demands, or materials. Graphic organizers and modifications to homework, notetaking, and assignments are described next.

Graphic Organizers　Academic information can be clarified with a graphic organizer. In a graphic organizer, relationships between and among facts and concepts are illustrated in a concrete way. Graphic organizers can be used to support students before, during, and after units of instruction; during the brainstorming of ideas; and when defining concepts.

Homework　Teachers cite several homework problems for students with AS. Lost, incomplete, or late homework is common with individuals who have AS. An essential accommodation is the Homework Checklist (Myles & Adreon, 2001), which is a formal identification of supports that facilitates success for individuals with AS (see Figure 6.3). This document is completed for each subject by the IEP or 504 team at the beginning of each year or semester, depending on when new classes are introduced. The second item on the Homework Checklist refers to a homework planner. This is an organizational system that helps the student keep homework assignments in one place. Examples include Mead's Trapper Keeper and IntelliGear.

Notetaking　Taking notes is often a problem for individuals with AS because of deficits in fine motor skills. Educators can assist with notetaking by providing one of the following supports (Myles & Adreon, 2001):

- A teacher-developed outline that includes the main idea and supporting details
- A teacher-developed skeletal outline that outlines the main idea and leaves spaces for the student to fill in supporting details
- A peer-constructed outline developed by a student volunteer
- Outlining software that allows the student to take notes on the main idea and details

Assignments　Assignment modifications commonly used for students with other disabilities can be effective for students with AS. Assessing the student's needs and strengths is essential when developing modifications for assignments. Common assignment modifications include increased time for assignment completion, shortened assignments, step-by-step instructions, and samples of completed assignments. Table 6.1 further details possible academic modifications.

Social Supports

Social supports for children and adolescents with AS usually follow one of two forms: instructional strategies or interpretive strategies.

Instructional Strategies　Instructional strategies directly teach students social rules and how to act in social situations. The Power Card Strategy (Gagnon, 2001) and Social Stories (Gray, 2000) are two forms of social support that meet these criteria.

Homework Checklist

1. Decide whether to (check one)
   __ Assign homework
   __ Provide a homework time during the day

2. Select homework planner that has (check all that apply)
   __ Enough space for the student to write
   __ A specific place to write assignments for each class

3. Decide whether (check one)
   __ Teacher(s) provide the student with written homework assignment descriptions rather than having the student write down homework assignments
   __ Teacher(s) prompt the student to write down assignments in his or her planner

4. If the student writes down the assignment (check all that apply)
   __ Teacher(s) fill in the details that the student has omitted
   __ Specific aspects of homework assignments not written by the student are identified, and a system is taught for that portion (e.g., due date)
   __ Teacher(s) reinforce the student's efforts to write down homework

5. Homework assignments (check all that apply)
   __ Are presented in written form in the same manner and place every day
   __ Are specific enough for the student's parents to understand the assignment requirements solely from the written information provided
   __ Include models of assignments whenever possible

6. The home routine for homework completion includes (check all that apply)
   __ A designated location that is free from distractions
   __ A specific time for completing homework
   __ Special considerations for the student (specify: _____)
   __ Use of textbooks that are kept at home for easy reference

7. A method for clarifying homework is in place and includes (check all that apply)
   __ A homework hot line
   __ Faxing or e-mailing assignments to the parents at home
   __ A peer buddy who can be called to clarify assignments

8. The plan to monitor completing and turning in homework includes (check all that apply)
   __ Having a parent sign the homework planner nightly
   __ Parent-assisted organization of homework assignments in the student's backpack
   __ Teacher prompts to turn in homework
   __ Weekly parental notification of assignments that have not been turned in

Figure 6.3. Sample Homework Checklist. (From Myles, B.S., & Adreon, D. [2001]. *Asperger syndrome and adolescence: Practical solutions for school success* [p. 75]. Shawnee Mission, KS: Autism Asperger Publishing Company; adapted by permission.)

Power Card Strategy   The visually based Power Card Strategy uses a "hero" related to the child's special interest to facilitate understanding of social situations, routines, and language (Gagnon, 2001). This intervention contains two components: a script and a Power Card. A teacher, speech-language pathologist, or parent develops a brief script. The script is written at the child's comprehension level and details the problem and how the hero solves the problem. The Power

Table 6.1. Academic modifications for children and adolescents with Asperger syndrome

Modify the environment	Use proximity setting.
	Seat the student in an area free of distraction.
	Keep the student's space free of unnecessary materials.
	Use checklists to help the student get organized.
	Provide opportunities for the student to move around.
Modify time demands	Increase the student's allowed time for completing assignments.
	Teach the student time management skills.
	Create short work periods spaced with breaks or changes of task.
	Set up a specific routine and stick with it.
	Give the student a specific task to perform within a specific time period.
Modify the materials	Let the student type, record, or orally reply instead of requiring him or her to handwrite answers.
	Provide the student with a copy of the lecture notes.
	Familiarize the student with new vocabulary before teaching a lesson.
	Utilize visual aids to supplement visual information.
	Illustrate vocabulary words.
	Adapt text for the student.
	Use manipulatives for math.
	Color-code assignments.
Modify the presentation	Break assignments into shorter tasks.
	Allow the student to use a computer or calculator.
	Highlight important concepts to learn.
	Schedule frequent, short conferences with the student to check for comprehension.
	Model skills in various ways.
	Use alternative assignments.
	Relate information to the student's experience.
	Provide consistent reviews before introducing new information.
	Monitor the rate at which information is presented.

Card contains a picture representing the child's special interest and a summary of the solution. The Power Card is the size of a business card or trading card, making it portable for promoting generalization. The Power Card can be carried; attached with Velcro inside a book, notebook, or locker; or placed on the corner of the child's desk (Gagnon, 2001). Figure 6.4 provides a sample Power Card script used to help a 10-year-old boy who continually blurted out answers in class. The script is based on the boy's special interest in a particular game show, so the game show host serves as the story's hero.

Social Stories   A Social Story is individualized and describes a specific social situation from the student's perspective. The description may include where and why the situation occurs, how others feel or react, or what prompts others' feelings and reactions (Gray, 2000; Gray & Garand, 1993). Social Stories may be exclusively written documents or can be paired with pictures, audiotapes, or videotapes (Swaggart et al., 1995). They may be created by mental health professionals,

---

How Jim Barton Became the Host of *Know the Price*

Jim Barton loves being the host of *Know the Price*. Sometimes, he reflects on lessons he has learned in his life that have helped him become the man he is today. One of the difficult lessons he learned was when and where it is appropriate to ask questions and make comments. This was a challenge for Jim because he loves to talk.

When Jim was in elementary school, he had a bad habit of blurting out in class. He would often blurt out an answer to a question without raising his hand or ask questions unrelated to the topic. These interruptions upset his teacher and the other kids in class. He met with his teacher before school one day and was given the following advice:

1. Raise your hand and wait for the teacher to acknowledge you before you speak.
2. Before asking a question, ask yourself, "Can this question wait until later?"
3. If you decide that a question can wait, consider writing it down.

Just like Jim, future talk show hosts can follow these three steps to prevent blurting out answers in class. Jim would be proud of young men who learn when and where to speak.

Figure 6.4.   Sample text from a Power Card. (*Source:* Gagnon, 2001.)

educators, and parents and often include student input. The basic Social Story formula generally consists of four types of sentences: 1) descriptive, 2) directive 3) perspective, and 4) affirmative (Gray, 2000). Descriptive sentences define a social setting and what people typically do in a particular situation. Directive sentences guide an individual to engage in an appropriate response in a defined situation and often begin with the phrase "I will work on," "I will try," "I have a choice," or "I may." Perspective sentences refer to the internal status of the person for whom the Social Story is written. Finally, affirmative sentences express a shared opinion or value. Figure 6.5 contains a Social Story for an adolescent with AS who has difficulty taking school field trips.

Interpretive Strategies   Interpretive strategies form another type of social supports. These help an individual with AS understand a social situation with which he or she experienced difficulties. Cartoons, Situations-Options-Consequences-Choices-Strategies-Simulation (SOCCSS), and sensory-based interventions are among the myriad types of interpretive strategies.

Cartoons   Cartoons promote social understanding by incorporating simple figures and other symbols in a comic strip format. The visual symbols found in cartoons enhance social understanding by turning abstract and elusive events into something tangible and static that can be reflected upon (Hagiwara & Myles, 1999; Kuttler, Myles, & Carlson, 1998). Used as a generic term, *cartooning* has been implemented by speech-language pathologists for many years to enhance pragmatic and semantic understanding in their clients. Several different interventions use cartoon figures as an instructional medium: Comic Strip Conversations (Gray, 2000), mind-reading (Howlin, Baron-Cohen, & Hadwin, 1999), and pragmaticism (Arwood & Brown, 1999).

Field Trips

Sometimes we go on field trips. Field trip days are different from other days at school and give students a chance to be flexible.

Every field trip is a little different. This is okay. If I feel apprehensive about the field trip, I can ask my teacher for a schedule of the day's special events. I can carry this schedule with me and cross off each event as it happens. If I have any questions about the day, I can ask my teacher to clarify the schedule. My teacher or one of the field trip chaperones will be happy to answer any questions I have.

The night before the field trip, my mother will give me the details so that I will know what to expect. She will write them down for me so that I can look at them as many times as I wish.

I will try to be calm and relaxed and enjoy the field trip. If I begin to feel anxious, I need to let an adult know immediately so he or she can help me.

Field trips can be fun if I am prepared.

Figure 6.5. Sample Social Story. (*Source:* Gray, 2000.)

Situation-Options-Consequences-Choices-Strategies-Simulation SOCCSS helps students with social disabilities understand social situations and develop problem-solving skills by putting social and behavioral issues into a sequential form (Roosa, as cited in Myles & Southwick, 1999). Specifically, this teacher-directed strategy helps students understand cause and effect and realize that their decisions can influence the outcome of many situations. The strategy can be used one to one with a student or can be a group activity, depending on the situation and the students' needs. SOCCSS contains six steps (see Table 6.2) that help students understand a social situation, realize that they have many behavior options from which to choose in each situation, understand cause and effect, and learn problem-solving strategies. SOCCSS can be used before a social situation that a teacher knows will be problematic for a certain student. The teacher can address the difficulties using SOCCSS, thereby giving the student a plan before he or she encounters the situation. This technique can also be used following a social situation to help a student understand what occurred (Myles & Simpson, 2003; Myles & Southwick, 1999).

Sensory-Based Interventions Many individuals with AS exhibit sensory differences and may require environmental modifications. The visual, auditory, proprioceptive, vestibular, olfactory, and gustatory systems all affect learning. If these systems do not work appropriately, the learning process is impaired (Dunn et al., 2002). Several programs can be used with children and adolescents who have AS. For example, *How Does Your Engine Run: The Alert Program for Self-Regulation* (Williams & Shellenberger, 1996) helps individuals recognize their sensory issues, particularly in relation to arousal or awareness. This self-empowering program

Table 6.2. Description of each Situation-Options-Consequences-Choices-Strategies-Simulation (SOCCSS) step

Step	Description
Situation	This step includes identifying who, what, when, where, and why regarding the problem situation. Although the goal is encouraging the student to relate these variables to each other, the teacher initially will need to prompt and identify (when necessary) the answers to these questions.
Options	At this step, the teacher works with the student to generate a list of possible behavioral options to address the social problem. The student is encouraged to relate any options without evaluation from the teacher.
Consequences	In this step, a consequence is listed for each behavioral option generated. The teacher asks the student, "So what would happen if you [name option]?" Because it is difficult for students with AS to generate consequences, the teacher may need to take an active role in identifying the cause–effect relationship.
Choices	This step involves prioritizing options and consequences by using a numerical sequence or a yes/no response. Following prioritization, the student is prompted to select the option that he or she thinks is realistic and will most likely achieve his or her desired outcome.
Strategies	The Strategies step involves developing a plan or tactic to carry out the option. Although this may be a collaborative effort between the teacher and the student, the student should be encouraged to generate and own the plan.
Simulation	During this phase, the student practices the strategy that he or she identified. Practice may involve 1) using imagery, 2) talking with someone else about the plan, 3) writing down the plan, or 4) role-playing. The simulation should be evaluated to ensure that it gave the student the skills and confidence to carry out the plan.

teaches children and adolescents to change their level of alertness in response to academic or social demands. *Tool Chest: For Teachers, Parents, and Students* (Henry Occupational Services, 1998) emphasizes behavior as a means of communication and helps teachers and parents develop sensory strategies that prevent behavioral problems. Two videotapes supplement the program by demonstrating interventions for sensory issues. *Asperger Syndrome and Sensory Issues: Practical Solutions for Making Sense of the World* (Myles et al., 2000) provides an overview of how sensory integration dysfunction affects the academic, social, and behavioral domains of children and adolescents with AS. It also contains instruments to assess social issues and discusses strategies to address these concerns for effective social and academic functioning.

CONCLUSION

Children with AS can learn to manage their environments effectively but only with the proper supports in place. These supports vary slightly with each individual and change over the life span because the characteristics of the syndrome change with their development. A comprehensive approach encompassing the family, health professionals, and school staff is vital for successful intervention. Even elementary school students with AS are keenly aware of their differences or difficulties with fitting in, and they would gladly do a better job if they just knew how. With perseverance and willingness to look outside of conventional norms when planning intervention strategies, knowledgeable and caring adults at home and school can make all the difference. Remembering that one size does not fit all, appropriate modifications can put these children on the path of future happiness and independence.

REFERENCES

American Psychiatric Association. (1994). *Diagnostic and statistical manual of mental disorders* (4th ed.). Washington, DC: Author.

American Psychiatric Association. (2000). *Diagnostic and statistical manual of mental disorders* (4th ed., text rev.). Washington, DC: Author.

Arwood, E.L., & Brown, M.M. (1999). *A guide to cartooning and flowcharting: See the ideas.* Portland, OR: Apricot.

Asperger, H. (1944). Die 'Autistischen Psychopathen' im Kindesalter [Autism psychopathy in children]. *Archiv fur Psychiatrie und Nervenkrankheiten, 117,* 76–136.

Barnhill, G., Hagiwara, R., Myles, B.S., & Simpson, R.L. (2000). Asperger syndrome: A study of the cognitive profiles of 37 children and adolescents. *Focus on Autism and Other Developmental Disabilities, 15,* 146–153.

Barnhill, G.P., Hagiwara, T., Myles, B.S., Simpson, R.L., Brick, M.L., & Griswold, D.E. (2000). Parent, teacher, and self-report of problem and adaptive behaviors in children and adolescents with Asperger syndrome. *Diagnostique, 25*(2), 147–167.

Barnhill, G.P., & Myles, B.S. (2001). Attributional style and depression in adolescents with Asperger syndrome. *Journal of Positive Behavior Interventions, 3,* 175–183.

Carpenter, L.B. (2001). Travel Card. In B.S. Myles & D. Adreon, *Asperger syndrome and adolescence: Practical solutions for school success* (pp. 92–96). Shawnee Mission, KS: Autism Asperger Publishing Company.

Charak, D.A., & Stella, J.L. (2001–2002). Screening and diagnostic instruments for identification of autism spectrum disorders in children, adolescents, and young adults: A selective review. *Assessment for Effective Intervention, 27*(1 & 2), 5–18.

Church, C., Alisanki, S., & Amanullah, S. (2000). The social, behavioral, and academic experiences of children with Asperger syndrome. *Focus on Autism and Other Developmental Disabilities, 15,* 12–20.

Dunn, W., Myles, B.S., & Orr, S. (2002). Sensory processing issues associated with Asperger syndrome: A preliminary investigation. *The American Journal of Occupational Therapy, 56*(1), 97–102.

Education for All Handicapped Children Act of 1975, PL 94-142, 20 U.S.C. §§ 1400 *et seq.*

Ehlers, S., Gillberg, C., & Wing, L. (1999). A screening questionnaire for Asperger syndrome and other high-functioning autism spectrum disorders in school age children. *Journal of Autism and Developmental Disorders, 29,* 129–142.

Filipek, P.A., Accardo, P.J., Baranek, G.T., Cook, E.H., Dawson, G., Gordon, B., Gravel, J.S., Johnson, C.P., Kallen, R.J., Levy, S.E., Minshew, N.J., Prizant, B.M., Rapin, I., Rogers, S.J., Stone, W.L., Teplin, S., Tuchman, R.F., & Volkmar, F.R. (1999). The screening and diagnosis of autistic spectrum disorders. *Journal of Autism and Developmental Disorders, 29,* 439–484.

Fombonne, E., Bolton, P., Prior, J., Jordan, H., & Rutter, M. (1997). A family study of autism: Cognitive patterns and levels in parents and siblings. *Journal of Child Psychology and Psychiatry, 38,* 667–683.

Fombonne, E., & Tidmarsh, L. (2003). Epidemiologic data on Asperger disorder. *Child and Adolescent Psychiatric Clinics of North America, 12,* 15–22.

Gagnon, E. (2001). *The Power Card Strategy: Using special interests to motivate children and youth with Asperger syndrome and autism.* Shawnee Mission, KS: Autism Asperger Publishing Company.

Ghaziuddin, M. (2002). Asperger syndrome: Associated psychiatric and medical conditions. *Focus on Autism and Other Developmental Disabilities, 17,* 138–144.

Ghaziuddin, M., & Butler, E. (1998). Clumsiness in autism and Asperger syndrome: A further report. *Journal of Intellectual Disability Research, 42,* 43–48.

Gray, C. (2000). *Writing Social Stories with Carol Gray.* Arlington, TX: Future Horizons.

Gray, C.A., & Garand, J.D. (1993). Social Stories: Improving responses of students with autism with accurate social information. *Focus on Autistic Behavior, 8,* 1–10.

Griswold, D.E., Barnhill, G.P., Myles, B.S., Hagiwara, T., & Simpson, R.L. (2002). Asperger syndrome and academic achievement. *Focus on Autism and Other Developmental Disabilities, 17*(2), 94–102.

Hagiwara, T., & Myles, B.S. (1999). A multimedia Social Story intervention: Teaching skills to children with autism. *Focus on Autism and Other Developmental Disabilities, 14,* 82–95.

Henry Occupational Services. (1998). *Tool chest: For teachers, parents, and students.* Youngstown, AZ: Author.

Howlin, P., Baron-Cohen, S., & Hadwin, J. (1999). *Teaching children with autism to mind-read: A practical guide.* New York: John Wiley & Sons.

Individuals with Disabilities Education Act Amendments of 1997, PL 105-17, 20 U.S.C. §§ 1400 et seq.

Jones, V.F., & Jones, L.S. (1995). *Comprehensive classroom management: Creating positive learning environments for all students* (4th ed.). Boston: Allyn & Bacon.

Kadesjo, B., Gillberg, C., & Hagberg, B. (1999). Autism and Asperger syndrome in seven-year-old children: A total population study. *Journal of Autism and Developmental Disorders, 29,* 327–332.

Klin, A., Volkmar, F., & Sparrow, S. (2000). *Asperger syndrome.* New York: The Guilford Press.

Konig, C., & McGill-Evans, J. (2001). Social and language skills in adolescent boys with Asperger syndrome. *Autism: The International Journal of Research and Practice, 5,* 23–36.

Kuttler, S., Myles, B.S., & Carlson, J.K. (1998). The use of Social Stories to reduce precursors to tantrum behavior in a student with autism. *Focus on Autistic Behavior, 13,* 176–182.

Lord, C., Rutter, M., DiLavore, P.C., & Risi, S. (2001). *Autism Diagnostic Observation Scale (ADOS).* Los Angeles: Western Psychological Services.

Lord, C., Rutter, M., & LeCouteur, A. (1994). Autism Diagnostic Interview–Revised (ADI-R): A revised version of a diagnostic interview for caregivers of individuals with possible pervasive developmental disorder. *Journal of Autism and Developmental Disorders, 24,* 659–685.

Moore, S.T. (2002). *Asperger syndrome and the elementary school experience: Practical solutions for academic and social difficulties.* Shawnee Mission, KS: Autism Asperger Publishing Company.

Myles, B.S., & Adreon, D. (2001). *Asperger syndrome and adolescence: Practical solutions for school success.* Shawnee Mission, KS: Autism Asperger Publishing Company.

Myles, B.S., Adreon, D., & Stella, J. (2003). *Asperger syndrome and assessment: Practical solutions for identifying students' needs.* Shawnee Mission, KS: Autism Asperger Publishing Company.

Myles, B.S., Bock, S.J., & Simpson, R.L. (2000). *Asperger Syndrome Diagnostic Scale.* Austin, TX: PRO-ED.

Myles, B.S., Cook, K.T., Rinner, L., Robbins, L.A., & Miller, N.E. (2000). *Asperger syndrome and sensory issues: Practical solutions for making sense of the world.* Shawnee Mission, KS: Autism Asperger Publishing Company.

Myles, B.S., Hilgenfeld, T.D. Barnhill, G.P., Griswold, D.E., Hagiwara, T., & Simpson, R.L. (2002). Analysis of reading skills in individuals with Asperger syndrome. *Focus on Autism and Other Developmental Disabilities, 17,* 44–47.

Myles, B.S., Huggins, A., Rome, M., Hagiwara, T., & Barnhill G.P. (2003). *The written language profile of children and youth with Asperger syndrome.* Manuscript submitted for publication.

Myles, B.S., & Simpson, R.L. (2003). *Asperger syndrome: A guide for educators and parents* (2nd ed.). Austin, TX: PRO-ED.

Myles, B.S., Simpson, R.L., & Becker, J.K. (1994–1995). An analysis of characteristics of students diagnosed as having higher-functioning autistic disorder. *Exceptionality, 5*(1), 19–30.

Myles, B.S., & Southwick, J. (1999). *Asperger syndrome and difficult moments: Practical solutions for tantrums, rage, and meltdowns.* Shawnee Mission, KS: Autism Asperger Publishing Company.

O'Neill, R.E., Horner, R.H., Albin, R.W., Sprague, J.R., Storey, K., & Newton, J.S. (1997). *Functional assessment and program development for problem behavior: A practical handbook.* Belmont, CA: Brooks/Cole.

Paul, R. (2003). Promoting social communication in high functioning individuals with autistic spectrum disorders. *Child and Adolescent Psychiatric Clinics of North America, 12,* 87–106.

Plotts, C., & Webber, J. (2001–2002). The role of developmental histories in the screening and diagnosis of autism spectrum disorders. *Assessment for Effective Intervention, 27*(1 & 2), 19–26.

Pope, K.K. (1993). The pervasive developmental disorder spectrum: A case illustration. *Bulletin of the Menninger Clinic, 57,* 110–117.

Raja, M., & Azzoni, A. (2001). Asperger's disorder in the emergency psychiatric setting. *General Hospital Psychiatry, 23,* 341–348.

Rehabilitation Act of 1973, PL 93-112, 29 U.S.C. §§ 701 *et seq.*

Rinner, L. (2000). *Asperger syndrome and autism: Comparing sensory processing in daily life.* Unpublished master's thesis, University of Kansas.

Sattler, J.M. (1998). *Clinical and forensic interviewing of children and families: Guidelines for the mental health, education, pediatric, and child maltreatment fields.* La Mesa, CA: Jerome M. Sattler, Publisher.

Savner, J.L., & Myles, B.S. (2000). *Making visual supports work in the home and community: Strategies for individuals with autism and Asperger syndrome.* Shawnee Mission, KS: Autism Asperger Publishing Company.

Smith, I. (2000). Motor functioning in Asperger syndrome. In A. Klin, F. Volkmar, & S. Sparrow (Eds.), *Asperger syndrome* (pp. 97–124). New York: The Guilford Press.

Swaggart, B.L., Gagnon, E., Bock, S.J., Quinn, C., Myles, B.S., & Simpson, R.L. (1995). Using Social Stories to teach social and behavioral skills to children with autism. *Focus on Autistic Behavior, 10,* 1–16.

Wilde, L.D., Koegel, L.K., & Koegel, R.L. (1992). *Increasing success in school through priming: A training manual.* Santa Barbara: University of California, Graduate School of Education.

Williams, M.S., & Shellenberger, S. (1996). *How does your engine run: A leader's guide to the alert program for self-regulation.* Albuquerque, NM: Therapy Works.

Wing, L. (1981). Asperger syndrome: A clinical account. *Psychological Medicine, 11,* 115–129.

7

Psychotic Disorders

Rochelle Caplan

· ·

Chapter Concepts

- The various symptoms of psychosis
- Underlying psychoses that cause the symptoms
- How these symptoms and psychoses might be manifested in classrooms
- How these symptoms are also seen in nonpsychotic disorders
- Treatments options, including medication, hospitalization, and family and child therapy
- Strategies for rehabilitation in school and society

Psychosis is a relatively rare event that occurs in less than 1% of children and adolescents. Nevertheless, it is important for teachers to be aware of this syndrome and how it might appear in the classroom. Early recognition leads to early intervention, ensures the safety of the child and others, and decreases the child's suffering. After defining psychosis and how it presents in children, this chapter describes the disorders in which psychosis can occur in childhood, the particular symptoms of psychosis in these disorders, and classroom behaviors that might alert teachers to psychosis and to the underlying disorder. It then describes commonly used treatment approaches and the impact that teachers can have on these interventions.

DEFINITIONS OF DIAGNOSTIC CRITERIA

According to diagnostic criteria in the text revision of the *Diagnostic and Statistical Manual of Mental Disorders, Fourth Edition* (DSM-IV-TR; American Psychiatric Association, 2000), having one of the following clinical manifestations indicates psychosis: hallucinations, delusions, or disorganized thinking. The same diagnostic criteria are used for children, adolescents, and adults.

Hallucinations involve impaired perception and reality testing for auditory, visual, olfactory, and tactile sensations. A child who hears voices even though no one is there or has spoken to the child is hallucinating (i.e., impaired perception). The child also interprets these sensations as real rather than imaginary (i.e., poor reality testing).

Delusions are impairments that occur in the content of thoughts and include erroneous beliefs or misinterpretations. An example would be when a child thinks that the children in his class are looking at him because they believe he smells bad. In this case, the child's erroneous belief leads to a misinterpretation of the fact that his peers are looking at him.

Disorganized thinking is an impairment in how an individual presents thoughts (i.e., the form of the thoughts) to the listener. The listener has difficulty following the speaker's illogical thoughts, non sequiturs, and unpredictable changes in topic (i.e., loose associations). Due to decreased use of linguistic ties to connect ideas across sentences (i.e., lack of cohesion); unclear references to people, objects, and events; and poor monitoring and correction of linguistic and thought-organization errors (i.e., lack of repair), the listener is unable to determine who and what the child is talking about (Caplan, Guthrie, Tang, Komo, & Asarnow, 2000; Caplan et al., 2001). See Table 7.1 for definitions and examples of thought disorder.

In addition to hallucinations, delusions, and disorganized thinking, the individual's motor behavior can range from hyperactive and agitated to motionless. A person might relate to others or withdraw into a world of his or her own. Aggression to self and others might also occur, particularly if the individual is scared and provoked. Additional behavioral features and associated symptoms depend on the nature of the underlying disorder and the severity of the psychosis.

Table 7.1. Measures, definitions, and examples of thought disorder

Areas of thought disorder	Measures	Definitions	Examples
Formal thought disorder			
	Illogical thinking	Contradiction or inappropriate reasoning	I left my hat there because her name is Mary.
	Loose association	Unpredicted topic change to an unrelated topic	Interviewer: What's that? Student: I call my mom sweetie.
Underuse of cohesion			
	Conjunction	Ties together contiguous clauses	The witch gets burned and the story ends.
	Referential cohesion	Pronoun, demonstrative, definite article, or comparative reference mentioned in prior spoken text	A boy called Peter saw a ghost. He was scared.
	Unclear reference	Pronoun, demonstrative, definite article, or comparative reference previously unmentioned	I went and looked at the guy to see what they did.
	Ambiguous reference	Referent applies to more than one person or object	Her mom made a costume and she was happy.
	Exophora	Reference to the environment rather than to the conversation	Interviewer: Did you like that story? Student: Open this toy.
	Lexical cohesion	Use of word repetition, synonyms, and antonyms to connect ideas	The kids were bad. Tim was bad, too.
Underuse of repair: organization of thoughts			
	Repetition	Clarification of what was said by repeating word(s)	Cause he want cause he want to play with him.
	Postponement	The addition of background information to clarify referent	She knew when she saw the cat she knew that was what was making the girl happier.
	False starts	Starting but not completing an idea	And, um I don't, John said but I can play.
	Fillers	Word(s) that fill pauses without changing meaning	Well, like, I don't know; it's just scary.
Underuse of repair: revision of linguistic elements			
	Referential repair	Clarifies the referent	She would have Anne would have to take care of her.
	Word choice	Modifies word choice	Play with him and make give him some wishes.
	Syntactic repair	Corrects syntactic error	The picture you're drawing you drew looks funny.

EXPRESSIONS OF PSYCHOTIC SYMPTOMS IN CHILDHOOD

This section details how each of the previously discussed diagnostic criteria—hallucinations, delusions, and disorganized thinking—may be manifested in childhood.

Hallucinations

From the developmental perspective, hallucinations are rare in children younger than 7 years of age (Egdell & Kolvin, 1972; Garralda, 1984c; Kemph, 1987; Kostopulos, Kanigsberg, & Fiedorowicz, 1987). By age 5 years, children are well aware that if they hear or see things, there is an obvious source for these perceptions. Similarly, if they smell something or feel something on their skin, they generally understand that there is an obvious source for this perception.

It is important to be sure that developmental phenomena, such as imaginary friends, are not confused with hallucinations. Although children younger than age 5 years may have imaginary friends, they are aware of the imaginary nature of these friends. If children older than 5 years of age see and hear imaginary friends talking to them and are convinced that others can see and hear them, they are experiencing hallucinations. Other normal developmental phenomena that need to be differentiated from hallucinations include fantasies, fears, and hallucinations that occur while falling asleep or waking up (Edgell & Kolvin, 1972). In addition, it is important to remember that most children at some time experience their imagination playing tricks on them. They might think they hear someone talking to them when no one is there. However, they are aware of the imaginary nature of this experience.

To assess hallucinations, clinicians need to determine whether the child comprehends the clinician's questions; is not trying to please or get attention; realizes the experience is unusual; will act on the basis of the hallucination; and feels fear, dread, or elation while experiencing the hallucination. In terms of comprehending the clinician's question ("Do you hear voices?" or "Are you hearing voices?"), most children will say yes unless the interviewer clarifies that the child hears voices when no one else hears voices and when no one is there. Similarly, most children try to please the adults around them. If they think adults want to hear that they hear voices, they might say yes.

A hallucinatory experience causes fear because it challenges the reality testing of children, making them uncertain of their reality. For this reason, children usually do not share these experiences readily. A child's sense that he might act on the basis of the hallucinatory perception also causes extreme fear. If children report hearing voices or seeing things, in the absence of subjective distress they might not be having a hallucination. (See the exception to this rule in the later discussion on dissociative disorders.)

Delusions

Delusions, like hallucinations, are rare in children younger than 7 years of age (Bettes & Walker, 1987; Volkmar, Cohen, Hoshino, Rende, & Rheas, 1988). When delusions occur, they tend to be single and include irrational fears and cosmic threats (Eggers, 1978). For example, a child might believe that ghosts are trying to hurt her when she is by herself. Unlike adults, if children have several delusions, the delusions typically do not have a common integrating theme (Kolvin, Ounsted, Humphrey, & McNay, 1971; Russell, 1994). Yet, this can occur. For example, an 11-year-old believed that American and British children are despicable because they use the "C" word (i.e., *cool*). He also was convinced that Adolf Hitler was his personal protector and would help him kill these children.

Like hallucinations, delusions need to be differentiated from normal developmental phenomena, such as magical thinking and fantasies. When a child believes that having a thought is equivalent to carrying out the thought, this is magical thinking. For example, a 6-year-old child was angry at her father and wished that he would die. The child then became scared that her father might die. Children normally have fantasies about many different things. Unlike children with delusions, they are able to recognize the imaginary basis of their fantasies (Jordan & Prugh, 1971). If magical thoughts and fantasies are pervasive and the child acts on them, the thoughts are considered delusions (Russell, Bott, & Sammons, 1989).

Disorganized Thinking

Young children acquire the ability to organize and present their thoughts to a listener in a coherent and cohesive manner as they mature throughout childhood and adolescence (Caplan et al., 2000). The speech of typically developing children younger than age 7 years can be incoherent because young children change conversational topics in an unpredictable manner (i.e., make loose associations) and use illogical reasoning as they speak (see Table 7.1). After age 7 years, children use significantly less illogical thinking and no loose associations (Caplan et al., 2000). Illogical thinking is infrequent in children older than age 10. By early adolescence, individuals organize their thoughts in a coherent manner.

During middle childhood and adolescence, the repertoire and use of cohesive devices—such as conjunctions, referential devices (e.g., pronouns, demonstratives, articles), substitution of phrases for words, and others—increase (Caplan et al., 2000). Similarly, as they mature, children do a better job of monitoring their speech for linguistic errors and communication breakdowns, and they employ a wider range of linguistic devices to repair these errors (Caplan et al., 2001). It becomes easier for listeners to follow who and what children are talking about as these higher-level linguistic skills develop.

The disorganized thinking (i.e., thought disorder) found in children with psychosis reflects impairments of these higher-level discourse skills. It can involve overuse of loose associations or illogical thinking along with underuse of cohesive and repair devices (Caplan, Guthrie, & Komo, 1996; Caplan et al., 2000).

UNDERLYING DISORDERS

Two underlying causes for psychotic symptoms are explored in this chapter. First, disorders associated with psychosis are discussed. Then, the relationship of psychotic symptoms to disorders not normally associated with psychosis is discussed. Classroom manifestations of the disorders are discussed as well. (See also Table 7.2 for tips on addressing symptoms of psychosis in children.)

Disorders Associated with Psychosis

The most common disorders associated with psychosis are schizophrenia, mood (affective) disorders, dissociative disorders, drug-induced psychosis, various disorders with transient psychotic-like features, and psychosis associated with neurological disorders.

Schizophrenia Schizophrenia can have an insidious (i.e., gradual) or acute (i.e., sudden) onset. Several studies have shown that auditory hallucinations occur in approximately 80%–100% of children with schizophrenia (Eggers, Bunk, & Krause, 2000; Gordon et al., 1994; Green et al., 1984; Kolvin et al., 1971; McKenna et al., 1994; Russell, 1994; Russell et al., 1989; Spencer & Campbell, 1994). Such hallucinations can involve the children hearing other people talking about them, saying they are trying to do bad things to them; hearing bad things or curses said to them about themselves or people close to them; commands telling them to hurt others or themselves; and hearing a super being or religious entity telling them about themselves or what will happen to the world. Approximately 30%–80% of these children also have visual hallucinations (Eggers et al., 2000; Gordon et al., 1994; Green et al., 1984; Kolvin et al., 1971; McKenna et al., 1994; Russell et al., 1989), 21% have olfactory hallucinations, and 37% have tactile hallucinations (Gordon et al., 1994; McKenna et al., 1994).

Table 7.2. Tips for addressing symptoms of psychosis in children

Symptoms	Tips
Unusual behaviors	Do not single the child out in front of the class about these behaviors.
	Inform the child's parents (and/or physician, if permission has been received to do so).
	Do not call on the child to answer questions in front of the rest of the class if he or she appears very self-conscious.
	If the child appears afraid to be near peers, make sure that the peers keep their distance from the child and hurry along so he or she can feel less anxious.
Anger	Allow the child to be alone to calm down and regroup.
	If the child's behavior might be dangerous to others or to him- or herself, inform school authorities, parents (and/or physician, if permission has been received to do so). If necessary, call the police.
Unusual motor activity	If the child seems "slowed down," give him or her more time to get classwork done.
	If the child is having difficulty sitting and needs to stand repeatedly, let the parents (and/or physician, if permission has been received to do so) know as soon as possible.
	If the child has stiff or jerky movements, tic-like movements, or tremors, inform his or her parents (and/or physician, if permission has been received to do so).
Tiredness	Inform the child's parents (and/or physician, if permission has been received to do so).

Delusions occur in approximately 60%–95% of children with schizophrenia (Eggers et al., 2000; Gordon et al., 1994; Greene et al., 1984; Kolvin et al., 1971; McKenna et al., 1994; Russell et al., 1989; Spencer & Campbell, 1994). These delusions might be bizarre with no apparent connection to what is happening in the child's life. Typically, the delusions are persecutory in nature (i.e., people trying to harm the child), involve physical complaints or bodily concerns, represent the child's conviction that he or she has magical powers, or demonstrate a belief that people are looking at the child and thinking bad thoughts about him or her (Eggers, 1978; Gordon et al., 1994; Greene et al., 1984; McKenna et al., 1994; Russell et al., 1989). Early in the development of schizophrenia, some children have pervasive morbid fantasies involving gruesome and violent thoughts.

Children with schizophrenia evidence loose associations and illogical thinking more often than expected for their age (Caplan et al., 2000). They also use conjunctions and referential devices infrequently but use unclear and ambiguous references more frequently than typically developing children (see Table 7.1; see also Caplan et al., 2000). In addition, in comparison with typically developing children, children with schizophrenia use fewer types of fillers and often abandon a thought before completing it (Caplan et al., 1996). As a result, the listener experiences variable difficulty in following the child's speech, which might be incoherent, idiosyncratic, and unusual—or normal.

From the motor perspective, children with schizophrenia might appear agitated or withdrawn. They may evidence unusual postures or rituals or movements that are slow, rigid, or somewhat jerky. Their attention and concentration are typically distracted, and they might appear preoccupied with internal stimuli punctuated by occasional inappropriate laughing and gazing to the side. They might speak a lot or refrain from speaking. Schizophrenia can also reduce the child's ability to express emotions, both in terms of facial expression and the prosody (i.e., tone) of speech. In addition, schizophrenia is often associated with decreased motivation and interest in things that previously interested the child, as well as an inability to enjoy things. Impaired facial expression of affect (i.e., emotions), motivation, interest, and enjoyment develop over time and might not be apparent at the onset of the illness.

Classroom Behaviors Prior to diagnosis, teachers might notice increasing difficulties with concentration and academic performance. The child may display odd behavior or withdrawal from peers. Furthermore, he or she may make unusual statements or use non sequiturs. Other symptoms that might be seen in the classroom include changes in handwriting, bizarre or slowed movements, increasing agitation or irritability, inappropriate laughing, talking to oneself, unkempt appearance, and preoccupation with unusual topics.

Mood Disorders Several types of mood disorders can also include psychotic symptoms: depression, mania, and bipolar disorder. Although these disorders are discussed at length in Chapter 11, it is important to cover their relationship to psychosis.

Depression Depression in children and adolescents frequently includes psychotic symptoms (Bashir, Russell, & Johnson, 1987; Carlson, 1990; Ryan et al.,

1987; Ulloa et al., 2000; Werry, McClellan, & Chard, 1991). Because young children cannot verbalize their feelings, depression is often externalized as anger, irritability, aggression, and explosive behavior (Carlson, 1990; Pataki & Carlson, 1990).

The hallucinations of children with depression, like those of children with schizophrenia, can tell them to do things (i.e., command hallucinations), say bad things about them (i.e., commenting voices hallucinations), or threaten to harm them (i.e., persecutory hallucinations) (Chambers, Puig-Antich, Tabrizi, & Davies, 1982; Ryan et al., 1987; Ulloa et al., 2000). The delusions of children with depression can involve repeated irrational thoughts about bad things happening to them and to the world around them (Chambers et al., 1982). Unlike children with schizophrenia, the content of hallucinations and delusions in children who are depressed is congruent with their mood. The hallucinations and delusions include themes that fit in with the child's sad mood, such as being bad, being undeserving, needing punishment, or causing trouble to everyone. For example, a child with depression might have hallucinations to kill him- or herself and delusions that he or she is the source of family problems. In contrast, a child with schizophrenia might try to commit suicide in response to command hallucinations and a bizarre delusion that he or she is an alien and needs to die to go home. It is important to note that the presence of suicidal ideas or actions does not occur only in depression.

Although not systematically studied, bizarre delusions with thought control, thought insertion, and other disturbances of thought content seem to be more characteristic of schizophrenia than affective psychosis (psychosis associated with mood disorders) in childhood. In the single study conducted on disorganized thinking in hospitalized adolescents with depression, the absence of bizarre verbalizations is what differentiated their thought disorder from that of children with schizophrenia (Makowski et al., 1997). Thus, the impaired facial expression (i.e., displaying no affect) and lack of interest, motivation, ability to enjoy things, and curiosity that are found in children with depression need to be differentiated from the negative signs found in children with schizophrenia.

Classroom Behaviors   Children with depression might increasingly express sadness through frequent crying and withdrawal from peers in the classroom, but these are more noticeable on the playground. As previously noted, children who are depressed can present with anger, irritability, and aggression. They have difficulty concentrating, doing schoolwork in the classroom and at home, and waking up and getting to school on time. Their motivation and interest in schoolwork and other areas, including peer relationships, might decrease. Because depressed children have difficulty falling asleep at night and/or staying asleep, they might appear tired and listless during class. The early morning hours are sometimes the most difficult for children (particularly adolescents) with depression, and their mood and activity level might improve during the course of the day. Oppositional behavior or substance abuse can be first signs of depression in children and adolescents.

Mania or Bipolar Disorder   Children with mania or bipolar disorder can also present with psychotic symptoms (Ulloa et al., 2000). As described for children with depression, the hallucinations and delusions of children with mania are also consistent with their overall mood, which can be either happy or, more frequently, angry and irritable. Thus, these children can have grandiose delusions (in the case of euphoria) or paranoid delusions (in the case of irritability). In contrast, the grandiose delusions of a child with schizophrenia might be bizarre and do not fit with the child's mood. For example, a child with schizophrenia might plan to rule the world so that he can kill all the people who have made fun of him. In contrast, a child with mania might think that she should run the world so she can make everyone have a good time.

The psychotic manifestations of children with bipolar disorder include auditory hallucinations (i.e., commanding, commenting) and delusions of reference that make them assume others can read, know, or hear their thoughts (Ulloa et al., 2000). Auditory hallucinations vary, and a child might sometimes show more depressive symptoms and at other times show more manic and paranoid symptoms. For adolescents with mania, there is a high rate of receiving different psychiatric diagnoses prior to the diagnosis of mania; this is not as apparent in adolescents who evidence mania and psychotic symptoms (Kafantaris, Coletti, Dicker, Padula, & Pollack, 1998).

In addition, similar high rates of irritability, negative mood, and disruptive behavior disorders—including attention-deficit/hyperactivity disorder (ADHD), oppositional defiant disorder, and conduct disorder—are found in children with bipolar disorder, schizophrenia, and psychotic disorder not otherwise specified (McClellan, McCurry, Spelz, & Jones, 2002; Paillere-Martinot, Aubin, Martinot, & Colin, 2000). Thus, the quality of the mood alone does not necessarily help differentiate between these disorders (McClellan et al., 2002).

Associated characteristics, such as the content of thought, sleep patterns, appetite, speech patterns, and judgment, as well as history prior to the onset of the illness, might assist the mental health worker in suggesting the nature of the underlying disorder. Before the onset of illness, more children with schizophrenia than children with bipolar disorder or depression are perceived as odd by their peers; this perception is related to children with schizophrenia having poor levels of sociability and the nature of their peer relationships, scholastic achievement, school adaptation, and interests (Asarnow & Ben-Meir, 1988; Eggers & Bunk, 1997; Werry et al., 1991).

Classroom Behaviors For children with mania or bipolar disorder, teachers might observe increasing distractibility, poor academic performance, impulsivity, irritability, poor judgment, verbosity with frequent interruptions, grandiosity, aggression, and suspiciousness. Hypersocial and hypersexual behavior are possible as well.

Dissociative Disorder Children with dissociative disorder have transient changes in consciousness varying from sudden loss of their train of thought and difficulty remembering things that have happened to them in the past to frank psychosis with hallucinations and delusions. These children have a history of physical or sexual abuse and often present with numerous unsuccessfully treated psychiatric diagnoses before the onset of their psychotic symptoms (Famularo, Fenton, Kinscherff, & Augustyn, 1996; Putnam, 1991). Children with psychosis not otherwise specified (i.e., psychosis not associated with any of the disorders described in this chapter) have a higher rate of posttraumatic stress disorder (PTSD) than children with schizophrenia or bipolar disorder (McClellan et al., 2002).

In terms of psychotic symptoms, children with dissociative disorder have complex hallucinations that can be both auditory and visual. The auditory hallucinations frequently include distinct, familiar voices talking to them—one threatening and the other protecting them (Hornstein & Putnam, 1992; Putnam, 1991). The auditory command hallucinations of children with dissociative disorders involve internalized, distinctive voices of specific people that command them to hurt themselves or other people (Hornstein & Putnam, 1992). The visual hallucinations usually involve seeing scary and threatening apparitions (Hornstein & Putnam, 1992).

Unlike the children with the previously described diagnoses, children with dissociative disorder sometimes do not demonstrate subjective affective distress when they describe their hallucinations. Disorganized thinking and a sense of having thoughts taken out of or put into their head might occur transiently. These children do not have delusions, and their facial expression of affect is normal. Suicidal ideation is found in approximately 15% of children with PTSD (Famularo et al., 1996). Some children with PTSD might develop psychosis that is dissociative.

Classroom Behaviors   Children with a history of trauma who have a dissociative disorder might demonstrate poor concentration in the classroom, as they experience transient changes in consciousness. They might exhibit poor body boundaries in their relationships with their peers, sexual acting out, and irritability. They might also show increased emotional lability, with a tendency to be excitable and frequent crying, anger, or happiness. Teachers might note increased or decreased motor activity. Relationships with peers might be erratic.

Drug-Induced Psychosis   During psychosis, there is an increased activation of neurotransmitters (chemical compounds that facilitate information flow between nerve cells), including dopamine, adrenaline, noradrenaline, acetylcholine, glutamate, gamma-aminobutyric acid, and others. As a result, both illegal and legal drugs that activate these neurotransmitters can cause psychosis. Street drugs that cause psychosis include methamphetamine, cocaine, amphetamine, methylenedioxymethamphetamine (MDMA, or "ecstasy"), jimsonweed, trumpet tea plant, ketamine, opium and its derivatives, and hallucinogens such as lysergic acid diethylamide (LSD) (Holtmann, Becker, Hartmann, & Schmidt, 2002). Because very high doses of cannabis (marijuana) are needed to cause psychosis, it is still unclear whether cannabis-associated psychosis only occurs in youth with a predisposition toward schizophrenia (Fleischhaker, Priemer, Schultz, & Remschmdit, 2002; Hall & Degenart, 2000). McClellan, Breiger, McCurry, and Hlastala (2003) reported substance abuse (i.e., marijuana and alcohol) in 44% of adolescents with psychotic disorders—such as schizophrenia, bipolar disorder presenting with psychosis, and psychosis not otherwise specified—1.8 years before the onset of psychosis.

Among legal drugs, stimulants—such as methylphenidate (Concerta, Ritalin), dextroamphetamine (Dexedrine), and a mixture of levoamphetamine and dextroamphetamine (Adderall), which are used to treat ADHD—rarely induce hallucinations and paranoid delusions in children (see review in Greenhill et al., 2002). Although the drugs commonly used to treat depression and anxiety disorders—selective serotonin reuptake inhibitors (SSRIs), such as fluoxetine (Prozac), paroxetine (Paxil), and sertraline (Zoloft), and catecholamine reuptake inhibitors, such as bupropion (Wellbutrin), trazodone (Desyrel), and venlafaxine (Effexor)—can induce mania and psychosis in adults (Fortunati, Mazure, Preda, Wahl, & Bowers, 2002), there are no clinical reports of psychosis in children.

Finally, psychosis is described, albeit infrequently, in children with epilepsy who are treated with antiepilepsy drugs—such as topiramate (Topamax), zonisamide (Zonegran), levetiracetam (Keppra), or vigabatrin (Sabril) (see review in Besag, 2001). Despite use of these same medications to stabilize mood in children with mood disorders (Riddle, Kastelic, & Frosch, 2001), their use does not appear to be associated with psychosis.

Classroom Behaviors Children who develop psychosis from illicit drugs may show a downhill academic course, irritability, tiredness, and distractibility along with evidence of impaired judgment, poor reality testing, and suspiciousness. Teachers should be aware of which students are being treated with any of the previously described medications. If these individuals show signs that suggest the onset of psychosis, teachers should consider the possibility of medication-induced psychosis.

Disorders with Transient or Psychotic-Like Features Transient or psychotic-like features can accompany multidimensionally impaired disorder (Kumra et al., 1998) and schizotypal personality disorder (Russell, 1994), which are presented in this section, or multiplex complex developmental disorder (van der Gaag et al., 1995), which is described later in the section on developmental disorders. Children with these disorders appear to have hallucinations, delusions, and disorganized thinking, with variable reality testing regarding the verity of their hallucinations and delusions. They think these are imaginary experiences sometimes but are convinced that they are real at other times. Children who are multidimensionally impaired also have impaired impulse control, attention, and affective control (Kumra et al., 1998) and may initially receive diagnoses of ADHD, impulse control disorder, or bipolar disorder (Kumra et al., 1998).

The cognitive, neurophysiological, and brain magnetic resonance imaging (MRI) findings of children with these disorders are similar to those of children with schizophrenia (Kumra, Giedd, et al., 2000; Kumra, Wiggs, et al., 2000). Outcome studies suggest that within 2–8 years of diagnosis, 50% of these children are diagnosed with psychosis not otherwise specified (Nicolson et al., 2001).

The unusual perceptual experiences, impaired thought content (i.e., ideas of reference, unusual beliefs, magical thinking, telepathy, and ideas of mind control), odd speech, and behavior of children with schizotypal personality disorder are sometimes difficult to differentiate from the delusions, hallucinations, formal thought disorder, and disorganized behavior of children with schizophrenia. Russell (1994) found similarities in the clinical manifestations of children who met DSM-III (APA, 1980) criteria for schizophrenia and schizotypal personality disorder. The groups differed, however, in the severity of their symptoms. For example, the children with schizotypal personality disorder had perceptual disturbances or bizarre preoccupations, whereas the children with schizophrenia had frank hallucinations or delusional beliefs. Asarnow et al. (1988) described similar dysfunction prior to the onset of illness and long-term prognosis in children with schizotypal personality disorder and schizophrenia.

Caplan, Perdue, Tanguay, and Fish (1990) found no statistically significant differences between the illogical thinking and loose associations scores of mental-age matched children who had schizophrenia and schizotypal personality disorder. Children with schizotypal personality disorder, however, had a narrower range of less severe discourse deficits (i.e., thought disorder) than children with schizophrenia (Caplan & Guthrie, 1992). Despite fluctuations in the degree of impaired reality testing, the unusual perceptual experiences and odd thinking of these children are pervasive and affect overall functioning.

Classroom Behaviors Teachers might be aware of children who demonstrate impulsive, volatile, and explosive behavior along with attentional difficulties. These children might be overly suspicious of their peers, frequently taking offense at things other children do that actually have nothing to do with them. Their imagination might run away with them, and their thoughts and speech are difficult to follow. Some of these children might appear socially anxious and withdrawn; others might interact with other children but with poor social skills.

Psychosis Associated with Neurological Disorders Approximately 10% of children with a type of epilepsy that involves the temporal lobe of the brain develop psychotic symptoms (Caplan et al., 1998; Lindsay, Ounsted, & Richards, 1979). These symptoms include hallucinations, delusions, and disorganized thinking. Unlike children with schizophrenia and depression, these children have no changes in the ability to express emotion or in motivation, interest, and curiosity level. Psychotic symptoms might be more predominant when the children are having poorly controlled seizures (Caplan, Shields, Mori, & Yudovin, 1991). As described in the subsection on drug-induced psychosis, the medications used to treat epilepsy can also sometimes cause psychosis in children (Besag, 2001).

In the early stages of some degenerative neurological disorders, prior to obvious cognitive decline, children might exhibit hallucinations, delusions, and disorganized thinking along with subtle signs of cognitive deficits (Caplan, Tanguay, & Szekely, 1987). Whereas symptoms wax and wane in children with schizophrenia, mood disorders, and dissociative disorders, these children have continuous symptoms and their behavior, cognition, and language undergo a downhill course. That is, their thoughts become progressively more disorganized with incoherent and unintelligible speech, they lose basic cognitive skills, and their behavior might be impulsive and inappropriate. Some authors have used the term *disintegrative psychosis* to describe this condition (Mouridsen, Rich, & Isager, 2000).

Classroom Behaviors Decreased attention, spacing out, withdrawal, increased irritability, and declining cognitive performance could be the first signs of psychosis in a child with epilepsy or the early stages of a degenerative neurological disorder.

Other Disorders Associated with Psychosis

A number of nonpsychotic disorders can also include hallucinations, delusions, and/or disorganized thinking. Several of the more common ones are discussed in the following subsections.

Autism and Multiplex Complex Developmental Disorder Chapters 5 and 6 provide a more complete treatment of autism and Asperger syndrome. Because a few children with autism also have psychoses, however, it is described here as well.

The rate of schizophrenia in children with autism (0.6%) is no higher than that of the general population (Volkmar & Cohen, 1991). Children with autism who have severe language delay or impairment and/or mental retardation, as well as most children with high-functioning autism or Asperger syndrome, do not have hallucinations and delusions.

A subgroup of these children, however, develops hallucinations and delusions with or without disorganized thinking. These children have what has also been called *multiplex complex developmental disorder* (van der Gaag et al., 1995). Unlike other children with autism or pervasive developmental disorder (Buitelaar & van der Gaag, 1998; van der Gaag et al., 1995), they have impaired regulation of affective state (i.e., aggression, anxiety, panic, unusual fears) and thought disorders (i.e., confusion of reality and fantasy, irrationality, magical thinking, overvalued ideas that defy logic and reality). Their impairments in social interaction and communication, as well as their stereotyped and rigid behaviors, are less severe than those in children with autism only.

These children are unaware of the imaginary nature of their unusual perceptual experiences and erroneous, overvalued beliefs. For example, a child was preoccupied with vampires and dragons and could see them, hear them, and feel them doing bad things to him. He believed that they wanted to kill him and that he could protect himself from them by having the Egyptian god of death in him. His specific interests focused on fantasy play with time machines. Whereas he was able to appreciate the imaginary nature of his time machine fantasies, that was not the case for his perceptions and thoughts about the vampires, dragons, and the Egyptian god of death.

Classroom Behaviors Children with multiplex complex developmental disorder have variable difficulties relating to other children in the classroom, including impaired turn taking (e.g., interrupting, not responding) and poor eye contact with people during conversation. Although the children might get very irritable when others intrude into their space, they can be quite intrusive and unaware of other people's body boundaries. During recess, they might be loners or interact with children who have similar, specific, and circumscribed interests. They might talk about their hallucinations and delusions repeatedly, as well as other specific topics, even though their peers show no interest. While they speak, these children use few gestures and minimal modulation of affect. They also exhibit repeated stereotyped movements, such as jumping, hand flapping, or twirling.

Language Disorders   Although children with language disorders do not have hallucinations or delusions, their thinking might appear disorganized. This is usually associated with their linguistic difficulties.

Classroom Behaviors   Children with language disorders might have obvious speech difficulties and language-related learning disorders. Frequently, however, the language difficulties of these children go unnoticed and they first present with behavior difficulties, such as poor attention span, hyperactivity, impulsivity, aggression, and poor academic performance (Cohen, Barwick, Horodezky, Vallance, & Im, 1998).

Anxiety Disorders   Some children who have anxiety disorders present with hallucinations (Cassano, Pini, Saettoni, & Dell'Osso, 1999; Kostopoulos et al., 1987; Ulloa et al., 2000). Psychotic symptoms might be more prominent in children with anxiety disorders who also have depressive symptoms (Ulloa et al., 2000). The fears of children with separation anxiety disorder (i.e., concern about being separated from their parents) typically involve realistic fears, such as robbers, kidnappers, and accidents. Sometimes they involve imaginary beings, and the possibility of an underlying psychosis should be ruled out. For example, while alone in her room at night, a child sees monsters and ghosts who threaten to harm her. During the day, however, she has good reality testing for her fears. In the absence of any other evidence of psychosis, it is plausible that this child has a separation anxiety disorder related to sleeping apart from her parents. For a child with separation anxiety, it is also important to ensure that the fears of separation from the parents do not stem from hallucinations and delusions that scare the child.

Similarly, when children with generalized anxiety disorder (i.e., tendency toward exaggerated worrying) report repeated worries, it is essential to ascertain that these repeated thoughts are in fact worries rather than delusions or hallucinations. For instance, for a child who worries that something terrible will happen to her because voices are telling her that she will die, the worrying is based on a hallucination rather than anxiety.

Finally, hallucinations and delusions could underlie what might appear to be phobias (i.e., fear and avoidant behavior from social situations or specific objects), as well as the repeated thoughts (i.e., obsessions) and rituals (i.e., compulsions) of children with obsessive-compulsive disorder (OCD). For example, a shy child avoided being around, walking near, or looking at people. Although he was diagnosed as having a social phobia, his avoidance of contact with people was based on a delusion that people were trying to control his thinking. In another case, an adolescent who believed that other people thought he was a homosexual engaged in elaborate rituals before going through doorways and in repeated hand washing. The adolescent was initially diagnosed as having OCD, but his compulsive behaviors were associated with delusions and hallucinations in which he heard people saying that he was homosexual.

Classroom Behaviors Typically, teachers are unaware of children's anxiety disorders because children often keep this information to themselves and do not present behavioral problems in the classroom. Nonetheless, some behaviors might suggest the presence of anxiety. A child with a separation disorder might have great difficulty separating from his or her parents in the morning before coming into the school building. A child who becomes very concerned before or after a test or if he or she is picked up a little late after school might have a generalized anxiety disorder or a separation anxiety disorder, respectively. Repeated erasing of work and perfectionism are also found in children with generalized anxiety disorder and OCD.

Disruptive Behavior Several studies have shown that some children with disruptive behavior have hallucinations and delusions (Del Beccaro, Burke, & McCauley, 1988; Fard, Hudgens, & Welner, 1978; Garralda, 1984a; McClellan et al., 2002). Continued hallucinations and delusions at the 2- to 7-year follow-ups were associated with marked dysfunction both at work and in social situations but not with a diagnosis of schizophrenia (Del Beccaro et al., 1988; Fard et al., 1978; Garralda, 1984b; McClellan et al., 2002).

McGee, Williams, and Poulton (2000) found hallucinations in 8.4% of a large community sample of 788 nonreferred 11-year-old children. In this community sample, significantly more children with hallucinations had inattention, a psychiatric diagnosis (e.g., ADHD, anxiety disorder, conduct disorder, depression, oppositional defiant disorder), intrusive thoughts, and bad dreams compared with children without hallucinations. Thus, hallucinations in children might be an indicator of a wide range of behavioral difficulties rather than of the specific behavioral disturbances associated with a disorder such as schizophrenia.

Forty percent of children whose parents have schizophrenia have violent aggression, school problems, and a diagnosis of ADHD prior to a diagnosis of psychosis (Ross & Compagnon, 2001; Schaeffer & Ross, 2002). Although approximately 9% of these children have psychotic symptoms (Ross & Compagnon, 2001), they often are treated with antianxiety, antidepressant, and stimulant drugs prior to receiving this diagnosis.

Classroom Behaviors Classroom behavior does not usually suggest the presence of hallucinations in children with disruptive disorders. As described in Chapters 4 and 14, children with ADHD, conduct disorder, and oppositional defiant disorder may display the following: difficulty sitting still, inattentiveness, distractibility, impulsiveness, arguing with adults, attempting retribution when anyone upsets them, refusing to do what others request of them, and breaking rules (with conduct disorder).

TREATMENT

This section briefly describes the main approaches used to treat children with psychosis: medication, hospitalization, therapy for the child and his or her parents, educational rehabilitation, and social rehabilitation. Together these treatment approaches target the psychotic symptoms, the underlying disorder, and long-term deficits resulting from the psychosis and underlying disorder while optimizing the child's functioning at home, at school, and with peers.

Medication

The drugs used to control psychotic symptoms are called neuroleptics (see reviews in Campbell, Rapoport, & Simpson, 1999; Findling, McNamara, & Gracious, 2000; Schur et al., 2003). Older neuroleptic drugs—such as chlorpromazine (Thorazine), thioridazine (Mellaril), haloperidol (Haldol), thiothixene (Navane), and lozapine (Loxitane)—act primarily through the D2 dopamine neurotransmitter, which is thought to be activated or relatively increased in psychosis. The newer, atypical neuroleptics—such as risperidone (Risperdal), olanzapine (Zyprexa), quetiapine (Seroquel), ziprasidone (Geodon), and clozapine (Clozaril)—act through both the D2 dopamine and the serotonin neurotransmitters.

Both groups of drugs target psychotic symptoms and decrease hallucinations, delusions, disorganized thinking, and the associated agitation, irritability, aggression, and insomnia. Unlike the older neuroleptics, the atypical neuroleptics also prevent and reduce the symptoms of schizophrenia.

Although most of the neuroleptics have immediate calming effects, their antipsychotic effects take time and are dose dependent (i.e., the patient needs to be receiving an adequate dose of the drug). The full impact of the newer atypical neuroleptics takes several months, particularly for cognitive impairments and negative symptoms in individuals with schizophrenia (Frazier et al., 1994; Kumra et al., 1996).

In terms of side effects, the older neuroleptics have movement-related adverse effects, such as increased stiffness of muscles, as well as involuntary movements, including tremors, a need to move all the time, and tic-like movements. These side effects occur less frequently with the atypical neuroleptic drugs. In both cases, the side effects can be treated with drugs, such as benztropine (Cogentin) or trihexyphenidyl (Artane).

Additional side effects include tiredness, which occurs mainly when the drugs are first started and their dosage is increased. Slowing of cognitive processing might occur if a child's dosage is too high. This effect should be differentiated from continued cognitive impairment due to inadequate dosage (i.e., too low) and from poor response to the drug. In the former case, the child needs an increase in the dosage of medication; in the latter case, the child needs a medication change.

Increased appetite and weight gain are frequent side effects, particularly in individuals treated with atypical neuroleptic drugs, such as risperidone and olanzapine. Dizziness, drooling, increased skin sensitivity to sunlight, constipation, decreased frequency of urination, urinary incontinence, and metabolic side effects (e.g., impaired liver function; increased fasting glucose, cholesterol, and blood fats) are other less frequent side effects.

Classroom Behaviors Teachers should be aware of the positive and negative effects of drugs used to treat psychosis, as this is an important potential source of information for a child's treating psychiatrist. In terms of target symptoms, teachers can take note if the child becomes less agitated, irritable, or withdrawn, as well as more organized in his or her thinking, with improved concentration. Alternatively, lack of change in these behaviors, despite treatment at a constant dosage for several weeks, can suggest the need for a dosage increase. Regarding side effects, teachers might notice that the child appears sleepy or slow; lacks facial expression; or has tremors, grimaces, tic-like movements, or stiffness. It is important to communicate this information to the child's parents or directly to his or her physician, if the parents have provided written permission to release information.

Hospitalization

Children and adolescents with psychosis are hospitalized if ongoing treatment does not adequately control their symptoms. A child with psychosis often becomes a danger to him- or herself or to others because of aggression, suicidal behavior, or other dangerous behaviors. Hospitalization is also indicated if the psychosis affects all areas of the child's functioning and the child is unable to function at school or at home. Information that teachers give the parents and/or the physician is often essential in making this decision.

Therapy for the Child and His or Her Parents

While in an active psychotic stage, most children and adolescents benefit from supportive therapy. Therapy provides them hope that the symptoms will go away, information about what to do when experiencing psychotic symptoms, ways to address the fear that they will act on these symptoms (e.g., carry out a command hallucination to hurt someone), and methods for dealing with the demands of everyday life. Once the psychotic symptoms have subsided, these children might benefit from individual therapy to promote self-esteem, problem solving, and coping skills at home, at school, and with peers.

Supportive therapy is essential for increasing parents' ability to deal with their anxieties about their child's illness while they help the child. Parent education is helpful regarding the nature of the symptoms, the underlying disorder, the therapeutic effects and side effects of the medications used to treat the child, the time course of the treatment and the underlying disorder, and ways to prevent additional psychotic bouts. To ensure early intervention and prevention, parents should be made aware of warning signs that suggest subsequent psychotic episodes.

Educational Rehabilitation

If the child's cognitive functioning has been affected by psychosis, the school should devise an individualized education program (IEP) with input from parents and mental health professionals. The IEP should take into consideration the child's ongoing academic problems, as unrealistic high academic demands can exacerbate psychosis. Alternatively, expectation below the child's level of functioning can further increase the child's demoralization and poor self-esteem. Therefore, the program should be reevaluated and modified based on changes in the child's condition. In planning the child's educational program, it is important to bear in mind that his or her academic performance directly affects self-esteem and the ability to cope with the impact of the illness on his or her life.

Social Rehabilitation

Some children with psychosis, particularly those with schizophrenia, acquire significant social deficits as a result of their illness. Children with schizophrenia may become socially withdrawn and have difficulty initiating and carrying on a conversation. They might become anxious about contact with people and feel self-conscious about how they look, feel, and present themselves to others.

Social rehabilitation studies involving adults with schizophrenia have shown that certain aspects of cognitive function (e.g., executive function) (Brekke, Kohrt, & Green, 2001) and the ability to predict the mental state (Pollice et al., 2002) and affect recognition (Hooker & Park, 2002) predict social functioning. Despite the important impact of social deficits on children's quality of life, there have been no studies on social rehabilitation in children with schizophrenia. However, use of atypical neuroleptic drugs and the associated improvement in facial expression of affect, motivation, and curiosity make these children more amenable to social skills intervention.

CONCLUSION

Psychosis is infrequent in childhood and adolescence. Nonetheless, its presenting symptoms—hallucinations, delusions, and disorganized thinking—can occur with other psychiatric disorders, including schizophrenia, mood disorders (e.g., mania, bipolar disorder, depression), disorders with transient psychotic features (e.g., schizotypal personality disorder, multidimensionally impaired disorder), dissociative disorder, substance abuse, and neurological disorders (with and without epilepsy). Other psychiatric disorders—such as separation anxiety disorder, generalized anxiety disorder, specific phobias, and OCD—can have symptoms that mimic psychotic symptoms. Developmental disorders—such as high-functioning autism, Asperger syndrome, multiplex complex developmental disorder, and language disorders—also need to be ruled out when a child shows psychotic symptoms.

Correct identification of psychotic symptoms and diagnosis of the underlying disorder is the first step in determining a treatment plan. Teachers' awareness of possible classroom behaviors associated with each disorders (e.g., changes in concentration, work habits, and mood; irritability; social withdrawal; bizarre behavior; worsening of grades) can provide important diagnostic information and alert parents to the importance of having their child receive a psychiatric examination. Treatment approaches include medication, therapy, educational rehabilitation, and social rehabilitation. Input from teachers provides important information on both treatment efficacy and side effects.

REFERENCES

American Psychiatric Association. (1980). *Diagnostic and statistical manual of mental disorders* (3rd ed.). Washington, DC: Author.

American Psychiatric Association. (2000). *Diagnostic and statistical manual of mental disorders* (4th ed., text rev.). Washington, DC: Author.

Asarnow, J.R., & Ben-Meir, S. (1988). Children with schizophrenia spectrum and depressive disorders: A comparative study of premorbid adjustment, onset pattern, and severity of impairment. *Journal of Child Psychology and Psychiatry and Allied Disciplines, 29,* 477–489.

Asarnow, J.R., Goldstein, M.J., Carlson, G.A., Perdue, S., Bates, S., & Keller, J. (1988). Childhood-onset depressive disorders: A follow-up study of rates of rehospitalization and out-of-home placement among child psychiatric inpatients. *Journal of Affective Disorders, 15,* 245–248.

Bashir, M., Russell, J., & Johnson, G. (1987). Bipolar affective disorder in adolescence: A 10-year study. *The Australian and New Zealand Journal of Psychiatry, 21,* 36–43.

Besag, F.M. (2001). Behavioural effects of the new anticonvulsants. *Drug Safety, 24,* 513–536.

Bettes, B.A., & Walker, E. (1987). Positive and negative symptoms in psychotic and other psychiatrically disturbed children. *Journal of Child Psychology and Psychiatry, 28,* 555–568.

Brekke, J.S., Kohrt, B., & Green, M.F. (2001). Neuropsychological functioning as a moderator of the relationship between psychosocial functioning and the subjective experience of self and life in schizophrenia. *Schizophrenia Bulletin, 27,* 697–708.

Buitelaar, J.K., & van der Gaag, R.J. (1998). Diagnostic rules for children with PDD-NOS and multiple complex developmental disorder. *Journal of Child Psychology and Psychiatry and Allied Disciplines, 39,* 911–919.

Campbell, M., Rapoport J.L., & Simpson, G.M. (1999). Antipsychotics in children and adolescents. *Journal of the American Academy of Child and Adolescent Psychiatry, 38,* 537–545.

Caplan, R., Arbelle, S., Magharious, W., Guthrie, D., Komo, S., Shields, W.D., Chayasirisobhon, S., & Hansen, R. (1998). Psychopathology in pediatric complex partial and primary generalized epilepsy. *Developmental Medicine and Child Neurology, 40,* 805–811.

Caplan, R., & Guthrie, D. (1992). Communication deficits in childhood schizotypal personality disorder. *Journal of the American Academy of Child and Adolescent Psychiatry, 35,* 961–967.

Caplan, R., Guthrie, D., & Komo, S. (1996). Conversational repair in schizophrenic and normal children. *Journal of the American Academy of Child and Adolescent Psychiatry, 35,* 950–958.

Caplan, R., Guthrie, D., Komo, S., Chayasirisobhon, S., Mitchell, W., & Shields, W.D. (2001). Conversational repair in pediatric complex partial seizure disorder. *Brain and Language, 78,* 82–93.

Caplan, R., Guthrie, D., Tang, B., Komo, S., & Asarnow, R.F. (2000). Thought disorder in childhood schizophrenia: Replication and update of concept. *Journal of the American Academy of Child and Adolescent Psychiatry, 39,* 771–778.

Caplan, R., Perdue, S., Tanguay, P.E., & Fish, B. (1990). Formal thought disorder in childhood onset schizophrenia and schizotypal personality disorder. *Journal of Child Psychology and Psychiatry and Allied Disciplines, 31,* 1103–1114.

Caplan, R., Shields, W.D., Mori, L., & Yudovin, S. (1991). Middle childhood onset of interictal psychoses: Case studies. *Journal of the American Academy of Child and Adolescent Psychiatry, 30,* 893–896.

Caplan, R., Tanguay, P.E., & Szekely, A.G. (1987). Subacute sclerosing panencephalitis presenting as childhood psychosis: A case study. *Journal of the American Academy of Child Psychiatry, 26,* 440–443.

Carlson, G.A. (1990). Child and adolescent mania—diagnostic considerations. *Journal of Child Psychology and Psychiatry, and Allied Disciplines, 31,* 331–342.

Cassano, G.B., Pini, S., Saettoni, M., & Dell'Osso, L. (1999). Multiple anxiety disorders comorbid in patients with mood spectrum disorders with psychotic features. *The American Journal of Psychiatry, 156,* 474–476.

Chambers, W.J., Puig-Antich, J., Tabrizi, M.A., & Davies, M. (1982). Psychotic symptoms in prepubertal major depressive disorder. *Archives of General Psychiatry, 39,* 921–927.

Cohen, N.J., Barwick, M.A., Horodezky, N.B., Vallance, D.D., & Im, N. (1998). Language, achievement, and cognitive processing in psychiatrically disturbed children with previously identified and unsuspected language impairments. *Journal of Child Psychology, Psychiatry, and Allied Disciplines, 39,* 865–877.

Del Beccaro, M., Burke, P., & McCauley, E. (1988). Hallucinations in children: A follow-up study. *Journal of the American Academy of Child and Adolescent Psychiatry, 27,* 462–465.

Egdell, H.G., & Kolvin, I. (1972). Childhood hallucinations. *Journal of Child Psychology and Psychiatry, 13,* 279–287.

Eggers, C. (1978). Course and prognosis in childhood schizophrenia. *Journal of Autism and Childhood Schizophrenia, 8,* 21–36.

Eggers, C., & Bunk, D. (1997). The long-term course of childhood-onset schizophrenia: A 42-year follow-up. *Schizophrenia Bulletin, 23,* 105–117.

Eggers, C., Bunk, D., & Krause, D. (2000). Schizophrenia with onset before the age of eleven: Clinical characteristics of onset and course. *Journal of Autism and Developmental Disorders, 30,* 29–38.

Famularo, R., Fenton, T., Kinscherff, R., & Augustyn, M. (1996). Psychiatric comorbidity in childhood post traumatic stress disorder. *Child Abuse and Neglect, 20,* 953–961.

Fard, K., Hudgens, R.W., & Welner, A. (1978). Undiagnosed psychiatric illness in adolescents: A prospective study and seven-year follow-up. *Archives of General Psychiatry, 35,* 279–282.

Findling, R.L., McNamara, N.K., & Gracious, B.L. (2000). Pediatric uses of atypical antipsychotics. *Expert Opinion on Pharmacotherapy, 1,* 935–945.

Fleischhaker, C., Priemer, K., Schulz, E., & Remschmidt, H. (2002). Z Kinder jugendpsychiatr psychother [Psychotic disorders and drug abuse in adolescents]. *Zeitschrift Fur Kinder Und Jugendpsychiatrie Und Psychotherapie, 30,* 87–95.

Fortunati, F., Mazure, C., Preda, A., Wahl, R., & Bowers, M., Jr. (2002). Plasma catecholamine metabolites in antidepressant-exacerbated mania and psychosis. *Journal of Affective Disorders, 68,* 331–334.

Frazier, J.A., Gordon, C.T., McKenna, K., Lenane, M.C., Jih, D., & Rapoport, J.L. (1994). An open trial of clozapine in 11 adolescents with childhood-onset schizophrenia. *Journal of American Academy of Child and Adolescent Psychiatry, 33,* 658–663.

Garralda, M.E. (1984a). Hallucinations in children with conduct and emotional disorders: I. The clinical phenomena. *Psychological Medicine, 14,* 589–596.

Garralda, M.E. (1984b). Hallucinations in children with conduct and emotional disorders: II. The follow-up study. *Psychological Medicine, 14,* 597–604.

Garralda, M.E. (1984c). Psychotic children with hallucinations. *British Journal of Psychiatry Supplement, 145,* 74–77.

Gordon, C.T., Frazier, J.A., McKenna, K., Giedd, J., Zametkin, A., Zahn, T., Hommer, D., Hong, W., Kaysen, D., & Albus, K.E. (1994). Childhood-onset schizophrenia: An NIMH study in progress. *Schizophrenia Bulletin, 20,* 697–712.

Green, W.H., Campbell, M., Hardesty, A.S., Grega, D.M., Padron-Gayol, M., Shell, J., & Erlenmeyer-Kimling, L. (1984). A comparison of schizophrenic and autistic children. *Journal of the American Academy of Child Psychiatry, 4,* 399–409.

Greenhill, L.L., Pliszka, S., Dulcan, M.K., Bernet, W., Arnold, V., Beitchman, J., Benson, R.S., Bukstein, O., Kinlan, J., McClellan, J., Rue, D., Shaw, J.A., & Stock, S. (2002). Practice parameter for the use of stimulant medications in the treatment of children, adolescents, and adults. *Journal of the American Academy of Child and Adolescent Psychiatry, 41,* 26S–49S.

Hall, W., & Degenhardt, L. (2000). Cannabis use and psychosis: A review of clinical and epidemiological evidence. *The Australian and New Zealand Journal of Psychiatry, 34,* 26–34.

Holtmann, M., Becker, K., Hartmann, M., & Schmidt, M.H. (2002). Is there a temporal correlation between substance abuse and psychosis in adolescents? *Zeitschrift Fur Kinder Und Jugendpsychiatrie Und Psychotherapie, 30,* 97–103.

Hooker, C., & Park, S. (2002). Emotion processing and its relationship to social functioning in schizophrenia patients. *Psychiatry Research, 112,* 41–50.

Hornstein, N.L., & Putnam, F.W. (1992). Clinical phenomenology of child and adolescent dissociative disorders. *Journal of the American Academy of Child and Adolescent Psychiatry, 31,* 1077–1085.

Jordan, K., & Prugh, D.G. (1971). Schizophreniform psychosis of childhood. *American Journal of Psychiatry, 128,* 323–331.

Kafantaris, V., Coletti, D.J., Dicker, R., Padula, G., & Pollack, S. (1998). Are childhood psychiatric histories of bipolar adolescents associated with family history, psychosis, and response to lithium treatment? *Journal of Affective Disorders, 51,* 153–164.

Kemph, J.P. (1987). Hallucinations in psychotic children. *Journal of the American Academy of Child and Adolescent Psychiatry, 26,* 556–559.

Kolvin, I., Ounsted, C., Humphrey, M., & McNay, A. (1971). Studies in the childhood psychoses: I. The phenomenology of childhood psychoses. *British Journal of Psychiatry Supplement, 118,* 385–395.

Kostopoulos, S., Kanigsberg, J., Cote, A., & Fiedorowicz, C. (1987). Hallucinatory experiences in nonpsychotic children. *Journal of the American Academy of Child and Adolescent Psychiatry, 26,* 375–380.

Kumra, S., Frazier, J.A., Jacobsen, L.K., McKenna, K., Gordon, C.T., Lenane, M.C., Hamburger, S.D., Smith, A.K., Albus, K.E., Alaghband-Rad, J., & Rapoport, J.L. (1996). Childhood-onset schizophrenia. A double-blind clozapine-haloperidol comparison. *Archives of General Psychiatry, 53,* 1090–1097.

Kumra, S., Giedd, J.N., Vaituzis, A.C., Jacobsen, L.K., McKenna, K., Bedwell, J., Hamburger, S., Nelson, J.E., Lenane, M., & Rapoport, J.L. (2000). Childhood-onset psychotic disorders: Magnetic resonance imaging of volumetric differences in brain structure. *American Journal of Psychiatry, 157,* 1467–1474.

Kumra, S., Jacobsen, L.K., Lenane, M., Zahn, T.P., Wiggs, E., Alaghband-Rad, J., Castellanos, F.X., Frazier, J.A., McKenna, K., Gordon, C.T., Smith, A., Hamburger, S., & Rapoport, J.L. (1998). "Multidimensionally impaired disorder": Is it a variant of very early-onset schizophrenia? *Journal of the American Academy of Child and Adolescent Psychiatry, 37,* 91–99.

Kumra, S., Wiggs, E., Bedwell, J., Smith, A.K., Arling, E., Albus, K., Hamburger, S.D., McKenna, K., Jacobsen, L.K., Rapoport, J.L., & Asarnow, R.F. (2000). Neuropsychological deficits in pediatric patients with childhood-onset schizophrenia and psychotic disorder not otherwise specified. *Schizophrenia Research, 42,* 135–144.

Lindsay, J., Ounsted, C., & Richards, P. (1979). Long-term outcome in children with temporal lobe seizures: III. Psychiatric aspects in childhood and adult life. *Developmental Medicine and Child Neurology, 21,* 630–636.

Makowski, D., Waternaux, C., Lajonchere, C.M., Dicker, R., Smoke, N., Koplewicz, H., Min, D., Mendell, N.R., & Levy, D.L. (1997). Thought disorder in adolescent-onset schizophrenia. *Schizophrenia Research, 23,* 147–165.

McClellan, J., Breiger, D., McCurry, C., & Hlastala, S.A. (2003). Premorbid functioning in early-onset psychotic disorders. *Journal of the American Academy of Child and Adolescent Psychiatry, 42,* 666–672.

McClellan, J., McCurry, C., Speltz, M.L., & Jones, K. (2002). Symptom factors in early-onset psychotic disorders. *Journal of the American Academy of Child Adolescent Psychiatry, 41,* 791–798.

McGee, R., Williams, S., & Poulton, R. (2000). Hallucinations in nonpsychotic children. *Journal of the American Academy of Child and Adolescent Psychiatry, 39,* 12–13.

McKenna, K., Gordon, C.T., Lenane, M., Kaysen, D., Fahey, K., & Rapoport, J.L. (1994). Looking for childhood-onset schizophrenia: The first 71 cases screened. *Journal of the American Academy of Child and Adolescent Psychiatry, 33,* 636–644.

Mouridsen, S.E., Rich, B., & Isager, T. (2000). A comparative study of genetic and neurobiological findings in disintegrative psychosis and infantile autism. *Psychiatry and Clinical Neurosciences, 4,* 441–446.

Nicolson, R., Lenane, M., Brookner, F., Gochman, P., Kumra, S., Spechler, L., Giedd, J.N., Thaker, G.K., Wudarsky, M., & Rapoport, J.L. (2001). Children and adolescents with psychotic disorder not otherwise specified: A 2- to 8-year follow-up study. *Comprehensive Psychiatry, 42,* 319–325.

Paillere-Martinot, M.L., Aubin, F., Martinot, J.L., & Colin, B. (2000). A prognostic study of clinical dimensions in adolescent-onset psychoses. *Schizophrenia Bulletin, 26,* 789–799.

Pataki, C.S., & Carlson, G. (1990). Affective disorders in children and adolescents. In B.J. Tongue, G.D. Burrows, & J.S. Werry (Eds.), *Handbook of studies on child psychiatry* (pp. 137–160). New York: Elsevier Science.

Pollice, R., Roncone, R., Falloon, I.R., Mazza, M., De Risio, A., Necozione, S., Morosini, P., & Casacchia, M. (2002). Is theory of mind in schizophrenia more strongly associated with clinical and social functioning than with neurocognitive deficits? *Psychopathology, 35,* 280–288.

Putnam, F. (1991). Dissociative disorders in children and adolescents: A developmental perspective. *Psychiatric Clinics of North America, 14,* 519–531.

Ran, M.S., Xiang, M.Z., Chan, C.L., Leff, J., Simpson, P., Huang, M.S., Shan, Y.H., & Li, S.G. (2003). Effectiveness of psychoeducational intervention for rural Chinese families experiencing schizophrenia: A randomised controlled trial. *Social Psychiatry and Psychiatric Epidemiology, 38,* 69–75.

Riddle, M.A., Kastelic, E.A., & Frosch, E. (2001). Pediatric psychopharmacology. *Journal of Child Psychology and Psychiatry and Allied Disciplines, 42,* 73–90.

Ross, R.G., & Compagnon, N. (2001). Diagnosis and treatment of psychiatric disorders in children with a schizophrenic parent. *Schizophrenia Research, 50,* 121–129.

Russell, A.T. (1994). The clinical presentation of childhood onset schizophrenia. *Schizophrenia Bulletin, 20,* 631–646.

Russell, A.T., Bott, L., & Sammons, C. (1989). The phenomenology of schizophrenia occurring in childhood. *Journal of the American Academy of Child and Adolescent Psychiatry, 28,* 399–407.

Ryan, N.D., Puig-Antich, J., Ambrosini, P., Rabinovich, H., Robinson, D., Nelson, B., Iyengar, S., & Twomey, J. (1987). The clinical picture of major depression in children and adolescents. *Archives of General Psychiatry, 44,* 854–861.

Schaeffer, J.L., & Ross, R.G. (2002). Childhood-onset schizophrenia: Premorbid and prodromal diagnostic and treatment histories. *Journal of the American Academy of Child and Adolescent Psychiatry, 41,* 538–545.

Schur, S.B., Sikich, L., Findling, R.L., Malone, R.P., Crismon, M.L., Derivan, A., MacIntyre, J.C., Pappadopulos, E., Greenhill, L., Schooler, N., Van Orden, K., & Jensen, P.S. (2003). Treatment recommendations for the use of antipsychotics for aggressive youth (TRAAY). Part I: A review. *Journal of the American Academy of Child and Adolescent Psychiatry, 42,* 132–144.

Spencer, E.K., & Campbell, M. (1994). Children with schizophrenia: Diagnosis, phenomenology, and pharmacotherapy. *Schizophrenia Bulletin, 20,* 713–725.

Ulloa, R.E., Birmaher, B., Axelson, D., Williamson, D.E., Brent, D.A., Ryan, N.D., Bridge, J., & Baugher, M. (2000). Psychosis in a pediatric mood and anxiety disorders clinic: Phenomenology and correlates. *Journal of the American Academy of Child and Adolescent Psychiatry, 39,* 337–345.

van der Gaag, R.J., Buitelaar, J., van den Ban, E., Bezemer, M., Njio, L., & van Engeland, H. (1995). A controlled multivariate chart review of multiple complex developmental disorder. *Journal of the American Academy of Child and Adolescent Psychiatry, 34,* 1096–1106.

Volkmar, F.R., & Cohen, D.J. (1991). Comorbid association of autism and schizophrenia. *American Journal of Psychiatry, 148,* 1705–1707.

Volkmar, F.R., Cohen, D.J., Hoshino, Y., Rende, R.D., & Rheas, P. (1988). Phenomenology and classification of the childhood psychoses. *Psychological Medicine, 18,* 191–201.

Werry, J.S., McClellan, J.M., & Chard, L. (1991). Childhood and adolescent schizophrenic, bipolar, and schizoaffective disorders: A clinical outcome study. *Journal of the American Academy of Child and Adolescent Psychiatry, 30,* 457–465.

Biologically and/or Psychologically Based Disorders

Larry B. Silver

Mental health disorders can have psychosocial causes. For example, anxiety or depression can be caused by family stress, the loss of a loved one, or academic failure. Some individuals have biological predispositions that make them more vulnerable to these factors or influence the way that they react to stress. These same mental health disorders can be caused by a biologically based neurochemical deficiency that is probably inherited. Therefore, although stress might contribute to or exacerbate the disorder, the underlying biologically based problem causes it. Still other disorders might start because of psychological stresses; however, these stresses might lead to biological changes within the brain or within other body systems, causing the disorder to persist or to become more severe. It is not easy to clarify where biology and psychosocial issues begin and end. Often, there is a blend of the two. Thus, clinicians approach treatment by trying to recognize the presenting disorder. Treatment approaches might be biological (medication), psychological (psychotherapy, behavioral management), and social (family therapy, environmental changes).

Four types of such mental health disorders are discussed in Section III. The biological influences, neurochemical changes, and social factors related to substance abuse are discussed in Chapter 8. Heredity and psychosocial issues also can influence the development of eating disorders, anxiety disorders, and mood disorders, which are detailed in Chapters 9, 10, and 11, respectively.

8

Substance Use and Abuse

Deborah R. Simkin with Larry B. Silver

Chapter Concepts

- The high incidence of substance use among students
- Factors that place some students at risk for substance use and abuse
- Types of substances used by students
- Ways to recognize a possible problem
- What to do if a substance abuse problem is suspected
- The essential role of the classroom teacher in addressing substance use and abuse

Unfortunately, middle and high school students commonly experiment with various substances. For many peer groups, using alcohol, nicotine, or other drugs constitutes socially acceptable behavior. For most young people, this experimentation is limited in amount and to specific social situations. However, this social use sometimes moves into substance misuse, and students use these substances more often than in social situations. Personality, behavior, and school performance are affected. For some students, substance misuse expands into substance abuse. Substance abuse leads to significant changes in personality, behavior, and school performance as well as to substance dependency. The need for drugs results in more self-destructive behaviors and, possibly, legal problems. This shift is often subtle and missed by both parents and teachers.

This chapter focuses on substance use and abuse as related to school settings and classroom teachers. The scope of the problem, the types of substances used, and the behaviors that might be noted in the classroom are discussed. Early recognition and appropriate intervention, which are critical to helping these students, are discussed as well because the classroom teacher plays an important role with each task.

PREVALENCE

Drug use has not yet climbed to the heights of the 1970s and 1980s. Marijuana was used by one in two high school seniors in 1979, as compared with one in four in 1996. Nonetheless, from 1996 through 2001, illicit drug use reached levels not seen since the previous usage peaks in the late 1970s and early 1980s. Among 12- to 17-year olds, illicit drug use "within the last month" doubled from 1992 to 1995 (National Institute of Drug Abuse [NIDA], 1996, 2002).

In 2001, the lifetime use rates for illicit drugs other than marijuana among eighth graders were below their 1996 lifetime peaks (approximately 20%) (NIDA, 1996, 2002). Yet, in 1996, 66% of high school seniors reported lifetime use of any illicit drug, and more than 85% of all adolescents had tried alcohol and other drugs by the time they finished high school (Johnston, 1996). Of seniors surveyed that same year, 85% had some experience with alcohol, and 31% had five or more drinks per month. Two percent of high school seniors reported trying heroin.

In 1996, inhalants were the fourth most common drug used by high-school students. Inhalants also are popular among middle school students: Inhalant use was almost twice as high among eighth graders than among tenth or twelfth graders. Furthermore, 21% of eighth graders had tried inhalants at least once (NIDA, 1996). Although the numbers for inhalant use are decreasing, it is startling that a greater number of adolescents are engaging in the use of this drug. This finding is probably due to the availability of inhalants.

In 1996, usage of lysergic acid diethylamide (LSD) and phencyclidine (PCP) approached its late 1970s and early 1980s peak. LSD use among high school seniors increased from a low of 8.3% in 1989 to 12.6%, and the general use of hallucinogens rose to 14% for lifetime prevalence. Approximately 42% of twelfth graders and 19% of eighth graders surveyed stated that LSD is easily accessible (NIDA, 1996, 2002).

Marijuana is the most common illicit drug used among youth, with increases in use beginning to show during 1992. In 1996, lifetime annual and current use doubled in eighth graders, with 11% reporting use within the last month and 5% reporting daily use. Although marijuana use has fallen among older students, it is troubling that adolescents and young teens are now experimenting with it. This observation is particularly worrisome because research has shown that earlier use of marijuana indicates a greater risk for later development of substance abuse and substance dependency.

Alcohol use rates were surveyed in the context of binge drinking. Among twelfth graders, the percentages of students who engaged in binge drinking were as follows: 41% in 1983, 28% in 1992, and 32% in 1998. Among eighth graders, the rate was 13% in 1992 and 16% in 1998. For tenth graders, the rate was 21% in 1992 and 25% in 1998. In 2000, the percentage of eighth graders who had gotten drunk in the past year was 18.5%; in 2001, that rate decreased to 16.6%. Disappointingly, the rate of daily use by seniors increased from 2.9% to 3.5%. (Johnston, 1996; NIDA, 1996, 2002).

On an encouraging note, cigarette usage rates have continued a downward trend. In 1976, 39% of twelfth graders had used cigarettes in the previous month. By 1992, the rate had decreased to 28%. From 2000 to 2001, past-month use declined among eighth graders from 14.6% to 12.2%. Use across these years declined from 23.9% to 21.3% among tenth graders and from 7.4% to 5.5% among twelfth graders. The risk of using cigarettes increased, however: to 38% for eighth graders, to 46% for tenth graders, and to 45% for twelfth graders.

These statistics show the widespread nature of substance use and abuse. The properties and effects of the specific substances mentioned, as well as those of other abused substances, are discussed later in this chapter under the heading "Substances of Abuse."

BIOPSYCHOSOCIAL MODEL FOR UNDERSTANDING SUBSTANCE PROBLEMS

Substance use and abuse can be understood in both a specific and a general manner. Specifically, one must know the precise physical and psychological impacts of the substances used. Yet, one also must have a general understanding of the addictive qualities of these substances. These addictive qualities can lead an individual from substance use to substance dependency and abuse. Understanding these problems requires studying the biological, psychological, and social factors involved over time (Chatlos, 1996; Jaffe & Simkin, 2002). One must look at predisposing or risk factors, enabling systems, and the biological and psychological impacts of the drug used.

Before relaying specific information about substance abuse problems, however, it is helpful to understand the initiation into first alcohol or drug use. At this point, psychological and social factors are important. Initiation is usually not a coping method for dealing with stress. Instead, use for coping is a learned response that develops with greater use. Biological and psychological factors interact to contribute to this behavior. Strong positive reinforcement from drug euphoria and lack of reinforcement in abstinence also contribute to the progression, which follows the specific stages described next.

Stage 1: Experimentation—Learning the Mood Swing

The experimentation stage usually begins with peer pressure in middle school and involves drinking beer, smoking marijuana, or sniffing inhalants. This activity typically occurs on the weekend at the student's home, while hanging out at a friend's house, or at a party, and it often fulfills the desires to be accepted by peers and to feel grown up. During this stage, small amounts of the drug are needed to get high, so the person usually returns to a normal mood quickly with no problems. At this point, the individual has learned to use drugs to affect mood and to stimulate the pleasure centers of the brain. To many young people, what feels good must be good, and possible negative effects often are not considered.

Stage 2: Regular Use—Seeking the Mood Swing

More regular substance use begins, for example, with progression to hard liquor or bouts of drinking to get drunk. At this stage, use becomes associated with coping with stress. Use begins occurring during the week, and more of the drug is needed as the body develops tolerance. Minor problems arise, such as being late for school or work or not performing well on a sports team because of hangovers. The individual tries different drugs at this point and may progress to using hallucinogens and pills. During this stage, friends who do not use drugs may be dropped. In addition, more money may be needed to acquire substances, possibly leading to stealing from family members and lying to hide drug use. The individual's moods may change rapidly and without explanation; he or she might be irritable, happy, angry, or even depressed. Interest in usual activities may change as well.

Stage 3: Substance Abuse—Harmful Consequences with Repeated Use

As the extent of drug use progresses, problems develop in additional areas of the person's life. Drug use becomes a central focus, resulting in the failure to fulfill major obligations at home, school, or work. This evolving preoccupation involves drug use in physically hazardous situations (e.g., driving while intoxicated) and may include recurrent substance-related legal problems. Nonetheless, use continues despite these persistent interpersonal and social problems. Mood and behavior changes that occur at this point may be due to withdrawal from certain drugs.

Stage 4: Substance Dependence—Compulsive Use

This final stage of addiction involves larger amounts of substances as tolerance increases. Hard, or more dangerous, drugs (e.g., heroin) may be used at this point.

The individual continues using the substance despite his or her knowledge of physical or psychological problems caused or exacerbated by the substance. The person is increasingly preoccupied with obtaining the substance, using it, and recovering from its use. Important social, occupational, and recreational activities are reduced or given up. Attempts to cut down or quit are often unsuccessful. Drug-using friends may contribute to the person's cognitive distortions or denial of the problem. Even with denial, however, guilt, shame, and self-hatred may lead to suicidal thoughts and suicide attempts. At this point, the individual cannot control his or her drug use, and life becomes unmanageable. Often, use is continued to avoid withdrawal and, thus, to feel "normal."

RISK FACTORS

No one risk factor leads to substance abuse. Rather, the more risk factors that an individual has, the greater his or her risk of developing the disorder. Different combinations of risk factors and the strength and nature of the individual risk factors lead to varying potentials for negative outcomes. Specific risk factors have a greater influence at certain developmental stages. Cultural and societal elements may influence risk factors throughout all developmental states (Newcomb, 1995; Pandina, Johnson, & Labouvie, 1992). In this context, three types of risk factors are discussed: interpersonal, psychobehavioral, and biogenetic.

Interpersonal

Interpersonal factors might reflect family issues, peer influences, or individual personality factors. These interpersonal risk factors have the most influence during childhood and adolescence. They include the effects of parental modeling, parental belief in the harmlessness of certain substances, lack of monitoring by parents, physical abuse, family disruption (e.g., divorce), negative communication patterns, lack of anger control by a family member, parental lack of involvement with children's activities, parental passivity, and low academic aspirations by parents.

As examples of these factors, the impact of parent monitoring in initiating alcohol, tobacco, and other drug use has the greatest influence with children younger than age 11. A higher risk for initiating marijuana, cocaine, and inhalant drugs occurs in children who are seldom monitored during middle childhood (ages 10–12). Parental smoking is a form of modeling that influences children's initiation of smoking. When coupled with lack of school success, low parental monitoring, and easy access to cigarettes, children who start smoking at a young age are more likely to continue smoking.

Monitoring by parents is particularly an issue because many families have two working parents. The time of least parent monitoring is often considered to be on weekends, when children and adolescents hang out with their friends. Parent supervision should be present; however, it is not always easy to supervise situations. Children and adolescents are at risk when together on weekend evenings without close parental supervision. However, the time period of 3:00 P.M.– 7 P.M. on weekdays presents an equal risk. Many students are on their own after school and until parents return from work. They often go to friends' houses or have friends come to their houses. Often, there is no parent supervision during this time. Increased experimentation with alcohol and other drugs; sexual activity; and delinquent behaviors, such as breaking into homes and stealing, often take place during this often unsupervised after-school time.

Peer influence also plays an important role. Peer attitudes may predict the initiation of alcohol and other substance use. In predicting susceptibility to substance abuse during adolescence, strong peer attachment has a greater influence than parental attachment. Peer influence also plays a strong role in predicting relapse: 90% of teens who relapse do so because of peer pressure.

Psychobehavioral

During childhood and adolescence, age at first use is likely to influence the onset of substance problems. Youth who begin drinking at an early age (11–12 years) have a higher probability of developing substance dependency (15.9%) or abuse (13.5%) as compared with those who begin drinking at age 13 or 14 years (13.7% and 9.0%, respectively). Those who start to drink at age 19 or 20 have even lower rates (2% and 1%). It is important to note that rapid progression of alcohol and drug use disorders occur most often with earlier age of onset and increased frequency of use (DeWitt, Adlaf, Offord, et al., 2000; Lee & DeClemente, 1985).

In addition, lack of peer acceptance and limited academic success often result in low self-esteem and a poor self-image. In turn, these factors may contribute to risk for substance use. It is critical, therefore, that risk factors such as poor social skills and learning disabilities (which are related to lack of peer acceptance and limited academic success) are recognized early. Appropriate assessments and interventions must be conducted as early as possible.

Furthermore, substance use problems and psychiatric disorders have a high comorbidity rate. The question is whether these other disorders contribute to the student's vulnerability to use substances, whether these other disorders are a consequence of substance abuse, or if the answer is a mixture of both. Another question is whether the student might be using alcohol or other drugs to self-medicate an underlying psychiatric disorder. It is important for the professionals working with this student to clarify which theme might be relevant.

Depression and anxiety disorders have been found to be higher among students who have substance problems. Anger control problems, such as intermittent explosive disorder, or bipolar disorder are also found to be comorbid with substance problems. Disruptive behavioral disorders, such as conduct disorder and oppositional defiant disorder, as well as attention-deficit/hyperactivity disorder are often present before the onset of any substance use. In addition, individuals with certain eating disorders, such as bulimia, seem to be at greater risk for substance abuse than individuals with anorexia. An analysis of adolescents who committed suicide showed that 70% were drug and alcohol users (Shoffi et al., 1988). Among 10- to 19-year-olds, suicide was 4.9 times more likely to have occurred while drinking (Brent, Perper, & Allman, 1987).

Finally, substance abuse and physically dangerous behavior are connected. People who started drinking before age 14, as well as those who started at each intervening age up to 21, were significantly more likely to be injured while under the influence of alcohol (Hingson, Heeren, Jamanka, & Howland, 2000). The relationship between alcohol and/or drug use and automobile accidents is well established in highway safety literature.

Biogenetic

Inherited susceptibility can play a role once a person begins to use substances. Those who have a greater genetic predisposition to develop substance abuse may be more susceptible to the influence of alcohol or the impact of alcohol on gene expression (Nestler, 2001a, 2001b).

There is another genetically based concern related to specific areas of the brain. Constant exposure to alcohol and other drugs may create permanent changes in the internal messenger system inside the cells in these areas. These changes might influence the turning on of specific genes, which, in turn, may influence the drive mechanism toward substance use.

SUBSTANCES OF ABUSE

Nicotine

Nicotine is one of the most addictive substances known. Use of cigarettes introduces adolescents to behaviors associated with use. They learn to hide the use, lie about their use, and begin to develop tolerance and the pleasure associated with use. Smoking is often considered the gateway drug. Students who use marijuana and, later, other drugs often start with cigarettes. Smoking can decrease the rate of lung development, and chewing tobacco can cause tooth loss and oral cancer. Of interest to educators, a correlation has been shown between cigarette use and low academic achievement.

Alcohol

Alcohol continues to be the most commonly used psychoactive substance. As noted previously, one study showed that approximately one third of high school seniors have had a binge drinking episode (five or more drinks) in the past month. The psychological and behavioral effects are related to the blood alcohol level (BAL). In adolescents who have not developed alcohol tolerance, impaired judgment occurs at a BAL of 0.06%, impaired motor coordination at 0.08%, impaired reaction time at 0.10%, impaired balance at 0.15%, and confusion or unconsciousness at 0.30%. Excessive intake at any age (BAL 0.40%–0.50%) can cause death. The BAL level for driving while intoxicated varies with each state and is usually between 0.08% and 0.10%.

Drinking alcohol causes a two-phased response. The initial rising of BAL is associated with arousal, excitement, and increased confidence. This is always followed by falling BALs, which are associated with fatigue and dysphoria (i.e., unease and depression). Tolerance to alcohol decreases the initial stimulating effects and increases the secondary depressant effects. Pathologic intoxication occurs when, in contrast to his or her usual temperament, an individual becomes violent and aggressive after drinking alcohol.

Adolescents who abuse alcohol may develop nausea, vomiting, peptic ulcer disease, and gastrointestinal hemorrhaging. Alcohol withdrawal, when present, may yield the following symptoms: nausea and vomiting, tremors, increased heart rate, elevated blood pressure, sweating, anxiety, irritability, and seizures. Adolescents who abuse alcohol have the problems seen in adults who chronically abuse alcohol, such as cirrhosis of the liver or specific neurological disorders. However, the brain of an adolescent undergoes major changes during development. These changes influence cognitive abilities, memory, and planning, as well as the area of the brain involved in the pleasure experienced by alcohol's effects. Therefore, the effects of alcohol on a developing individual's brain are different from its effects on an adult's mature brain. For instance, there might be a reduction in the size of specific areas of the brain, resulting in memory problems or other processing difficulties.

Marijuana

Marijuana is the most commonly abused illegal drug. The active ingredient, cannabis, may remain in the body for up to 8 days. Acute physiological effects may include increased heart rate, conjunctival injection (bloodshot eyes), sensitivity to light, dry mouth, and tremors. Acute psychological effects include euphoria or apathy; sensation of slowed time and intensified perception; and, often, increased appetite. For adolescents, the most dangerous effects are in the areas of cognition and psychomotor performance. Short-term memory loss might persists for 6 weeks after the last drug use. This loss, combined with decreased attention, may markedly impair the adolescent's ability to learn and to do schoolwork. A single marijuana cigarette can impair complex visual-motor functioning for up to 24 hours. It is disconcerting that many individuals are often not aware of these difficulties. For instance, many adolescents and teenagers do not realize that after smoking marijuana, their driving is impaired. Yet, there is extensive evidence linking fatal accidents to cannabis use.

Abrupt cessation after long-term, heavy use may result in insomnia, irritability, restlessness, drug craving, body aches, and general malaise. In addition, there may be depression, anxiety, tremors, nausea, muscle twitches, and increased sweating.

Cocaine

Cocaine can be administered by snorting, injecting, and smoking. Crack is the common street name given to cocaine after it has been changed to a free base for smoking. The effects of cocaine use include constricted peripheral blood vessels, dilated pupils, increased body temperature, increased heart rate, and elevated blood pressure. High doses over a prolonged time may cause paranoia. Habitual snorting may cause ulcerations of the mucous membrane of the nose. The immediate danger in using cocaine is that death can occur secondary to cardiac arrest and/or respiratory arrest.

Opiates

Opiates are processed from a naturally occurring substance known as morphine, which is produced from opium poppies. Opiates include opium, opium derivatives, and synthetic substitutes. These substitutes include codeine, fentanyl, meperidine (Demerol), and oxycodone (OxyContin). They are used medically for pain relief, cough suppression, and diarrhea relief. Thus, adolescents might seek opiates or synthetic substitutes in the form of prescription pain relievers or cough syrups (often found in the family medicine cabinet).

Acute physiologic effects of opiates include drowsiness, constricted pupils, reduced cough reflex, and constipation. Higher doses may produce nausea, vomiting, and respiratory depression. Acute intoxication or overdose produces "pinpoint pupils" and respiratory and central nervous system depression. A lowered body temperature, lowered blood pressure, and slowing of breathing rate might occur. Overdoses can occur from opiates alone or in combination with alcohol or sedatives.

Heroin is the usual drug of choice for opiate addicts because it is short-acting, which gives it a quick peak effect with intense euphoria. Euphoria is experienced within 30 minutes after snorting, 15 minutes after subcutaneous injection, and 16 seconds after intravenous injection. Heroin produces rapid tolerance, so increased doses are needed to give the same euphoric effect. Physical dependence evolves, and a characteristic withdrawal syndrome develops when heroin use is terminated. Acute withdrawal symptoms begin within 8 hours, peak at 48–72 hours, and decrease over the next 4–7 days. Withdrawal symptoms include agitation, goose bumps, rapid heart rate, mild hypertension, and constricted pupils. Sweating, vomiting, diarrhea, and urinary frequency also occur. At 8–12 hours after termination of heroin use, anxiety is high, and tremors, shakes, muscle cramps, and joint pain develop. Although uncomfortable, the withdrawal state is not life-threatening. Chronic heroin users may experience other serious outcomes, such as collapsed veins, infectious diseases (e.g., HIV/AIDS, hepatitis), heart valve infections, and other infections involving the skin or muscles.

Inhalants

Inhalants are breathable, chemical vapors that produce mind-altering effects. Inhalants are easily accessible and, thus, commonly used to achieve this outcome through sniffing (or "huffing"). Abuse of inhalants is highest in the early adolescent years.

There are three major classes of inhalants: solvents, gases, and nitrites. Solvents include household products such as paint thinners, degreasers, dry-cleaning fluids, gasoline, and glues. Solvents may also be found in certain office supplies such as correction fluids (e.g., Wite-Out), felt-tip marker fluid, and air cleaners. Gases can be found in household products such as butane lighters and propane tanks, aerosol (e.g., for whipping cream), and refrigerant gases. Household aerosol products such as spray paints, hair or deodorant sprays, and fabric protector sprays may be used as a source of these gases. Nitrites are available in the public as cyclohexl nitrite, a cleaning solution. Medical anesthetic gases—such as ether, chloroform, halothane, and nitrous oxide—are other nitrite sources. Amyl nitrite is only available by prescription, and butyl nitrite is classified as an illegal substance.

Inhalant abuse may produce excitation followed by depression, confusion, and disorientation. It may produce severe irreversible consequences, including hearing loss, peripheral nerve damage, central nervous system brain damage, limb spasms, and bone marrow deterioration. Serious but potentially reversible effects include liver and kidney damage and blood oxygen depletion.

Inhalant abuse can easily result in death. *Sudden sniffing death* occurs when someone huffing an inhalant is suddenly startled by another person and dies of cardiovascular collapse (a condition related to a sudden drop in blood pressure). Inhaling the substance from a paper or plastic bag or in a closed area (often done deliberately to heighten effects) greatly increases the chances of suffocation. Furthermore, fluorocarbons and butane-type gases can displace oxygen in the lungs, causing suffocation.

Hallucinogens

LSD is odorless, colorless, and has a slightly bitter taste. It is often added to absorbent paper, such as blotter paper, and divided into small squares, each representing one dose (or "hit"). The strength of LSD has been reduced since the 1960s. The sugar-cube dosage of the 1960s contained three to four times more LSD than the 1-inch square blotter-paper dosage of the 1990s.

The experience of being under the influence of LSD is commonly called a *trip*. Physical effects of a trip include increased heart rate, increased blood pressure, dilated pupils, sweating, loss of appetite, dry mouth, lethargy, and tremors. Bad trips may be experienced as a rapid swing in emotions. Higher doses may produce visual hallucinations and delusions, and panic may result. These sensations begin to clear after about 12 hours. However, flashbacks may occur up to 1 year after use.

Milder hallucinogens used by adolescents include mescaline, from the peyote cactus, and psilocybin, which comes from a certain type of mushrooms. In addition, chewing the seeds of jimsonweed may produce a hallucinatory experience. These substances might produce the same side effects as noted for LSD.

Steroids

Common generic forms of oral anabolic-androgenic steroids include methandrostenolone, stanozol, oxandrolone, methyltestosterone, fluoxymesterone, and oxymetholone. These steroids are illegal, and possession is a felony offense. They are banned by major sports organizations and in all competitions.

The physical consequences of abuse in males include reduced sperm production, shrinking of the testicles, infertility, baldness, and irreversible growth of breasts. In females, abuse may cause viriling effects (e.g., deepening voice, hair growth, male-pattern baldness). In younger users, there is an initial increase of skeletal growth followed by a premature closure of the skeletal plates. The mental effects of abuse may include increased aggression and, in some cases, mania. Depression is possible.

Club Drugs

Methylenedioxymethamphetamine (MDMA, or "ecstasy"), flunitrazepam (Rohypnol, or "rophies"), gamma hydroxybutyrate (GHB), and ketamine ("Special K") are among the so-called club drugs used by teens and young adults who attend bars or raves (all-night dance parties) or are part of the trance scene (groups that gather to experience a relaxed trance-like experience). These drugs can be added to a beverage without changing its taste because they are often colorless, tasteless, and odorless. The person ingesting this drink does not know of the added drug and is susceptible to trance-like behavior. In this state, the person is suggestible and vulnerable to sexual abuse. Congress passed the Drug-Induced Rape Prevention and Punishment Act of 1996 (PL 104-305) after these drugs became a popular way to commit date rape.

Phencyclidine

PCP is a white crystalline powder that is soluble in water and has a bitter taste. It is usually snorted, smoked, or eaten, resulting in a perceived state of excitement. However, low doses cause shallow breathing, flushing, and profuse sweating. Numbness of the extremities may occur, along with lack of coordination. Increased doses may cause the physical symptoms of dizziness, drop in blood pressure, drooling, blurred vision, nausea, and vomiting. Seizures, coma, and death may even occur. Hallucinations and illusions are also possible. Thinking can be disordered and paranoid. Long-term use results in difficulties with speech and memory. Thus, the accumulation of these effects with chronic use of PCP may cause problems with the learning process.

CLASSROOM SIGNS OF POSSIBLE SUBSTANCE PROBLEMS

Certain clues might alert general education teachers to a substance abuse problem, although these hints often are general. More common signs include motor vehicle accidents, a decline in grades, truancy, a reduction in class preparation or performance, and a loss of interest or a decline in performance in previously enjoyed activities (e.g., sports). Furthermore, the student might engage in activities—such as fighting, having unprotected sex, breaking the law, or running away from home—that he or she would have avoided if not under the influence or dealing with a substance problem.

Another pattern relates to friends. The student's friends who do not use substances may voice disapproval of the student's behavior. The student may gravitate toward peers who are considered trouble makers or members of a fringe peer group. This student might also change his or her choice of clothing style, music, or activities.

ASSESSMENT

It is important to remember that few adolescents seek help for a substance abuse problem. More often, parents, teachers, or friends become concerned. Thus, any assessment must include these people. Intervention will be based on what is learned during the assessment.

The assessment of substance use should determine the stage in which the adolescent is actively engaged (experimentation, regular use, substance abuse, or substance dependence). Once the stage of use is determined, the clinician begins the difficult task of assessing the individual's readiness to change and his or her motivation for treatment. The individual often rationalizes the problem, minimizing the seriousness of his or her substance use. This person may also deny any direct relationship between the negative consequences associated with substance use and his or her behaviors.

There are many screening and assessment approaches to assist in this task. The student's teacher might be asked to complete specific forms or rating scales as part of this process. He or she might also be asked about the school's general peer environment and the specific group of friends with which the student associates.

Urine Drug Screening

Urine drug tests are commonly used to detect recent use of illegal drugs, but their many limitations can restrict their assessment role. Urine must be obtained under observed conditions to make sure that it is the test subject's sample or that a foreign substance (e.g., apple juice) has not been substituted. It is also important to ensure that the sample has not been adulterated. This is necessary because many teenagers are well versed in ways to beat urine drug screens. Adding a small amount of bleach or blood may make the results negative. Taking a diuretic with enormous amounts of fluid often makes urine drug screen results negative as well. In fact, simply drinking large amounts of water will yield a very diluted urine sample and may make the sample negative.

The urine drug test is limited to the length of time that specific drugs stay in the body and, therefore, are present in urine. Stimulants may be detected for up to 48 hours after last use, cocaine and its metabolites may be detected for up to 3 days, and opiates may appear for up to 2 days. Short-acting barbiturates are detected for 1 day. Marijuana, which is stored in fatty tissue, may be detected in the urine for up to 4 days in recreational users and for up to a month in chronic daily users.

For these reasons, urine drug screenings are not conducted on a routine basis. They are done only when drug use is suspected. Adolescents may resist giving a urine sample by claiming the test violates independence and privacy. Unfortunately, such resistance is usually related to hiding the use of drugs.

Confidentiality

Medical and mental health professionals have standard and acceptable practices, including rules about confidentiality during assessments. Thus, breaking confidence is not easy for professionals who have a therapeutic relationship with a child or adolescent. If a child's or adolescent's behavior is dangerous to self or others, however, confidentiality should be broken to inform appropriate individuals. For example, if suicide or homicide is a concern, the student's parents must be told. Driving while intoxicated or under the influence of other drugs is another reason for informing parents. When possible, the individual is encouraged to discuss these thoughts or behaviors during a planned family session.

Such clear standards do not exist for classroom teachers. This lack of guidelines often puts the classroom teacher in a dilemma. A student might confide in a trusted teacher. Classmates might inform a teacher because of concern for a friend. The teacher, in turn, wants to ensure that a student gets the needed help. The best advice for the teacher is to meet with the school counselor, social worker, or psychologist. The teacher and counselor may need to brainstorm about the best thing to do. They need to consider whether the parents should be told and if the parents would even believe that their child has a potential problem.

Next, it might be necessary for the teacher, mental health professional, and a school administrator to meet. When a school system has a firm no-tolerance policy, revealing what a teacher knows to a school administrator might initiate a break in confidence and a punitive action. Yet, not revealing what is known puts the teacher at risk if the student does something harmful. Ideally, the driving force should be how to get help for the student in need. Yet, the teacher is expected to follow school policy. Often, this conflict between wanting to do what is best for the student and following school policy results in no action. Example 3 in Chapter 17 explores this situation.

INTERVENTION

Many levels of intervention are available. The ideal intervention is prevention through educational programs and early recognition efforts. Some students may be helped through outpatient programs. Others may require intensive, integrated services in day-treatment programs, comprehensive wrap-around programs (programs that cover all parts of the student's day and all possible situations), or hospitalization. It may be necessary for some to participate in longer-term alcohol and/or drug rehabilitation programs. Family involvement is a critical part of any treatment plan. Each program focuses on the individual and his or her family, peer influences, and community issues. In turn, interventions are designed to address each area, particularly emphasizing the individual and the family.

Once a student returns to school, it is essential that a recovery maintenance and health management program is in place. Often, help with finding a new peer group is needed. Urine drug screenings might be used. There might be a need for observations and feedback from school professionals. In addition, twelve-step programs such as Alcoholics Anonymous (AA) and Narcotics Anonymous (NA) may be helpful. These programs use a positive group process and support to encourage clear steps toward recovery. Many intervention programs are designed for adolescents.

Prevention

As noted previously, prevention is the ideal form of intervention. One of the earliest efforts at decreasing drug use was the Anti-Drug Abuse Act of 1988 (PL 100-690). This law provided funds to schools and communities to decrease drug use. Some of the decline of drug use in the early 1990s may be attributed to such legislation. Because drug use began another upward trend in the mid-1990s, however, it is clear that the effects of these programs were not long term.

Most prevention strategies emphasize research to find effective programs with long-term results. These studies stress the need for prevention programs to include a specific program focus, a particular delivery technique, an evaluation process, training for those involved in the program, and support. Of particular interest is the concept of *program focus*, which describes the expected outcome. Early programs were well meaning but focused only on the desired outcome, not on how to best reach this outcome. D.A.R.E. (Drug Abuse Resistance Education) was such an effort. Results demonstrated that drug use in control schools and those using the D.A.R.E. program were almost equal. Thus, there were no substantial positive outcomes in schools that implemented D.A.R.E. Other programs were tried. In general, programs that had an informational or affective component had very little effect, whereas those that used social influence approaches or life skills approaches with social influence approaches were most effective. Examples of such programs are Project SMART (Johnson, Hansen, Flay, & Sobel, 1983) and Project STAR.

The shift was made to programs that were based on research data regarding the variables that had a strong statistical relationship to drug use (e.g., drug use by peers, previous drug use). Later, the focus was on themes that adolescents might consider important. For example, programs demonstrated health consequences, such as injury or death in motor vehicle accidents. Another approach was telling the child or adolescent what to do, such as "Just say no!" None of the research-based models have been successful in achieving a decrease in drug use, which is a source of concern among professionals in the drug prevention field.

A more recent prevention effort focuses on the importance of parents in monitoring their children, claiming that "mothers are the best prevention." Classroom teachers should know about school-based and/or community-based programs that are actively being used in their area.

CONCLUSION

Substance use, misuse, dependency, and abuse are major concerns with middle school and high school students. Because school is the life work of children and adolescents, the impact of substance problems may first become apparent in school. Academic performance and grades might drop. The student might miss classes. Teachers might note changes in personality and behaviors. A change in the student's choice of friends might be of concern. The classroom teacher may be one of the first people to notice the problem's effects, or the student's friends may tell the teacher about the problem. Thus, it is essential that all educators are knowledgeable about substance use and abuse because early recognition and early, appropriate intervention are critical to students' academic success and well-being.

REFERENCES

Anti-Drug Abuse Act of 1988, PL 100-690, 21 U.S.C. §§ 1501 et seq.

Brent, D.A., Perper, J.A., & Allman, C.J. (1987). Alcohol, firearms, and suicide among youth. *JAMA: The Journal of the American Medical Association, 257,* 3369–3372.

Chatlos, J.C. (1996). Recent trends and a developmental approach to substance abuse in adolescents. *Child and Adolescent Psychiatric Clinics of North America, 31,* 1041–1045.

DeWitt, D.J., Adlaf, E.M., Offord, D.R., et al. (2000). Age of first alcohol use: A risk factor for the development of alcohol disorders. *American Journal of Psychiatry, 157,* 745–750.

Drug-Induced Rape Prevention and Punishment Act of 1996, PL 104-305, 21 U.S.C. §§ 841 et seq.

Hingson, R.W., Heeren, T., Jamanka, A., & Howland, J. (2000). Age of drinking onset and unintentional injury involvement after drinking. *JAMA: The Journal of the American Medical Association, 284*(12), 1527–1533.

Jaffe, S.L., & Simkin, D.R. (2002). Alcohol and substance abuse in children and adolescents. In M. Lewis (Ed.), *Child and adolescent psychiatry: A comprehensive textbook* (3rd ed., pp. 895–911). Philadelphia: Lippincott Williams & Wilkins.

Johnson, C.A., Hansen, W.B., Flay, B.R., & Sobel, J.L. (1983). *Project SMART: A social approach to drug abuse prevention: Teacher's guide* (2nd ed.). Los Angeles: Health Behavior Research Institute, University of Southern California.

Johnston, L. (1996, December). The rise in drug use among American teens continues in 1996: Monitoring the future. *News and Information Services.* Ann Arbor: University of Michigan.

Lee, G.P., & DeClemente, C.C. (1985). Age of onset versus duration of problem drinking on the Alcohol Use Inventory. *Journal of Studies on Alcohol, 46,* 298–402.

National Institute on Drug Abuse. (1996). *Monitoring the future: NIDA Capsules: Facts about teenagers and drug abuse* (NIH Publication No. C83-07). Bethesda, MD: Author.

National Institute on Drug Abuse. (2002). *Monitoring the future: Overview of key findings* (NIH Publication No. 02-5105). Bethesda, MD: Author.

Nestler, E.J. (2001a). Delta FB: A sustained molecular switch for addiction. *Proceedings of the National Academy of Sciences (USA), 98*(20), 11042–11046.

Nestler, E.J. (2001b). Molecular neurobiology of addiction. *American Journal on Addictions, 10,* 201–217.

Newcomb, M.D. (1995). Identifying high risk youth: Prevalence and patterns of adolescent drug abuse. In E. Rahdert & D. Czechowicz (Eds.), *Adolescent drug abuse: Clinical assessment and therapeutic interventions* (NIH Publication No. 96-113949, pp. 7–38). Washington, DC: U.S. Department of Health and Human Services.

Pandina, R.J., Johnson, V., & Labouvie, E.W. (1992). Affectivity: A central mechanism in the development of drug dependence. In M. Glantz & R. Pickens (Eds.), *Vulnerability to drug use* (pp. 179–209). Washington, DC: American Psychological Association.

Shoffi, M., Steltz-Linarsky, J., Derrick, A.M., et al. (1988). Comorbidity of mental disorders in the post-mortem diagnosis of completed suicides in children and adolescents. *Journal of Affective Disorders, 15,* 227–233.

9

Eating Disorders

John Thoburn and Anne Hammond-Meyer

Chapter Concepts

- Characteristics of normal and problem eating
- Physical factors of eating disorders, including how they manifest in schools
- Diagnoses and characteristics of various eating disorders
- A model of eating disorders
- Various treatment regimens
- Prevention techniques

Although eating disorders are relatively common, they are often misunderstood. The following vignettes illustrate differences between problem eating and eating disorders. They also illustrate risk factors in the development of eating disorders.

Carla, age 11, is in the 60th percentile for her height and the 95th percentile for weight. Her mother has put her on a diet. Carla complains that she does not like any of the food that her mother has told her she can eat. She also complains that she is hungry. Her mother's response is one of tough love: "Do you want the boys at school to continue teasing you? Do you like that?"

* *

Carla's 9-year-old sister, Monica, has confided that she has a problem with "stuffing her face" when she gets upset, which she says is all the time. She secretly told Carla, "I gorge myself; later, I feel really terrible about it and I want to throw up."

* *

Sheri, age 19, is a sophomore at a private college. She is 5'6" tall and weighs 82 pounds. She is listless, slurs her speech, and has difficulty concentrating. In addition, her body is covered with a fine hair and she has not menstruated for a year. She only allows herself to eat a quarter inch of string cheese per meal and only drinks vitamin-fortified water. However, she insists on cooking for the other women with whom she shares a house. When told that she is dangerously thin, she points out that she needs to lose a few more pounds because her stomach is paunchy. Secretly, she views her roommates as "disgustingly fat."

Sheri was admitted to an inpatient program for most of the summer between her freshman and sophomore years. Although she had regained some weight by the end of that summer, her weight is now back down to what it was at the end of her freshman year. The dean of student life has called a conference with Sheri's parents to discuss having her take a leave of absence from the college until she "deals with her illness."

* *

Carla, Monica, and Sheri are representative of the world of problem eating and eating disorders. Carla does not technically have an eating disorder, but she displays many of the risk factors for developing one: dieting at an early age, feeling deprived of food, being teased by peers about her weight, and conflict with a parent over food issues (Striegel-Moore & Smolak, 2001a). Monica displays binge eating behavior, a precursor to bulimia nervosa (hereafter called *bulimia*)

(Wade, Bulik, & Sullivan, 2000). Sheri is in the throes of full-blown anorexia nervosa (hereafter called *anorexia*), slowly starving herself to death.

Other mental health disorders affect broader segments of the population, but bulimia and anorexia are associated with significant impairments in physical, psychological, and social functioning. People with eating disorders have the highest rates of treatment seeking, inpatient hospitalization, and suicide attempts of all psychiatric disorders and a mortality rate of 5.9% (Garvin & Striegel-Moore, 2001). The ongoing severity of eating disorders is equally distressing. Only one third of individuals with anorexia are likely to resume normal eating 4–8 years following diagnosis, 36% may continue to suffer severe eating disturbances beyond 11 years, and another 11% will die during that time from factors related to dysfunctional eating (Deter & Herzog, 1994; Hsu, 1980; Suldo & Sandberg, 2000).

What is most compelling for educators is that during the school-age years, young girls—and, increasingly, young boys—are most susceptible to risk factors implicated in the development of eating disorders. Most diagnoses of eating disorders occur with adolescents or young adults (Striegel-Moore & Smolak, 2001a). Dieting behavior is highly implicated as a precursor to eating disorders; by age 13, 80% of North American girls and 10% of North American boys have already begun a weight-loss program (Mellin, Scully, & Irwin, 1992). In another study, 40% of female adolescents surveyed considered themselves overweight when only 4% actually were according to commonly accepted medical standards (Davis & Furnham, 1986). A study on dieting conducted in London showed that after 1 year, 38% of the participants were still dieting, 33% had stopped, and 20% had progressed to an eating disorder—compared with 3% of nondieters (Patton, Johnson-Sabine, & Wood, 1990).

The lifetime prevalence for anorexia that meets all diagnostic criteria is 0.5% (American Psychiatric Association [APA], 2000a). The prevalence for bulimia is 1%–3% (APA, 2000a). However, 4%–6% of the general population is diagnosed with an atypical eating disorder—that is, one that does not meet all criteria for a diagnosis of anorexia or bulimia but has most of the features (often lacking just one criterion for the diagnosis of anorexia or bulimia).

Once considered a problem of the Caucasian middle class, eating disorders are now found among all races in industrialized societies. The sociocultural factor that is most strongly implicated is the emphasis on thinness as a standard of beauty. Cultures or subcultures that stress the thin ideal have a high incidence of eating disorders in relation to cultures in which the standard for beauty allows for diversity and values inner states such as character (Nichter & Vuckovic, 1994; Parker, Nichter, et al., 1995). Ninety percent of individuals with eating disorders are women (Sands, 2003).

Anorexia most frequently develops between the ages of 14 and 18 years. Bulimia typically develops in the late teens to early twenties; however, bulimics often try to manage the disorder themselves for several years before seeking professional help, which may explain the older age demographics for bulimia (Johnson, Lewis, & Hagman, 1984; Merriam & Murray, 1997; Mitchell, Pyle, & Eckert, 1981). Personal and environmental factors that correlate with bulimia include parental alcoholism, low parental contact with paradoxically high parental expectations, low self-esteem, a history of weight fluctuation, an external locus of control, and strong neuroticism (Kendler, MacLean, Neale, Kessler, Heath, & Eaves; 1991; Wade et al., 2000). Individuals with anorexia have high incidences of overprotective, chaotically enmeshed families; negative outlooks on life; impulsivity; disordered eating habits; and avoidance-of-harm strategies (Foulkes, 1996; Horesh et al., 1996; Schmidt, Humfress, & Treasure, 1997).

These statistics highlight why educators need to understand the features, risk factors, treatment, and prevention of eating disorders.

CHARACTERISTICS OF TYPICAL EATING AND PROBLEM EATING

Eating disorders fall along a continuum. At one end is simply eating to live, in the middle is a healthy enjoyment of eating, and at the extreme other end is a compulsion to eat and to organize one's life around eating. People with normal, balanced weight regulation have an internal orientation to the regulation of food intake. In determining eating behavior, normal eaters predominately attend to body cues such as appetite, hunger, and satiation rather than to feelings. Normal eaters generally maintain weight stability. When they decide to reduce their weight, however, it is a voluntary action rather than an obligatory or compulsory act. People with normal eating behaviors have the ability to give up the food restriction freely when weight goals have been met or when they tire of the regimen. These individuals tend to have moderate to high self-esteem regarding their bodies. People with normal eating habits also tend to have an easygoing temperament, above average intelligence, strong problem-solving skills, and adequate social skills. They are generally optimistic, academically competent, spiritual, and creative. Relationships with their parent(s) tend to be good, their extended family network is perceived to be supportive, there is a relatively low level of family stress, and their parents are considered authoritative rather than authoritarian (Striegel-Moore & Smolak, 2001a). Normal eaters tend to have positive school experiences, well-developed peer friendship networks, responsibilities outside the home, involvement in extracurricular activities (e.g., sports), and positive relationships with adults outside the home. Individuals with normal eating behaviors also tend to have a non-Caucasian worldview, reside in a rural community, and come from a culture that recognizes and celebrates size diversity while viewing weight and size as being mostly beyond an individual's control (Crago, Shisslak, & Estes, 1996).

Those who move away from the middle of the eating behaviors continuum begin to manifest problem eating attitudes and behaviors. Mid-range problem eaters generally externalize food regulation and have heightened external standards imposed for weight control. These people are detached from internally generated body cues and have moderate to low self-esteem about their bodies, with moderate to severe body distortion (Satter, 2002).

Those who fall at the extreme of the continuum manifest crisis-level or chronically disturbed eating behavior. Crisis-level eaters generally have a history of eating and growth problems. Crisis-level eating problems are characterized by external regulation of food behavior; a rigid adherence to external weight standards; and an insensitivity to body cues regarding appetite, hunger, and satiation. Obsessive concerns with food selection and amount of food (eaten or refused) highlight the overwhelming concern with weight and size. The inability to regulate weight and eating exemplifies chronically failed weight-reducing attempts, which lead to increased unwillingness to take risks with weight. Generally, there is a severe distortion of body image and low self-esteem. Eating is commonly associated with compensatory behaviors such as overexercising (e.g., being unwilling to miss a daily workout regardless of injury) or exercising for several hours after eating a "forbidden" food (Beumont, Arthur, Russell, & Touyz, 1994).

CHARACTERISTICS OF EATING DISORDERS

Among individuals of the same height, there are great variations in skeletal structure and body frame size. Therefore, an unhealthy weight for one person may not be unhealthy for another. Cultural perceptions about what is attractive and what is healthy vary over time, potentially giving rise to weight concerns by people of normal weight. This point is shown in the following vignette.

Mary, an attractive woman in her twenties, complained to her therapist that she could not control her eating and considered herself fat. Mary had been a high school cheerleader and married the high school quarterback. She was a large-boned woman of Scandinavian ethnicity who fell at the high end of the normal range for weight-to-height ratio. When the therapist asked Mary what she wanted to look like, Mary pulled out a women's fashion magazine to reveal a picture of a thin, waifish model— someone she could never have looked like, even if she had lost half her body weight. Mary was convinced that the model represented the perfect woman's body.

What constitutes an eating disorder—as opposed to problem eating behavior, which, although unusual, still falls within the category of "normal"? Some professionals use Metropolitan Life Insurance height and weight tables or the Centers for Disease Control and Prevention's Pediatric Growth Chart for norms for height, weight, and age groupings to make a diagnosis of anorexia. However, the text revision of the *Diagnostic and Statistical Manual of Mental Disorders, Fourth Edition* (DSM-IV-TR), makes it clear that these are only guidelines for the clinician because "it is unreasonable to specify a single standard for minimally normal weight" (American Psychiatric Association [APA], 2000a, p. 584). As a result, final clinical diagnosis is often subjective in nature. If a person has the stomach flu and makes him- or herself throw up, is that an eating disorder? Is a body builder who has a body mass index of 28 but a fat percentage of 11% obese? (Body mass index, or BMI, is a measure of total body fat based on a person's weight and height.) Does the person who sometimes gorges him- or herself during special occasions have problems with bingeing? As long as eating disorders and normal eating are placed in distinct categories, there will be difficulties with such diagnostic questions. Eating disorders are best understood by viewing eating patterns along a continuum from healthy to unhealthy or normal to pathological. People diagnosed with an eating disorder will be scattered along the continuum, anywhere from having somewhat unhealthy attitudes, thoughts, and behavior about food to extremely distorted thoughts, feelings, and behaviors toward food and outward appearance (Merriam & Murray, 1997).

One telltale indicator for an eating disorder is differentiating between behaviors done in private versus those done in public. Behavior that is primarily public often reflects a food fad or phase—for example, picking at food in a restaurant with friends but eating normally at home with one's family. Habits that are both public and private tend to reflect a person's true orientation. People with eating problems often isolate their eating, regulating it as a private enterprise out of shame and embarrassment (Merriam & Murray, 1997). People with anorexia tend to have distorted, even magical ideas about food: A sense of rigid control over food can substitute for a sense of control over one's life. It also is important to consider how much of a person's life is taken up by food issues. Is the person's life organized around food—thinking about it, planning what to eat or not to eat, or cooking for others but not for him- or herself? It is a myth that individuals with anorexia have no interest in food. On the contrary, they are consumed with and fixated on food and food issues (Merriam & Murray, 1997).

Another consideration is whether a person's behavior is chronic or acute. Eating disorders tend to follow a discrete pattern of development. There is a strong correlation between the culmination of a first successful diet and anorexia. Anorexia can manifest acutely or progress slowly (Merriam & Murray, 1997). Bulimia tends to develop incrementally over time, moving from a light stage of gorging to a heavier stage of bingeing coupled with purging behavior that becomes increasingly frequent. At first, the bingeing and purging is secret, but it becomes so pervasive that the individual is eventually unable to hide it. In most cases of bulimia, bingeing predates purging behavior by about 2 years (Stice, Killen, Hayward, & Taylor, 1998). In both cases, the prognosis is best when treatment is initiated in the early phases of the disorder (Merriam & Murray, 1997).

The precipitating factors for eating-disordered behaviors are many and varied. The behavior may be avoidance or a response to anger. It may manifest at certain times of the day (e.g., late at night), with certain moods (e.g., when feeling sad, lonely, guilty, bored, or anxious), or in certain places (e.g., only at home). In bulimia, the behavior tends to grow, encompassing more emotional states over time (Merriam & Murray, 1997).

Eating disorders have both a perceived and actual effect on relationships, emotions, academic functioning, goals for the future, and general sense of well-being. One young woman left bags of vomit in her gym locker, her school locker, the school bathroom, and her bedroom. The behavior disgusted her locker mates and friends, who slowly withdrew their friendship. Another young woman, weighing 76 pounds, was asked to leave her college after it was reported that she could not concentrate well enough to take her exams, was missing most classes, and presented a dismal distraction to the other students. She was extremely angry, maintaining that there was nothing wrong with her, even as her parents packed her bags to leave.

People with eating disorders often perceive benefits of the behavior. The most obvious benefit is weight loss. Other perceived payoffs include anxiety reduction, avoidance of responsibility, and procrastination. Anxiety reduction may have to do with a response to social pressure, social events, and avoidance of conflict. Secondary benefits may not be conscious, such as avoidance of maturation, continued dependence on parents, or avoidance of making major decisions, such as trying to decide on a job or college upon finishing high school (Merriam & Murray, 1997).

PHYSICAL ASPECTS OF EATING DISORDERS

There are numerous debilitating physical consequences of eating disorders. Among individuals with bulimia, 81%–94% vomit and 63% use laxatives for purging (Merriam, & Murray, 1997). Vomiting causes a loss of stomach acid, and stomach acid can burn the esophagus and mouth, destroy tooth enamel, and lead to a swelling of the parotid glands (the largest salivary glands), leaving the cheeks swollen and puffy. Vomiting upsets body chemistry at the cellular level. Body pH increases, and weakness and fatigue ensue; the individual also develops headaches, urinary tract infections, and an intolerance for cold. Hypoglycemic tingling and muscle cramping are also by-products of purging. Purging leads to an imbalance in electrolytes and the loss of minerals, including calcium. Potassium is usually lost through vomiting and laxative and diuretic use, too, leading to fatigue, anxiety, and depression. Heart arrhythmias and cardiac arrest are often thought to be the severe consequences of anorexia alone, but they can be part of the effects of purging behavior as well. Laxative use may deplete body minerals, cause dehydration, and affect the proper functioning of the intestinal tract. With bingeing, the stomach may enlarge, and the individual may experience reactive hypoglycemia from the large intake of carbohydrates (Merriam, & Murray, 1997).

Starvation brings its own physical problems. Individuals with anorexia develop hypothyroidism, decreased blood pressure, and a fine body hair called *lanugo*. Furthermore, depending on age, puberty or the menstrual cycle ceases. Among people with anorexia, 50% also display symptoms of bulimia—resulting in a disorder called *bulimarexia*. No psychiatric disorder has a higher death rate than bulimarexia (Pope, Hudson, & Yurgelun-Todd, 1984).

The physical aspects of a student's eating disorder manifest in schools primarily through weight loss. Educators should be aware of significant changes in physical appearance and/or disproportionately low weight-to-height ratios. The other physical manifestations of eating disorders—loss of stomach acid, burning of mouth and esophagus, deterioration of tooth enamel, swelling of salivary glands, disrupted menses, hypothyroidism, and so forth—are less apparent to external observers. Thus, although educators may make referrals for eating disorders, diagnosing eating disorders requires the experience, wisdom, and examination of experienced mental health and medical professionals.

DIAGNOSIS OF EATING DISORDERS

There are four primary diagnostic categories for eating disorders: anorexia nervosa, bulimia nervosa, eating disorder not otherwise specified, and binge eating disorder (an area currently under research investigation by the APA). Although the DSM-IV-TR does not list obesity as an eating disorder, it is included as a fifth category in this chapter because obesity is a common eating-oriented problem.

Anorexia Nervosa

As noted in the DSM-IV-TR, the core features of anorexia nervosa are "the refusal to maintain . . . a normal body weight" and "an intense fear of . . . becoming fat" (APA, 2000a, p. 589). Other symptoms include thoughts and feelings that produce a distorted body image (i.e., feeling overweight when not), denial of having a seriously low body weight (i.e., fear of gaining any weight), relentless pursuit of thinness (i.e., by a failure to maintain body weight or to gain weight), and the onset of amenorrhea (i.e., cessation of the menstrual cycle). Appendix A at the end of this book contains the official DSM-IV-TR diagnostic criteria for anorexia nervosa. There are two subcategories for the diagnosis: restricting type and binge-eating/purging type. Approximately 50% of those diagnosed with anorexia also display binge eating and purging (APA, 2000a).

Bulimia Nervosa

The prevalence of bulimia has dropped as the diagnosis has become more specific (Ben-Tovim, 1988). According to the DSM-IV-TR, "The essential features of bulimia nervosa are binge eating and inappropriate compensatory measures to prevent weight gain" (APA, 2000a, p. 589). The major question regarding diagnosis is, "What constitutes bingeing?" The DSM-IV-TR defines *bingeing* as "eating, in a discrete period of time (e.g., within any 2-hour period), an amount of food that is definitely larger than most people would eat during a similar period and under similar circumstances" (APA, 2000a, p. 594). Bingeing might be better defined by dysphoric (sad) mood and the eater's loss of control (Garner, Shafer, & Rosen, 1992). Bulimics tend to place great emphasis and value on weight and body shape in their struggle for improved self-esteem. There are two subcategories for the diagnosis of bulimia: purging type and nonpurging type (APA, 2000a). Appendix A contains the official DSM-IV-TR diagnostic criteria for bulimia nervosa.

Eating Disorder Not Otherwise Specified

The DSM-IV-TR category of eating disorder not otherwise specified (NOS) is reserved for eating disorders that do not meet the full criteria for a diagnosis of anorexia or bulimia. Also called *atypical eating disorder,* this diagnosis has become more common as the criteria for anorexia and bulimia have become more specific. Eating disorder NOS probably represents 25%–50% of individuals diagnosed with an eating disorder, which involves 4%–6% of the general population. See Appendix A for the official DSM-IV-TR diagnostic criteria for eating disorder NOS.

Binge-Eating Disorder

The DSM-IV-TR includes binge-eating disorder as a suggested category for further research. Binge eating, a subjective feeling of lack of control over eating, and feelings of distress characterize binge-eating disorder (APA, 2000a). Inappropriate compensatory behaviors, such as the vomiting or laxative use that indicate bulimia, are not present. The DSM-IV-TR lists "eating very rapidly" and "eating until uncomfortably full" as typical indicators of this disorder (APA, 2000a, p. 785). Distress, another hallmark of the disorder, is evident during and after bingeing episodes and involves the individual's worries about the effect of long-term bingeing on weight and body shape (APA, 2000a). Because purging behavior is absent, individuals with binge-eating disorder are more likely to be obese than those with bulimia. Research criteria for binge-eating disorder are listed in Appendix Λ.

Obesity

Obesity may be defined as surplus body fat in individuals who are 20% over ideal body weight for height (Jeffrey & Knaus, 1981). By this definition, approximately 34 million Americans are overweight, incurring serious health and psychological consequences (Bray, 1986; Brownell, 1982; Burton, Foster, Hirsch, & Van Itallie, 1985). Middle-age Americans who are 50% overweight suffer a 90% increase in mortality. This is because obesity is associated with increased risk of disease, including hypertension (high blood pressure), hyperglycemia (high blood sugar), hyperlipidemia (high cholesterol), and non–insulin-dependent diabetes mellitus (Bray, 1986; Brownell, 1982; Burton et al., 1985; Hubert, Feinleib, McNamara, & Castelli, 1983; Keys, 1979).

As noted previously, the most common criterion of obesity is 20% over ideal weight for height (Jeffrey & Knauss, 1981). Thus, although most obese individuals are overweight, not all individuals who are overweight are obese (Bray, 1986). To some extent, such cutoffs are arbitrary. Each person's body weight and body fat composition may be viewed as falling along a continuum (that includes all members of the population) from low to high.

Among children, those who are more than 20% overweight based on the 50th BMI percentile are considered obese (Must, Dallal, & Dietz, 1991). Although this cutoff is used widely, it is being challenged. Experts suggest that a child and his or her parents are served more effectively by comparing the child's current growth with past patterns rather than with a normative sample that has arbitrary cutoffs (Satter, 2000). By appreciating each child's unique growth pattern, it is possible to support positive feeding and parenting practices. This practice avoids the institution of restrictive eating protocols that disrupt the child's internal regulation, introduce stress into the parent–child relationship, and distort growth that is positive, albeit at the upper end of the percentile. By knowing and observing each individual child's growth pattern, clinicians can monitor and document growth over time, making it easier to identify individual growth problems.

Research on and clinical observation of child growth patterns have demonstrated that individual growth varies greatly and that childhood growth is an interactive process of many complex factors. Some children grow consistently and well at the 95th percentile, whereas others children grow consistently and well at the 50th percentile (Satter, 2000). Therefore, a case exists for appreciating consistent growth while ensuring that other biological, psychological, and social factors are intact. By monitoring the child's growth pattern in a nonreductive perspective, it is possible to be confident that the child is growing according to his or her inherited constitution. If a child's growth begins an inconsistent pattern or diverges significantly upward or downward, then these changes should be observed and related specifically to the child in question. Once a growth pattern has been identified as problematic, the clinician can investigate the factor(s) responsible for the divergence (Satter, 2000).

When there is a problem, the best approach is one that honors the complexity of the child. Biological, psychological, and social factors influence a child's growth pattern and can lead to problematic growth changes. For example, illness or another medical condition may cause a child's growth to deviate from his or her normal patterns. Prescribed medication may affect appetite, hunger, and weight stability. Changes in family finances may affect food sufficiency and nutritional status. Psychosocial issues such as divorce, sibling conflict, school and peer adjustment problems, or a death in the family may influence the child's well-being and, therefore, growth (Satter, 2000).

Finally, feeding dynamics play an important role in a child's level of eating competence. If the child has experienced poor learning around food—that is, if he or she has experienced enforced food restriction, over- or undermanagement of the feeding relationship, or poor structure (e.g., lack of regular mealtimes)—then he or she may respond by over- or undereating. This deregulated eating may result in problematic growth. All of these potential problems must be addressed separately. Redefining obesity as weight that diverges from consistent growth allows the isolation of factors that truly require intervention and the provision of effective assistance to the child and his or her parents (Satter, 2000).

Educator's Role in Diagnosis

As mentioned previously, an accurate diagnosis can only be accomplished through examinations by experienced mental health or medical professionals. Educators can assist in this task by communicating clearly and specifically what they have observed. (See Table 9.1 for examples of such observed behavior.) For instance, an educator's information about changes in body shape can confirm the family's report. In the unlikely event that an educator directly observes behavior related to the eating disorder (e.g., purging), he or she should obviously include this information in the referral or communicate it if diagnosis has already been made. The other symptoms of eating disorders are less behavioral and, thus, can be directly observed by a diagnosing professional.

INTEGRATIVE INTERPERSONAL MODEL FOR EATING DISORDERS

The integrative interpersonal model is biopsychosocial—that is, the elements that lead to health problems or neurosis about feeding and eating are the result of biological, intrapersonal, and interpersonal processes. Biological processes include genetic predisposition and chemical balances (or imbalances), as well as neurological development that occurs outside of the womb. Intrapersonal processes refer to the impact of nonconscious memory; subjective emotional experiences regarding self, others, and life; and the development of internal cognitive models regarding relationships. Interpersonal processes refer to an individual's embeddedness and learning through social networks—family, friends, school, community, and culture. Biopsychosocial processes are recursive. This means that each aspect of the system strengthens the other in mutually reinforcing feedback loops. Finally, biopsychosocial processes are multifactorial. No single factor can be solely implicated in the development of an eating disorder. Rather, there is a confluence of nested systemic factors that when present, lead to obsessive thinking and compulsive behavior around feeding and eating issues (Bruch, 1981; Ericsson, Poston, & Foreyt, 1996; Hsu, 1990; Strober & Humphrey, 1987; Suldo & Sandberg, 2000). Figure 9.1 provides a visual representation of a biopsychosocial model of eating disorders.

RISK FACTORS FOR DEVELOPING EATING DISORDERS

Heredity

It is estimated that more than 50% of the risk for developing an eating disorder can be attributed to genetic factors (Kendler et al., 1991; Klump, McGue, & Iacono, 2000; Wade et al., 2000; Klump, Miller, Keel, McGue, & Iacono, 2001). This statistic includes the symptoms and diagnoses of anorexia, bulimia, binge eating, weight preoccupation, disordered eating attitudes, body dissatisfaction, and compensatory measures for weight control (Bulik, Sullivan, Kendler, & Kenneth, 1998; Kendler et al., 1991; Klump et al., 2001; Klump, McGue, & Iacono, 2000; Rutherford, McGuffin, & Katz, 1993; Sullivan, Bulik, & Kendler, 1998; Wade et al., 2000). Grilo and Pogue-Geile (1991) found an overall similarity of weight and BMI between identical twins, with little impact from the environment. Heredity is likely a

Table 9.1.   Appropriate actions for educators regarding eating disorder problems, behaviors, and attitudes

Potential problem	Observed behavior	Attitude	Appropriate actions
A student appears to be gaining or losing weight.	The student's lunches are inadequate in nutrition, or the student does not have a lunch or lunch money. The student appears to eat compulsively or picks at food and refuses to eat.	The student expresses disinterest in food and eating or is preoccupied with food and eating.	Speak with the parents about possible psychosocial changes occurring in the family. Encourage the child to eat consistent, nutritious lunches. Document events. Make referrals when needed.
A student is not taking time to eat lunch or is snacking quickly but not taking time for a meal.	The student becomes tired, inattentive, and cranky after the lunch break.	The student expresses a desire to play, not to eat.	Make eating a priority. Build eating into classroom the structure. Model competent, internally regulated eating to students. Encourage students to enjoy good food, but do not dichotomize food into good and bad categories.
A student is preoccupied with weight and size.	The student frequently discusses his or her body size. The student refuses to change clothes for physical education class.	The student expresses dissatisfaction with his or her appearance, size, and weight.	Model body acceptance. Encourage students to love and appreciate the bodies they were born with. Celebrate size diversity in the classroom. Emphasize body function rather than esthetics. Represent all sizes when using images with students.
A student feels shame about his or her size and experiences teasing in the classroom or on the playground.	The student is teased by peers for being heavier or thinner than average.	The student expresses the desire to be alone, yet he or she feels ostracized.	Preserve the child's dignity by protecting him or her from teasing. Model size acceptance and diversity in the classroom. Establish a no-tolerance rule for teasing. Provide consequences for violations of a classmate's dignity.

Potential problem	Observed behavior	Attitude	Appropriate actions
A colleague demonstrates size bias with students.	A student is treated differently from others because he or she is heavier or thinner than average.	The colleague expresses strong feelings that certain sizes are not acceptable or always indicate a problem.	Educate colleagues about weight and size diversity.
			Encourage colleagues to think of size diversity in the same way they consider ethnic or racial diversity.
			Help colleagues provide a size diversity "safe zone" for all children.
			Encourage colleagues to practice respect and dignity to all children.
			Teach colleagues that weight and size are functions of complex biopsychosocial factors, not failures in a child's character.
The school disrespects family mealtimes.	School meetings and sporting events are commonly scheduled during the family dinner times.	Family dinner time is not considered important.	Encourage school administrators to see that healthy eating is an outgrowth of biopsychosocial wellness.
			Encourage school administrations to do their part in supporting the social wellness of students and families by supporting family mealtimes.
			Suggest moving activities to times that do not interfere with families gathering for dinner.
A student does not want to participate in physical activities.	The student demonstrates distaste toward physical activity. The student is selected last for teams or opts to stand on the sidelines.	The student expresses a lack of self-efficacy regarding athletics.	Present an activity philosophy that communicates that movement can be fun.
			Provide multiple movement opportunities that are noncompetitive.
			Model an attitude that different body types have different strengths, and introduce children to a wide variety of activity choices.
			Encourage the joy of movement without connecting activity to weight loss or compensatory/obligatory motivations.
			Emphasize movement for functional rather than esthetic goals.

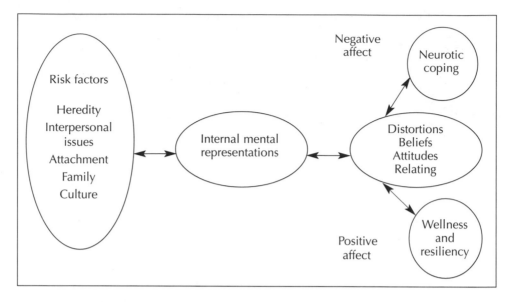

Figure 9.1. Integrative interpersonal model of eating disorders.

predisposing factor for eating-disordered behavior, but this behavior appears to be triggered by environmental factors that might include the mother–child relationship, parental conflict, and a family focus on weight. Research suggests a genetic vulnerability for eating disorders among all females, but pathological behavior is expressed when an individual 1) is influenced by environmental risk factors and 2) begins exhibiting precursor behavior (e.g., dieting, bingeing) that can lead to an eating disorder (Wade et al., 2000).

Interpersonal Issues

Individuals with eating disorders often have difficulties with peers, poor social adjustment, and long-term interpersonal problems (Johnson & Larson, 1982; Norman & Herzog, 1984). They tend to be overly competitive and overachieve in school to prove their competence. Individuals with anorexia tend to cling to family members and isolate themselves from others. They often experience problems with dating and may display poor social skills, driving potential friends away by being too controlling. People with anorexia generally avoid dealing with sexuality, display confusion and ambivalence regarding sexual development, and have difficulty being admired for their sexual appearance. Sexist comments, remarks about weight, or a focus on curves may lead to feelings of anxiousness. Sexual harassment and sexual abuse are correlated with eating disorders. The internalization of the societal standard of the woman as object may lead women to objectify themselves. Rape or incest can precipitate an eating disorder (Bowlby, 1969; Garvin & Striegel-Moore, 2001; Jacobson & Robbins, 1989; Pruitt, Kappius, & Gorman, 1992). Individuals with bulimia may have more friends than those with anorexia, but the relationships tend to be superficial. People with bulimia compete socially and are easily influenced by peer pressure. Bingeing and purging are often considered a response to the relentless pressure to compete socially. Eating issues have a special social context; students often engage in "fat talk," and parents may reinforce the thin ideal (Nichter & Vuckovic, 1994).

Attachment

Studies of children ranging from toddler to college age have clearly shown the relationships among attachment, weight concerns, and eating disorders (Broberg, Hjalmers, & Nevonen, 2001; Chatoor, Ganiban, Colin, Plummer, & Harmon, 1998; Cole-Detke & Kobak, 1996; Friedberg & Lyddon, 1996; Heesacker & Neimeyer, 1990; O'Kearney, 1996; Salzman, 1997; Sharpe et al., 1998). Attachment is related to a child's natural desire to maintain proximity with a caregiver for safety and security. However, safety is only one issue in the attachment relationship. The quality of attachment is implicated in an infant's neurological development and in subjective expectations about relating to self and others. Child-rearing interactions play a significant part in shaping childhood self-image and, consequently, the way that a child interacts with others (Ainsworth, 1989; Amini, Lewis, Lannon, & Louie, 1996; Bowlby, 1973; Schore, 1997). Being loved in a healthy way—having needs met, receiving soothing for hurts, and experiencing patience in the face of mistakes—leads to the expectation of similar treatment from others and to high self-esteem. Unmet needs or suffocating love lead to incomprehension of healthy attitudes toward self and others (Lewis, Amini, & Lannon, 2000).

Bartholomew (1990) created a four-factor model of attachment that focuses on the individual's relationship to self and others. *Securely attached* individuals have a sense of personal worthiness ("lovability") and the expectation that others are generally accepting and responsive. *Preoccupied* individuals have a sense of personal unworthiness and are self-critical but evaluate others positively. Preoccupied individuals tend to be more dependent and externally focused, constantly seeking from others the affirmation that is lacking within (Bartholomew, 1990; Friedberg & Lyddon, 1996). *Fearful* individuals have a sense of personal unworthiness and believe that others are rejecting. Fearful individuals do not trust themselves or others, avoid close relationships, and are insecure (Bartholomew, 1990; Friedberg & Lyddon, 1996). *Dismissing* individuals have a personal sense of self-worth but judge others as unworthy, disappointing, and unworthy of trust. This attachment style is characterized by limited expression of emotion and independence (Bartholomew, 1990; Friedberg & Lyddon, 1996).

Individuals who are securely attached tend to have a healthy orientation toward food. Conversely, the research implicates a preoccupied attachment style in the etiology of eating disorders. First, inconsistent parenting or lack of parental availability can lead to the failure to develop a positive self-image while maintaining a positive view of others. The individual seeks to be positively viewed by others but is overly critical of him- or herself (e.g., regarding appearance) and, as a result, may be particularly susceptible to sociocultural pressures for thinness (Suldo & Sandberg, 2000). Self-esteem becomes rigidly tied to externals such as body weight, shape, and appearance. As a result, the child requires and receives more attention than his or her siblings but has the lowest self-esteem. Second, the child fails to develop a sense of autonomy and protects him- or herself against the fear of abandonment and/or independence. With the increasing psychosocial demands of adolescence to shift attachment from parents to peers, individuals who pursue thinness literally and figuratively stave off the physical and psychosocial elements of puberty (Armstrong & Roth, 1989; Bell, Billington, & Becker, 1986; Kenny & Hart, 1992; Mallinckrodt, McCreary, & Robertson, 1995; O'Kearney, 1996; Rhodes & Kroger, 1992; Tucker, McNamara, Claremont University Center, & Monsour Counseling Center, 1995).

Role of Internal Mental Representations

Biopsychosocial factors work together to develop each person's unique, neurologically based perspective about him- or herself, others, and life. The quality of an individual's first human relationship(s) becomes the prototype for all other intimate relationships (Horner, 1984). How children relate to others in the future is determined in large measure by how they respond initially to patterns in their environment. Children have an inborn, autonomous, biological affinity for organizing experiences into patterns (Horner, 1984). These patterns, or mental pictures, are organized into patterns of patterns and then into schemas, which become consolidated and stabilized through repetition. A *schema* is a mental representation that when generalized, becomes an internal working model, or a basic structure, of the mind that is fundamental to establishing a sense of self. Schemas of self and others are developed through interpersonal transactions between infants and caregivers. These transactions mediate the psychological tasks of child development, including attachment, differentiation of self, the formation of core beliefs, and attitudes toward and manner of relating to self and others; the interactions also shape plans and goals for attaining attachment needs and goals (Collins & Read, 1994; Main, Kaplan, & Cassidy, 1985; O'Kearney, 1996).

A child's internalized memories of attachment experiences become working models that form healthy or unhealthy core beliefs and influence ongoing affective states. O'Kearney (1996) noted,

> The premise of these applications of attachment theory to psychopathology in adults and adolescents is that the behavioral, cognitive, and affective features of the attachment system are central to the progress toward adaptive functioning and personality formation. These features impact on the development of beliefs and competencies about interpersonal functioning on the merging sense of self, self-efficacy, and self-esteem, on the capacity to regulate affective life, and on motivation. (p. 117)

Poorly formed internal mental representations or representations formed out of anxiety lead to distorted attitudes, beliefs, and feelings toward self, others, and life. Whereas securely attached individuals form internal mental representations that are whole and adhere closely to reality, resulting in little distortion, insecure attachment leads to distortions and negative feelings about self and others. These feelings include loneliness, abandonment, guilt, shame, and fear. Negative affect (mood) leads to neurotic coping styles represented by the obsessive thinking and compulsive behavior that are demonstrated in eating disorders.

Family

Individuals with eating disorders often come from families where there is a high emphasis on achievement. Connections among family members may be tenuous, and there are fluctuations in the family between overinvolvement and abandonment. Reliance on external achievement develops as a means to attain a sense of worth in the family.

Families may also exhibit an overconcern with beauty, appearance, and thinness. For instance, too much family time spent talking about weight, appearance, and superficial behaviors can reinforce a daughter's focus on beauty as a way to compensate for low self-esteem. Daughters in particular get the sense that they are valued for their looks, and womanhood may be as devalued in the family as it often is in society at large (Rodin, Silberstein, & Striegel-Moore, 1984).

Families facing an eating disorder may display separation problems between mother and child, with the child placed in the role of caring for the parent emotionally; this type of relationship is seen in 31%–39% of families in which a member has an eating disorder (Beaumont, Mayes, & Rugg, 1978; Kalucy, Crisp, & Harding, 1977). The child's father may be emotionally or physically distant. Achievement becomes a way to get love because being loved for who one is does not seem enough. Parents themselves often have mental health disorders, with phobic avoidance noted in 33% of mothers, depression in 33% of mothers, obsessiveness in 29% of fathers, and excessive alcohol use in 19% of fathers (Kalucy et al., 1977). Many parents have concerns about their own weight, and these concerns are transferred to the child.

As in families of alcoholics, families affected by a member's eating disorder may display loyalty and rigidity. Family members seek to maintain the status quo out of anxiety and fear. Roles are rigidly maintained, and no family member is allowed to develop autonomy. Direct conflict is avoided, though the eating disorder exacerbates tension, resentment, and chaos. Parent–child coalitions are common, in which the child is forced into an alliance with one parent against the other. A typical theme is collusion, whereby parents submerge their own conflict to focus on the child's illness. Research indicates that prior to a child's receiving an eating disorder diagnosis, 34% of fathers and 19% of mothers threatened parental separation (Kalucy et al., 1977).

Culture

Culture appears to play a significant role in the development eating disorders. It is not uncommon for girls to gain weight prior to the onset of puberty. At this time, girls also are becoming aware of their bodies and looking to societal norms for validation or devaluation of themselves. The first diet often is started in response to the initial signs of puberty. This diet is an effort at self-control; if successful, it can be reinforcing and is highly significant in the formation of an eating disorder (Polivy & Herman, 1985). Dieting can set in motion a trend to mistrust internal regulation, deny hunger, sacrifice nutritional needs, and seek media-reinforced images that lead to body disparagement. Approximately 90% of people affected by eating disorders are women. Both men and women deal with binge eating (Johnson & Togrud, 1996), and body dysmorphia (an unflatteringly distorted view of one's body image) may be equally common in men and women. However, gender role expectations seem to be implicated to a degree in the formation of an eating disorder. Whereas the male gender role is agentic, emphasizing assertiveness and independence, the female gender role is communal, fostering interpersonal relationships. The Superwoman role (Murnen, Smolak, & Levine, 1994) suggests that women should have it all: a good career, a happy marriage, healthy children, an active social life, and good looks. Those who seek to achieve in all of these domains are often seeking social approval and extrinsic reward. In Westernized cultures, these domains potentially require thinness for success. For example, thinner people are more likely to be hired and promoted, to go on more dates, and to be thought of as more attractive than their counterparts who are not thin (Blaine, DiBlasi, & Connor, 2002).

Mass media are an important part of most children's and adolescents' daily lives (Arnett, 1995; Harris, 1994) and are highly influential. For example, Caucasian women in the media are unusually thin, presenting the thin ideal to Caucasian girls and young women. These individuals often do not grasp that media are often digitally enhanced and that highly sophisticated advertising is meant to manipulate consumers. Levine and Smolak (1998) stated, "Media messages serve multiple intents such as entertainment, socialization, information management, social organization, education, government and—lest we forget—frequent opportunities for businesses to sell many different things to an extraordinarily large number of potential consumers" (p. 24). However, mass media do not brainwash people. Rather, as Levine and Smolak (1998) noted, "Media provoke a complex process of attention and interpretation by individuals who, depending on their developmental stage, their personality, and their immediate situation, and other sociocultural contexts, bring various motives and information processing strategies to the task" (p. 25). That is, media interact with other biopsychosocial factors in the development and exacerbation of problem eating.

TREATMENT

Treatment for eating disorders once focused on a combination of cognitive behavioral therapy and psychotropic medication (Agras et al., 1994; Agras, Schneider, & Arnow, 1989; Fairburn, Peveler, Jones, Hope, & Doll, 1993). However, more recent research points to a multifactorial etiology for eating disorders, and treatment has become more comprehensive, with new therapies taking an integrative approach that focuses on cognition, interpersonal schemas, family dynamics, emotional responses, and cultural factors (Fairburn et al., 1995; Fairburn, Marcus, & Wilson, 1993; Treasure & Ward, 1997).

Collaboration

The serious nature of eating disorders makes treatment very important, and earlier intervention promises a more positive outcome. Parents and teachers are often the first to notice problematic changes in individuals, so input from both is critical to timely treatment. The most effective treatment is a multiteam approach with appropriate coordination of care, usually through a physician. Possible team members include but are not limited to inpatient care providers; treating psychiatrist, psychologist, or social worker; family therapist; nutritionist; teacher(s); school nurse; school counselor; clergy member or other spiritual advisor; and parents. There is a need for communication among all parties, especially with regard to matters of referral, evaluation, diagnosis, and treatment. Lack of communication may result in assumptions about who is attending to certain treatment areas. It also can lead to unconscious collusion with the eating disorder, pitting team members against each other as the person with the disorder blocks efforts to help. Thus, clear, unambiguous communication among all team members is imperative. Collaboration among team members might include the following:

- A teacher notices a particular student's odd eating behavior, such as hoarding food (food insecurity), avoiding eating (enforced dieting or self-restriction), or frequent trips to the bathroom following eating (purging behavior) and refers the student to the school nurse. Nurses play an important role in assessment and screening for students with all kinds of concerns. In addition to offering knowledge, nurses often know the child, can help document behavior concerns, and facilitate parent contact. The school nurse seeks to convince the individual to get help. Depending on the age of the child, the school nurse provides age-appropriate steps to help advocate for the child as needed.

- The teacher supports the school nurse and the individual—for example, by not allowing teasing to occur in the classroom or on the playground.

- The student's parents are called for consultation. The school nurse makes a referral to a particular doctor.

- The doctor monitors the student's health and weight. The physician also acts as the gatekeeper for collateral treatment, evaluating the student for the potential to harm him- or herself, life-threatening physical state and the potential need for inpatient treatment, stabilization of food intake, and possible medication to stabilize mood (as an augment to psychotherapy). The physician then refers the person for individual, family, and nutrition therapies.

- The student's therapist administers first-order cognitive behavior therapy and addresses second-order attachment issues. The family's therapist addresses second-order family issues of differentiation. (See the ensuing discussion under the subsection "First- and Second-Order Change.") The nutritionist addresses dietary needs.

- A spiritual component, based on the religious practices of the individual and his or her family, may be added to the treatment protocol.

- The multidisciplinary team exhibits appropriate helping attitudes—that is, they do not judge behaviors (e.g., showing disgust at bingeing and purging behavior).

First- and Second-Order Change

Under the integrative interpersonal model of treatment, goals for addressing eating disorders include first- and second-order change. *First-order change* refers to modifications in thoughts, feelings, and behaviors through skills acquisition and greater understanding of self, others, and the environment. First-order treatment includes cognitive restructuring, encapsulating neurotic concerns, identifying and defusing internalized negativity, building reliance on internal regulation, developing resilient thinking and positive filters, and challenging distorted thinking and attitudes about self (e.g., poor body image) and others. Behavioral change includes systematically shaping positive and competent behavior, thereby developing a wellness lifestyle characterized by self-care and intrinsic, rather than extrinsic, motivation.

Second-order change refers to growth and transformation at more dynamic levels. It focuses on individuation facilitated through the therapeutic relationship, affect regulation, interpersonal competence, and modification of internal mental representations, with a corresponding ability to form more healthy attachments. Developing a sense of self-autonomy, increasing self-esteem, and processing deep attachment feelings serve to shift the individual's locus of control from external influences to inward trust processes. Differentiation among family members increases a personal sense of autonomy. *Differentiation* refers to the ability of each family member to 1) distinguish between "me" and "we" and 2) respond to rather than emotionally react to one another. A decrease in reactive communication among family members reduces family anxiety and allows family members to focus on consistent family communication of care.

Therapy Goals[1]

Treatment for eating disorders utilizes psychoeducation and cognitive behavioral therapy to enhance motivation, explore distortions in perceptions and attitudes, and begin the process of normalizing eating behaviors through increased trust

---

[1]This section on therapy goals is adapted from Wonderlich, S.A., Mitchell, J.E., Peterson, C., & Crow, S. (2001). Integrative cognitive therapy for bulimic behavior. In R. Striegel-Moore & L. Smolak (Eds.), *Eating disorders: Innovative directions in research and practice* (pp. 182–184). Washington, DC: American Psychological Association. Copyright © 2001 by the American Psychological Association. Adapted with permission.

in self. Therapy supports the process of internal regulation through systematic desensitization techniques and nutritional education, along with affective processing and family and interpersonal therapies. Therapy seeks to identify repetitive reactive interpersonal patterns, make connections between distortions and interpersonal/cognitive styles, modify internal mental representations, and decrease family anxiety. Therapy ends with a focus on relapse prevention and lifestyle management, solidifying the ability to self-regulate affect, reviewing nonreactive methods for relating to family, planning for relapse, and reviewing coping strategies. Therapy serves to provide support and reassurance and to help the individual maintain a positive balance with eating (e.g., strong permission to feed oneself well, balanced with not giving in to every impulse). In other words, self-regulation becomes the following: One is never deprived but does not need to always say "yes" to every presentation of food.

Educator's Role in Treatment

The educator helps uphold the primary and secondary goals established by the treatment team. As mentioned previously, the educator's main role is to support the student and family. Direct confrontations about eating are not usually beneficial and may develop into power struggles that deteriorate the student–teacher relationship. The most effective thing that an educator can do is develop and preserve a strong, appropriate relationship with the student, characterized by a caring attitude. This type of relationship can be particularly beneficial in support of the secondary goals established by the team. For example, educators can work directly and indirectly to increase interpersonal competence through social skills development. Educators also can reinforce healthy mental representations of the ideal body types. Perhaps most important, educators can assist in establishing a healthy internal locus of control by giving real choices, mediating student attributions toward internal control, providing opportunities for success, and recognizing and attributing success to the student's hard work.

Overall, educators can be key, although not primary, members of an eating disorders treatment team. Frequent communication with the team facilitator will help coordinate efforts toward a student's successful treatment.

PREVENTION AND CHANGE

In addition to the previously discussed team participation, prevention is a natural area in which educators can have a positive impact on eating disorders. Prevention strategies seek to prevent eating disorders before they start by changing attitudes and understanding about self, others, and the environment or by altering current inappropriate behaviors through education, heightened awareness, and training (Smolak, 1999).

The educator must decide whether his or her students need education on prevention or change. If the strategies are to focus on prevention, then the educator must intervene at an early age, when there is a low rate of target behavior (e.g., dieting). The educator must conduct a preliminary sample of the students to see whether the behavior is low enough to justify a prevention program. He or she must recognize that long-term outcome is the only effective measure for the validity of a prevention program. Furthermore, outcome data must be collected when the target behavior would most likely emerge (Smolak, 1999). This entails schools following students throughout grades to rate the effectiveness of a program.

If the educator wants to focus on change, then he or she must be aware that in the classroom, some risk factors are more amenable to change than others—for example, teasing (Heinberg, 1996), life and coping skills, and the ability to withstand peer and media pressure (Levine, 1999). Factors such as family dynamics and individual dieting behavior are less ably tackled in the classroom. Most prevention programs have been developed for adolescents (Butler & Neuman, 1985; Carter, Stewart, Dunn, & Fairburn, 1997; Piran, Levine, & Steiner-Adair, 1999; Shisslak, Crago, & Neal, 1990); however, there is a need to develop prevention curricula for elementary school children, prior to the onset of dysfunctional behavior. Elementary school curricula can prepare girls for the transition to puberty, attacking issues that are most salient to female emotional development (Frost & Forrest, 1995; Levine, Schermer, Smolak, & Etling, 1996). Educators must keep in mind that aspects of adolescent-based prevention programs are not suitable for elementary school, such as curricula that require abstract reasoning and/or personal evaluation (Phelps & Johnston, 1999). Sound programs create learning environments that accentuate didactic and experiential learning and discussion as well as individual study and group collaboration.

Prevention programs should focus equally on positive (e.g., positive physical attributes, competencies) and negative (e.g., dieting, body dissatisfaction) factors. Self-esteem plays a large role in the etiology of eating disorders, with a general drop in female self-esteem during early adolescence being a precursor to eating problems (Nolen-Hoeksema & Girgus, 1994). Female self-esteem is linked to appearance throughout the school years and into early adulthood (Akan & Grilo, 1995; Grilo, Wilfley, Jones, Brownell, & Rodin, 1994). Curricula should stress building up individuals in this area (Shisslak, Crago, & Gray, 1998) and teaching coping skills and self-efficacy (National Institute of Mental Health Committee, 1995). Sexuality issues and sexual harassment, as well as peer pressure regarding appearance and behavior, increase at puberty and continue throughout adolescence and early adulthood. Among middle school girls, 41.5% talk with friends about weight, shape, and dieting (Nichter & Vukovic, 1994). Individuals who mature early tend to start dieting earlier and are more at risk for dysfunctional eating behavior (Graber, Brooks-Gunn, Paikoff, & Warren, 1994). Curricula to explore issues around dating and relating to the opposite sex can be useful, although coeducational training appears less successful than education in a homogenous classroom setting (Levine & Smolak, 1996).

The media's influence on individual attitudes toward weight—that is, the thin ideal—is well documented (Gordon, 1990; Levine et al., 1996; Murray, Touyz, & Beumont, 1996; Nichter & Vuckovic, 1994). Furthermore, body dissatisfaction is the single strongest predictor of eating disorders (Button, 1990; Leon, Fulkerson, Perry, & Cudeck, 1993). Phelps, Dempsey, Sapia, and Nelson defined *body dissatisfaction* as the internalization of "a culturally determined body ideal" and the determination that one's body diverges from that ideal (1999, p. 164). Two areas of self-concept are related to body dissatisfaction, and changing these leads to changes in the internalization of the thin ideal. The first area is related to increased recognition of positive physical features; the second concerns an increase in a sense of personal competence and empowerment (Phelps et al., 1999, p. 165).

Just as insight in therapy is not enough to change behavior, knowledge-focused curricula alone is not enough to change individual action. Prevention programs must include critiques of sociocultural mores; clarification of personal values; and interactive lessons, including group discussion, problem solving, and cooperative exercises to enhance resilience. As noted previously, curricula must also focus on personal competence and self-esteem issues (Phelps et al., 1999).

The two dominant models for preventing eating disorders are the Disease Specific Pathways model (DSP) and the Non-specific Vulnerability Stressor model (NSVS). The DSP emphasizes the role of negative body image, weight and shape concerns, calorie-restrictive dieting, and negative feelings (Killen et al., 1993; Stice, 2001). This model considers eating disorders diseases, and education emphasizes the danger of focusing on nutrition and exercise for weight control, the danger of calorie-restrictive dieting, and the need to analyze and resist cultural factors (e.g., media messages, weight-related teasing). Individuals who struggle with eating concerns often use nutritional knowledge and exercise in a punitive fashion. For a student with an eating disorder, nutrition can become simply another form of food restriction—greater knowledge leads to an increased list of forbidden foods. Rather than thinking of nutrition as a strategy to support internal regulation (appetite, hunger, and satiety) as normal eaters do, people with eating disorders use nutrition to become even more externally controlled. Furthermore, exercise is often a conflict for those who have eating concerns. Rather than moving primarily for functional fitness and health, people with eating disorders often use exercise in obligatory and compensatory ways. Exercise can then become another part of restriction or be used as a form of purging. These individuals often overexercise and suffer from overuse injuries. The DSP provides education on the hazards of eating disorders themselves, potentially dangerous developmental factors (e.g., pubertal weight gain), and the thin ideal.

The NSVS focuses on stress, poor health, lack of coping skills, lack of social support, and information on the development and manifestation of eating disorders (Albee & Gullotta, 1997). This model emphasizes sound nutrition and exercise for healthier lifestyle (versus weight management). Life skills such as relaxation and assertive decision making are stressed, along with critical thinking about gender issues and improvement of self-esteem and sense of competence (Shisslak, Crago, Renger, & Clark-Wagner, 1998).

The reality is that prevention training has had little impact on stemming the tide of eating disorders, primarily because prevention protocols tend to emphasize behavior change more than knowledge and life skills acquisition, such as media literacy and changes in attitudes (Levine & Piran, 2001). For example, some school-based programs teach the adverse effects of dieting and other weight-control methods as well as life skills training to resist social pressure to diet. Prevention programs that include life skills training have an 85% success rate, as opposed to the 56% success rate of programs without life skills training (Striegel-Moore & Smolak, 2001b). Prevention curricula goals are more effective when tailored to individual needs. For instance, self-worth may vary among individuals and within each student's relationships. Mastery of social skills in one domain does not guarantee mastery in others; therefore, educators should stress individually tailored development in promoting resilience, competence, and evaluative thinking. Clearly formulated prevention-related messages should be present in the curriculum and classroom materials, along with explicit rules prohibiting teasing and peer pressure. This is accomplished by presenting expectations that indicate gossiping and teasing are not acceptable, setting clear consequences for breaking these rules, and modeling acceptance.

CONCLUSION

Eating disorders are devastating and predominantly affect adolescents and young adults. Eating behavior is best understood as existing along a continuum, in which extremes of over- or undereating bookend normal eating behavior. It appears that individuals have a genetic predisposition for anorexia nervosa, bulimia nervosa, and obesity; however, eating disorders may be precipitated by a variety of environmental factors. These factors affect intrapersonal development and interpersonal relationships and, ultimately, lead to negative affect, obsessive thinking, and compulsive behavior. More salient warning signs include early dieting behavior, low self-esteem, eating for comfort, rigid or chaotic families, little parental support, mood disorders such as depression or anxiety, and the culture-bound media emphasis on the thin ideal.

To be effective, treatment needs to begin as early as possible. It also must reflect a biopsychosocial perspective and multidisciplinary approach, in which teachers can play a vital role in early detection, exposure, and referrals for appropriate health care. Successful treatment focuses on affective processing; cognitive restructuring; behavioral change; differentiation of self from family; development of healthier attachments; and generation of more realistic internal mental representations of self, others, and life.

Teachers play a pivotal role in the prevention of eating disorders. They are uniquely trained to provide didactic and experiential learning experiences to change problematic behavior and, more important, to change attitudes and increase personal and interpersonal life skills. Teachers can provide an enriched environment—in the classroom, in the lunchroom and on the playground—where teasing and harassment are not tolerated and people are respected for who they are, not simply for their achievements. To this end, teachers need to be trained in listening actively, offering nonjudgmental feedback, and providing information without lecturing (Phelps & Johnston, 1999). Teachers must address their own attitudes and possible prejudices regarding eating issues, the thin ideal, and children with eating problems. Individuals with eating disorders often evoke anger, hostility, stress, and hopelessness in caregivers (Kaplan, Allan, & Garfinkel, 1999). Therefore, educators must examine themselves, engage in training whenever possible, and seize the opportunity to teach students social skills that emphasize tolerance and broad-mindedness.

REFERENCES

Agras, W.S., Rossiter, E.M., Arnow, B., Telch, C.F., Raeburn, S.D., & Bruce, B. (1994). One-year follow-up of psychosocial and pharmacologic treatments for bulimia nervosa. *Journal of Clinical Psychiatry, 55*, 179–183.

Agras, W.S., Schneider, J.A., & Arnow, B. (1989). Cognitive-behavioral treatment with and without exposure plus response prevention in the treatment of bulimia nervosa: A reply to Leitenberg and Rosen. *Journal of Consulting and Clinical Psychology, 57*(6), 778–779.

Ainsworth, M.S. (1989). Attachment beyond infancy. *American Psychologist, 44*(4), 709–716.

Akan, G.E., & Grilo, C.M. (1995). Sociocultural influences on eating attitudes and behaviors, body image, and psychological functioning: A comparison of African-American, Asian-American, and Caucasian college women. *International Journal of Eating Disorders, 18*, 181–187.

Albee, G.W., & Gullotta, T.P. (1997). Primary prevention's evolution. In G.W. Albee & T.P. Gullotta (Eds.), *Primary prevention works* (pp. 3–22). Thousand Oaks, CA: Sage Publications.

American Psychiatric Association. (2000a). *Diagnostic and statistical manual of mental disorders* (4th ed., text rev.). Washington, DC: Author.

American Psychiatric Association. (2000b). *Practice guidelines for the treatment of patients with eating disorders* (2nd ed.). Arlington, VA: Author.

Amini, R., Lewis, T., Lannon, R., & Louie, A. (1996). Affect, attachment, memory: Contributions toward psychobiologic integration. *Psychiatry: Interpersonal and Biological Processes, 59*(3), 213–239.

Armstrong, J., & Roth, D. (1989). Attachment and separation difficulties in eating disorders: A preliminary investigation. *International Journal of Eating Disorders, 8*, 141–155.

Arnett, J.J. (1995). Adolescents' use of media for self-socialization. *Journal of Youth and Adolescence, 24*, 519–533.

Bartholomew, K. (1990). Avoidance of intimacy: An attachment perspective. *Journal of Social and Personal Relationships, 7*(2), 147–178.

Bartholomew, K., & Horowitz, L.M. (1991). Attachment styles among young adults: A test of a four-category model. *Journal of Personality and Social Psychology, 61*(2), 226–244.

Beaumont, J.G., Mayes, A.R., & Rugg, M.D. (1978). Asymmetry in EEG alpha coherence and power: Effects of task and sex. *Electroencephalography and Clinical Neurophysiology, 45*(3), 393–401.

Bell, M.D., Billington, R., & Becker, B. (1986). A scale for the assessment of object relationships: Reliability, validity, and factorial invariance. *Journal of Clinical Psychology, 42*(5), 733–741.

Ben-Tovim, D.I. (1988). DSM-III, draft DSM-III-R, and the diagnosis and prevalence of bulimia in Australia. *American Journal of Psychiatry, 145*, 1000–1002.

Berg, F.M. (2000). *Women afraid to eat: Breaking free in today's weight-obsessed world.* Hettinger, ND: Healthy Weight Network.

Beumont, P.J.V., Arthur, B., Russell, J.D., & Touyz, S.W. (1994). Excessive physical activity in dieting disorder patients: Proposals for a supervised exercise program. *International Journal of Eating Disorders, 15*, 21–36.

Blaine, B.E., DiBlasi, D.M., & Connor, J.M. (2002). The effect of weight loss on perceptions of weight-control ability: Implications for prejudice against overweight people. *Journal of Applied Biobehavioral Research, 7*(1), 44–56.

Bowlby, J. (1969). *Attachment and loss: Vol. 1. Attachment.* New York: Basic Books.

Bowlby, J. (1973). *Attachment and loss: Vol. 2. Separation.* New York: Basic Books.

Bray, G.A. (1986). Effects of obesity on health and happiness. In K.D. Brownell & J.P. Foreyt (Eds.), *Handbook of eating disorders: Physiology, psychology, and treatment of obesity, anorexia, and bulimia* (pp. 1–44). New York: Basic Books.

Broberg, A.G., Hjalmers, I., & Nevonen, L. (2001). Eating disorders, attachment and interpersonal difficulties: A comparison between 18- to 24-year-old patients and normal controls. *European Eating Disorders Review, 9*(6), 381–396.

Brownell, K.D. (1982). Obesity: Understanding and treating a serious, prevalent, and refractory disorder. *Journal of Consulting and Clinical Psychology, 50*(6), 820–840.

Bruch, H. (1981). Teaching and learning of psychotherapy. *Canadian Journal of Psychiatry, 26*, 86–92.

Bulik, C.M., Sullivan, P.F., Kendler, K.S., & Kenneth, S. (1998). Heritability of binge-eating and broadly defined bulimia nervosa. *Biological Psychiatry, 44*(12), 1210–1218.

Burton, B.T., Foster, W.R., Hirsch, J., & Van Itallie, T.B. (1985). Report of conference proceedings. Health implications of obesity: NIH Consensus Development Conference. *International Journal of Obesity, 9*, 155–169.

Butler, R., & Neuman, O. (1985). Effects of task and ego achievement goals on help-seeking behaviors and attitudes. *Journal of Educational Psychology, 87*(2), 261–271.

Button, E. (1990). Self-esteem in girls aged 11–12: Baseline findings from a planned prospective study of vulnerability to eating disorders. *Journal of Adolescence, 13*, 407–413.

Carter, J.C., Stewart, D.A., Dunn, V.J., & Fairburn, C.G. (1997). Primary prevention of eating disorders: Might it do more harm than good? *International Journal of Eating Disorders, 22*, 167–172.

Chatoor, I., Ganiban, J., Colin, V., Plummer, N., & Harmon, R.J. (1998). Attachment and feeding problems: A reexamination of nonorganic failure to thrive and attachment insecurity. *Journal of the American Academy of Child and Adolescent Psychiatry, 37*(11), 1217–1224.

Cole-Detke, H., & Kobak, R. (1996). Attachment processes in eating disorder and depression. *Journal of Consulting and Clinical Psychology, 64*, 282–290.

Collins, N.L., & Read, S.J. (1994). Cognitive representations of attachment: The structure and function of working models. In K. Bartholomew & D. Perlman (Eds.), *Attachment processes in adulthood: Vol. 5. Advances in personal relationships* (pp. 53–90). London: Jessica Kingsley Publishers.

Crago, M., Shisslack, C.M., & Estes, L.S. (1996). Eating disturbances among American minority groups: A review. *International Journal of Eating Disorders, 19*(3), 239–248.

Davis, E., & Furnham, A. (1986). Body satisfaction in adolescent girls. *British Journal of Medical Psychology, 59*, 279–289.

Deter, H., & Herzog, W. (1994). Anorexia nervosa in a long-term perspective: Results of the Heidelberg-Mannheim study. *Psychosomatic Medicine, 56*(1), 20–27.

Ericsson, M., Poston, W.S.C., & Foreyt, J.P. (1996). Common biological pathways in eating disorders and obesity. *Addictive Behaviors, 21*(6), 733–743.

Fairburn, C.G., Marcus, M.D., & Wilson, G.T. (1993). Cognitive-behavioral therapy for binge eating and bulimia nervosa: A comprehensive treatment manual. In C.G. Fairburn & G.T. Wilson (Eds.), *Binge eating: Nature, assessment, and treatment* (pp. 361–404). New York: The Guilford Press.

Fairburn, C.G., Norman, P.A., Welch, S.L., O'Connor, M.E., Doll, H.A., & Peveler, R.C. (1995). A prospective study of outcome in bulimia nervosa and the long-term effects of three psychological treatments. *Archives of General Psychiatry, 52*, 304–312.

Fairburn, C.G., Peveler, R.C., Jones, R., Hope, R.A., & Doll, H.A. (1993). Predictors of 12-month outcome in bulimia nervosa and the influence of attitudes to weight and shape. *Journal of Counseling and Clinical Psychology, 26*, 57–63.

Foulkes, P.V. (1996). Eating disorders, families and therapy. *Australian Journal of Psychotherapy, 15*(2), 28–42.

Friedberg, N.L., & Lyddon, W.J. (1996). Self-other working models and eating disorders. *Journal of Cognitive Psychotherapy, 10*(3), 193–203.

Frost, J., & Forrest, J. (1995). Understanding the impact of effective teenage pregnancy prevention programs. *Family Planning Perspectives, 27*, 188–195.

Garner, D.M., Shafer, C.L., & Rosen, L.W. (1992). Critical appraisal of the DSM-III-R diagnostic criteria for eating disorders. In S.R. Hooper, G.W. Hynd, & R.E. Mattison (Eds.), *Child psychopathology: Diagnostic criteria and clinical assessment* (pp. 261–303). Mahwah, NJ: Lawrence Erlbaum Associates.

Garvin, V., & Streigel-Moore, R.H. (2001). Health services research for eating disorders in the United States: A status report and a call to action. In R.H. Striegel-Moore & L. Smolak (Eds.), *Eating disorders: Innovative directions in research and practice* (pp. 135–152). Washington, DC: American Psychological Association.

Gordon, R. (1990). *Anorexia and bulimia: Anatomy of a social epidemic.* Malden, MA: Blackwell Publishers.

Graber, J.A., Brooks-Gunn, J., Paikoff, R.L., & Warren, M.P. (1994). Prediction of eating problems: An 8-year study of adolescent girls. *Developmental Psychology, 30*(6), 823–834.

Grilo, C.M., & Pogue-Geile, M.F. (1991). The nature of environmental influences on weight and obesity: A behavior genetic analysis. *Psychological Bulletin, 110*(3), 520–537.

Grilo, C.M., Wilfley, D.E., Jones, A., Brownell, K., & Rodin, J. (1994). The social self, body dissatisfaction, and binge eating in obese females. *Obesity Research, 2*(1), 24–27.

Harris, R.J. (1994). *A cognitive psychology of mass communication* (2nd ed.). Mahwah, NJ: Lawrence Erlbaum Associates.

Heesacker, R.S., & Neimeyer, G.J. (1990). Assessing object relations and social cognitive correlates of eating disorder. *Journal of Counseling Psychology, 37*(4), 419–426.

Heinberg, L.J. (1996). Theories of body image disturbance: Perceptual, developmental, and sociocultural factors. In J.K. Thompson (Ed.), *Body image, eating disorders, and obesity: An integrative guide for assessment and treatment* (pp. 27–47). Washington, DC: American Psychological Association.

Horesh, N., Apter, A., Ishai, J., Danziger, Y., Miculincer, M., & Stein, D. (1996). Abnormal psychosocial situations and eating disorders in adolescence. *Journal of the American Academy of Child and Adolescent Psychiatry, 35*, 921–927.

Horner, A.J. (1984). *Object relations and the developing ego in therapy.* Northvale, NJ: Jason Aronson.

Hsu, L.K. (1980). Outcome of anorexia nervosa: A review of the literature (1954–1978). *Archives of General Psychiatry, 37*(9), 1041–1046.

Hsu, G.L. (1990). Experiential aspects of bulimia nervosa: Implications for cognitive behavioral therapy. *Behavior Modification, 14*(1), 50–65.

Hsu, L.K.G., Chesler, B.E., & Santhouse, R. (1990). Bulimia nervosa in eleven sets of twins: A clinical report. *International Journal of Eating Disorders, 9*, 275–282.

Hubert, H.B., Feinleib, M., McNamara, P.M., & Castelli, W.P. (1983). Obesity as an independent risk factor for cardiovascular disease: A 26-year follow-up of participants in the Framingham heart study. *Circulation, 67*, 968–977.

Jacobson, R., & Robbins, C.J. (1989). Social dependency and social support in bulimic and nonbulimic women. *International Journal of Eating Disorders, 8*, 665–670.

Jeffrey, D.G., & Knauss, M.R. (1981). The etiologies, treatments, and assessments of obesity. In S.N. Haynes & L. Gannon (Eds.), *Psychosomatic disorders: A psychophysiological approach to etiology and treatment* (pp. 269–319). Westport, CT: Praeger Publishers.

Johnson, C., & Larson, R. (1982). Bulimia: An analysis of moods and behavior. *Psychosomatic Medicine, 44*, 341–351.

Johnson, C.L., Lewis, C., & Hagman, J. (1984). The syndrome of bulimia: Review and synthesis. *Psychiatric Clinics of North America, 7*(2), 247–273.

Johnson, W., & Torgrud, L. (1996). Assessment and treatment of binge eating disorder. In J.K. Thompson (Ed.), *Body image, eating disorders, and obesity: An integrative guide for assessment and treatment* (pp. 321–344). Washington, DC: American Psychological Association.

Kalucy, R.S., Crisp, A.H., & Harding, B. (1977). A study of 56 families with anorexia nervosa. *British Journal of Medical Psychology, 50*(4), 381–395.

Kaplan, A.S., Allan, S., & Garfinkel, P.E. (1999). Difficulties in treating patients with eating disorders: A review of patient and clinician variables. *Canadian Journal of Psychiatry, 44*(7), 665–670.

Kendler, K.S., MacLean, C., Neale, M.C., Kessler, R., Heath, A.C., & Eaves, L. (1991). The genetic epidemiology of bulimia nervosa. *American Journal of Psychiatry, 148*, 1627–1637.

Kenny, M.E., & Hart, K. (1992). Relationship between parental attachment and eating disorders in an inpatient and a college sample. *Journal of Counseling Psychology, 39*(4), 521–526.

Keys, A. (1979). Is overweight a risk factor for coronary heart disease? *Cardiovascular Medicine, 4,* 1233–1242.

Killen, J.D., Taylor, C.B., Hammer, L.D., Litt, I., Wilson, D.M., Rich, T., Hayward, C., Simmonds, B., Kraemer, A., & Varady, A. (1993). An attempt to modify unhealthful eating attitudes and weight regulation practices of young adolescent girls. *International Journal of Eating Disorders, 13,* 369–384.

Klump, K.L., McGue, M., & Iacono, W.G. (2000). Age differences in genetic and environmental influences on eating attitudes and behaviors in preadolescent and adolescent female twins. *Journal of Abnormal Psychology, 109*(2), 239–251.

Klump, K.L., Miller, K.B., Keel, P.K., McGue, M., & Iacono, W.G. (2001). Genetic and environmental influences on anorexia nervosa syndromes in a population-based twin sample. *Psychological Medicine, 31*(4), 737–740.

Leon, G.R., Fulkerson, J.A., Perry, C.L., & Cudeck, R. (1993). Personality and behavioral vulnerabilities associated with risk status for eating disorders in adolescent girls. *Journal of Abnormal Psychology, 102,* 438–444.

Levine, M.P. (1999). Prevention of eating disorders, eating problems, and negative body image. In R. Lemberg (Ed.), *Controlling eating disorders with facts, advice, and resources* (2nd ed., pp. 64–72). Phoenix, AZ: Oryx Press.

Levine, M.P., & Piran, N. (2001). The prevention of eating disorders: Toward a participatory ecology of knowledge, action, and advocacy. In R.H. Striegel-Moore & L. Smolak (Eds.), *Eating disorders: Innovative directions in research and practice* (pp. 233–253). Washington, DC: American Psychological Association.

Levine, M.P., Schermer, F., Smolak, L., & Etling, C. (1996). *Eating smart, eating for me.* Columbus: Ohio Department of Education.

Levine, M.P., & Smolak, L. (1996). Media as a context for the development of disordered eating. In L. Smolak & M.P. Levine (Eds.), *The developmental psychopathology of eating disorders* (pp. 235–257). Mahwah, NJ: Lawrence Erlbaum Associates.

Levine, M.P., & Smolak, L. (1998). The mass media and disordered eating: Implications for primary prevention. In W. Vandereycken & G. Noordenbos (Eds.), *The prevention of eating disorders* (pp. 23–56). New York: New York University Press.

Lewis, T., Amini, F., & Lannon, R. (2000). *A general theory of love.* New York: Vintage Books.

Main, M., Kaplan, N., & Cassidy, J. (1985). Security in infancy, childhood, and adulthood: A move to the level of representation. *Monographs of the Society for Research in Child Development, 50*(1–2), 66–104.

Mallinckrodt, B., McCreary, B.A., & Robertson, A.K. (1995). Co-occurrence of eating disorders and incest: The role of attachment, family environment, and social competencies. *Journal of Counseling Psychology, 42*(2), 178–186.

Mellin, L., Scully, S., & Irwin, C. (1992). Prevalence of disordered eating in girls: A survey of middle-class children. *Journal of the American Diet Association, 92,* 851–853.

Merriam, B.W., & Murray, M.K. (1997). Eating disorders: Identification, prevention, and treatment. In T.N. Fairchild (Ed.), *Crisis intervention strategies for school-based helpers* (2nd ed., pp. 323–369). Springfield, IL: Charles C Thomas.

Mitchell, J.E., Pyle, R.L., & Eckert, E.D. (1981). Frequency and duration of binge-eating episodes in patients with bulimia. *American Journal of Psychiatry, 138*(6), 835–836.

Murnen, S., Smolak, L., & Levine, M.P. (1994). *Development of a scale to measure adherence to the "Superwoman" construct.* Unpublished manuscript.

Murray, S.H., Touyz, S.W., & Beumont, P.J.V. (1996). Awareness and perceived influence of body ideals in the media: A comparison of eating disorder patients and the general community. *Eating Disorders: The Journal of Treatment and Prevention, 4,* 33–46.

Must, A., Dallal, G.E., & Dietz, W.H. (1991). Reference data for obesity: 85th and 95th percentiles of body mass index (wt/ht^2) and triceps skinfold thickness. *American Journal of Clinical Nutrition, 53,* 839–846.

Nichter, M., & Vukovic, N. (1994). Fat talk: Body image among adolescent girls. In N. Sault (Ed.), *Many mirrors: Body image and social relations* (pp. 109–131). Piscataway, NJ: Rutgers University Press.

National Institute of Mental Health Committee on Prevention Research. (1995). *A plan for prevention research for the National Institute of Mental Health (A report to the National Advisory Mental Health Council).* Washington, DC: Author.

Nolen-Hoeksema, S., & Girgus, J. (1994). The emergence of gender differences in depression during adolescence. *Psychological Bulletin, 115,* 424–443.

Norman, D.K., & Herzog, D.B. (1984). Persistent social maladjustment in bulimia: A 1-year follow up. *American Journal of Psychiatry, 14*(3), 444–446.

O'Kearney, R. (1996). Attachment disruption in anorexia nervosa and bulimia nervosa: A review of theory and empirical research. *The International Journal of Eating Disorders, 20*(2), 115–127.

Parker, S., Nichter, M., Nichter, M., Vuckovic, N., Sims, C., & Ritenbaugh, C. (1995). Body image and weight concerns among African American and White adolescent females: Differences that make a difference. *Human Organization, 54,* 103–114.

Patton, G.C., Johnson-Sabine, E., & Wood, K. (1990). Abnormal eating attitudes in London schoolgirls: A prospective epidemiological study: Outcome at twelve month follow-up. *Psychological Medicine, 20*(2), 99–108.

Phelps, L., Dempsey, M., Sapia, J., & Nelson, L. (1999). The efficacy of a school-based eating disorder prevention program: Building physical self-esteem and personal competencies. In N. Piran, M.P. Levine, & C. Steiner-Adair (Eds.), *Preventing eating disorders: A handbook of interventions and special challenges* (pp. 163–174). Philadelphia: Brunner/Routledge.

Phelps, L., & Johnston, L.S. (1999). Prevention of eating disorders: Identification of predictor variables. *The Journal of Treatment & Prevention, 7*(2), 99–108.

Piran, N., Levine, M.P., & Steiner-Adair, C. (Eds.). (1999). *Preventing eating disorders: A handbook of interventions and special challenges.* Philadelphia: Brunner/Routledge.

Polivy, J., & Herman, C.P. (1985). Dieting and bingeing: A causal analysis. *American Psychologist, 40,* 193–201.

Pope, H.G., Hudson, J.I., & Yurgelun-Todd, D. (1984). Prevalence of anorexia nervosa and bulimia in three student populations. *International Journal of Eating Disorders, 3*(3), 45–51.

Pruitt, J.A., Kappius, R.E., & Gorman, P.W. (1992). Bulimia and fear of intimacy. *Journal of Clinical Psychology, 48*(4), 472–476.

Rhodes, B., & Kroger, J. (1992). Parental bonding and separation-individuation difficulties among late adolescent eating disordered women. *Child Psychiatry and Human Development, 22*(4), 249–263.

Rodin, J., Silberstein, L., & Striegel-Moore, R. (1994). *Nebraska Symposium on Motivation: Vol. 32* (pp. 267–307). Lincoln: University of Nebraska Press.

Rutherford, J., McGuffin, P., & Katz, R.J. (1993). Genetic influences on eating attitudes in a normal female twin population. *Psychological Medicine, 23*(2), 425–436.

Salzman, J.P. (1997). Ambivalent attachment in female adolescents: Association with affective instability and eating disorders. *International Journal of Eating Disorders, 21*(3), 251–259.

Sands, S.H. (2003). The subjugation of the body in eating disorders: A particularly female solution. *Psychoanalytic Psychology, 20*(1), 103–116.

Satter, E. (2000). *Child of mine: Feeding with love and good sense.* Boulder, CO: Bull Publishing.

Satter, E. (2002). *Treating the dieting casualty workshop.* Madison, WI: Ellyn Satter Institute.

Schmidt, U., Humfress, H., & Treasure, J. (1997). The role of general family environment and sexual and physical abuse in the origins of eating disorders. *European Eating Disorders Review, 5*(3), 184–207.

Schore, A.N. (1997). Early organization of the nonlinear right brain and development of a predisposition to psychiatric disorders. *Development and Psychopathology, 9*(4), 595–631.

Sharpe, T.M., Killen, J.D., Bryson, S.W., Shisslak, M., Estes, L.S., Gray, N., Crago, M., & Taylor, C.B. (1998). Attachment style and weight concerns in preadolescent and adolescent girls. *International Journal of Eating Disorders, 23*(1), 39–44.

Shisslak, C.M., Crago, M., & Gray, N. (1998). The McKnight Foundation prospective study of risk factors for the development of eating disorders. In W. Vandereycken & G. Noordenbos (Eds.), *The prevention of eating disorders* (pp. 56–74). London: Althone.

Shisslak, C.M., Crago, M., & Neal, M.E. (1990). Prevention of eating disorders among adolescents. *American Journal of Health Promotion, 5,* 100–106.

Shisslak, C.M., Crago, M., Renger, R., & Clark-Wagner, A. (1998). Self-esteem and the prevention of eating disorders. *Eating Disorders: Journal of Treatment and Prevention, 6,* 105–117.

Smolak, L. (1999). Elementary school curricula for the primary prevention of eating problems. In N. Piran, M.P. Levine, & C. Steiner-Adair (Eds.), *Preventing eating disorders: A handbook of interventions and special challenges* (pp. 37–55). Philadelphia: Brunner/Routledge.

Stice, E. (2001). Risk factors for eating pathology: Recent advances and future directions. In R. Striegel-Moore & L. Smolak (Eds.), *Eating disorders: Innovative directions for research and practice* (pp. 57–73). Washington, DC: American Psychological Association.

Stice, E., Killen, J., Hayward, C., & Taylor, C. (1998). Support for the continuity hypothesis of bulimic pathology. *Journal of Consulting and Clinical Psychology, 66,* 784–790.

Striegel-Moore, R.H., & Smolak, L. (2001a). Conclusion: Imaging the future. In R.H. Striegel-Moore & L. Smolak (Eds.), *Eating disorders: Innovative directions in research and practice* (pp. 271–278). Washington, DC: American Psychological Association.

Striegel-Moore, R.H., & Smolak, L. (2001b). *Eating disorders: Innovative directions in research and practice.* Washington, DC: American Psychological Association.

Strober, M., & Humphrey, L. (1987). Familial contributions to the etiology and course of anorexia nervosa and bulimia. *Journal of Consulting and Clinical Psychology, 55,* 754–759.

Suldo, S.M., & Sandberg, D.A. (2000). Relationship between attachment styles and eating disorder symptomatology among college women. *Journal of College Student Psychology, 15*(1), 59–73.

Sullivan, P.F., Bulik, C.M., & Kendler, K.S. (1998). The epidemiology and classification of bulimia nervosa. *Psychological Medicine, 28*(3), 599–610.

Sullivan, P.F., Bulik, C.M., Kendler, K.S., & Kenneth, S. (1998). Genetic epidemiology of binging and vomiting. *British Journal of Psychiatry, 173,* 75–79.

Treasure, J., & Ward, A. (1997). A practical guide to the use of motivational interviewing in anorexia nervosa. *European Eating Disorders Review, 5,* 102–114.

Tucker, T.W., McNamara, K., Claremont University Center, & Monsour Counseling Center. (1995). Assessing the relationship between parents' object relations and their daughters' eating. *Eating Disorders: The Journal of Treatment and Prevention, 3*(4), 311–323.

Wade, T.D., Bulik, C.M., & Sullivan, P.F. (2000). The relation between risk factors for binge eating and bulimia nervosa: A population-based female twin study. *Health Psychology, 19*(2), 115–123.

Wonderlich, S.A., Mitchell, J.E., Peterson, C., & Crow, S. (2001). Integrative cognitive therapy for bulimic behavior. In R. Striegel-Moore & L. Smolak (Eds.), *Eating disorders: Innovative directions in research and practice.* Washington, DC: American Psychological Association.

10

Anxiety Disorders

Christopher A. Sink and Cher N. Igelman

• •

Chapter Concepts

- Types and characteristics of anxiety disorders
- Prevalence rates
- Examination of etiological issues
- Diagnostic process
- Common interventions
- School-based applications and the educator's role

With tears and terror in his eyes, Isaac and his mother approach the kindergarten classroom on the first day of school. The enthusiastic new teacher, with a big smile on her face, comes to greet them at the door. Isaac is trembling and tightly holding his mother's hand. Then Isaac begins to sob loudly, clinging to his mother and begging her not to leave. The teacher tries to coax him into the room to meet the other children. Isaac turns around and dashes out of the classroom, with his mother chasing him.

• •

Teachers of school-age children may have had their own "Isaacs"—students who view school as a frightening place where they are left in the hands of strangers. Although separation anxiety disorder is uncommon at age 5, Isaac may exhibit some symptoms of the disorder if his behavior persists at this intensity level for many months (i.e., chronic inappropriate behavior). Such anxiety disorders obviously affect a student's mental health and learning, as well as his or her family's general well-being, and, potentially, the self-confidence of the teacher and other staff members. Educators want success for all students, so difficulty reaching a particular child can lead to irrational—but natural—feelings of failure. Unfortunately, anxiety disorders encompass a host of complex issues that cannot be fully addressed in the school environment. Therefore, this chapter is not intended to prepare educators to diagnose anxiety disorders. Rather, its goal is to equip teachers to communicate effectively with mental health professionals, both within and outside schools, and to assist them in the identification of students who may benefit from additional services to support their educational success. To realize this goal, the chapter explores these concepts in a way that provides educators with a basic understanding of anxiety disorders and practical classroom strategies to assist children with these concerns.

TYPES, CHARACTERISTICS, AND PREVALENCE OF ANXIETY DISORDERS

Fear, stress, and tension are also quite normal in children and youth. As individuals progress through the developmental stages, anxiety exhibits itself in disparate ways. Anxiety is therefore part of the maturational process and, in reasonable amounts, may help students to push themselves a little harder when preparing for a test, competing in a sporting event, or performing in a school play. Yet, some students display signs of severe apprehension and discomfort that considerably exceed cultural and societal norms for appropriate nervous behavior in children. This section explains the impact of anxiety disorders and reviews the types usually seen in school-age children and youth. Characteristics and prevalence rates of the disorders are discussed as well.

Impact of Anxiety Disorders in General and in School

As noted by the text revision of the *Diagnostic Statistical Manual of Mental Disorders, Fourth Edition* (DSM-IV-TR; American Psychiatric Association [APA], 2000), anxiety disorders compose a broad category of mental health disorders that may begin in childhood and adolescence. However, educators may have difficultly separating the symptoms associated with anxiety disorders from those linked with depression; as a general rule, these internalizing disorders have similar symptoms and commonly co-occur in children (Merrell, 2001; Office of the Surgeon General, 1999). For example, each disorder involves the recurring, intense internal or emotional distress over a period of months or years and unreasonable fear and anxiety, melancholy, and low self-esteem or feelings of worthlessness (Office of the Surgeon General, 1999). Highly anxious students can exhibit many of the following characteristics (American Academy of Child & Adolescent Psychiatry, 2000; APA, 1999; Merrell, 2001):

- Frequent and excessive worries about things before they take place

- Constant fretting or concern about schoolwork and performance, friends, or activities (e.g., sports)

- Recurring thoughts and actions (obsessions and/or compulsions)

- Negative and unrealistic thoughts

- Feelings of panic

- Physiological arousal (e.g., increased heart rate)

- Excessive fears of embarrassment or making mistakes

- Hypersensitivity to physical cues (e.g., bright lights, loud noises)

- A consistent sense of being uptight

- Nausea and profuse sweating

- Shaking or tremors

- Recurring nightmares

- A strong need for reassurance and support

- Worries that interfere with daily activities at school and at home

In describing the commonalities among anxiety disorders, Merrell (2001) created a model involving 1) subjective feelings (e.g., discomfort, worry, fear, dread), 2) overt behaviors (e.g., school avoidance, withdrawal, repetitive actions), and 3) physiological responses (e.g., sweating, nausea, muscle tension and aches, shaking or tremors).

These symptoms are troubling to students who experience them, as well as to their family and close friends. Many factors influence whether educators without training on mental health issues will notice the students' problems. Unfortunately, severe anxiety can have long-term debilitating consequences. If students do not receive appropriate intervention early, anxiety disorders can lead to any of the following (Center for Mental Health Services, 1998):

- Missed school days or an inability to finish school (e.g., dropping out)

- Impaired relationships with peers, friends, and family members

- Permanent self-esteem problems

- Use of alcohol or other drugs

- Poor performance on school assignments and related activities

- Problems adjusting to work situations

- Anxiety disorders in adulthood

With timely identification and treatment, anxiety disorders can be ameliorated and perhaps even eliminated. Hence, the teacher's role in the identification and ongoing support processes is vital (Merrell, 2001).

Specific Anxiety Disorders

The APA (1999, 2000) has identified these specific anxiety disorders: generalized anxiety disorder (GAD), obsessive-compulsive disorder (OCD), panic disorder (PD), phobias (i.e., specific phobia, social phobia, agoraphobia), posttraumatic stress disorder (PTSD), and separation anxiety disorder (SAD). The following subsections provide an overview of these disorders in nontechnical language, using descriptions from various publications (Allen, Liebman, Park, & Wimmer, 2001; American Academy of Child & Adolescent Psychiatry, 2000; APA, 1999, 2000; Anxiety Disorders Association of America, 2002a; Center for Mental Health Services, 1998; Dacey & Fiore, 2000; National Institute of Mental Health [NIMH], 2000b; Office of the Surgeon General, 1999; Stein & Hollander, 2002). It should be noted that the DSM-IV-TR symptoms characterizing a specific type of anxiety disorder may overlap with those of another anxiety disorder (Laurent & Potter, 1998; Merrell, 2001). Appendix A at the end of the book provides the DSM-IV-TR diagnostic criteria for these disorders.

Generalized Anxiety Disorder GAD can seem to strike out of the blue, but more often, the symptoms surface over time. Students with GAD normally have intense, irrational worries that 1) are not directly connected to recent events and 2) seriously hamper their ability, for instance, to do their schoolwork, maintain social relationships, or participate in important daily living activities. In other words, over a long-term period (at least 6 months), a student with GAD experiences unjustifiable anxiety, worry, and apprehension that strongly interferes with school and home life. In a way, these learners tend to "worry about worrying"— that is, they view themselves as anxious people who cannot cope well with their worries, so they eventually develop "additional anticipatory anxiety when . . . faced with even the possibility of being in an uncomfortable situation" (Dacey & Fiore, 2000, p. 37).

Students with GAD may seem very insecure and stressed, need extra support and encouragement, and complain about psychosomatic maladies (e.g., headaches, stomachaches, aching muscles). In addition, as indicated in the DSM-IV-TR (APA, 2000) and by Dacey and Fiore (2000), GAD is accompanied by restlessness, tiredness, difficulty concentrating, irritability, and sleep problems. Perhaps the best way to spot a student with symptoms of GAD is excessive worrying about grades, sports performance, punctuality, family issues, potential disasters (e.g., terrorist attacks, earthquakes), and health. Students with GAD also can be perfectionists who are very hard on themselves, sometimes redoing their schoolwork repetitively (Anxiety Disorders Association of America, 2002a).

Obsessive-Compulsive Disorder   OCD is another form of debilitating anxiety. Students with this disorder feel locked into a cycle of repetitive thoughts and behaviors. Often, individuals with OCD admit that their thoughts (or *ideations*) and behaviors are pointless and upsetting, but the obsessions and compulsions seem out of their control. Compulsive behaviors (i.e., things individuals feel that they must do) may include excessive hand washing, counting, praying, and hoarding and the extreme need for orderliness (e.g., continuously reorganizing objects on one's desk). Allen et al. (2001) described obsessions as "intrusive worries about being touched by someone such as in shaking hands, possibly having hit someone while driving, or having left home without locking up or turning off the lights" (p. 52). Obsessions also can be images, thoughts, or impulses (Office of the Surgeon General, 1999). Students with OCD often feel compelled to perform repetitive behaviors (i.e., compulsions) so that they can relieve the anxiety and the tensions caused by their obsessive thoughts (Dacey & Fiore, 2000). It is interesting to note that the compulsions are comforting, in a sense, but very disruptive to the individuals' daily functioning.

OCD normally begins in the teenage or early adult years, and the onset tends to be gradual. From time to time, the disorder is found in children. The diagnosis of OCD is generally not made unless the obsessions and compulsions produce significant distress in the individual, are chronic, are time-consuming (i.e., take up more than 1 hour per day), and hinder daily routines (i.e., those related to school, work, or relationships) (Allen et al., 2001; APA, 2000).

Panic Disorder   PD is frightening because it is characterized by panic attacks, or episodes of overpowering fear. These recurrent attacks occur unexpectedly; emerge without any discernible reason; and are marked by periodic times of intense fear of one's death, losing control, or going crazy. People can also feel a sense of "unrealness" or disconnectedness with their surroundings (Allen et al., 2001). Physiological manifestations of PD may include a pounding in the chest, sweating, dizziness or lightheadedness, nausea or stomachache, trembling, shortness of breath, tingling sensations, numbness, chills, or hot flashes (APA, 1999). Going through such a terrifying experience can make someone live in fear of having another attack. As a result, a student with PD expends a lot of energy trying to avoid situations that seem likely to trigger a panic attack (e.g., going to school, using the school restroom, walking to class in a very crowded hallway).

Clearly, the student's life is significantly disrupted by avoiding potentially fearful situations. PD tends to emerge from late adolescence to the mid-thirties, so high school educators need to be ready to intervene.

Phobias Phobias involve unrealistic and intense fear of, for example, spiders, snakes, or open spaces. Thus, a phobia can be defined as an uncontrollable, irrational, and persistent fear of various circumstances or activities or of certain animate or inanimate objects (APA, 1999). Although debilitating phobias largely emerge in the late teenage years to the mid-30s, children or youth have been known to develop phobias that are severe and long lasting. Fortunately, most phobias that develop in childhood generally disappear with time and maturity (Dacey & Fiore, 2000). An individual who has an extreme phobia often desperately tries to evade the root of the dread, thus limiting his or her day-to-day functioning and relationships at school and home. Researchers have identified three subtypes of phobias, which are summarized next (Allen et al., 2001; Anxiety Disorders Association of America, 2002a; see also APA, 2000).

Specific Phobia Specific phobia arises fairly often in 6- to 9-year-olds and involves excessive fear of a particular object or situation that is not harmful under normal circumstances. Students with specific phobias are intensely afraid of, for instance, certain animals (e.g., dogs), common medical procedures (e.g., shots), insects (e.g., bees, spiders), storms (e.g., thunder claps, tornados), water, heights, or particular situations (e.g., being confined in an enclosed space). Of course, specific phobias may arise from a traumatic event. For instance, a child might acquire a strong fear of riding in a car after being involved in an automobile accident or become intensely scared of all dogs after being injured by a pit bull. If the trauma is severe, students can develop PTSD (detailed discussion to follow).

Social Phobia Because social phobia (previously known as *social anxiety disorder*) has such profound implications for school behavior, it is presented in more depth than other phobias. Although social phobia mainly develops in teenagers, younger children—particularly extremely shy ones—have been known to exhibit social phobia (Dacey & Fiore, 2000). With this phobia, children and adolescents are terrified of various social situations in which they can be criticized, embarrassed, ridiculed, or judged by others. A mental health report by the Office of the Surgeon General (1999) provided examples of social situations at school that might cause physical reactions (e.g., shaking, sweating, diarrhea, blushing, muscle tension, heart palpitations) or outright panic attacks: speaking in class; conversing with peers; and eating, drinking, or writing in public places.

Although teenagers recognize that their social fears are largely unwarranted and excessive, elementary-age children are less able to identify their disproportionate anxiety. Younger children usually cannot voice their fears as well; instead, they may cry, act out, "freeze," cling to their parents, or respond to uncomfortable social situations with extremely timid or avoidance behaviors. In rare cases, younger children with social phobia may become selectively mute, withdrawing by not speaking in uncomfortable social situations such as school activities (Anxiety Disorders Association of America, 2002a).

The impact of social phobias on school life can be substantial. Students may miss a significant number of school days, fall behind, and avoid situations requiring social interaction. If the problems are not resolved in a timely fashion, social phobia may produce lifelong severe isolation, depression, and substance abuse (Anxiety Disorders Association of America, 2002a; Dacey & Fiore, 2000; Office of the Surgeon General, 1999).

In summary, educators should look for these potential symptoms of social phobia (Anxiety Disorders Association of America, 2002a):

- Fear of at least one social situation (e.g., recess) or performance situation (e.g., taking a test)

- Noticeable fear when interacting with classmates or with adults

- Anxiety symptoms (e.g., sweating, pounding heart, stomachache, dizziness, crying, acting out, tantrums) when faced with a feared situation

- Evasion or intense dread of situations that elicit fear

- Interference with school performance and attendance, the ability to socialize with peers, or the ability to form and keep relationships

Agoraphobia According to the DSM-IV-TR (APA, 2000), agoraphobia is the third major phobia category. This is almost an extreme form of social phobia. It tends to be rare in young children, more likely developing between the adolescent and young adult years. Students with this disorder generally do not participate in social situations, avoiding places that may be disturbing, such as school assemblies, crowded hallways, classrooms without windows, tunnels, and so on. In a worst-case scenario, these students may even become housebound, shunning uncomfortable places altogether (APA, 1999; Dacey & Fiore, 2000). In addition, agoraphobia can emerge when students begin avoiding places associated with an earlier panic attack or circumstances that they think they could not escape if they experienced a panic attack (Anxiety Disorders Association of America, 2002a).

Posttraumatic Stress Disorder Because of its negative impact on students' daily lives, one of the most serious anxiety disorders, PTSD, can develop in children or adolescents after they experience a very stressful event, such as physical or sexual abuse, being a victim of or witnessing violence, or experiencing a disaster (e.g., a bombing, a hurricane). During the event, children imprint the trauma in their minds as they feel intense fear, helplessness, or horror. Fortunately, many students who experience trauma do not develop or even experience signs of PTSD. A diagnosis of PTSD is made only if the symptoms last longer than 1 month. Recovery time varies. Some children and youth recover within 6 months, whereas others have the symptoms for much longer and develop PTSD as a chronic disorder. It is also important to note PTSD may not emerge until many years after the trauma (NIMH, 2000b).

People with PTSD tend to relive the event through painful memories, flashbacks, and upsetting thoughts. Consequently, those with PTSD may try to avoid anything associated with the trauma. Other potential symptoms of PTSD that tend to emerge within 3 months of the trauma are ongoing nightmares, an inability to recall the details of the traumatic event(s), physical or emotional disengagement from others, limited affect (mood), a sense of imminent doom or early death, numbness about daily activities and events, agitation, touchiness, feelings of being on guard, jitteriness, aggression, problems with concentration, and a quick startle reaction (Allen et al., 2001; APA, 1999; Dacey & Fiore, 2000; NIMH, 2000b). In addition, PTSD can affect school performance and attendance and can manifest in the classroom. For example, incidental events like a loud popping noise may trigger a significant anxiety attack, causing the child to leave school for many days and miss assignments and perhaps even negatively affecting his or her course grades. Finally, PTSD is often accompanied by depression, substance abuse, or one or more other anxiety disorders (NIMH, 2000b).

Separation Anxiety Disorder Anxious behavior (e.g., being clingy, being afraid of strangers) upon separation from one's parents or home is a normal developmental characteristic of infants, toddlers, and preschoolers. In time, these behaviors usually fade almost completely. A potential problem emerges when children ages 4 and older feel an immense level of stress when separating from their caregivers in familiar surroundings. In fact, this chapter's opening vignette suggests that Isaac shows early signs of SAD. However, the DSM-IV-TR indicates that to make a diagnosis of SAD, the anxiety or fear must produce such distress that it begins to negatively affect the individual's social, academic, or job function-ing and must last at least 1 month (APA, 2000). Moreover, separation anxiety is often correlated with symptoms of depression (e.g., sadness, withdrawal, apathy, difficulty in maintaining focus), tends to be more common in girls than boys, leads to total school avoidance in very severe cases, and can be a precursor to developing PD or agoraphobia later in life (Office of the Surgeon General, 1999).

To overview, the following lifestyle-related symptoms are very good indica-tors of SAD (Anxiety Disorders Association of America, 2002a). Children and youth with SAD tend to:

- Have a difficult time falling asleep while alone, so they demand that someone stay with them at bedtime or go to their parents' bedroom during the night
- Follow a parent around
- Have nightmares about being separated from loved ones
- Show significant fears about the health and safety of their caregivers
- Pass up going places by themselves
- Refuse to go to school or camp
- Demonstrate extreme homesickness (i.e., feelings of misery at not being with loved ones)
- Be reluctant or refuse to participate in sleepovers with friends

An initial report of one of these signs does not necessarily mean that a child is in beginning stages of SAD. The symptoms need to be persistent and sufficiently debilitating over the course of many weeks to result in a diagnosis of SAD.

Prevalence Rates

According to a mental health report by the Office of the Surgeon General (1999), anxiety disorders are among the most common mental health issues that manifest during the school years. Specifically, the 1-year combined prevalence for all anxiety disorders in children and adolescents (ages 9–17) is 13% (Office of the Surgeon General, 1999). More than 1 in 10 students may have some type of anxiety disorder. Overall, more teenage girls than boys have an anxiety disorder. In addition, approximately 50% of the children and adolescents with one anxiety disorder have another type of anxiety disorder or an accompanying mental health disorder, such as depression (Anxiety Disorders Association of America, 2002a).

Although the prevalence rates for particular anxiety disorders are difficult to nail down, especially for school-age children, the Surgeon General's mental health report (Office of the Surgeon General, 1999) provided these estimates:

- GAD: 1-year prevalence rate for all individuals with the disorder is approximately 3%

- OCD: 0.2%–0.8% of children and up to 2% of teenagers

- SAD: 4% of children and young adolescents

- Social phobia: lifetime prevalence can range (depending on the context) from 3% to 13%, and the majority of individuals with the disorder are female

ASSESSMENT AND DIAGNOSIS

When does anxiety become a debilitating factor in a student's life? When is it considered a mental health disorder? Even though educators generally notice which students are overly stressed and pressured, they are not expected to provide answers to these questions. Research has shown that identifying a potential anxiety disorder and initiating suitable interventions are multistep and multidimensional processes requiring a great deal of training in mental health issues (Merrell, 2001; Office of the Surgeon General, 1999; Wagner, 2003). Nonetheless, the identification process often begins in the classroom.

Teachers should first review the previously discussed characteristics of anxiety disorders and ensure that they are familiar with the more obvious signs of severe anxiety. As students begin to show inklings of stress, educators should observe them carefully, perhaps confidentially taking notes. Observations should highlight:

- *Which* signs were observed (e.g., shaking, freezing, withdrawal)

- *When* they were observed (e.g., end of first period, at 8:30 A.M., before singing a song)

- *Where* they occurred (e.g., in the classroom, in the hallway, in the locker room).

If possible, educators should also estimate how long the signs lasted (e.g., 5 seconds, 1 minute) and indications of their intensity level (e.g., only one of the student's legs trembled, student curled up into a ball, student strongly gripped the railing and would not let go). The educator must see the school's mental health representative (e.g., school counselor, school social worker, school psychologist, intervention specialist) as soon as possible. If the student's symptoms persist, the educators should update the appropriate school personnel. Because anxiety must be chronic to reflect a disorder, these records can be critical in making a diagnosis.

Once a confidential referral is made, the school psychologist should coordinate further assessment, aid in the diagnostic process, and manage interventions. Ideally, this person keeps all relevant parties posted and provides suggestions for working with the child. Most likely, the school psychologist will conduct further observations, interview relevant persons, and consult with others at school (e.g., the school counselor and relevant teachers) and in the mental health profession. If the child shows symptomatic behavior and requires additional professional help, he or she is referred to a child clinical psychologist, child psychiatrist, clinical social worker, or licensed mental health counselor to begin the formal assessment process.

This clinician attempts to learn about the child's unique functional characteristics and to look for symptoms that suggest a mental health disorder (see Office of the Surgeon General, 1999, for further information). As indicated previously, the child may be experiencing another problem (e.g., depression) as well as anxiety. The diagnostic process largely involves informal and standardized testing, environmental assessments (e.g., at school, at home), interviews (e.g., with the child and his or her parents, teachers, pediatricians, and counselors), observations, review of medical records, and so forth. If appropriate, the clinician will use the DSM-IV-TR to make a diagnosis, then devise a treatment plan and provide a prognosis. Generally, this process includes oral and written reports about the expected pattern of distress and its limitations to the child's functioning as well as the course of the disorder and recovery. A confidential copy of the written report should then be forwarded to the school for review by a trained mental health professional (e.g., the school psychologist).

Depending on who is managing the case (i.e., the outside mental health professional or the school psychologist), this individual generally consults with the child's teachers and other pertinent educators. He or she also should inform all educators about providing emotional support and academic assistance to the student. The students' teachers may alter time constraints for submitting assignments and reduce the workload to a reasonable level. The school counselor may develop a practical, school-based intervention plan that includes teachers, the school nurse, the librarian, administrators, and custodians. Because diagnosis and treatment are ongoing confidential processes, an educator is expected to be one of the educational liaisons between the school and outside responsible party (e.g., the clinical psychologist working with the child and parents). When in doubt, the educator should ask questions and remain informed.

POTENTIAL CAUSES OF ANXIETY DISORDERS

The precise etiology of most anxiety disorders probably cannot be pinpointed, but neuroscientific and behavioral research suggest significant risk factors that involve both nature and nurture (Office of the Surgeon General, 1999). A person's basic temperament (e.g., being very shy and reserved in unfamiliar circumstances) and other biological/genetic factors can play a role in the development of childhood and adolescent anxiety disorders (Center for Mental Health Services, 1998; Office of the Surgeon General, 1999). Other predictors appear to include environmental concerns involving aspects of family life (e.g., severe family problems, a parent's mental health disorder or criminal behavior, parenting style). Maladaptive peers and sibling rivalry also may be risk factors. Finally, child abuse tends to be related to mental health disorders, including anxiety. Although knowing the "why" aids mental health professionals in their treatment planning, educators do not need to know the cause of students' anxiety to lend support and to assist with the referral process.

INTERVENTION

As mentioned previously, the mental health professional who conducts the assessment creates a timely and appropriate treatment plan. Interventions are usually comprehensive and reflect the severity and nature of the anxiety symptoms experienced. Some students acknowledge mild to severe symptoms on a periodic basis and find that they are able to manage their anxiety without using prescribed drugs. Others may receive medication but elect not to receive counseling. Still other children and youth take medication and participate in therapy to learn appropriate skills for handling their anxiety. The research literature has not promoted one standard of care; rather, several approaches have emerged as acceptable and effective interventions (e.g., Barton, 2002; Office of the Surgeon General, 1999; Seligman, 1998; White, 1998). The following subsections are the mainstays of anxiety treatment: psychotherapy, psychotropic medication, and combination therapy.

Psychotherapy

An important approach to assisting students with anxiety disorders is psychotherapy. Generally, this is a "talking" intervention, by which the psychotherapist, who may be, for example, a clinical psychologist or a mental health counselor, works with the individual for an extended period of time (e.g., 3 or more months) to help alleviate his or her symptomic behavior and possibly get to the primary cause of the disorder. There are several major orientations to psychotherapy for children and adolescents with anxiety disorders. The three leading approaches for addressing anxiety are cognitive therapy, behavioral therapy, and cognitive behavioral therapy.

Cognitive Therapy   Cognitive therapy has two basic assumptions. First, individuals with an anxiety disorder are trapped in a negative way of thinking about their situation. Second, they can be freed from these distorted thoughts by identifying, evaluating, and modifying dysfunctional thinking as well as the underlying beliefs (Reilly, Sokol, & Butler, 1999). Originally applying this to depression, Beck,

Emery, and Greenberg (1985) later used various cognitive therapy techniques in the treatment of anxiety disorders. This approach has since gained widespread acceptance.

Behavioral Therapy The primary goal of behavioral therapy in the treatment of anxiety is utilizing specific behavioral techniques to reduce and manage stress. Examples include progressive muscle relaxation, meditation, and biofeedback (Seligman, 1998). Behavioral therapy alone is not considered as effective in the treatment of anxiety as cognitive therapy or cognitive behavioral therapy (Seligman, 1998).

Cognitive Behavioral Therapy Cognitive behavioral therapy is the combination of both cognitive and behavioral therapy techniques. The literature supports this intervention as the best of the nonmedication approaches, because 1) it combines two helpful psychotherapy methods into one intervention, 2) the efficacy studies document higher success rates, and 3) clients report better long-term outcomes (e.g., Ballenger, 1999; Seligman, 1998).

Psychotropic Medications

Pharmacological approaches have long been considered a useful way to treat many mental health issues, including anxiety disorders (Anxiety Disorders Association of America, 2002a, 2002b; Barton, 2002). Three basic drug groups have emerged as effective drug treatments for anxiety disorders: benzodiazepines (BZs), azapirones, and selective serotonin reuptake inhibitors (SSRIs) (Conner & Davidson, 1998; Gitlin, 1990; Maxmen & Ward, 1995). See Table 10.1 for a summary of the major medications used to treat anxiety disorders.

BZs have received the most attention in the literature (Ballenger, 1999; Conner & Davidson, 1998; Stahl, 1999). Until the late 1990s, BZs were considered a first-line treatment for GAD, whereas now BZs are used as second-line or augmentation medication (Stahl, 1999). This drop in status is most likely due to the relapse rate after discontinuing medication (50%–70% in first year), potential for abuse, withdrawal symptoms, sedation, memory impairment, and lack of research available regarding potential side effects of long-term use (Conner & Davidson, 1998; Hantouche & Vahia, 1999).

Azapirones have also been documented as effective in the treatment of anxiety (Rickels, DeMartinis, & Aufdembrinke, 2000; Sussman, 1987). Although not as fast acting (the full effect requires 4–6 weeks, in comparison with the immediate effects of BZs), this drug group is favored, as it does not cause drug dependency, withdrawal symptoms, or other serious side effects (Maxmen & Ward, 1995). Drawbacks include ineffectiveness in the treatment of insomnia and the inability to be taken as needed (Gitlin, 1990). Although past clinical trials deemed buspirone, the most prominent azapirone, as effective as BZs in the treatment of anxiety, later research found it to be far less effective (Rickels et al., 2000). In addition, individuals who have previously taken BZs are less likely to benefit from buspirone.

Table 10.1. Medications commonly used to treat anxiety disorders

Drug class	Generic name(s)	Brand name(s)	Target disorder	How the drugs may work on the brain	Benefits	Side effects
Anticonvulsants	Gabapentin	Neurontin	SAD	Affect GABA	Usually effective within 2–4 weeks[a]	Sedation
Azapirones	Buspirone	BuSpar	GAD	Enhance the activity of serotonin	Effective for many people; less sedating than benzodiazepines	Work slowly
Benzodiazepines (BZs)	Lorazepam Prazepam Flurazepam Clonazepam Triazolam Chlordiazepoxide Halazepam Temazepam Oxazepam Clorazepate Diazepam Alprazolam	Ativan Centrax Dalmane Klonopin Halcion Librium Paxipam Restoril Serax Tranxene Valium Xanax	GAD, PD, SAD	Enhance the function of GABA	Fast acting; some people feel better the first day	Potentially habit forming; can cause drowsiness; can produce withdrawal symptoms; should be discontinued slowly
Beta blockers	Propranolol Atenolol	Inderal Tenormin	SAD	Reduce ability to produce adrenaline	Fast acting; not habit forming	Should not be used with certain preexisting medical conditions, such as asthma, congestive heart failure, diabetes, vascular disease, hypothyroidism, and angina pectoris
Monoamine oxidase inhibitors (MAOIs)	Selegiline Isocarboxazid Phenelzine Tranylcypromine	Eldepryl Marplan Nardil Parnate	PD, PTSD, SAD	Block the effect of an important brain enzyme, preventing the breakdown of both serotonin and noradrenaline	Effective for many people, especially for those not responding to other medications; 2–6 weeks for improvement[a]	Strict dietary restrictions and potential drug interactions; moderate weight gain

(continued)

Table 10.1. *(continued)*

Drug class	Generic name(s)	Brand name(s)	Target disorder	How the drugs may work on the brain	Benefits	Side effects
Selective serotonin reuptake inhibitors (SSRIs)	Citalopram Fluvoxamine Paroxetine Fluoxetine Sertraline	Celexa Luvox Paxil Prozac Zoloft	GAD, OCD, PD, SAD	Affect the concentration of the neurotransmitter serotonin, a chemical in the brain thought to be linked to anxiety disorders	Effective with fewer side effects than other medications; 4–6 weeks for improvement[b]	Possible nausea, nervousness
Tricyclic antidepressants (TCAs)	Doxepin Clomipramine Nortriptyline Amitriptyline Imipramine Maprotiline Desipramine Trimipramine Protriptyline	Adapin Sinequan Anafranil Aventyl Pamelor Elavil Janimine Tofranil Ludiomil Norpramin Pertofrane Surmontil Vivactil	PD, PTSD; OCD (Anafranil only)	Regulate serotonin and/or noradrenaline in the brain	Effective for many people; 2–6 weeks for improvement[b]	Dry mouth; constipation; blurry vision; difficulty urinating; dizziness; low blood pressure; moderate weight gain
Other antidepressants	Trazodone Venlafaxine Nefazodone	Desyrel Effexor Serzone	GAD, OCD, PD, SAD	Affect the concentration of the neurotransmitter serotonin, a chemical in the brain thought to be linked to anxiety disorders	Effective with fewer side effects than other medications; 4–6 weeks for improvement[b]	Possible nervousness

From Anxiety Disorders Association of America. (2002b). Chart. Retrieved October 30, 2003, from http://www.adaa.org/AnxietyDisorderInfor/Medications.cfm; adapted by permission.

[a]This period of time is usually needed for the body's neurophysiological system to adjust to the medication's effect.

[b]The body's neurophysiological system normally takes several weeks to adjust to powerful effects of SSRIs. Physicians and psychiatrists may prescribe other faster-acting drugs (e.g., benzodiazepines) to clients for more immediate relief of symptoms.

Key: GABA: gamma-aminobutyric acid (an inhibitory neurotransmitter that is prevalent throughout the central nervous system; GABA and benzodiazepines can act at different sites on the same complex receptor to produce inhibition in nerve cells); GAD: generalized anxiety disorder; OCD: obsessive-compulsive disorder; PD: panic disorder; PTSD: post-traumatic stress disorder; SAD: social anxiety disorder

Disclaimer: This information is for educational purposes only. Use this chart only as a rough outline of medications to treat anxiety disorders. Always speak with a qualified doctor about any of these medications and their use with children, adolescents, and adults.

Finally, several SSRI medications (e.g., Fluoxetine [Prozac], sertraline [Zoloft], paroxetine [Paxil], citalopram [Celexa], fluvoxamine [Luvox]) are prescribed by physicians to treat various anxiety disorders. Although these medications perhaps take up to 12 weeks for clients to feel their full effects, they can be very beneficial (Barton, 2002). For example, they are proving to be effective to alleviate anxiety in adults and children, are nonaddictive, and generally have relatively minor side effects (e.g., dry mouth, drowsiness) (NIMH, 2002a). NIMH (2002a) listed antidepressant and antianxiety medications approved for use with children and youth (see Table 10.2). Some are SSRIs and others are not. Other antidepressant medications (monoamine oxidase inhibitors, tricyclic antidepressants) and even other drugs (e.g., beta blockers, anticonvulsants) are listed in Table 10.1. Unlike the medications in Table 10.2, however, these are not recommended for treating anxiety disorders in children and youth.

Physicians or psychiatrists prescribe medications. The correct dosage and frequency of use should be scrupulously followed. Teachers should ask the school nurse (or the student's doctor, if permission has been received to contact the physician directly) about how these medications affect classroom learning and behavior (e.g., intermittent drowsiness and lack of concentration) and about side effects. It should also be noted that children and adults receive different medicines based on the drugs' effectiveness and side effects with different age groups. One size does not fit all.

Combination Therapy

The debate regarding the most effective treatment for anxiety (i.e., drug therapy versus nondrug therapy) has encouraged researchers to consider the possibility that a combined approach is superior and/or has synergistic effects when compared with either treatment intervention alone (Ballenger, 1999; Barlow & Lehman,

Table 10.2. Antidepressant and antianxiety medications approved for use with children and youth

Generic	Brand name	Approved age (in years)
clomipramine	Anafranil	10 and older (for OCD)
buspirone	BuSpar	18 and older
venlafaxine	Effexor	18 and older
fluvoxamine	Luvox (SSRI)	8 and older (for OCD)
paroxetine	Paxil (SSRI)	18 and older
fluoxetine	Prozac (SSRI)	18 and older
nefazodone	Serzone (SSRI)	18 and older
doxepin	Sinequan	12 and older
imipramine	Tofranil	6 and older (for bedwetting)
bupropion	Wellbutrin	18 and older
sertraline	Zoloft (SSRI)	6 and older (for OCD)

Source: National Institute of Mental Health (2002a).
Key: OCD = obsessive-compulsive disorder; SSRI = selective serotonin reuptake inhibitor

1996; Hantouche & Vahia, 1999). Most children and youth are treated with the combination therapy approach.

APPLICATION TO EDUCATION: ROLE OF THE TEACHER

Because of the extended time spent with students, a classroom educator is potentially one of the most influential forces in students' lives. This is especially true for learners with anxiety disorders. Although teachers may not have extensive training in the diagnosis and treatment of anxiety or other mental health disorders, they tend to know their students very well and can advocate for them.

As mentioned previously, it is important to be aware of the impact that anxiety disorders have on students' social functioning, academic performance, and behavior. Depending on where his or her symptoms fall on the spectrum of anxiety disorders, a learner may be dramatically impaired or only periodically display symptoms. It is also helpful to know how the various anxiety disorders are perhaps manifested in the classroom.

There are two types of students with anxiety—those with and without a formal diagnosis. Particular issues accompany each type, and teachers need to support these students regardless of whether or not a diagnosis has been made.

Diagnosed Anxiety Disorder

When a diagnosis has been made and a treatment plan is in place, teachers can provide feedback to support people such as the school counselor, parents, community mental health providers, and others. Teachers should inform these individuals of the student's progress and potential challenges to his or her social and academic success. As noted previously, teachers may be asked to provide reports or documentation to assist with medication evaluation, diagnosis, or treatment progress. Teachers can observe behavior and identify potential neglect or misuse of medication, self-medicating behaviors, or inadequate or ineffective medication.

Medication can pose other issues in school. Students who take medication for anxiety disorders often have access to their prescriptions via the school nurse, and anecdotal reports indicate that elementary-age students are periodically bullied or coerced into sharing or giving their medication to others. To help prevent this, educators should require caregivers to inform the school of which medications are being brought to school, as well as their dosages, times taken, and possible side effects. A monitoring form could be devised and kept by both the caregiver and relevant school personnel (e.g., nurse). Medications should only be delivered to the school by a responsible adult, never by the child. Finally, appropriate child-safe packaging should always be used.

Some students with anxiety disorders have the false impression that if one pill helps them feel better, two will make them feel great. Prescriptions for anxiety disorders are based on weight, ethnicity, gender, and other issues, and it is imperative that the student closely follows protocol. Overuse of medication may have serious medical consequences and can potentially lead to substance dependence. It is important to note that in addition to or in lieu of medication, adolescent students may abuse alcohol and other drugs as a means of self-medicating their disorder. To assist with preventing this additional problem, educators should be aware of the side effects of medications and note behaviors that are inconsistent with those side effects. Typically, antianxiety medications will not drastically interfere with normal school functioning, but when combined with drugs and alcohol use, students may show signs such as diminished motivation, infrequent school attendance, and a sudden decline in grades. Any of these behaviors or other disturbing actions should be reported immediately to the school counselor or school psychologist. Confidentially documenting these behaviors is always a good idea. The educator should note specifically when, where, and how frequently the actions took place.

Undiagnosed Anxiety Disorder

This group of students includes individuals who have anxiety disorders that have yet to be diagnosed and those who display anxiety symptoms but do not meet the criteria for an anxiety disorder. Some students with symptoms of anxiety may be only mildly affected, and their anxiety is undetectable except in extremely stressful situations. Other students' symptoms are more obvious and may have a daily impact on their lives.

Teachers may be students' only connection to potential intervention and treatment. Many parents are unaware of the academic and social implications of anxiety disorders. A parent may be apprehensive about seeking intervention from a mental health professional or may lack resources to do so. Parents often mistake anxiety disorder symptoms as signs that their child is high strung or nervous rather than as signs of a disorder that needs medical and mental health intervention. In addition, with the unbalanced ratio of students to counselors, it is unreasonable to rely solely on school counselors for identifying students who have the potential for anxiety disorders.

Thus, teachers who suspect that a child may have anxiety issues can and should refer the student to the school counselor or school psychologist. School counselors have limited training related to mental health diagnoses; however, these individuals have the resources to make an appropriate referral. It is not the teacher's responsibility to diagnose or provide counseling for a student with anxiety disorders. It is hoped that through gaining an understanding of anxiety issues and other mental health disorders, educators can help identify and refer students to the appropriate personnel. By acting as the classroom liaison, teachers become a key link between students needing support services and those providing the services.

The following two fictional vignettes illustrate the educator's important role in working with students who have anxiety disorders. In the first vignette, the student has been diagnosed with an anxiety disorder; in the second one, the student has not received a formal diagnosis but displays symptoms of anxiety. For further reflection, a brief discussion of the teacher's role follows each vignette.

Joey   *Joey is an 8-year-old of European American ethnicity. He is a second-grade student at Shady Tree Elementary School. He lives with his father, who is a single parent. Joey's mother died last year of cancer.*

The school counselor informed the classroom teacher that Joey has been diagnosed with SAD. According to the counselor, Joey also had numerous absences in his first-grade year because of illness. Also, when Joey's father attempted to bring him to school, Joey would kick, scream, and shake violently. When Joey did attend school, he appeared distracted and often expressed concern for his father's safety.

Due to his lack of attention in the classroom and numerous absences, Joey fell behind. The school psychologist ruled out learning disabilities. In addition, Joey's physician performed a thorough medical examination and found no physical basis for Joey's difficulties. Although Joey has yet to show the symptoms seen in his first-grade year, the school counselor is concerned that Joey is behind academically and may be at risk for relapse as he progresses through school and experiences significant transitions between grades and school levels.

• •

Discussion   SAD is often identified when a child refuses to attend school. Joey's behavior in second grade illustrates that he was most likely experiencing ongoing trauma because of his mother's death. Clinging to his father was likely an effort to avoid further abandonment. If Joey was emotionally unprepared for his mother's death (which is likely, due to his age), he may have feared that his father was more vulnerable for an untimely death. Joey may have felt the need to stay with his father as much as possible to protect him. By doing so, Joey was affirming to himself that his father was healthy and alive. The distractions that Joey experienced while at school were likely related to his concern for his father's well-being.

To assist Joey, the teacher needs to be reassuring and supportive of his concerns and pain while encouraging him to participate and interact with his peers as much as possible. The teacher does not want to reinforce any distracting or attention-seeking classroom behavior that will disrupt the learning environment, nor does the teacher want to yield to any inappropriate demands (e.g., excessive time away from peers, repeatedly wanting to stay inside with the teacher or other adults during recess). In addition, the teacher needs to be supportive of Joey's father and provide him with appropriate referrals to outside parent support groups, encouraging him to speak with the school counselor and school psychologist as needed. As Joey moves on to the next grade level, his third-grade teacher needs to be aware of continuing indicators of SAD (e.g., excessive shyness, dependency on adults, clinginess, inappropriate emotional outbursts). If these are recognized, consultation with the school counselor and school psychologist is warranted.

Anna   *Anna is a 13-year-old Latina. She is a seventh-grade student at Winding Road Junior High School. Anna's maternal great-grandparents immigrated to the*

United States when they were newlyweds, and Anna is a fourth-generation Mexican American.

Anna has a history of academic excellence and is an outgoing person. She has been involved in school sports and other extracurricular activities. Over the past 7 months, however, Anna has demonstrated excessive worry about a number of areas of her life. As a result, her teacher contacts the school counselor. The school counselor sets up weekly meetings with Anna, allowing Anna to discuss her concerns about school, friendships, family, and health. Anna describes her anxiety as uncontrollable and shares that it often impedes her ability to focus in the classroom. In addition, Anna reports that her anxiety has affected her ability to sleep, making her tired at school. As a result, Anna's problems with concentration and alertness have begun to affect her grades.

• •

Discussion Even though Anna has not been formally identified as having an anxiety disorder, symptoms of anxiety are evident. Anna's anxiety is not limited to a particular situation or event and, regrettably, has begun to affect her grades. Anna might have GAD; however, it is imperative that the school counselor makes appropriate referrals to ensure that Anna's needs are properly identified and addressed. Once a referral is made, the teacher should obtain permission from Anna's parents to contact the outside mental health professional. Table 10.3 lists questions that the teacher could ask to make the educator–mental health professional collaboration more effective.

Summary of the Teacher's Role

It is the chapter authors' desire that teachers become a strong support system for students with anxiety disorders. Table 10.4 provides a summary of ideas for supporting students with anxiety. As they work with these students, educators may find that they may need more information. Appendix C at the end of the book provides resources for further information.

Table 10.3. Questions for educators to ask mental health providers

Is a written release of information available for us to communicate directly with each other?

As the classroom teacher, how should I support the student educationally?

In general, what services is the student currently receiving from you?

Is the student receiving psychotherapy? If so, in what form? If the student is receiving medication, how might it affect learning?

Which school-related services might be beneficial for the student?

Would it be helpful if I periodically submit a report to you regarding the student's educational status and classroom behavior? If so, how should I submit this information?

Table 10.4. Suggestions for working with students who have anxiety disorders

Do not share the student's diagnosis with other students or staff who are not providing services to the student. As with any disability, the student's diagnosis should remain confidential and should not be shared.

Obtain a release of information from the student's parent if an outside mental health professional requests information.

Do not give the student unusual or preferential treatment. If the student qualifies for assistance under the Individuals with Disabilities Education Act (IDEA) Amendments of 1997 (PL 105-17) or the Americans with Disabilities Act (ADA) of 1990 (PL 101-336), consult with special education professionals, school officials, and (if needed) legal counsel to identify which special education services and/or classroom accommodations should be provided.

Remember:
  The effects of substance abuse often look like severe anxiety.
  Individuals with anxiety disorders may self-medicate with alcohol or other drugs.
  There is a high comorbidity of anxiety and depression.
  Consult with knowledgeable mental health professionals whenever questions arise.

CONCLUSION

It is often said that art mirrors culture. The same may be said of the classroom. According to NIMH, anxiety disorders are the number one mental health problem in the United States, affecting perhaps one in seven Americans (Lerner, 2000). Given the widespread nature of anxiety in U.S. society, it is little wonder that anxiety manifests itself in the classroom.

A sign in a colleague's office reads, "As long as there are tests, there will be prayer in schools!" The creator of this amusing thought obviously is aware of the anxiety that high-stakes testing generates in students. Classroom teachers may be challenged when attempting to differentiate "normal" anxiety related to exams, social situations, and new environments from debilitating anxiety disorders. It is hoped that this chapter has provided readers with a basic overview of the diagnostic criteria associated with anxiety disorders, leading interventions, and practical recommendations for teachers. Understanding the symptoms that are closely related to anxiety disorders should enable teachers to help identify students who need additional services.

REFERENCES

Allen, T.E., Liebman, M.C., Park, L.C., & Wimmer, W.C. (2001). *A primer on mental disorders: A guide for educators, families, and students.* Lanham, MD: Scarecrow Press.

American Academy of Child and Adolescent Psychiatry. (2000). *The anxious child.* Retrieved January 31, 2003, from http://www.aacap.org/publications/factsfam/anxious.htm

American Psychiatric Association. (1999). *Let's talk facts about anxiety disorders.* Retrieved January 31, 2003, from http://www.psych.org/public_info/anxiety.cfm

American Psychiatric Association. (2000). *Diagnostic and statistical manual of mental disorders* (4th ed., text rev.). Washington, DC: Author.

Americans with Disabilities Act (ADA) of 1990, PL 101-336, 42 U.S.C. §§ 12101 *et seq.*

Anxiety Disorders Association of America. (2002a). *Anxiety disorders in children and adolescents.* Retrieved January 31, 2003, from http://www.adaa.org/AnxietyDisorderInfor/ChildrenAdo.cfm

Anxiety Disorders Association of America. (2002b). *Medications: Chart.* Retrieved January 25, 2003, from http://www.adaa.org/AnxietyDisorderInfor/Medications.cfm

Ballenger, J.C. (1999). Current treatments of the anxiety disorders in adults. *Biological Psychiatry, 46,* 1579–1594.

Barlow, D.H., & Lehman, C.L. (1996). Advances in the psychosocial treatment of anxiety disorders. *Archives of General Psychiatry, 53,* 727–735.

Barton, S. (2002). *Clinical evidence: Mental health.* London: BMJ Publishing.

Beck, A.T., Emery, G., & Greenberg, R.L. (1985). *Anxiety disorders and phobias: A cognitive perspective.* New York: Basic Books.

Center for Mental Health Services. (1998, December). *Children's mental health facts: Anxiety disorders in children and adolescents.* Retrieved January 31, 2003, from http://www.mental health.org/publications/allpubs/CA-0007/default.asp

Conner, K.M., & Davidson, J.R.T. (1998). Generalized anxiety disorder: Neurobiological and pharmacotherapeutic perspectives. *Biological Psychiatry, 44,* 1286–1294.

Dacey, J.S., & Fiore, L.B. (2000). *Your anxious child: How parents and teachers can relieve anxiety in children.* San Francisco: Jossey-Bass.

Gitlin, M.J. (1990). *The psychotherapist's guide to psychopharmacology.* New York: The Free Press.

Hantouche, E.G., & Vahia, V.N. (1999). Interactions between psychotherapy and drug therapy in generalized anxiety disorder. *Human Psychopharmacology, 14,* S87–S93.

Individuals with Disabilities Education Act Amendments of 1997, PL 105-17, 20 U.S.C. §§ 1400 *et seq.*

Laurent, J., & Potter, K.L. (1998). Anxiety-related difficulties. In T.S. Watson & F.M. Gresham (Eds.), *Handbook of child behavior therapy* (pp. 371–392). New York: Plenum.

Lerner, M.E. (2000, September 29). Facing your fear. *USA Weekend,* pp. 8–11.

Maxmen, J.S., & Ward, N.G. (1995). *Psychotropic drugs fast facts.* New York: W.W. Norton.

Merrell, K.W. (2001). *Helping students overcome depression and anxiety: A practical guide.* New York: The Guilford Press.

National Institute of Mental Health. (2002a). *Medications.* Retrieved October 28, 2003, from http://www.nimh.nih.gov/publicat/medicate.cfm#ptdep8

National Institute of Mental Health. (2000b). *Mental disorders in America: Anxiety disorders.* Retrieved January 28, 2003, from http://www.nimh.nih.gov/publicat/numbers.cfm

Office of the Surgeon General. (1999). Children and mental health. In *Mental health: A report of the Surgeon General* (Chap. 3). Retrieved January 16, 2003, from http://www. surgeongeneral.gov/library/mentalhealth/pdfs/C3.pdf

Reilly, C.E., Sokol, L., & Butler, A.C. (1999). A cognitive approach to understanding and treating anxiety. *Human Psychopharmacology, 14,* S16–S21.

Rickels, K., DeMartinis, N., & Aufdembrinke, B. (2000). A double-blind, placebo-controlled trial of abecarnil and diazepam in the treatment of patients with generalized anxiety disorder. *Journal of Clinical Psychopharmacology, 20,* 12–18.

Seligman, L. (1998). *Selecting effective treatments: A comprehensive, systematic guide to treating mental disorders.* San Francisco, CA: Jossey-Bass.

Stahl, S.M. (1999). Mergers and acquisitions among psychotropics: Antidepressant takeover of anxiety may now be complete. *Journal of Clinical Psychiatry, 60,* 282–283.

Stein, D.J., & Hollander, E. (Eds.). (2002). *Textbook of anxiety disorders.* Washington, DC: American Psychiatric Publishing.

Sussman, N. (1987). Treatment of anxiety with buspirone. *Psychiatry, 17,* 114–120.

Wagner, W.G. (2003). *Counseling, psychology, and children: A multidimensional approach to intervention.* Upper Saddle River, NJ: Prentice Hall.

White, J. (1998). "Stress control" large group therapy for generalized anxiety disorder: Two year follow-up. *Behavioural and Cognitive Psychotherapy, 26,* 237–245.

RECOMMENDED READINGS

The following sources from the preceding reference list are recommended for readers who want a more in-depth review of anxiety disorders from a scientific perspective: Laurent and Potter (1998) and Stein and Hollander (2002). For readers who are interested in learning more about the day-to-day issues of anxiety disorders, Dacey and Fiore (2000) and Merrell (2001), which also are on the reference list, are a good place to start.

11

Mood Disorders

Janine Jones

• •

Chapter Concepts

- Characteristics and behavioral indicators of mood disorders in children
- Impact of mood disorders in school settings
- Traditional clinical approaches used to treat mood disorders
- Information to assist diagnosis and treatment

This chapter describes mood disorders that may affect children. Using the terminology of the text revision of the *Diagnostic and Statistical Manual of Mental Disorders, Fourth Edition* (DSM-IV-TR; American Psychiatric Association, 2000), the following disorders are detailed in the chapter: dysthymic disorder, major depressive disorder, bipolar disorder, cyclothymic disorder, and schizoaffective disorder. Each section focuses on a specific disorder to give the educator an understanding of the disorder's features, subtypes, and effect on a child's behavior in the classroom. Because of its relationship to mood disorders, suicide is covered as well. The chapter also presents information on treating mood disorders, including classroom-based interventions.

DYSTHYMIC DISORDER

Dysthymic disorder—a long-term, low-grade form of depression—is the most common mood disorder seen in children and adolescents. A student who is often sad or withdrawn may have dysthymic disorder. Dysthymic disorder is a formal name for what is commonly called "depression."

Characteristics

Dysthymic disorder is typically characterized by a depressed mood in the child for most of the day as observed by others. In adults, this depressed mood must exist for 2 years; however, in children, the depressed mood must exist for a minimum of 1 year (in children and adolescents, the mood may also reflect irritability). During this time period, the child may experience any of the following symptoms: changes in appetite, sleep problems, lethargy (tiredness), low self-esteem, poor concentration, and the feeling of hopelessness.

Children may experience appetite changes in two directions. Some children may begin overeating and experience excessive weight gain. Other children may lose their appetite and become unable to maintain a healthy diet, as demonstrated by excessive weight loss.

Some children may also experience sleep problems. Changes in sleep pattern are also bidirectional. Children with dysthymic disorder may be sleeping excessively (e.g., needing 10 or more hours of sleep each night). Or they may experience insomnia, sleeping 5 or fewer hours each night. The sleep changes are debilitating and may exacerbate symptoms of irritability.

A typical characteristic of dysthymic disorder is lethargy. This is particularly common when children experience insomnia. They seem tired all the time, regardless of the amount of sleep they receive. They lack energy most of the day and resist activities that require high levels of physical output. Their lethargy may even cause them to perceive everyday, low-energy tasks as requiring high levels of physical exertion. For example, a child or adolescent who usually takes the stairs and carries his or her backpack may suddenly feel that these tasks are too exhausting and request assistance.

Low self-esteem is also a common indicator of dysthymic disorder. Children with the disorder tend to experience a great deal of self-doubt and believe that they do not have the ability to be successful. Educators are usually the first to notice this characteristic because school activities require intense focus and expose the child to a variety of opportunities for success. When a child has low self-esteem, finishing work can become a problem, and other related depressive symptoms may appear. For instance, when an educator requests completion of an assignment, the child may cry, say, "I can't do it," and resist completing the work.

Similarly, poor concentration can be a symptom of dysthymic disorder in children. The child or adolescent may be unable to focus during lessons and may become preoccupied with depressive thoughts. These concentration problems may be exhibited both at home and school and usually are a source of frustration for all adults working with the child.

The final potential symptom of dysthymic disorder in children and adolescents is a sense of hopelessness, which is usually manifested as sadness or a general sense of giving up. Adults around the child may interpret the change as a lack of motivation rather than an endogenous symptom of depression.

Any of the previously mentioned symptoms may indicate dysthymic disorder in children and adolescents. For a diagnosis to be made, the child must have at least two symptoms that are present most of the time. The child may experience remission, but unless the remission exceeds 2 months, dysthymic disorder cannot be ruled out.

Classroom Behavior

There is no typical course of classroom behavior for children and adolescents who have dysthymic disorder. Their behavior is usually closely related to the specific symptoms that they experience daily. Children who exhibit symptoms of sadness and low self-esteem may be socially withdrawn in the classroom. They may be rarely noticed because they are not disruptive and remain focused on their schoolwork. Other children with dysthymic disorder may be irritable and, in turn, in conflict more often than other children. They may be disruptive and draw attention to themselves. Thus, it is essential that educators note changes in behavior that occur over time. When the child is disruptive, for instance, educators may experience frustration and doubt their ability to manage the classroom. In such a case, educators should recognize that the child's behavior is a symptom of emotional suffering rather than an intentional effort to disrespect the educator.

Because symptoms of dysthymic disorder must be present for 1 year for a diagnosis to be made, educators must communicate across grades. Otherwise, one educator may not see the behavioral changes associated with this disorder and simply assume that the behavior is normal for the child. This point is illustrated by the following vignette.

Tyler, age 10, lives with this mother and grandmother. One year ago, his father, the family's breadwinner, passed away in a car accident. In third grade, Tyler was a

gregarious, outgoing child with many friends. Educators described him as an enjoy-
able, stellar student. Now in fourth grade, Tyler's behavior has changed substantially.
He is withdrawn, quiet, and unsure of himself. He has trouble completing his assign-
ments on time and, as a result, is receiving low grades. He rarely speaks and does
not respond when educators ask him questions. In addition, he appears tired most
of the time.

Some educators may expect a child who is depressed to cry often. Although he
does not cry, Tyler shows the following symptoms of dysthymic disorder: low
self-esteem, poor concentration, and lethargy. He is clearly affected by his loss.
Furthermore, this sense of loss appears to have lasted for more than 1 year.
Educators must not overlook the fact that Tyler's behavior has changed over
time, and depression is not solely manifested in tears and sadness. Tyler requires
emotional support to work through the loss of his father. An educator who
recognizes Tyler's pain may be the first to initiate these processes.

MAJOR DEPRESSIVE DISORDER

Major depressive disorder significantly affects daily functioning but has a shorter
duration than dysthymic disorder. With major depressive disorder, mood dysfunction occurs for a minimum of 2 weeks. This 2-week (or longer) period is referred to
as a *major depressive episode*. To receive the diagnosis of major depressive disorder, a
child or adolescent must experience one of the following: a depressed mood, a
loss of interest and pleasure, or an irritable mood. Although the duration is short,
symptoms of major depressive disorder are intense and may return numerous
times after the first depressive episode. The diagnosis of major depressive disorder
is usually made after a reoccurring major depressive episode.

Characteristics

In addition to the previously described mood change, other symptoms must be
present. These can include changes in appetite, sleep disturbance, excessive guilt,
activity disturbance, fatigue, poor concentration, or thoughts of death or suicide.
All of these symptoms must be abnormal in nature and observable by others.

The changes in appetite and sleep disturbance are similar to those seen in
dysthymic disorder. Both are bidirectional and can occur in either extreme. For
example, the changes in appetite may be represented by increased appetite that
results in overeating or decreased appetite that results in undereating. The same
pattern may occur with sleep.

Inappropriate or excessive guilt is a feature of major depressive disorder. This guilt may manifest itself in self-blame, increased worry, or unrealistic negative evaluations of self-worth. Children or adolescents with major depressive disorder often misinterpret trivial day-to-day events as evidence of personal faults. The sense of worthlessness or guilt is intense and can be entirely irrational.

To be an indicator of major depressive disorder, activity disturbance must be observable by other people. They may notice psychomotor agitation (abnormal level of activity/movement) or psychomotor retardation (atypically slow movement, speech, or thinking). Psychomotor agitation is sometimes confused with hyperactivity because of the child's inability to sit still, pacing, hand wringing, or pulling or rubbing the skin. In children and adolescents, psychomotor retardation may show as slowed reactions when answering questions in the classroom or as a slow gait when moving around the school. Because these symptoms can signify other disorders, a clinician must use interview data, observations, and historical information about the duration of behavioral change to filter out competing diagnoses.

The fatigue that occurs in major depressive disorder resembles the lethargy that accompanies dysthymic disorder. The individual is tired, has low energy, and has difficulty completing daily tasks. Small tasks require great effort and are exhausting.

Poor concentration, which is also a symptom of dysthymic disorder, is evident in people with major depressive disorder. Many individuals with major depressive disorder report an impaired ability to think, concentrate, or make decisions. They are unable to focus on daily activities and to grasp new concepts and information. This is particularly distressing for those who previously demonstrated high concentration levels along with high levels of school success. In children, poor concentration during a major depressive episode may lead to a sudden drop in grades.

The final and commonly distressing symptom of major depressive disorder is thoughts of death or suicidal ideation (thoughts about causing intentional self-injury or death). The individual is preoccupied with thoughts of dying and/or suicidal ideation, but this is not always obvious to others. Instead, it may be manifested in behaviors such as withdrawing from others, giving away prized possessions, or cutting one's skin (i.e., self-injury). If an educator suspects that a student is experiencing suicidal ideation, an immediate referral should be made to the school counselor or school psychologist. This action is absolutely necessary because suicidal ideation may be acted on at any time.

Classroom Behavior

The classroom behavior of a child or adolescent with major depressive disorder reveals dysfunction that may vary on a day-to-day basis. Students who were once successful may become disruptive, withdrawn, angry, or sad. They are no longer able to complete their work. Changes in social relationships may also be observed. The students' friendships may be strained, and they may be hypersensitive to criticism, become easily frustrated, or lack the desire to maintain cordial relationships with others.

BIPOLAR DISORDER

Bipolar disorder is a mood disorder that combines features of major depressive disorder and another disorder called *mania*. Bipolar disorder involves waves of dysfunction, during which the individual experiences symptoms of major depression at times and symptoms of mania or hypomania at other times. (Mania and hypomania are described in the "Definitions" subsection.) Once called *manic-depression,* the disorder was renamed to signify the symptoms that appear in two (bipolar) directions.

There is a second pattern of mood swings for some children and adolescents. In addition to cycling between depression and mania, the individual might cycle from a calm state to anger and rage. For example, moods might shift from depression to euphoria to normal to anger within the same day.

Definitions

The features of bipolar disorder include diagnostic criteria for several other mood disorders. This section focuses on defining the terms necessary to understand the characteristics of bipolar disorder: manic episode, hypomanic episode, and mixed episode.

A manic episode is a period of time during which the child or adolescent's mood is disturbed to significant degree. The mood may be disturbed by inflated self-esteem, a decreased need for sleep (e.g., 3 hours or less), pressured speech or increased talkativeness, racing thoughts, distractibility, or psychomotor agitation. These symptoms occur in conjunction with an expansive, elevated mood or an irritable mood. This episode may last 1 week or more and can include psychotic features (e.g., hallucinations, delusions, memory loss). During manic episodes, the child or adolescent's daily functioning is significantly impaired.

A hypomanic episode is similar to a manic episode; however, the intensity and level of pathology is reduced. The individual may experience increased talkativeness, decreased need for sleep, and inflated self-esteem, but the intensity of these changes is not as extreme as in a manic episode. In addition, psychotic features are never associated with a hypomanic episode. Although the symptoms of the hypomanic episode are the same as those for a manic episode, there is no obvious disturbance in daily functioning.

During a mixed episode, the individual simultaneously meets criteria for a manic episode and a major depressive episode. The mixed episode must also occur during a 1-week (or longer) period.

Characteristics

Diagnosing bipolar disorder is complicated and must be made by an experienced clinician. The diagnosis is more commonly given to adolescents and adults than to children. Bipolar disorder does exist in children, however; it is simply far less common at early developmental levels.

There are two subtypes of bipolar disorder: bipolar I and bipolar II. To receive a diagnosis of bipolar I, the individual must be experiencing (or must have recently experienced) a manic, hypomanic, mixed, or major depressive episode. Prior to the current episode, the person must have had at least one manic or mixed episode. Thus, there must be a history of experiencing the most debilitating forms of mania. The manic symptoms cannot be due to drugs or the effects of any other substance. To receive a diagnosis of bipolar II, the individual must have the history of having at least one major depressive episode as well as one hypomanic episode. A person with bipolar II disorder has never experienced a manic or mixed episode.

Classroom Behavior

Individuals with bipolar disorder experience a variety of symptoms depending on the phase of the disorder. For example, an adolescent who is in a manic phase of bipolar I disorder may become extremely talkative and more able to complete multiple tasks within a short period of time. He or she may appear to be impulsive and may seek pleasure without regard for the consequences. When in a depressed phase, however, sadness, tiredness, and suicidal ideation may be present. The educator needs to take note of extreme changes in behavior that appear to be without transition. The following vignette exemplifies such changes.

Lisa is a 15-year-old whose personality has changed significantly in the past 2 years. Her parents and teachers had originally attributed this change to puberty but have recently begun to suspect that the problem is related to something else. Lisa goes through periods in which she is unresponsive, irritable, and withdrawn. She disconnects from her friends, family, and teachers and is resentful when people try to pull her out of her shell. These phases last for a few months or longer.

Over the past year, Lisa's parents noticed two occasions during which Lisa's mood peaked. During a 2-week period, Lisa was "like a tornado." She hardly slept, was in a fantastic mood, and talked for hours on end. Her father was concerned that she was taking drugs, but drug test results indicated that she was not using any illicit substances. This was confusing for Lisa's parents because there was no explanation for her abrupt change in mood.

bipolar I

• •

Scenarios like Lisa's are common in adolescents with bipolar I disorder. Because a significant change in behavior occurs for a short period of time, adults usually assume that drug use is a factor. The peak in Lisa's mood and the tornado description suggest a classic manic episode during a 2-week hiatus from depressive symptoms.

It is important to note that in addition to the swings from depression to mania shown in Lisa's case, some children and adolescents swing from being pleasant to being angry. It is not uncommon for students with bipolar disorder to have either type of mood swing within the same day.

CYCLOTHYMIC DISORDER

Cyclothymic disorder is less commonly known. It is best described as mood swings that are frequent and chronic and have existed for at least 1 year in children and adolescents.

Characteristics

frequent but less extreme

Cyclothymic disorder shares features with bipolar II disorder and is characterized by numerous periods with hypomanic symptoms as well as numerous periods with depressive symptoms. However, the depressive symptoms do not rise to the severity of a major depressive disorder. Furthermore, during the 1-year period, the child or adolescent may not be without the symptoms for more than 2 months at a time. Thus, the child has not experienced a major depressive disorder, a manic episode, or a mixed episode during the course of this mood disturbance.

Classroom Behavior

The classroom behavior of a child or adolescent with cyclothymic disorder is similar to that of an individual with bipolar II disorder. The primary difference is that with cyclothymic disorder, the behaviors are less extreme and the duration of each behavioral phase is shorter. For example, a preadolescent with bipolar II disorder may show depressive symptoms for 3 weeks and then show hypomanic symptoms for 1 week. In cyclothymic disorder, symptoms may vary every few days. The moods seem to sway back and forth like a pendulum.

SCHIZOAFFECTIVE DISORDER

Individuals with schizoaffective disorder have symptoms of bipolar I disorder while having some of the symptoms of schizophrenia. Thus, while experiencing feelings of sadness and other depressive symptoms, the individual also displays psychotic symptoms. The psychotic symptoms may appear in the form of auditory or visual hallucinations or delusional thoughts (irrational thoughts or fears that are unfounded and without evidence). The onset of schizoaffective disorder is typically in adolescence or early adulthood.

Characteristics

During the course of schizoaffective disorder, there is an uninterrupted period of time during which the person experiences a major depressive episode, a manic episode, or a mixed episode while also experiencing periods with delusions, hallucinations, disorganized speech, disorganized behavior, or emotional flatness (the lack of emotional expression). The symptoms are typically considered bizarre and alarming to individuals around the person. To meet the criteria for diagnosis, the features of schizophrenia must exist for least 2 weeks without the presence of the mood symptoms.

Classroom Behavior

Because schizoaffective disorder includes features of schizophrenia, it is easier for educators to notice the student's behavior. These children or adolescents usually are socially isolated and demonstrate unusual behaviors in the classroom. An educator might see the students regularly talk to themselves or respond to voices that no one else hears. The students may also describe bizarre thoughts or create unusual drawings that are uncharacteristic for a child or adolescent their age. In short, these children draw attention to themselves by their odd behavior and social awkwardness, as shown in the following vignette.

Ryan is a 16-year-old high school student who has a history of limited friendships, social awkwardness, and withdrawn behavior. The school psychologist has been monitoring Ryan for the past few months because he has shown increasingly odd behavior at school. Although he has always seemed depressed, he recently began to exhibit a strong odor. Ryan apparently had stopped showering and washing his face and hair. He also has reportedly been standing in the shadows talking to himself. The other students call Ryan "weird" and have become increasingly afraid of him. The school psychologist has decided to make an immediate appointment with Ryan and his parents to discuss a referral for mental health services.

- -

It is clear that Ryan has been struggling emotionally for some time. The new behaviors became a red flag for the school staff. It appears that Ryan is exhibiting symptoms of schizoaffective disorder; however, a referral is necessary because only a psychologist or psychiatrist can make a definitive diagnosis.

SUICIDE

Among 15- to 24-year-olds, suicide is the third leading cause of death. Among 5- to 14-year-olds, it is the sixth leading cause of death (American Academy of Child and Adolescent Psychiatry, 1998). It is essential that educators are aware of this problem and alert to clues that a student might be at risk for suicide.

Suicidal behavior in children and adolescents includes suicidal ideation and acts that cause intentional self-injury (suicide attempt) or death (suicide). Suicidal behavior among children and adolescents involves a continuum of nonsuicidal behavior to suicidal ideas, suicide attempts, and suicide (Pfeffer, 1986).

Intent to harm oneself is an essential concept in defining suicidal behavior. This concept might be difficult to establish with children, who might not associate their threats (e.g., "I'm going to stab myself") with death. Children might say things only to upset their parents. Even if the reason or intent is unclear, however, the overt behavior is potentially life threatening. It is important for teachers to report any related comments or concerns to school officials and to let school-based mental health professionals determine the intent. Children and adolescents who commit self-injurious acts are potentially suicidal.

Children and adolescents may attempt suicide by shooting, hanging, suffocating, stabbing, burning, or drowning themselves; running into traffic; or ingesting harmful substances. Firearms are the most common means of youth suicide (Brent, Perper, & Allman, 1987), although this method is used more often among young men. Young women, who attempt suicide more frequently than young men, predominantly ingest lethal substances in suicide attempts. This gender difference in suicidal methods may account for why successful suicide is higher among men than among women.

Suicidal behavior is a complex problem and is influenced by cultural factors, the presence of psychiatric symptoms and psychiatric disorders, and stressful life events. Alcohol and drugs are a contributing factor. Youth suicide victims have a higher prevalence of drug abuse. In the San Diego Suicide Study, 53% of the younger people who committed suicide abused substances. The most frequently abused substances were alcohol, marijuana, and cocaine (Fowler, Rich, & Young, 1986; Rich, Young, & Fowler, 1986).

Mood disorders are frequently associated with suicidal ideation and actions. However, there are no known clinical findings to distinguish depressed youth who are suicidal from those who are not. Being depressed does not mean that a student has suicidal thoughts or intents, but educators should be alert to this possibility.

In youth, there is a significant relationship between suicidal behavior and stressful life events. Preadolescents who reported suicidal ideation or suicide attempts had higher rates of cumulative stressful life events than nonsuicidal preadolescents. Stressful events include family deaths, separation from relatives, family disruptions and discord, birth of siblings, illness, hospitalization, and multiple family moves. Similarly, compared with depressed nonsuicidal adolescents and adolescents who were not depressed, adolescents who attempted suicide had more lifetime and recent stressful life events (Pfeffer, 2002).

Efforts to prevent youth suicide must include programs in schools. Such prevention models focus on encouraging adolescents to seek help if they recognize suicide risk in their peers. Thus, students are encouraged to share their concerns with an adult if a friend expresses suicidal intent. Teachers must be sensitive to any suggestions that a student is at risk for suicide and must know where to take their concerns. A plan of intervention must be in place to explore whether suicide threats are representative of true intent.

Strong evidence suggests that the availability of firearms is significantly associated with youth suicide risk (Shah, Hoffman, Wake, & Marine, 2000). National efforts to prevent youth suicide should also require better consideration on how to protect children and adolescents from access to firearms.

TREATMENT OF MOOD DISORDERS

There are a variety of treatments for mood disorders. The method selected depends on the disorder in question, along with the particular nature of the symptoms expressed. This section describes individual and family therapy, pharmacological intervention, and school-based intervention.

Individual Therapy

Individual therapy is the frontline treatment for mood disorders. It is usually provided by a licensed clinician outside the school. The range of professionals who can provide this form of treatment include licensed psychologists, licensed mental health counselors, and licensed clinical social workers. The family usually acquires this form of assistance on its own, but there may times when the teacher or another school staff member recommends such an intervention to the student's parents.

Educator's Role in Providing Information   When a referral is made, the clinician typically meets with the family and child to obtain authorization for treatment. During the initial phase of treatment, collaboration with school staff is often helpful in creating an individual treatment plan. At this time, the clinician may contact educators to obtain more information. Prior to this contact, however, the clinician must have obtained a signed release from the student's parents or their authorization to release information. An appropriately completed release form allows the clinician and educator (or school staff) to have regular contact with one another for 90 days. If additional contact is needed after the initial 90 days, a new release should be signed and dated. It is recommended that the educator prepares a history of the child's behavior and emotional functioning at school. This is because at the time of initial clinician–educator contact, the clinician will want to know the reason for the referral, such as whether a specific event triggered the referral process. The educator then has the opportunity to share his or her perceptions of the child and a chronology of the changes in the child's behavior. This information should be discussed in detail because most mental health professionals value the expertise of educators and recognize that they are the best source of information for academic and social functioning concerns. To organize the information into a treatment plan, however, it is beneficial for educators to share only information that is pertinent to the referral questions. For example, if a referral is made due to changes in academic performance, specifics about performance before and after the change would be helpful. An example regarding a change in personality and behavior might note that an adolescent suddenly begins to wear only black to school and refuses to socialize with members of his or her regular peer group.

Concrete data collection also helps the development of individual treatment plans. On occasion, clinicians will ask educators to complete a behavior rating scale for a referred child or adolescent. Although behavior rating scales usually take 15–20 minutes to complete, the information obtained is invaluable to the clinician. Therefore, it is essential for the educator to complete it as soon as possible. When a behavior rating scale is not requested, other data may help the clinician. Frequency counts are an easy way for educators to collect information quickly and concisely. The educator can quickly document the frequency of a particular behavior by tallying its expression during a given period of time. In addition, if the school psychologist has been involved, he or she might complete a functional behavioral assessment (FBA). The FBA may supplement other data collected at school. Overall, data should concretely document the nature of the disorder. Observable data are the most valuable. Opinions can be helpful but should not be the primary source of information.

The conclusion of the clinician–educator conference is an appropriate time for the educator to ask questions about serving the child in the classroom. The educator may obtain initial recommendations at this time but will likely receive more feedback once the individual treatment plan has been defined. Ideally, the door for additional communication is now open and the educator is part of the treatment process, even though it occurs outside of the school setting. Table 11.1 may assist educators in their collaboration with mental health professionals.

Family Therapy

When treating mood disorders in children and adolescents, family therapy is typically provided as an adjunct to individual therapy. Family therapy is helpful in working through family dynamics that may contribute to the child or adolescent's symptoms. If there is a genetic predisposition to depression (e.g., a history of depression or mood disorders on both sides of the family), family therapy is helpful in determining which approaches have been useful in assisting other family members. Family therapy also helps promote empathy among family members and teaches all members to support one another during times of suffering. Furthermore, the initial evaluation in family therapy can help in determining

Table 11.1. Steps for educators conferring with mental health professionals

Request a copy of the signed release form for sharing information.

Explain the reason for the referral (if applicable).

Provide a history of the child's behavior and a chronology of behavioral changes.

Describe academic and social concerns.

Provide concrete data.

Inform the clinician about interventions attempted (if applicable).

Ask questions pertinent to assisting the child's daily functioning at school.

whether medication compliance is likely if medication is deemed necessary. Although family therapy is a needed treatment approach for children and adolescents, educators are rarely involved in the process. If the family wishes to have the clinician consult with the teacher, releases are signed and ongoing communication may occur between the clinician and teacher. These consultations are useful in developing and modifying the treatment plan.

Pharmacological Intervention

Medications for mood disorders are usually prescribed by a child and adolescent psychiatrist, but they may also be prescribed by a family practice physician who is working in collaboration with the treating clinician. A wide range of antidepressant medications may be used with children and adolescents (Bezchlibnyk-Butler & Jeffries, 2001). Appendix B at the end of this book lists antidepressant medications that may be prescribed for children and adolescents who have the disorders described in this chapter. These medications are usually prescribed when the child or adolescent has a long history of symptoms that are debilitating and interfere with all aspects of daily functioning. Pharmacological treatment is rarely done in isolation (i.e., without individual and family therapy) because medication alone will not increase coping skills. Medication typically helps manage the physical manifestations of the mood disorder (e.g., insomnia, appetite changes, irritability, elevating mood) but does not provide an outlet for the feelings and behaviors that have been internalized over time. Individual and family therapy can provide this outlet and a path to resolution of underlying conflicts that may have preceded the mood disorder symptoms.

School-Based Intervention

Mood disorders may affect the educational functioning of some children and adolescents. If a disorder influences a student's ability to learn, then he or she may be eligible to receive special education support from the school. According to the regulations for the Individuals with Disabilities Education Act (IDEA) Amendments of 1997 (PL 105-17), children with emotional or behavioral difficulties may be suffering from a "serious emotional disturbance," which is

> A condition exhibiting one or more of the following characteristics over a long period of time and to a marked degree that adversely affects a child's educational performance:
>
> a) An inability to learn that cannot be explained by intellectual, sensory, or health factors;
> b) An inability to build or maintain satisfactory interpersonal relationships with peers and teachers;
> c) Inappropriate types of behavior or feelings under normal circumstances;
> d) A general pervasive mood of unhappiness or depression; or
> e) A tendency to develop physical symptoms or fears associated with personal or school problems. ("Assistance to States," 2002)

A child with serious emotional disturbance qualifies for special education support services. The school psychologist can assist in the determination of special education eligibility. By completing a psychological evaluation that includes an FBA, the school psychologist provides data that can identify serious emotional disturbance. The school psychologist evaluates the student and collects data from a variety of sources before the decision is made. Using these data, special education eligibility is ultimately determined by a team of professionals that sometimes includes outside mental health professionals.

When the student qualifies for services under the serious emotional disturbance eligibility category, some schools offer support services through a change in educational placement. This may mean full-day educational placement in a special education classroom. A child who requires full-day placement usually exhibits behavioral problems that require frequent adult intervention. Special education classroom ratios offer better opportunities for the teacher and student to interact on a one-to-one basis. Other situations might include partial-day services, in which the student is in a special education classroom for the portions of the day that are most difficult for him or her and also receive counseling support from the school counselor or school psychologist. A third option is to use a full inclusion model. This model allows the student to remain in the general education classes full time and to receive ancillary services to meet his or her emotional needs. Such ancillary services may include—but are not limited to—weekly individual counseling with the school counselor or school psychologist or participation in a counseling group. The placement decision is made by the multidisciplinary special education team. As with other students who receive special education services, the team of professionals is required to place the child or adolescent in the least restrictive environment (LRE) to meet their educational needs. The LRE is the most appropriate setting for the student that provides the fewest special education services. Of the three aforementioned placement options, the inclusion model is the least restrictive and full-day placement is the most restrictive. The team is to choose the setting that is most appropriate for the student and has the fewest restrictions.

Classroom Intervention Strategies Although mood disorders are diagnosed and treated by mental health professionals, educators can play an important supportive role. Classroom interventions can be implemented to support a student with a mood disorder and to facilitate a more supportive learning environment. McCarney (1993) provided a useful manual to assist teachers and other education professionals in developing classroom interventions for a variety of behavioral problems. This section includes general classroom approaches as well as strategies to improve social skills in children or adolescents with mood disorders.

Keep a Consistent Routine Educators should plan the overall daily schedule carefully and stick to the routine. Children with mood disorders have difficulty adjusting to abrupt changes in routine or structure. Educators can prepare students for anticipated transitions by providing verbal warnings of upcoming changes and adequate time to complete tasks (Frieman, 2001; Pierangelo & Giuliani, 2001).

Watch Carefully for Student Status Changes   All preadolescent and adolescent students deal with peer conflicts at some point. Educators should observe social status changes over time and attempt to intervene if a child's popularity changes dramatically. For example, if a student who was always a leader and trendsetter suddenly loses his or her friendship network, it is appropriate for the educator to speak individually with the student. Such a conversation might provide information about the student's self-perception as well as his or her reactions to this new social situation. If appropriate, a classroom intervention may be implemented to develop solutions before there is escalation to a psychological problem. For example, teachers may create opportunities to have students compliment one another or teachers may encourage the student by acknowledging the child's strengths publicly.

Promote Organizational Skills   Classroom approaches that encourage consistent organization assist all students. Yet individuals with mood disorders often experience confusion and concentration problems, so strategies that assist in the development of better organizational skills can reduce the impact of such symptoms. Educators may teach strategies such as the use of time management charts, homework notebooks, and schedule books or organizers to encourage better organization. For younger children, responsibility charts are an optimal approach to promoting both organization and adherence to a routine. These charts should include all of the activities that need to be completed as the day progresses (Rhode, Jenson, & Reavis, 1997).

Develop Positive Social Skills   Many students with mood disorders have difficulty connecting socially with their peers. As a result, strategies need to be implemented to support the development of positive social skills. Although individuals with mood disorders experience extreme feelings, sometimes they are out of touch with the nature of their feelings. Thus, counseling interventions can support these students in learning how to communicate their feelings appropriately rather than "falling apart."

Encourage Appropriate Expression of Feelings   Children with mood disorders usually have difficulty regulating their emotions. Many have problems expressing their feelings in an appropriate way. Inappropriate expression of feelings includes behavior such as aggression and tantrums. More appropriate methods include clear communication and articulating emotions. During times of conflict, educators may remind students to stop and think about how their body feels. They may discuss how students can identify feelings by listening to their body signals. For example, when angry, students may feel hot or shaky. Once feelings are identified, the students may discuss alternative responses to conflicts while acknowledging the feelings of each person involved. Educators may regularly encourage such interactions by reinforcing students when they spontaneously express feelings in an appropriate manner.

Utilize Local Resources   Most schools have counselors who form groups to provide emotional support to several children at once. These are counseling groups where the children have a confidential forum to discuss their feelings. The groups may include a psychoeducational curriculum designed around a particular issue (e.g., grief). Similarly, an educator may ask the school counselor to develop, for example, a group for building social skills. This would allow the educator to refer students who are likely to benefit from such services.

Use Role-Play Opportunities to Promote Positive Social Connections   When using role-play activities, students learn how to behave in new situations that resemble past situations with which they struggled. For example, making friends is difficult for some children with mood disorders. A role-play activity allows them to practice approaching a new person and starting a friendship. Educators can first model the appropriate behavior and then provide coaching and feedback as the child practices the new behavior. The more opportunities the children have to practice, the more likely they will develop better social skills. Educators should make the classroom training realistic and closely relate the activities to the child's actual experiences.

Place Isolated Children in Leadership Roles   Children with mood disorders may withdraw and become unable to connect with others. In some cases, placing them in leadership roles increases their self-esteem. This leadership can occur in the form of tutoring, receiving a classroom responsibility, or participating in an extracurricular activity. The educator must be careful to ensure that the child possesses the skills (and/or has an interest) in the area before assigning any new responsibility. If chosen appropriately, the leadership opportunity may provide encouraging experiences from which the student can relearn positive social skills.

CONCLUSION

Dysthymic disorder and major depressive disorder are the most common manifestations of depression among children and adolescents. Bipolar disorder, consisting of depressive as well as manic or hypomanic symptoms, is less common in children and adolescents but is more severe because of the intensity of the mood swings and the need for medication. Cyclothymic disorder is similar to bipolar disorder in that there are symptoms of depression and hypomania; however, cyclothymic disorder includes more rapid cycling than bipolar disorder. Schizoaffective disorder rarely occurs in children and is the least common mood disorder in adolescents. It includes features of depression along with psychotic symptoms.

Mood disorders are usually treated by a combination of individual and family therapy, along with pharmacological intervention. The most successful interventions usually employ a multimodal, multimethod treatment approach. For example, an adolescent with bipolar I disorder may receive individual and family therapy, psychiatric monitoring with medication, and weekly counseling at school. Ideally, all adults working with this adolescent collaborate and coordinate his or her care. School-based interventions may also be provided through special education services. In younger children, this support may include placement with a teacher who has expertise in working with children who have what IDEA refers to as "serious emotional disturbance." Full-day inclusion classes are more common at the elementary level than in middle and high schools.

General educators may also assist children or adolescents with mood disorders. This assistance supports the students' coping skills and adaptability while supplementing the care provided by mental health professionals. Educators may work with children on the development of routines and organizational skills, and they may intervene when a child's social status changes. Educators may also employ interventions to increase social skills, such as practicing the appropriate expression of feelings, referring students to social skills groups, role-playing in the classroom, and assigning leadership roles to children who are isolated.

Overall, mood disorders are common in children and adolescents. With support from all adults working with a child, these disorders are treatable, and the child usually can recover fully. For this level of support to occur, collaboration among all stakeholders is essential. Educators must realize that most mental health professionals perceive educators as a valuable resource in supporting the treatment of mental health issues such as mood disorders.

REFERENCES

American Academy of Child and Adolescent Psychiatry. (1998). *Facts for Families No. 10: Teen suicide.* Retrieved October 28, 2003, from http://www.aacap.org/publications/factsfam/suicide.htm

American Psychiatric Association. (2000). *Diagnostic and statistical manual of mental disorders* (4th ed., text rev.). Washington, DC: Author.

Assistance to States for the Education of Children with Disabiliteis, 34 C.F.R. § 300 (2002).

Bezchlibnyk-Butler, K.Z., & Jeffries, J.J. (Eds.). (2001). *Clinical handbook of psychotropic drugs* (11th ed.). Kirkland, WA: Hogrefe & Huber Publishers.

Brent, D.A., Perper, J.A., & Allman, C.J. (1987). Alcohol, firearms, and suicide among youth: Temporal trends in Allegheny County, Pennsylvania, 1960–1983. *The Journal of the American Medical Association, 257,* 3369–3372.

Frieman, B.B. (2001). *What teachers need to know about children at risk.* New York: McGraw Hill.

Fowler, R.C., Rich, C.L., & Young, D. (1986). San Diego Suicidal Study: Substance abuse in youth cases. *Archives of General Psychiatry, 43,* 962–965.

Individuals with Disabilities Education Act (IDEA) Amendments of 1997, PL 105-17, 20 U.S.C. §§ 1400 *et seq.*

McCarney, S.B. (1993). *Pre-referral intervention manual: The most common learning and behavior problems encountered in the educational environment.* Columbia, MO: Hawthorne Educational Services.

Pfeffer, C.R. (1986). *The suicidal child.* New York: The Guilford Press.

Pfeffer, C.R. (2002). Suicidal behavior in children and adolescents: Causes and management. In M. Lewis (Ed.), *Child and adolescent psychiatry. A comprehensive textbook* (pp. 796–805). Philadelphia: Lippincott Williams & Wilkins.

Pierangelo, R., & Giuliani, G.A. (2001). *What every teacher should know about students with special needs: Promoting success in the classroom.* Champaign, IL: Research Press.

Rhode, G., Jenson, W.R., & Reavis, H.K. (1997). *The tough kid book: Practical classroom management strategies.* Longmont, CO: Sopris West.

Rich, C.L., Young, D., & Fowler, R.C. (1986). San Diego Suicidal Study: Young versus old subjects. *Archives of General Psychiatry, 43,* 577–582.

Shah, S., Hoffman, R.E., Wake, I., & Marine, W.M. (2000). Adolescent suicide and household access to firearms in Colorado. Results of a case-count control study. *Journal of Adolescent Health, 26*(3), 157–163.

U.S. Department of Education. (2000). *Twenty-second annual report to Congress on the implementation of the Individuals with Disabilities Education Act.* Washington, DC: Author.

Behavioral Disorders

Frank M. Kline

In some ways, the disorders covered in this section are the most familiar to educators. Schools are constantly confronted with discipline issues rooted in disputes between peers, poor adjustment to life issues, and challenging behaviors. Chapters 12, 13, and 14 seek to help educators understand these subjects in more depth.

Most students have problems getting along with their peers at some time. Chapter 12 explores peer problems, explaining the difference between typical peer disputes and ones that may require further intervention. The chapter helps educators discern when students may need further evaluation for peer problems.

As with peer issues, at some time almost all students face a crisis that could create adjustment problems. Chapter 13 seeks to equip educators to understand the difference between "normal" adjustment problems and those that might require referral to a mental health professional.

Finally, even generally well-behaved children occasionally have tantrums. When challenging behaviors manifest in school situations, educators must attend to them in a way that serves the child's best interests. Educators also need to know when those behavioral problems are severe enough to merit referral to another source of help. Chapter 14 provides information to help address these issues.

By using the concepts and vocabulary common to the mental health field, Section IV provides the background information necessary for educators to collaborate with mental health workers. Furthermore, the section provides an overview of diagnostic procedures and symptoms, better equipping educators to understand when referral is necessary. For behavioral disorders in particular, this distinction is critical.

12

Peer Problems

**Beverly J. Wilson, Kathleen Lehman,
Katherine S. Quie, and Tamara Buker Parrott**

Chapter Concepts

- Common methods of assessing children's social problems
- Likely etiologies of children's social problems
- Risk and protective factors related to children's social problems
- Role of educators in treatment and care of children with social problems
- Elements of successful intervention programs

Peer relationships are important for children's development. In addition to providing opportunities for play and intimacy, peers encourage language, cognitive, and moral development (Garvey, 1986; Hartup, 1978, 1983; Piaget, 1932/1965). Evidence also suggests that children who have difficulty in their peer relationships are at considerable risk for continuing problems throughout their development (Parker & Asher, 1987). They are more likely than other children to have academic problems and drop out of school early and are at risk for juvenile delinquency and adult crime. There is also evidence that girls with peer relationship problems are at increased risk for teen pregnancy (Underwood, Kupersmidt, & Coie, 1996). It is important to understand factors that contribute to children's peer relationship difficulties because this information helps educators and researchers identify and intervene with children who are at particular risk for continuing social and conduct problems.

This chapter discusses how to identify children with social problems, the characteristics of these children, and potential causes of social problems in children. The chapter also presents risk and protective factors within the child, family, and community that can contribute to or mitigate children's social problems. Characteristics of teachers and schools that may assist these children are a particular focus of this chapter. Finally, features of effective interventions for children with social problems are presented.

METHODS FOR ASSESSING CHILDREN'S SOCIAL PROBLEMS

Children with peer problems typically have deficits in the areas of social competence and social skills (Merrell, 2003), which are related but distinct concepts. Because these terms are used throughout the chapter, this section defines these terms. *Social competence* is a broad term used to describe children's ability to develop and maintain positive relationships with others and to appropriately end negative ones (Kupersmidt, Coie, & Dodge, 1990; Merrell, 2003; Parker & Asher, 1987). *Social skills* have been defined as a component of social competence and are the specific behaviors needed to achieve different social tasks, such as beginning a conversation or joining peers' play (Gresham, Sugai, & Horner, 2001). Figure 12.1 illustrates the relationship between social competence, social skills, and peer relationships (Merrell, 2003).

A number of different methods have been used to assess the quality of children's peer relationships. These include assessments of children's social competence and social skills as well as their social status with peers. Methods for gathering this information include teacher and parent ratings of children's peer relationships, peer assessments, and direct observations of children's interaction patterns with peers. These methods are discussed in the following subsections.

Teacher-Completed Assessments

Teacher rating scales have several advantages. They are less time intensive and more efficient than other assessments. These scales are good measures of long-standing behavioral and emotional problems (Sattler, 2002) and are useful tools

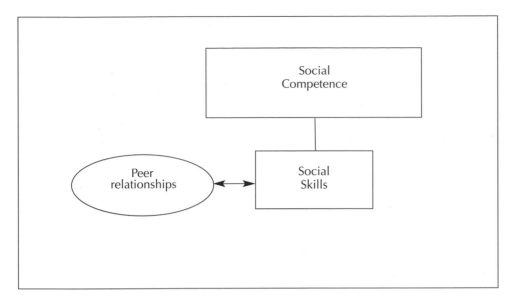

Figure 12.1. The relationship between social competence, social skills, and peer relationships. (From Merrell, K.W. [2003]. *Behavioral, social, and emotional assessment of children and adolescents* [2nd ed., p. 311]. Mahwah, NJ: Lawrence Erlbaum Associates; adapted by permission.)

for screening children who are at risk for or are just beginning to develop problems (Merrell, 2003). Some research indicates that teachers may be more accurate reporters than parents of children's social acceptance and conduct problems (Cole, Gondoli, & Peeke, 1998; Stanger & Lewis, 1993). Teachers also possess important and useful knowledge about the children in their classrooms and may be less biased than the child's peers about social skills and behavior because they are not part of the child's peer network (Rubin, Bukowski, & Parker, 1998). For example, teachers have numerous opportunities to observe children interacting with same-age peers in school settings such as in the classroom, playground, and lunchroom. Yet, as authority figures in the classroom, teachers are usually likely to make different value judgments about certain child behaviors than a child's peers. Teachers also are not privy to many events that peers experience outside the classroom.

Table 12.1 lists some of the most popular assessments that teachers (among others) may complete. These rating scales are discussed in the following subsections. It is important to note that information from rating scales should be interpreted by individuals with formal training in school assessments, such as school counselors or school psychologists.

Achenbach System of Empirically Based Assessment The Achenbach System of Empirically Based Assessment (ASEBA; Achenbach, 2001) contains a Child Behavior Checklist (CBCL), Teacher Report Form (TRF), and Youth Self-Report (YSR). The teacher-completed TRF measures areas of competence (i.e., social relations, school, and activities) and behavioral difficulties, including social problems and aggression. The TRF can be divided into two broad areas of concern: internalizing problems (e.g., anxiety, sadness) and externalizing problems (e.g., aggression, rule breaking).

Table 12.1. Common tools for assessing child behavior

Assessment	Rater(s)	Age or grade range
Achenbach System of Empirically Based Assessment (ASEBA; Achenbach, 2001)	Parent, teacher, child	$1^1/2$–18 years
Child Behavior Checklist (CBCL)	Parent	$1^1/2$–5, 6–18
Teacher Report Form (TRF)	Teacher	$1^1/2$–5, 6–18
Youth Self-Report (YSR)	Child	11–18
Behavior Assessment System for Children (BASC; Reynolds & Kamphaus, 1992)	Parent, teacher, child	4–18 years (8–18 for self-report)
School Social Behavior Scales (SSBS; Merrell, 1993)	Teacher	Kindergarten–grade 12
Social Skills Rating System (SSRS; Gresham & Elliott, 1990)	Parent, teacher	Preschool–grade 12 (grades 3–12 for self-report)

Behavior Assessment System for Children   The Behavior Assessment System for Children (BASC; Reynolds & Kamphaus, 1992) is similar to the TRF in that it measures areas of difficulties (i.e., behavioral and emotional problems) and competence (i.e., social, leadership, and study skills). In addition, the BASC divides the problems into internalizing behaviors (e.g., anxiety, withdrawal, sadness) and externalizing behaviors (e.g., rule breaking, aggression, hyperactivity).

School Social Behavior Scales   The School Social Behavior Scales (SSBS; Merrell, 1993) assess children's social behavior in the school setting. Its two components include social competence (i.e., self-management, academic achievement, and interpersonal skills) and problematic negative social behavior (i.e., aggression, irritability, hostility, demanding behaviors, and disruptive behaviors).

Social Skills Rating System   The Social Skills Rating System (SSRS; Gresham & Elliott, 1990) provides an assessment of children's social skills and problem behaviors. The social skills component measures children's assertion, self-control, and cooperation skills. The problem behaviors component of the SSRS includes externalizing problems (e.g., arguing, aggression), internalizing problems (e.g., anxiety, low self-esteem, sadness), and hyperactivity.

Peer-Completed Assessments

A second method that researchers and educators use to identify children with social problems involves investigating how well children are liked by their peers. To determine a child's social status with his or her peers, children in a particular group, such as a school classroom, are asked to identify a few children with whom they like to play with the most (positive nominations) and those they like to play with the least (negative nominations). Other versions of this interview ask children who they like or who they like to work with the most and the least. These are commonly referred to as *sociometric interviews,* and the results can be used to

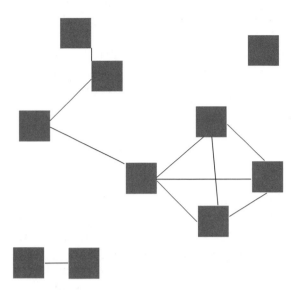

Figure 12.2. Sample sociogram. Squares represent different children, and lines represent associations between individual children. (From THE DEVELOPMENT OF CHILDREN by Michael Cole & Sheila Cole. © 1989, 1993, 1996, 2001 by Michael Cole and Sheila Cole. Used with permission of Worth Publishers.)

construct a *sociogram,* or a visual representation of how every child in the group feels about every other child (Rubin et al., 1998; see Figure 12.2). This technique is also used to categorize children into several different groups according to their popularity or social status within the group (see Coie, Dodge, & Coppotelli, 1982, for more information on these assessments). As can be seen in Table 12.2, *popular* children receive many positive nominations but no or very few negative nominations. These children are well liked and have many playmates. In contrast, children who receive many negative nominations and few positive nominations from peers have low social status and are commonly referred to as *peer-rejected* for research purposes. Children who receive a high number of positive and negative nominations are called *controversial.* Those who receive very few nominations, either positive or negative, are referred to as *neglected* (or socially isolated). These children can often be observed watching a group of peers from a distance but not interacting with them. The following subsections review the characteristics of children according to their social status with peers.

Popular Children Although a number of studies have found that children's social status with peers is related to their physical attractiveness (Boyatzis, Baloff, &

Table 12.2. Categorization of children into groups according to their popularity, per peer interview

Category	Positive nominations	Negative nominations
Popular	Many	Few or none
Peer-rejected	Few	Many
Neglected	Few	Few
Controversial	Many	Many

Durieux, 1998), their behavior with peers also plays a prominent role. In contrast with peer-rejected children, popular children are generally more socially skilled. They are better at initiating interactions with peers, engage in more prosocial and cooperative behavior, and are better able to regulate their emotions and behavior in social situations (Denham & Holt, 1993; Eisenberg et al., 1993; Ladd, Price, & Hart, 1988). Compared with less popular children, popular children tend to be more socially active and have higher cognitive and social skills. They are also less likely to engage in disruptive and aggressive behavior (Newcomb, Bukowski, & Pattee, 1993).

Peer-Rejected Children   Most of the behavior patterns and characteristics of popular children and of peer-rejected children are polar opposites. Peer-rejected children have lower social and cognitive skills and are more withdrawn and aggressive (Newcomb et al., 1993). Aggression is the most persistent behavior pattern associated with peer rejection. Approximately 50% of these children are rejected because of aggressive, disruptive, and impulsive behavior (French, 1990). Another important finding shows that peer-rejected children lack many of the positive social skills and behaviors that characterize popular children. Peer rejection is also associated with negative outcomes throughout development. In a meta-analysis of studies examining the outcomes of different social status, Parker and Asher (1987) found that peer-rejected children were at increased risk for having academic problems, dropping out of school, and committing crimes as adolescents and adults. This was not true for neglected children. Later research indicated that peer-rejected children are at risk for developing both externalizing and internalizing problems (Coie, Lochman, Terry, & Hyman, 1992; Kupersmidt, Coie, & Dodge, 1990; Zakriski & Coie, 1996).

Peer-rejected children who are also aggressive are at increased risk compared with those who are rejected but not aggressive. These children are more likely than nonaggressive peer-rejected children to overestimate their popularity with peers and to misinterpret the benign behaviors of peers as hostile (Dodge, 1980). These children tend to remain socially rejected even when they move to a new social setting (Asher & Dodge, 1986). Once they develop a reputation as being threatening or untrustworthy, they have a difficult time gaining peer acceptance, even when their behavior improves (Asher & Coie, 1990; Putallaz & Wasserman, 1990). For example, once their negative reputation is established in a group, group members tend to interpret the behavior of aggressive/rejected children as being aggressive or unfriendly, even when objective observations indicate it is not (Hymel, Wagner, & Butler, 1990). Thus, it is difficult for peer-rejected children to change their social status within a group. Over time, their lack of social success limits their options for developing peer relationships to other peer-rejected and aggressive children.

Controversial Children   Controversial children are actively disliked by some peers and well liked by others. These children tend to be highly aggressive but balance these negative behaviors with more positive ones, such as using humor or other social skills to maintain relationships with certain peers (Newcomb et al., 1993). Although controversial children are like peer-rejected children in that they have high levels of aggressive behavior, they have higher levels of the positive social qualities found in popular children. Their higher levels of sociability, cognitive skills, and positive social behavior appear to buffer them from peer rejection (Parkhurst & Asher, 1992). Controversial children are more likely to be identified by sociometric interviews with peers than by teacher report (Newcomb et al., 1993). It is likely that these children are more aware and better able to control their displays of aggression than rejected children. Thus, teachers and other adults are less likely to observe these negative behaviors than peers.

Controversial status is related to negative outcomes. Underwood and colleagues (1996) found that girls who had controversial social status in fourth grade were more likely than other girls, including rejected or aggressive girls, to become adolescent mothers. Controversial and aggressive girls who gave birth did so earlier in adolescence than other adolescent mothers.

Neglected Children Neglected children are generally less sociable than popular or average-status children (i.e., children whose social status falls between that of peer-rejected and popular children). They are also less aggressive than children in the other status groups, including children with average social status (Newcomb et al., 1993). Neglected children are not actively disliked or thought of as possessing negative traits; rather, they are simply not as well known by peers as more popular or average-status children. They also have better academic skills, fewer behavior problems in school, and are better liked by teachers than average-status children (Wentzel & Asher, 1995). The status of neglected children tends to be less stable over time than that of peer-rejected children (Asher & Coie, 1990; Cillessen, Vanijzendoorn, Van Lieshorst, & Hartup, 1992). Most research indicates that these children are not at increased risk for negative long-term outcomes (Newcomb et al., 1993).

Behavioral Observations of Children's Social Skills

A third way that researchers and educators investigate children's peer relationships involves examining their behavior during common social situations. To be most effective, these observations should be conducted by someone who is not aware of children's current social status or problems (i.e., a person who is "blind" to the target child's previous peer problems). Previous experiences with or knowledge about the child frequently influence one's perceptions. When blind observers are used, behavioral observations are thought to be the most valid way of assessing children's social skills (Elliott & Gresham, 1987). A number of structured observation systems have been developed to record these observations. Two of the most psychometrically sound and frequently used behavioral observation systems are the Peer Social Behavior Code (Walker & Severson, 1992) and the Target/Peer Interaction Code (Shinn, Ramsey, Walker, Steiber, & O'Neil, 1987). Readers should refer to Merrell (2003) for more information about behavioral assessments.

The way that young children solve problems inherent in social tasks is a central aspect of peer-related social competence. Therefore, kindergarten and elementary school teachers may also gather information about children's social skills by watching how they solve certain social tasks, such as how they resolve conflicts or, particularly, how they attempt to enter others' play.

Entry Behavior   Entry into the activities of others is a common task that serves as a prerequisite for further interaction with peers. To be successful at entry, children need to understand the frame of reference of others (i.e., their play theme) and incorporate this information into entry bids (Phillips, Shenker, & Revitz, 1951; Putallaz & Gottman, 1981). Strategies that communicate an understanding of a group's frame of reference include making group-oriented statements, imitation, and other behaviors that complement the group's activity. The following vignette highlights common difficulties experienced by children with peer problems when they attempt to join the play of others.

A group of children are building a Lego castle at a classroom table. Jimmy has just returned to the classroom after using the restroom. He is 6 years old and loves playing with Legos. He quickly walks toward a group of children building things with Legos and says, "Hey, the tower should be here and it needs a moat," as he takes Lego pieces off the castle and begins building his tower. The other children in the group become upset and tell Jimmy to leave because they do not want to play with him.

• •

Rejected children are less successful than more popular children at entering the play of others; they are less likely to use the group's frame of reference and are more likely to use entry bids that are disruptive and redirect the group's attention to themselves (Dodge, Schlundt, Schocken, & Delugach, 1983; Dodge & Somberg, 1987; Putallaz, 1983; Putallaz & Gottman, 1981). For example, these children are more likely than popular children to make self-referent statements, disagree with others, or make statements about their own wants and needs. These strategies result in high rates of entry failure. Children who tend to be neglected by peers are more likely than peer-rejected or popular children to hover in close proximity to others and watch their play, which usually results in their being ignored by other children (Dodge et al., 1983). Popular children are more successful at assessing information concerning the group's frame of reference and generating successful entry strategies (Dodge et al., 1983; Pettit, McClaskey, Brown, & Dodge, 1987; Putallaz, 1983; Putallaz & Gottman, 1981; Putallaz & Wasserman, 1989).

A second skill associated with successful entry into other's play involves delivering entry bids in a well-timed and appropriate manner. Children need to wait for breaks in the group members' conversations before making comments to the group. They also need to wait for others to physically make room for them rather than pushing their way into the group. Peer-rejected children and children with learning problems tend to deliver their entry attempts in a poorly timed and intrusive manner (Wilson, 1999, 2004). Such entry attempts can increase children's negative reputation with peers.

Clinicians and teachers frequently identify entry situations as being especially important and problematic for children (Dodge, McClaskey, & Feldman, 1985). Because the play interactions of young children are quite fragile and easily disrupted, children tend to protect these interchanges by discouraging the initial attempts of others to enter their play (Corsaro, 1979, 1981). Consequently, children seeking entry must frequently deal with disputes over access to the group and their activities. They must also anticipate rejection from the group because more than 50% of all initial entry attempts fail (Corsaro, 1979). This means that children who try to enter the ongoing activities of others must engage in multiple attempts and deal with rejection from members of the group before eventually succeeding. The ability to tolerate these frustrating events and to control their negative affect are central to the successful completion of this social task. Children who are unable to do this may engage in aggressive behavior against the group or withdraw from the group completely. Research indicates that children who are rejected or who have developmental delays tend to have more difficulty than popular children in controlling their negative affect and behavior after experiencing problems with entering the play of others (Wilson, 1999, 2003).

ETIOLOGY OF CHILDREN'S PEER PROBLEMS

A number of factors contribute to children's difficulties with peers. This section describes factors that increase or decrease children's risk for social problems. These are called *risk factors* or *protective factors,* respectively. Studies of children at risk for social problems indicate that three broad sets of variables function as risk or protective factors (see Garmezy, 1985, for a review). These variables include individual differences within the child, the child's family, and the child's community.

Risk and Protective Factors within the Child

Certain characteristics and behavior patterns can protect at-risk children from peer rejection. For example, although aggression is usually associated with peer rejection, the presence of positive qualities such as cooperation, trustworthiness, and kindness can protect these children from rejection by peers (Parkhurst & Asher, 1992). A study of fourth-, fifth-, and sixth-grade boys found that aggressive boys who were athletic and/or physically attractive were popular (Rodkin, Farmer, Pearl, & Van Acker, 2000). However, a lack of friendliness, prosocial orientation, or academic aptitude and the presence of internalizing behaviors are risk factors that increase the probability that aggressive boys will be rejected by peers. Another set of protective and risk factors involves individual differences in the ability to regulate attention and emotions effectively.

Regulating Attention Substantial research links children's social and conduct problems with their ability to manage attention (Eisenberg et al., 1995; Lahey,

Green, & Forehand, 1980; Pope, Bierman, & Mumma, 1989). For example, parent and teacher reports of children's attentional control (i.e., their ability to focus and shift attention) are related to social competence, prosocial behavior, and conduct problems in preschool and elementary school children (Eisenberg et al., 1996; Eisenberg, Fabes, Nyman, Bernzweig, & Pinuelas, 1994; Eisenberg et al., 2000). Furthermore, teacher-reported concentration problems predict aggressive behavior patterns in first-graders (Kellam et al., 1991).

To succeed with peers, children must be alert to opportunities for social engagement, attend to information that will help them gain entrance into others' play, watch for cues and feedback from others about the effectiveness of their behavior, and modify their behavior on the basis of this information. After initiating play with others, children must continue to attend to relevant social cues and to regulate their emotional responses. Successfully maintaining a joint play interaction is a particularly complex task. Children typically negotiate concerning roles, ownership of toys, and changes in activities. Attending to the affective signals of others and modifying behavior appropriately on the basis of these cues enables children to maintain their play activity despite periods of tension and disagreement. Good attention skills are critical to accomplishing these tasks (Wilson & Gottman, 1996).

Another reason why attention processes are important in children's social competence and social status with peers is that the ability to control attention provides children with an important avenue for regulating negative affect. For example, shifting attention away from a negative stimulus decreases negative affect and physiological arousal (Derryberry & Rothbart, 1988; Rothbart & Derryberry, 1981). This concept is further explored in the next subsection.

Regulating Emotions   Regulating strong affect in interpersonal settings is an important aspect of successful peer interaction (Eisenberg & Fabes, 1992; Hubbard & Coie, 1994; Sroufe, Schork, Motti, Lawroski, & LaFreniere, 1984). A number of studies suggest that compared with popular children, peer-rejected children have more difficulty in accomplishing this task. For example, peer-rejected children are less able than popular children to actively resist the provocation of peers (Eisenberg & Fabes, 1992). They are also less able to regulate their behavior during transitions from rough-and-tumble play (a context that elicits strong affect) to less rousing interactive play (Hubbard & Coie, 1994; Pellegrini, 1990). Pellegrini found that for peer-rejected children, transitions from rough-and-tumble play led to aggression 30% of the time, whereas with popular children, these transitions rarely led to aggression. Research also suggests that peer-rejected children express more verbal and nonverbal anger than popular children in provocative peer situations (Hubbard, 2001). The expression of negative affect also predicts the quality of children's peer relationships over time. Isley, O'Neil, and Parke (1996) found that children's expression of negative affect in kindergarten predicted their social competence with peers in first grade.

A number of child characteristics appear to protect children from peer rejection. Popular children are less aggressive than rejected children and also engage in more positive social behaviors. Furthermore, although aggression is typically associated with peer rejection, aggressive children who balance these negative behaviors with more positive attributes or behaviors, such as being prosocial or athletic, decrease their risk for peer rejection. Good attention and emotion-regulation skills also appear to buffer children from social problems. The ability to manage attention appropriately facilitates children's interactions with peers. Perhaps the most important reason for the positive associations between attention skills and children's social competence is the role of attention in facilitating children's ability to regulate negative affect.

Risk and Protective Factors within the Family

In addition to individual differences in children, factors in the family also influence children's social and conduct problems. The following section reviews research on family risk and protective factors for peer and conduct problems, including parenting behaviors, the family emotional milieu, the degree to which parents engage in emotion coaching of their children, and certain parental characteristics.

Parenting Behaviors Since the late 1970s, there has been a considerable amount of research on parental contributions to the development of childhood social and behavioral problems. One theoretical perspective that has been helpful for understanding the role of parenting in peer rejection and conduct problems is social learning theory. According to this theory, children learn how to get along with others as a result of observing behavior modeled in their social environments (Bandura, 1977). For example, after watching a set of videotaped vignettes involving a same-sex peer destroying a toy, peer-rejected children and their mothers were more likely than popular children and their mothers to make errors in processing social information; they both saw hostile intent in the other videotaped peers when none was present (Keane, Brown, & Crenshaw, 1990). Mothers of popular children also were more likely than mothers of peer-rejected children to provide prosocial resolutions to the stories (e.g., describing how they would teach their children to respond in a similar situation). These results suggest a relationship between mothers' and children's interpretation of and behavior about provocative social situations and children's peer status.

Numerous parenting behaviors have also been linked to children's social competence. For example, coercive, harsh parenting practices have been consistently associated with high levels of aggression and social problems in children (Dishion, 1990; Gottman & Katz, 1989; MacKinnon-Lewis, Lamb, Arbuckle, Baradaran, & Volling, 1992; Patterson, 1982; Putallaz & Heflin, 1990). Furthermore, parents who are highly intrusive in their children's lives tend to have children with lower levels of peer acceptance and independence than parents who use more gentle control and support with their children (MacDonald & Parke, 1984). Research also indicates that parents who are highly critical, disapproving, and generally rejecting tend to have children with behavior problems (Bandura & Walters, 1959; Lindahl, 1998; Loeber & Stouthamer-Loeber, 1986; Patterson, 1982).

The Family's Emotional Milieu Emotions expressed in families appear to play a prominent role in children's social and emotional development. Whereas emotional disengagement and negative affect appear to be especially prevalent in families of peer-rejected children (Boyum & Parke, 1995; Carson & Parke, 1996; Dekovic & Janssens, 1992; Dix, 1991; Forehand, Well, & Griest, 1980; Roopnarine & Adams, 1987), parents of popular children tend to be emotionally engaged and warm toward their children (Baumrind, 1967, 1971; Putallaz, 1987; Youngblade & Belsky, 1992). More specifically, results from Baumrind's research indicated that parents who are warm, responsive, consistent, and reasonable in their maturity demands tend to have children who are more socially competent than parents who are harsh, rejecting, inconsistent, or permissive. The influence of parental warmth also begins early in life and extends into childhood and beyond. For instance, Youngblade and Belsky found that children who had warm, sensitive bonds with their mothers at age 1 had more positive friendships 4 years later compared with children who had cold, insensitive relationships with their mothers.

Parental responsiveness to children's distress has also been linked to children's social competence (Roberts & Strayer, 1987; Zahn-Waxler, Radke-Yarrow, & Kind, 1979). For example, Zahn-Waxler and colleagues found that parents who responded positively to their children's distress tended to have children who responded positively to other children's distress and displayed prosocial behavior more often. Parents who are interested in their children's feelings appear to have children with high levels of social competence. For instance, mothers of popular children tend to be more expressive of their own thoughts and feelings during interactions with their children (Putallaz, 1987). Furthermore, mothers of popular children tend to be more concerned about their children's feelings and opinions than the mothers of children who had lower peer status (Putallaz, 1987). Parents who encourage their young children to express emotions (e.g., anger, fear, sadness) tend to have children with high levels of competence (Roberts & Strayer, 1987). These results suggest that parental solicitation and responsiveness regarding children's emotions contribute to their social competence.

Kopp (1989) suggested that children's emotion-regulation skills are facilitated by mothers who respond to their emotional distress and comfort or teach their children coping strategies. Not only do these parental behaviors reduce children's distress, they also help children learn emotion-regulation strategies. It is also likely that these episodes of soothing involve discussion of emotional experiences. The degree to which parents talk about emotions with their children relates to the likelihood that young children will talk about emotions on their own and that they will understand emotion-related events (Dunn, Bretherton, & Munn, 1987; Dunn, Brown, & Beardsall, 1991). Children with a better understanding of emotions tend to be more prosocial (Denham, 1986) and have better tolerance for frustration (Greenberg, Kusche, & Speltz, 1991). For example, Greenberg et al. found that 5-year-olds who had more emotional labels for stressful parent–child situations, such as separations, were better able to cope with frustrations during a waiting task.

There is also evidence that children learn about the regulation of emotions during interactions with their parents. This has been especially evident in research examining patterns in the physical play of peer-rejected and popular children and their parents (Carson & Parke, 1996; MacDonald, 1987; MacDonald & Parke, 1984). Physical play is a high-energy, fun activity for children and parents, but it is also a context in which overstimulation can easily occur. Thus, parents must carefully monitor the level of excitement and stimulation in this setting. Research indicates that the frequency of overstimulation is typically much higher for peer-rejected children and their parents than for popular children and their parents; this was especially true for boys and their fathers. Cycles of reciprocal negativity also characterized the exchanges of peer-rejected children and their parents, whereas with popular children and their parents, one member's negative behavior was likely followed with a positive or neutral behavior by the other (Carson & Parke, 1996). The play of popular children and their parents was filled with reciprocal positive affect involving laughter, smiles, teasing, and playful affection. These results suggest that peer-rejected children may be less likely than popular children to learn about repairing negative affect in the parent–child context.

Emotion Coaching Gottman and colleagues (1997) found that families develop specific belief systems about emotions, especially anger and sadness. The nature of these belief systems is related to whether parents notice and accept their children's emotions and whether they assist or coach their children when the children are experiencing a strong emotion. "Emotion-coaching" parents tend to notice low-intensity emotions in their children and see these as opportunities for teaching and building intimacy. These parents are accepting of their children's emotions but also set limits on behaviors associated with emotions. For example, emotion-coaching parents will accept their child's anger but require the child to not act aggressively toward the object of his or her anger. They also problem solve with their children about emotional experiences. In contrast, emotion-dismissing parents believe that negative emotions, such as sadness and anger, are dangerous and try to help their children get over these feelings as quickly as possible. Some emotion-dismissing parents also believe that these emotions are not important and that their children need to learn to ride out these affective states.

Gottman et al. (1997) found that parents who were more involved in coaching their children about emotional experiences (i.e., emotion-coaching parents) were less likely to engage in derogatory parenting behaviors such as criticizing and belittling children. This finding suggests that parenting behaviors form one mechanism through which emotion coaching may facilitate positive outcomes in children.

Longitudinal information on children with emotion-coaching or emotion-dismissing parents suggests that many positive outcomes are associated with having emotion-coaching parents. For example, children with emotion-coaching parents were better able to regulate their emotions, had less negative interactions with friends and peers at school, had fewer behavioral problems, and were rated more positively by their teachers (Gottman et al., 1997). Children with emotion-coaching parents also had lower heart rates and recovered more quickly from the physiological arousal associated with negative emotions than children with emotion-dismissing parents. At age 8, children with emotion-coaching parents had higher reading and mathematics scores in school, even when their general intelligence was controlled for at age 5. Thus, the family's emotional belief system has implications for a child's social and academic development. This is important because the child's emotional world and ability to regulate his or her own emotions are related to the development of peer-related social competence (Gottman, 1983; Gottman, Katz, & Hooven, 1996; Sroufe et al., 1984; Wilson & Gottman, 1996).

Parental Characteristics Certain parental characteristics have also been associated with children's social competence. For example, Patterson and Dishion (1985) found that the parents of children with social and conduct problems often experience chronic stress in numerous areas of their lives (e.g., financial problems, marital conflict, extended family conflict, limited social support), yet spend very little time problem solving or looking for solutions. These parents make negative attributions about their children, believing that their children intentionally try to make their lives miserable (Dix, 1991; Patterson, 1982). In addition, research shows that once parents of children with social and conduct problems become irritated, they also are more likely to use critical, insensitive commands and harsh, physical punishment in attempting to change their children's behavior (Patterson, 1982).

Several researchers have also found that parents with poor psychological and interpersonal functioning tend to have children with higher levels of peer rejection and aggression than parents with healthy psychological and interpersonal functioning (Forehand et al., 1980; Sameroff & Seifer, 1983). Strong negative emotions may interfere with parents' cognitive appraisal skills, undermining their ability to control their behaviors and to be sensitive to their child's needs (Dix, 1991). Therefore, when parents are overwhelmed by negative emotions, it becomes especially difficult for them to maintain control of their behavior and to provide comfort and support for their children.

Bidirectionality in Parent–Child Interactions It is important to note that although the studies cited in this section focused on the effect of parents' behaviors on their children, the parent–child relationship is bidirectional in nature (Bell, 1979). Thus, parents have a strong influence on their children's behavior and social competence, but children also affect their parents' behavior. A good example of bidirectionality in parent–child interactions comes from research examining the parenting behavior of mothers whose sons had conduct disorder (CD) and mothers of sons who did not have a behavioral disorder. No significant group differences were found in parenting behavior during play or structured tasks. This was true even when mothers from each group interacted with boys from the other group who were not their children (Anderson, Lytton, & Romney, 1986). Both groups of mothers gave more commands and negative responses to the boys with CD, and the boys with CD complied less with the mothers from both groups. These results indicate that parenting behavior and the noncompliant behavior of boys with CD were driven primarily by the child.

Summary Specific parenting behaviors are associated with children's social competence and status with peers. For example, positive parenting behaviors (e.g., modeling prosocial resolutions) are associated with peer acceptance, and negative parenting behaviors (e.g., coerciveness, intrusiveness) are associated with peer rejection. The emotional milieu of families also has been shown to play an important role in the social development of children. Research indicates that parents who are responsive to their children's distress and positive in their own affect tend to have popular children who are able to regulate their own emotions, focus their attention, and succeed academically. In contrast, parents who are unresponsive to their children's distress and negative in their affect tend to have children who are rejected by their peers and have poor emotion-regulation skills, attentional difficulties, and academic problems. Parents who encourage emotional expressiveness and teach their children appropriate skills for managing strong emotions also tend to have popular children, whereas emotion-dismissing parents tend to have children with social problems. Specific parental characteristics also are associated with peer rejection in children, such as poor interpersonal and psychological functioning, inadequate problem-solving skills, insensitivity toward their children's needs, and a tendency to view their children negatively.

Risk and Protective Factors within the Community

In addition to individual and family characteristics, research suggests that factors within the community influence children's relationships with peers and conduct problems. This research indicates that it is important for children to grow up in a community where they feel safe and secure (Garbarino, 1982). Greenberg, Lengua, Coie, and Pinderhughes (1999) found that children's neighborhoods have a "small but unique" effect on their behavior (as reported by their parents), acceptance of authority, and social competence (as reported by their teachers).

Most research on children and neighborhoods indicates a relationship between neighborhood safety and delinquency. For example, Stouhamer-Loeber, Loeber, Wei, Farrington, and Wikström (2002) found that living in a safe, higher socioeconomic status (SES) neighborhood protected 7- to 13-year-old boys from delinquency. In contrast, children and adolescents growing up in lower SES neighborhoods experienced more risk factors and fewer protective factors for delinquency. A study of African American sixth-graders in New York City found that children's aggressive behavior was directly related to the perceived dangerousness of their neighborhood and the law-breaking behavior of their friends (Griffin, Scheier, Botvin, Diaz, & Miller, 1999). Children who witnessed violence in their neighborhood were more likely to view aggression as an effective and acceptable response to "ambiguous peer provocation" (Schwartz & Proctor, 2000). In addition, Schwartz and Proctor suggested that a stronger relationship exists between community violence and children's peer problems when children both witness and directly experience violence.

When reviewing research on the links between neighborhoods and children's social and conduct problems, it is important to remember that not all children exposed to these risk factors develop problems (Cowen et al., 1992). In fact, research suggests that schools can play an important role in ameliorating the negative impact of living in a poor neighborhood. Cochran and Davila (1992) described a neighborhood as a "context for social relations" and stated that the link between schools and the neighborhood can either support or limit children's social relationships.

Teachers and Schools as Part of Children's Community Garbarino (1999) suggested that the accumulation of risk factors in the presence of few protective factors contributes to social and conduct problems in children and adolescents. He explained the role of these protective factors in children's lives by calling them *anchors*. Garbarino noted that one protective factor for boys is having "a stable positive emotional relationship with at least one person, someone absolutely committed to the child and to whom the child feels a strong positive attachment" (p. 161). The presence of a concerned, loving adult (e.g., grandparent, teacher) can serve to counteract the effects of unresponsive parents or marital conflict (Garmezy, 1991). Obviously, the more people who fit this definition, the more the child will be protected from developing violent behavior. Garbarino also noted that "positive social support from persons outside the family" (p. 168), such as teachers, can provide children with warm connections and promote prosocial behavior. Garmezy described the teacher as a "protective figure" developing competence in children from disadvantaged backgrounds.

A poignant example of the influential role of a teacher for an at-risk child is provided by Antwone Fisher in his memoir. Fisher wrote that his teacher for fourth through sixth grades "found something to compliment in each of us—a neat paper, a good attitude, an eager face—and rewarded the whole class for our positive efforts with impromptu parties, field trips, and other celebrations. We became a family" (2001, p. 124). Fisher described the effect of his teacher's encouragement and how it served to counterbalance his adverse home environment:

> Outside I shyly accept her praise, but inside I'm flying with the birth of revelation. It's the first time I've ever realized that there is something I can do to make things different for myself . . . that no matter how often someone says you can't do something, by simply working harder and trying, you can prove them wrong and actually change your circumstance. This lesson is a piece of gold I'll keep tucked in my back pocket for the rest of my life. (p. 127) (COPYRIGHT © 2001 BY ANTWONE QUENTIN FISHER AND MIM EICHLER RIVAS. Reprinted by permission of HarperCollins Publishers, Inc., WILLIAM MORROW.)

Researchers have evaluated the factors that contribute to children's attachment to their teachers. For example, Howes, Hamilton, and Philipsen (1998) reported that children form this foundation early in their school experience. The researchers found that 9-year-old children's connection to their teacher was predicted by the strength of their relationship with their preschool teacher and not by their attachment to their mother. In addition, Howes, Matheson, and Hamilton (1994) found that the strength of children's emotional connection to their preschool teacher was a better predictor of their social competence with school peers than their attachment to their mother. Children with strong connections to their preschool teacher interacted more cooperatively and participated in more elaborate social play. Similarly, Howe and colleagues (1998) noted that children's history of emotional connection to their teacher, combined with their previous friendship experiences, predicted how they viewed their relationships with peers at age 9. Another study found that a positive emotional connection with teachers positively influenced children's self-esteem, making the children less reactive to peer conflicts (Little & Kobak, 2003).

SCHOOL-BASED INTERVENTIONS

In addressing peer and conduct problems in children, it is important for schools to develop interventions that not only decrease risk factors but also improve protective factors (Walker et al., 1996). For children with peer relationship problems, intervention programs should focus on reducing children's maladaptive behaviors (e.g., aggression, bragging, disruptiveness) and increasing their adaptive skills (e.g., anger management, assertiveness, cooperation, supportiveness).

A variety of interventions have been developed to address the social problems of children and adolescents. In general, research indicates that the earlier social development interventions are initiated, the more beneficial it is for children on a long-term basis (Child Mental Health Foundations and Agencies Network, 2000; National Advisory Mental Health Council, 2001; Shonkoff & Phillips, 2000).

Educators have unique opportunities to make a significant difference in the lives of their students. For many children, school provides the first opportunity to participate in an environment outside of the home. Peer relationships become increasingly important throughout childhood and provide an important source of social support (Buhrmester, 1992; Parker & Gottman, 1989). Consequently, the classroom becomes a primary environment for children's social and emotional development, with educators playing a leading role.

Practicing Social Skills in the Classroom

Children benefit from practicing social skills in supervised situations, such as school classrooms, where their efforts will be rewarded and thus reinforced (Frey, Hirshstein, & Guzzo, 2000). Similarities exist between teaching social skills and teaching academic concepts in that the most effective teachers are those who model or demonstrate appropriate social behaviors, evoke imitation of these behaviors by children, and provide constructive feedback with opportunities for rehearsal (Elliot, 2001). Figure 12.3 provides a general model for teaching and reinforcing social skills with children. (See Sheridan, 1998, for more details on this model.)

Learning Social Skills from Peers

Peer pairing is relatively easy to implement in the classroom setting. It involves teaming children who have poor social skills with children who are more socially successful in structured and supervised play or work settings. Peer pairing is especially effective with socially neglected children (Morris, Messer, & Gross,

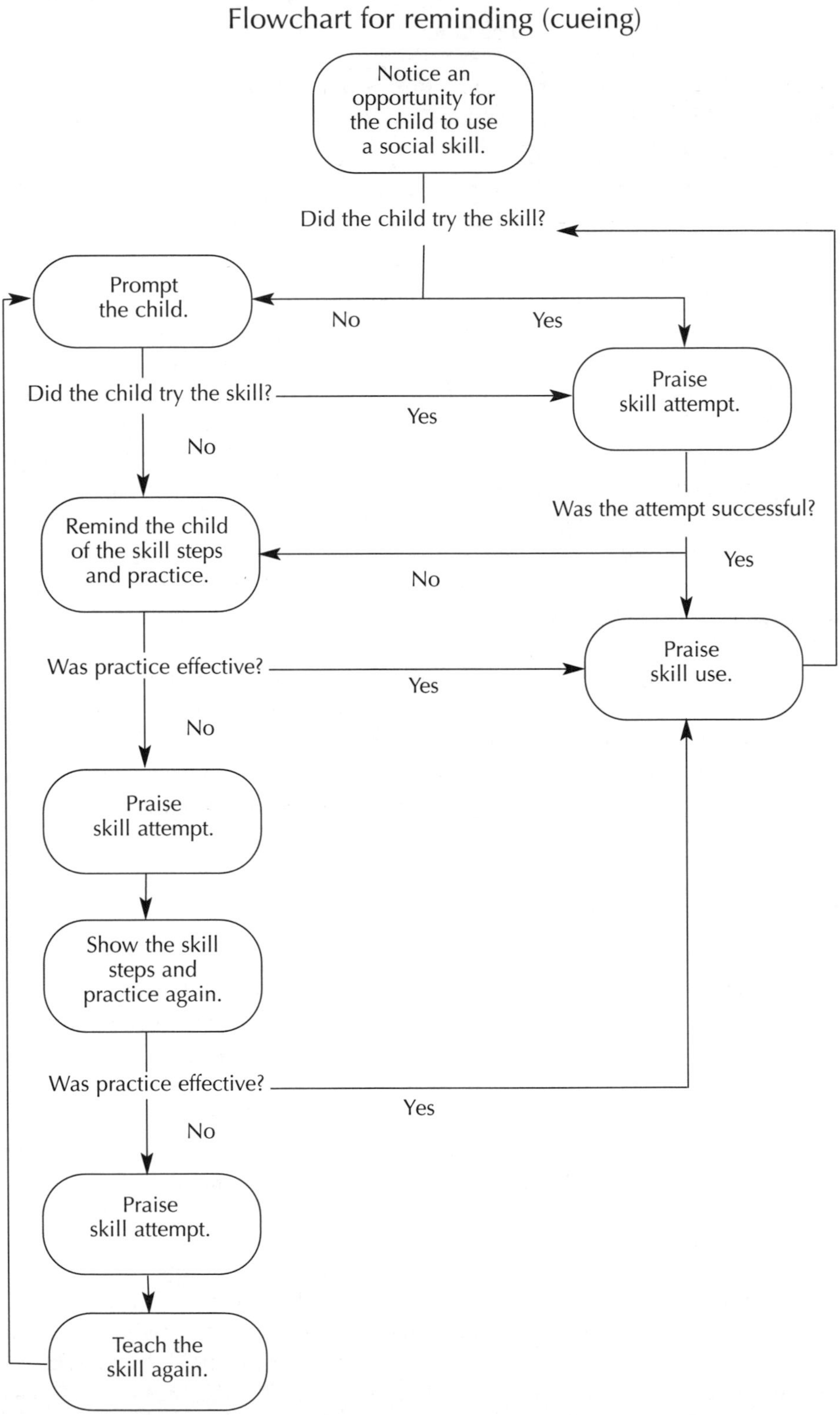

Flowchart for reminding (cueing)

Figure 12.3. A quick reference to help adults guide the enhancement of children's social skills. (Used with permission from Sopris West Educational Services, *Why don't they like me? Helping your child make and keep friends,* by Susan M. Sheridan, Copyright ©1998.)

1995). There is also some evidence that this technique can benefit (i.e., improve the social status of) children with other social and behavioral problems when combined with social skills training (Sancilio, 1987; Vaughn, McIntosh, & Spencer-Rowe, 1991).

It is important to note that pairing children with behavior problems together is generally not effective and may actually increase children's problems. Arnold and Hughes found that grouping such youth can be problematic and possibly cause more harm than good because it "may make shopping for a deviant interpersonal environment much easier" (1999, p. 110). Grouping youth with these problems can facilitate mutual identification between peers with social and conduct problems and may unintentionally affect their beliefs about the appropriateness of their problem behavior.

Elements of Successful Intervention Programs

Greenberg, Domitrovich, and Bumbarger (2001) identified common attributes of successful intervention programs, noting that the most compelling programs incorporate

> Long-term intervention strategies with repetitive or sustained support as the child continues to develop
>
> cross-situational programs that provide intervention in the home, school, and other community environments where the child is involved
>
> expansive models that enhance the interaction style of every person involved with the target child, as well as modifying each environment
>
> collaborative endeavors that integrate multiple systems' strategies with "school ecology" as the "central focus of intervention" for "school-aged children" (Best Practices in Prevention Programming section, para. 1)

Furthermore, intervention strategies that focus on risk and protective factors, rather than on specific problem behaviors, are more pragmatic because broad interventions can be just as effective and are more time- and cost-effective (Greenberg et al., 2001). Various effective intervention programs are summarized in Table 12.3. The following subsections detail a few of the programs for illustrative purposes.

Fast Track Fast Track is one example of an effective large-scale intervention program (Greenberg et al., 2001). The Fast Track model was developed by prevention research experts who recognized the need for a comprehensive intervention approach targeting elementary school children who are at high risk for problematic adolescent behaviors (Conduct Problems Prevention Research Group [CPPRG], 2000; Greenberg et al., 2001). Fast Track has three levels: 1) a school-based universal level; 2) family and child support for individual children who are at risk (identified during a kindergarten screening); and 3) individualized support as needed for the identified children and their families (CPPRG, 2000).

Table 12.3. Effective intervention programs for addressing peer problems

Name	Age range or grade level	Duration of effectiveness of intervention	Focus	Description
Adolescent Transition Program (ATP)	Teenagers	1-year follow-up	Multicomponent skills for child and family	Promotes self-regulation, through problem-solving skills, for students at risk for behavior problems and their parents
Anger Coping Program	Elementary and middle school	7-month follow-up comparison	Child anger and self-control	Addresses anger management for aggressive boys
Big Brothers Big Sisters of America	All ages (community based)	Not available	Adult mentoring	Develops mentoring relationships
Bullying Prevention Program (BPP)	Elementary and middle school	2-year follow-up comparison	Children's socioemotional and cognitive skill building	Prevents bullying at the individual child, classroom, and school levels
Child Development Project (CDP)	Elementary school	Not available	Children's socioemotional and cognitive skill building	Promotes cooperative learning with family–school partnerships
Earlscourt School-Based Program (ESP)	Ages 6–12	Not available	Multicomponent skills for child and family	Addresses aggressive and disruptive of children, as well as their parents and classrooms
Fast Track, with Promoting Alternative Thinking Strategies (PATHS) (Greenberg, Domitrovich, & Bumbarger, 2001)	Elementary school	Not available	Multicomponent skills for child and family	Promotes skills for children who are at risk for developing peer problems and addresses their peer groups, families, schools, communities
First Steps Program	Early childhood to kindergarten	Not available	Multicomponent skills for child and family	Promotes adaptive behavior in small groups, with optional parental guidance; meets two times per week for 12–15 weeks
I Can Problem Solve (ICPS) (previously called Interpersonal Cognitive Problem-Solving)	Preschool and elementary school	1-year follow-up comparison	Children's socioemotional and cognitive skill building	Focuses on language, thinking, and listening skills, then on interpersonal skills

Program	Age/Grade	Type/Focus	Follow-up	Description
Linking the Interests of Families and Teachers (LIFT)	All ages (multidomain)	Decreases risk and increase protective factors associated with delinquency and violence	Not available	Develops social and problem-solving skills for individual children; teaches parents how to supervise and discipline children effectively; school program comprises 20 sessions
Responding in Peaceful and Positive Ways (RIPP)	Middle school	Nonviolence	6-month follow-up comparison	Promotes nonviolence in adolescents; comprises 25 sessions
School Transitional Environment Project (STEP)	Grades 6–12	Children's socioemotional and cognitive skill-building	Multiple-year follow-up	Focuses on making successful transitions from elementary to middle schools or from middle to high schools
Seattle Social Development Project	All ages (multidomain)	Multicomponent (child, family, and school)	6-year follow-up comparison	Develops social skills for individual children and fosters bonding between their families and school
Second Step	Elementary school	Nonviolence	6-month follow-up comparison	Teaches anger management, empathy, and impulse control
Social Competence Promotion Program for Young Adolescents (SCPP-YA) (previously called Positive Youth Development Program [PYD] and Yale-New Haven Social Problem Solving Program)	Middle school	Children's socioemotional and cognitive skill building		Builds students' socioemotional and cognitive skills; comprises 45 sessions
Social Decision Making and Problem Solving (SDM/PS) Program (previously called Improving Social Awareness-Social Problem Solving [ISA-SPS])	Kindergarten through 8th grade	Children's socioemotional and cognitive skill building	6-year follow-up comparison	Teaches individual skill building to bolster student resilience; 2-year program

Source: Greenberg, Domitrovich, and Bumbarger (2001).
For more information about the programs, see Appendix C at the end of the book.

Fast Track's School-Based Program   Fast Track's school-based universal program, Promoting Alternative Thinking Strategies (PATHS), is of particular interest to educators. PATHS is also a research-based program that, as noted, identifies and provides intervention for elementary school children who are at risk (Greenberg, Kusche, Cook, & Quamma, 1995). The curriculum focuses on the identification, comprehension, and regulation of emotions. Empirical research has shown that PATHS is associated with socioemotional improvements in children with a variety of characteristics, from those requiring little support to those with physical disabilities (e.g., hearing impairments) or potential emotional disabilities (e.g., at risk for developing behavioral disorders). Greenberg et al. (1995) studied 286 second- and third-grade children in 30 classrooms and found that children at low and high risk showed improvements in their emotion management capabilities after only 1 year in the intervention program, with positive residual effects confirmed at 1- and 2-year follow-ups (Greenberg et al., 2001). Research on the long-term benefits of PATHS is still in progress.

Second Step   Second Step is another school-based intervention program for children's social and conduct problems. It is a classroom-based curriculum for preschool through ninth grade that is designed to reduce aggressive and impulsive behaviors and increase prosocial behavior in students by teaching empathy, problem solving, and anger management skills (McMahon, Washburn, Felix, Yakin, & Childrey, 2000). The program is used across the United States as well as in other countries, such as Canada (Frey et al., 2000). Each grade-level module contains units on empathy skills (i.e., the awareness of others' feelings), problem solving or impulse control, and anger management skills. Throughout each unit, the children role-play to practice these skills. An important component of Second Step is reinforcing students' use of these skills in the classroom and at home (through the use of parent education).

After the students learn to recognize feelings in themselves and others, they learn to problem solve. Problem-solving steps include identifying the problem; brainstorming solutions; and thinking about each solution in terms of its safety, effect on others' feelings, fairness, and effectiveness. Finally, students are taught to evaluate the success of their chosen solution and, if it did not work, to select another strategy. As noted previously, the final unit teaches students effective ways to manage their anger. The following vignette is an example of a student utilizing these skills in the classroom.

Suzie's teacher has given her permission to use the classroom computer. Suzie is 8 years old and is playing Mary's favorite game. Mary, who is also 8 years old, pushes Suzie aside and says, "I have the highest score on this game." Suzie stands and watches Mary for a moment. She notices her own bodily and emotional responses to this situation (recognizes feelings)—that she is squeezing her fists and feels like she wants to hit Mary. Suzie identifies that she is mad at Mary for pushing her off the computer (identifies the problem) and realizes that she needs to calm down before she can think of solutions. She takes three deep breaths and slowly counts to 10 (uses anger management skills). Suzie says to herself, "I could tell Mary that it is my turn because the teacher gave me permission. Another idea is that I could take the computer that Billy is using. Or I could tell the teacher." Suzie decides that telling Mary it is her turn is safe and fair and would not hurt Mary's feelings (thinks about the solutions). She says, "Mary, it's not fair that you pushed me off the computer because the teacher said I could use it and it's my turn now." Mary replies, "So what? What're you going to do about it?" Suzie is really mad now and begins the process of calming down and selecting another solution because her first choice did not work (thinks about the solution's level of success). She decides to ask the teacher for assistance. Her teacher has observed this interaction and praises Suzie for her efforts.

• •

Second Step's Parent Education Program Bronfenbrenner (1979) used the term "interconnectedness" to explain the importance of links among the different settings in which children participate on a daily basis, such as home, school, and community. In an effort to facilitate these connections, the Second Step program has an education component for parents of children in preschool through fifth grade. The program, Second Step Family Guide, aims to educate parents about the Second Step curriculum so that they can recognize and use the same words and strategies that their children are learning at school (Frey et al., 2000). This supports their children's use of social and problem-solving skills at home. In addition, parents are taught the skills so that they can learn ways to talk about feelings, problem-solving skills, and more effective ways to manage their own anger. This component enables them to better model these skills for their children (Committee for Children, 2002).

Evaluations of Second Step Several studies have evaluated the success of the Second Step program across different age groups. For example, McMahon and colleagues (2000) evaluated the effectiveness of Second Step with preschool and kindergarten students. Based on classroom observations (completed by observers who did not know which classrooms had used the Second Step program), problem behaviors such as verbal aggression, disruptive behavior, and physical aggression decreased following program completion. A second study, in which researchers conducted behavioral observations of elementary school children, found modest reductions in physical aggression and modest increases in neutral/prosocial behavior (Grossman et al., 1997). Finally, Van Schoiack-Edstrom and colleagues (2002) evaluated the effectiveness of the Second Step program for middle school students (grades six through eight) and found that students who participated in the program were less accepting of aggression and believed that implementing appropriate social skills was not difficult.

It is interesting to note that on the basis of teacher-completed behavioral ratings, teachers in the first two studies did not report changes in children's behavior, although unbiased observers did note these changes (Grossman et al., 1997; McMahon et al., 2000). Grossman and colleagues suggested that these teachers may have not seen improved student behavior because it often occurred outside the classroom (e.g., on the playground, in the cafeteria). Similarly, McMahon and colleagues suggested that behavioral rating scales may not be sensitive to changes in children's behavior over time. As noted previously, behavioral rating scales measure long-standing behavior, whereas behavioral observations measure more immediate and more subtle behavior changes (Sattler, 2002).

Summary

Educators play an important role in assisting children who have social and behavioral problems. School-based interventions provide an opportunity for teachers to intervene with children to increase their prosocial skills and decrease their problematic behavior (e.g., aggression, impulsivity).

CONCLUSION

Research suggests that peer relationship problems negatively influence children's social, emotional, and cognitive development and put them at risk for continuing problems as they develop. Children who are actively rejected by peers and children who are rejected and aggressive appear to be at highest risk for future problems. Multiple factors influence children's social and conduct problems, including the presence of negative behaviors (e.g., high levels of aggression) and the relative absence of more positive behaviors (e.g., prosocial behavior). Individual differences in attention and emotion-regulation skills also appear to facilitate children's relationships with peers. In addition to individual skills and characteristics of children, numerous family behaviors and characteristics influence children's social and conduct problems. Children with peer relationship problems tend to have parents who display more coercive and intrusive parenting approaches. Parents in these families tend to be less emotionally engaged with and responsive to their children and less likely to encourage their children to express their feelings. There is also evidence that peer-rejected children are less likely to learn effective strategies for regulating strong affect from their parents. Specific parental characteristics are associated with peer rejection in children, including poor interpersonal and psychological functioning and inadequate problem-solving skills. External support in community settings such as schools can play an important role in protecting children from social and conduct problems. For example, children who have strong attachments to their early school teachers tend to have better social relationships with peers. School-based intervention programs, such as Fast Track and Second Step, have also been shown to positively influence children's social competence through decreasing negative and increasing positive social behaviors in children. Early identification and intervention are important for intervening with children who have social problems. Early problems tend to increase over time, and children often become more resistant to intervention efforts as they progress through grade school (Conduct Problems Prevention Research Group, 2002).

This chapter also has highlighted the important role of schools and teachers in children's social development. Even when children have numerous individual, family, and community risk factors, caring and warm teachers can provide a protective function. Schools must have support systems in place to assist teachers in facilitating children's social and emotional development. Such supports include training opportunities for learning about children's social problems and the presence of school staff, such as school counselors and school psychologists, who are trained in the assessment and treatment of peer problems. Support from external agencies can also provide schools with tools to identify and implement effective interventions for children with peer problems. See Appendix C at the end of the book for web sites with additional information about children with social problems and resources for helping children with these problems.

REFERENCES

Achenbach, T.M. (2001). *Manual for the ASEBA school-age forms & profiles.* Burlington: University of Vermont, Department of Psychiatry.

Anderson, K.E., Lytton, H., & Romney, D.M. (1986). Mothers' interactions with normal and conduct-disordered boys: Who affects whom? *Developmental Psychology, 22,* 604–609.

Arnold, M.E., & Hughes, J.N. (1999). First do no harm: Adverse effects of grouping deviant youth for skills training. *Journal of School Psychology, 37,* 99–115.

Asher, S.R., & Coie, J.D. (1990). *Peer rejection in childhood.* New York: Cambridge University Press.

Asher, S.R., & Dodge, K. A. (1986) Identifying children who are rejected by their peers. *Developmental Psychology, 22,* 444–449.

Bandura, A. (1977). *Aggression: A social learning analysis.* Upper Saddle River, NJ: Prentice Hall.

Bandura, A., & Walters, R.H. (1959). *Adolescent aggression.* New York: Ronald Press.

Baumrind, D. (1967). Childcare practices anteceding three patterns of preschool behavior. *Genetic Psychology Monographs, 75,* 43–88.

Baumrind, D. (1971). Current patterns of parental authority. *Developmental Psychology Monograph, 4*(1, pt. 2).

Bell, R.Q. (1979). Parent, child, and reciprocal influences. *American Psychologist, 34,* 821–826.

Boyatzis, J., Baloff, P., & Durieux, C. (1998). Effects of perceived attractiveness and academic success on early adolescent peer popularity. *Journal of Genetic Psychology, 159,* 337–344.

Boyum, L.A., & Parke, R.D. (1995). The role of family emotional expressiveness in the development of children's social competence. *Journal of Marriage and the Family, 57,* 593–608.

Bronfenbrenner, U. (1979). *The ecology of human development: Experiments by nature and design.* Cambridge, MA: Harvard University Press.

Buhrmester, D. (1992). The developmental courses of sibling and peer relationships. In F. Boer & J. Dunn (Eds.), *Children's sibling relationships: Developmental and clinical issues* (pp. 19–40). Mahwah, NJ: Lawrence Erlbaum Associates.

Carson, J.L., & Parke, R.D. (1996). Reciprocal negative affect in parent-child interactions and children's peer competence. *Child Development, 67,* 2217–2226.

Child Mental Health Foundations and Agencies Network. (2000). *A good beginning. Sending America's children to school with the social and emotional competence they need to succeed.* Bethesda, MD: National Institute of Mental Health.

Cillessen, A.H.N., Vanijzendoorn, H.W., Van Lieshorst, C.F.M., & Hartup, W.W. (1992). Heterogeneity among peer-rejected boys: Subtypes and stabilities. *Child Development, 63,* 893–905.

Cochran, M., & Davila, V. (1992). Societal influences on children's peer relationships. In R.D. Parke & G.W. Ladd (Eds.), *Family–peer relationships: Modes of linkage.* Mahwah, NJ: Lawrence Erlbaum Associates.

Coie, J.D., Dodge, K.A., & Coppotelli, H. (1982). Dimensions and types of social status: A cross-age perspective. *Developmental Psychology, 18,* 315–336.

Coie, J.D., Lochman, J.E., Terry, R., & Hyman, C. (1992). Predicting early adolescent disorder from childhood aggression and peer rejection. *Journal of Consulting and Clinical Psychology, 60,* 783–792.

Cole, D.A., Gondoli, D.M., & Peeke, L.G. (1998). Structure and validity of parent and teacher perceptions of children's competence: A multitrait-multimethod-multigroup investigation. *Psychological Assessment, 10,* 241–249.

Cole, M., & Cole, S.R. (2001). *The development of children* (4th ed.). New York: Worth Publishers.

Committee for Children. (2002). *Second Step family guide.* Seattle: Author.

Conduct Problems Prevention Research Group. (2000). Merging universal and indicated prevention programs: The Fast Track model. *Addictive Behaviors, 25*(6), 913–927.

Corsaro, W. (1979). We're friends, right? Children's use of access rituals in a nursery school. *Language in Society, 8,* 315–336.

Corsaro, W.A. (1981). Friendship in the nursery school: Social organization in a peer environment. In S.R. Asher & J.M. Gottman (Eds.), *The development of children's friendships* (pp. 207–241). New York: Cambridge University Press.

Cowen, E.L., Work, W.C., Wyman, P.A., Parker, G.R., Wannon, M., & Gribble, P. (1992). Test comparisons among stress-affected, stress-resilient, and nonclassified fourth-through sixth-grade urban children. *Journal of Clinical Child and Adolescent Psychology, 20,* 200–214.

Dekovic, M., & Janssens, J.M.A.M. (1992). Parents' child-rearing style and child's sociometric status. *Developmental Psychology, 28,* 925–932.

Denham, S.A. (1986). Social cognition, social behavior, and emotion in preschoolers: Contextual validation. *Child Development, 57,* 194–201.

Denham, S., & Holt, R.W. (1993). Preschoolers' likability as cause or consequence of their social behavior. *Developmental Psychology, 29,* 271–275.

Derryberry, D., & Rothbart, M.K (1988). Affect, arousal, and attention as components of temperament. *Journal of Personality and Social Psychology, 55,* 958–966.

Dishion, T.J. (1990). The family ecology of boys' peer relations in middle childhood. *Child Development, 61,* 874–892.

Dix, T. (1991). The affective organization of parenting: Adaptive and maladaptive processes. *Psychological Bulletin, 110*(1), 3–35.

Dodge, K.A. (1980). Social cognition and children's aggressive behavior. *Child Development, 51,* 162–170.

Dodge, K.A., McClaskey, C.L., & Feldman, E. (1985). Situational approach to the assessment of social competence in children. *Journal of Consulting and Clinical Psychology, 53,* 344–353.

Dodge, K.A., & Somberg, D.R. (1987). Hostile attributional biases among aggressive boys are exacerbated under conditions of threat to the self. *Child Development, 58,* 213–224.

Dodge, K.A., Schlundt, D.G., Schocken, I., & Delugach, J.D. (1983). Social competence and children's social status: The role of peer group entry strategies. *Merrill-Palmer Quarterly, 29,* 309–336.

Dunn, J., Bretherton, I., & Munn, P. (1987). Conversations about feeling states between mothers and their young children. *Developmental Psychology, 23,* 132–139.

Dunn, J., Brown, J., & Beardsall, L. (1991). Family talk about feeling states and children's later understanding of others' emotions. *Developmental Psychology, 27,* 448–455.

Eisenberg, N., & Fabes, R.A. (1992). Emotion, regulation, and the development of social competence. In M.S. Clark (Ed.), *Review of personality and social psychology: Vol. 14. Emotion and social behavior* (pp. 119–150). Thousand Oaks, CA: Sage Publications.

Eisenberg, N., Fabes, R.A., Bernzweig, J., Karbon, M., Poulin, R., & Hanish, L. (1993). The relations of emotionality and regulation to preschoolers' social skills and sociometric status. *Child Development, 64,* 1418–1438.

Eisenberg, N., Fabes, R.A., Guthrie, I.K., Murphy, B.C., Maszk, P., Holmgren, R., & Suh, K. (1996). The relations of regulation and emotionality to problem behavior in elementary school children. *Development and Psychopathology, 8,* 141–162.

Eisenberg, N., Fabes, R.A., Murphy, B., Maszk, P., Smith, M., & Karbon, M. (1995). The role of emotionality and regulation in children's social functioning: A longitudinal study. *Child Development, 66,* 1360–1384.

Eisenberg, N., Fabes, R.A., Nyman, M., Bernzweig, J., & Pinuelas, A. (1994). The relations of emotionality and regulation to children's anger-related reactions. *Child Development, 65,* 109–128.

Eisenberg, N., Guthrie, I.D., Fabes, R.A., Shepard, S., Losoya, S., Murphy, B.C., Jones, S., Poulin, R., & Reiser, M. (2000). Prediction of elementary school children's externalizing problem behaviors from attentional and behavioral regulation and negative emotionality. *Child Development, 71,* 1367–1382.

Elliot, S.N. (2001). *Do social skills enable academic skills?* Greenfield, MA: Northeast Foundation for Children.

Elliott, S.N., & Gresham, F.M. (1987). Children's social skills: Assessment and classification practices. *Journal of Counseling & Development, 66,* 96–99.

Fabes, R.A., & Eisenberg, N. (1992). Young children's coping with interpersonal anger. *Child Development, 63,* 116–128.

Fisher, A.Q. (2001). *Finding fish. A memoir.* New York: Perennial.

Forehand, R., Well, K., & Griest, D. (1980). An examination of the social validity of a parent-training program. *Behavior Therapy, 11,* 488–502.

Frankel, F., & Myatt, R. (1994). A dimensional approach to the assessment of social competence in boys. *Psychological Assessment, 6,* 249–254.

French, D.C. (1990). Heterogeneity of peer-rejected girls. *Child Development, 61,* 2028–2031.

Frey, K.S., Hirshstein, M.K., & Guzzo, B.A. (2000). Second Step: Preventing aggression by promoting social competence. *Journal of Emotional and Behavioral Disorders, 8,* 619–701.

Garbarino, J. (1982). *Children and families in the social environment.* Hawthorne, NY: Aldine de Gruyter.

Garbarino, J. (1999). *Lost boys. Why our sons turn violent and how we can save them.* New York: Anchor Books.

Garmezy, N. (1985). Stress resistant children: The search for protective factors. In J.E. Stevenson (Ed.), *Recent research in developmental psychopathology* (pp. 213–233). New York: Pergamon Press.

Garmezy, N. (1991). Resiliency and vulnerability to adverse developmental outcomes associated with poverty. *American Behavioral Scientist, 34,* 416–430.

Garvey, C. (1986). Peer relationship and the growth of communication. In E.C. Mueller & C.R. Cooper (Eds.), *Process and outcome in peer relationships* (pp. 329–345). San Diego: Academic Press.

Gottman, J.M. (1983). How children become friends. *Monographs of the Society for Research in Child Development, 48*(3, Serial No. 201).

Gottman, J.M., & Katz, L.F. (1989). Effects of marital discord on young children's peer interaction and health. *Developmental Psychology, 25*(3), 373–381.

Gottman, J.M., Katz, L.F., & Hooven, C. (1996). Parental meta-emotion philosophy and the emotional life of families: Theoretical models and preliminary data. *Journal of Family Psychology, 10,* 243–268.

Gottman, J.M., Katz, L.F., & Hooven, C. (1997). *Meta-emotion: How families communicate emotionally.* Mahwah, NJ: Lawrence Erlbaum Associates.

Greenberg, M.T., Domitrovich, C., & Bumbarger, B. (2001). The prevention of mental disorders in school-aged children: Current state of the field. *Prevention and Treatment, 4.* Retrieved November 19, 2003, from http://journals.apa.org/prevention/volume4/pre0040001a.html

Greenberg, M.T., Kusche, C.A., Cook, E.T., & Quamma, J.P. (1995). Promoting emotional competence in school-aged children: The effects of the PATHS curriculum. *Developmental and Psychopathology, 7*(1), 117–136.

Greenberg, M., Kusche, C., & Speltz, M. (1991). Emotional regulation, self-control, and psychopathology: The role of relationships in early childhood. In D. Cicchetti & S. Toth (Eds.), *The Rochester Symposium on Developmental Psychopathology: Vol. 2. Internalizing and externalizing expressions dysfunction.* Mahwah, NJ: Lawrence Erlbaum Associates.

Greenberg, M.T., Lengua, L.L., Coie, J.D., & Pinderhughes, E.E. (1999). Predicting developmental outcomes at school entry using a multiple-risk model. Four American Communities. *Developmental Psychology, 35,* 403–417.

Gresham, F.M., & Elliot, S.N. (1990). *Social Skills Rating System manual.* Circle Pines, MN: American Guidance Service.

Gresham, F.M., Sugai, G., & Horner, R.H. (2001). Interpreting outcomes of social skills training for students with high-incidence disabilities. *Exceptional Children, 67,* 331–344.

Griffin, K.W., Scheier, L.M., Botvin, G.J., Diaz, T., & Miller, N. (1999). Interpersonal aggression in urban minority youth: Mediators of perceived neighborhood, peer, and parental influences. *Journal of Community Psychology, 27,* 281–298.

Grossman, D.C., Neckerman, H.J., Koepsell, T.D., Liu, P., Asher, K.N., Beland, K., Frey, K., & Rivara, F.P. (1997). Effectiveness of a violence prevention curriculum among children in elementary school. A randomized control trial. *Journal of the American Medical Association, 277,* 1605–1611.

Hartup, W.W. (1978). Peer interaction and processes of socialization. In M.J. Guralnick (Ed.), *Early intervention and the integration of handicapped and nonhanidcapped children* (pp. 27–51). Baltimore: University Park Press.

Hartup, W.W. (1983). Peer relations. In E.M. Hetherington (Ed.), *Handbook of child psychology: Vol. 4. Socialization, personality, and social development* (pp. 103–196). New York: John Wiley & Sons.

Howes, C., Hamilton, C.E., & Philipsen, L.C. (1998). Stability and continuity of child–caregiver and child–peer relationships. *Child Development, 69,* 418–426.

Howes, C., Matheson, C.C., & Hamilton, C.E. (1994). Maternal, teacher, and childcare history correlates of children's relationships with peers. *Child Development, 65,* 264–273.

Hubbard, J.A., & Coie, J.D. (1994). Emotional correlates of social competence in children's peer relationships. *Merrill-Palmer Quarterly, 40,* 1–20.

Hubbard, J.A. (2001). Emotion expression processes in children's peer interaction: The role of peer rejection, aggression, and gender. *Child Development, 72,* 1426–1438.

Hymel, S., Wagner, E., & Butler, L.J. (1990). Reputational bias: View from the peer group. In S.R. Asher & J.D. Coie (Eds.), *Peer rejection in childhood* (pp. 156–186). New York: Cambridge University Press.

Isley, S., O'Neil, R., & Parke, R.D. (1996). The relation of parental affect and control behaviors to children's classroom acceptance: A concurrent and predictive analysis. *Early Education & Development, 7,* 7–23.

Keane, S.P., Brown, K.P., & Crenshaw, T.M. (1990). Children's intention-cue detection as a function of maternal social behavior: Pathways to social rejection. *Developmental Psychology, 26,* 1004–1009.

Kellam, S.G., Werthamer-Larson, L., Dolan, L.J., Brown, C.H., Hendricks, C., Mayer, L.S., Rebok, G.W., Anthony, J.C., Laudolff, J., & Edelsohn, G. (1991). Developmental epidemiologically based preventive trials: Baseline modeling of early target behaviors and depressive symptoms. *American Journal of Community Psychology, 19,* 563–584.

Kopp, C.B. (1989). Regulation of distress and negative emotions: A developmental view. *Developmental Psychology, 25,* 343–354.

Kupersmidt, J.B., Coie, J.D., & Dodge, K.A. (1990). The role of poor peer relationships in the development of disorder. In S.R. Asher & J.D. Coie (Eds.), *Peer rejection in childhood* (pp. 274–305). New York: Cambridge University Press.

Ladd, G.W., Price, J.M., & Hart, C.H. (1988). Predicting preschoolers' peer status from their playground behaviors. *Child Development, 59,* 986–992.

Lahey, B.B., Green, K.D., & Forehand, R. (1980). On the independence of ratings of hyperactivity, conduct problems, and attention deficits in children: A multiple regression analysis. *Journal of Consulting and Clinical Psychology, 48,* 566–574.

Lindahl, K.M. (1998). Family process variables and children's disruptive behavior problems. *Journal of Family Psychology, 12*(3), 420–436.

Little, M., & Kobak, R. (2003). Emotional security with teachers and children's stress reactivity: A comparison of special-education and regular-education classrooms. *Journal of Clinical Child & Adolescent Psychology, 32,* 127–138.

Loeber, R., & Stouthamer-Loeber, M. (1986). Family factors as correlates and predictors of juvenile conduct problems and delinquency. In M. Tonry & N. Morris (Eds.), *Crime and justice: An annual review of research* (Vol. 7, pp. 29–149). Chicago: University of Chicago Press.

MacDonald, K. (1987). Parent-child physical play with rejected, neglected, and popular boys. *Developmental Psychology, 23,* 705–711.

MacDonald, K., & Parke, R. (1984). Bridging the gap: Parent-child play interaction and interactive competence. *Child Development, 55,* 1265–1277.

MacKinnon-Lewis, C., Lamb, M.E., Arbuckle, B., Baradaran, L.P., & Volling, B.L. (1992). The relationship between biased maternal and filial attributions and the aggressiveness of their interactions. *Development and Psychopathology, 4,* 403–415.

McMahon, S.D., Washburn, J., Felix, E.D., Yakin, J., & Childrey, G. (2000). Violence prevention: Program effects on urban preschool and kindergarten children. *Applied & Preventative Psychology, 9,* 271–281.

McMahon, S.D., Washburn, J., Felix, E.D., Yakin, J., & Childrey, G. (2000). Violence prevention: Program effects on urban preschool and kindergarten children. *Applied & Preventive Psychology, 9,* 271–281.

Merrell, K.W. (1993). *School Social Behavior Scales.* Austin, TX: PRO-ED.

Merrell, K.W. (2003). *Behavioral, social, and emotional assessment of children and adolescents* (2nd ed.). Mahwah, NJ: Lawrence Erlbaum Associates.

Morris, T.L., Messer, S.C., & Gross, A.M. (1995). Enhancement of the social interaction and status of neglected children: A peer-pairing approach. *Journal of Clinical Child Psychology, 24*(1), 11–20.

National Advisory Mental Health Council Workgroup on Child and Adolescent Mental Health Intervention Development and Deployment. (2001). *Blueprint for change: Research on child and adolescent mental health.* Bethesda, MD: National Institute of Mental Health.

Newcomb, A.F., Bukowski, W.M., & Pattee, L. (1993). Children's peer relations: A meta-analytic review of popular, rejected, neglected, controversial, and average sociometric status. *Psychological Bulletin, 113,* 99–128.

Parker, J.G., & Asher, S.R. (1987). Peer relations and later personal adjustment: Are low accepted children at risk? *Psychological Bulletin, 102,* 357–389.

Parker, J.G., & Gottman, J.M. (1989). Social and emotional development in a relational context: Friendship interaction from early childhood to adolescence. In T.J. Berndt & G.W. Ladd (Eds.), *Peer relations in child development* (pp. 15–45). New York: John Wiley & Sons.

Parkhurst, J.T., & Asher, S.R. (1992). Peer rejection in middle school: Subgroup differences in behavior, loneliness, and interpersonal concerns. *Developmental Psychology, 28,* 231–241.

Patterson, G.R. (1982). *A social learning approach: 3. Coercive family process.* Eugene, OR: Castalia.

Patterson, G.R., & Dishion, T.J. (1985). Contributions of families and peers to delinquency. *Criminology, 23,* 63–79.

Pellegrini, A.D. (1990). Elementary school children's playground behavior: Implications for children's social-cognitive development. *Children's Environments Quarterly, 7,* 8–16.

Pettit, G.S., McClaskey, C.L., Brown, M.M., & Dodge, K.A. (1987). The generalizability of laboratory assessments of children's socially competent behavior in specific situations. *Behavioral Assessment, 9,* 81–96.

Phillips, E.L., Shenker, S., & Revitz, P. (1951). The assimilation of the new child into the group. *Psychiatry, 14,* 319–325.

Piaget, J. (1965). *The moral judgment of the child* (M. Gabain, Trans.). New York: The Free Press. (Original work published 1932)

Pope, A.W., Bierman, K.L., & Mumma, G.H. (1989). Relations between hyperactive and aggressive behavior and peer relations at three elementary grade levels. *Journal of Abnormal Child Psychology, 17,* 253–267.

Putallaz, M. (1983). Predicting children's sociometric status from their behavior. *Child Development, 54,* 1417–1426.

Putallaz, M. (1987). Maternal behavior and sociometric status. *Child Development, 58,* 324–340.

Putallaz, M., & Gottman, J.M. (1981). An interactional model of children's entry into peer groups. *Child Development, 52,* 986–994.

Putallaz, M., & Helfin, A.H. (1990). Parent-child interaction. In S.R. Asher & J.D. Coie (Eds.), *Peer rejection in childhood* (pp. 189–216). New York: Cambridge University Press.

Putallaz, M., & Wasserman, A. (1989). Children's naturalistic entry behavior and sociometric status: A developmental perspective. *Developmental Psychology, 25,* 297–305.

Putallaz, M., & Wasserman, A. (1990). Parent-child interaction. In S.R. Asher & J.D. Coie (Eds.), *Peer rejection in childhood*. New York: Cambridge University Press.

Reynolds, C.R., & Kamphaus, R.W. (1992). *Behavioral Assessment System for Children manual*. Circle Pines, MN: American Guidance Service.

Roberts, W.L., & Strayer, J. (1987). Parents' responses to the emotional distress of their children: Relations with children's competence. *Developmental Psychology, 23,* 415–422.

Rodkin, P.C., Farmer, T.W., Pearl, R., & Van Acker, R. (2000). Heterogeneity of popular boys: Antisocial and prosocial configurations. *Developmental Psychology, 36,* 14–24.

Roopnarine, J.L., & Adams, G.R. (1987). Social interaction patterns of high, average, and low sociometric status children. *Journal of the American Academy of Child & Adolescent Psychiatry, 26,* 28–32.

Rothbart, M.K., & Derryberry, D. (1981). Development of individual differences in temperament. In M.E. Lamb & A.L. Brown (Eds.), *Advances in developmental psychology: Vol. 1* (pp. 37–86). Mahwah, NJ: Lawrence Erlbaum Associates.

Rubin, K.H., Bukowski, W., & Parker, J. (1998). Peer interactions, relationship, and groups. In W. Damon & N. Eisenberg (Eds.), *Handbook of child psychology: Vol. 3. Social, emotional, and personality development* (5th ed., pp. 619–700). New York: Wiley.

Rutter, M. (1987). Psychosocial resilience and protective mechanisms. *American Journal of Orthopsychiatry, 57,* 316–331.

Sameroff, A., & Seifer, R. (1983). Familial risk and child competence. *Child Development, 54,* 1254–1268.

Sancilio, M.F. (1987). Peer interaction as a method of therapeutic intervention with children. *Clinical Psychology Review, 7*(5), 475–500.

Sattler, J.M. (2002). *Assessment of children. Behavioral and clinical applications* (4th ed.). San Diego: Author.

Schwartz, D., & Proctor, L.J. (2000). Community violence exposure and children's social adjustment in the school peer. The mediating roles of emotion regulation and social cognition. *Journal of Consulting and Clinical Psychology, 68,* 670–683.

Searcy, S. (1996). Friendship interventions for the integration of children and youth with learning and behavior problems. *Preventing School Failure, 40*(3), 131–134.

Sheridan, S.M. (1998). *Why don't they like me? Helping your child make and keep friends.* Longmont, CO: Sopris West.

Shinn, M.R., Ramsey, E., Walker, H.M., Steiber, S., & O'Neil, R.E. (1987). Antisocial behavior in school settings: Initial differences in an at-risk and normal population. *Journal of Special Education, 21,* 69–84.

Shonkoff, J.P., & Phillips, D.A. (Eds.). (2000). *From neurons to neighborhoods: The science of early childhood development.* Washington, DC: National Academy Press.

Sroufe, A.L., Schork, E., Motti, F., Lawroski, N., & LaFreniere, P. (1984). The role of affect in social competence. In C.E. Izard, J. Kagan, & R.B. Zajonc (Eds.), *Emotions, cognition, and behavior* (pp. 289–319). New York: Cambridge University Press.

Stanger, C., & Lewis, M. (1993). Agreement among parents, teachers, and children on internalizing and externalizing behavior problems. *Journal of Clinical Child Psychology, 1,* 107–115.

Stouthamer-Loeber, M., Loeber, R., Wei, E., Farrington, D.P., & Wikström, P.H. (2002). Risk and promotive effects in the explanation of persistent serious delinquency in boys. *Journal of Consulting and Clinical Psychology, 70,* 111–123.

Underwood, M.K., Kupersmidt, J.B., & Coie, J.D. (1996). Childhood peer sociometric status and aggression as predictors of adolescent childbearing. *Journal of Research on Adolescence, 6,* 201–223.

Van Schoiack-Edstrom, L., Frey, K.S., & Beland, K. (2002). Changing adolescents' attitudes about relational and physical aggression: An early evaluation of a school-based intervention. *School Psychology Review, 31,* 201–216.

Vaughn, S., McIntosh, R., & Spencer-Rowe, J. (1991). Peer rejection is a stubborn thing: Increasing peer acceptance of rejected students with learning disabilities. *Learning Disabilities Research & Practice, 6*(2), 83–88.

Walker, H.M., Homer, R.H., Sugai, G., Bullis, M., Sprague, J.R., Bricker, D., & Kaufman, M.J. (1996). Integrated approaches to preventing antisocial behavior patterns among school-age children and youth. *Journal of Emotional and Behavioral Disorders, 4,* 194–209.

Walker, H.M., & Severson, H. (1992). *Systematic screening for behavior disorders* (2nd ed.). Longmont, CO: Sopris West.

Wentzel, K.R., & Asher, S.R (1995). The academic level of neglected, rejected, popular, and controversial children. *Child Development, 66,* 754–763.

Wilson, B.J. (1999). Entry behavior and emotion regulation abilities of developmentally delayed boys. *Developmental Psychology, 35,* 214–222.

Wilson, B.J. (2003). The role of attentional processes in children's prosocial behavior: Emotion and shifting attention. *Development and Psychopathology, 15,* 313–329.

Wilson, B.J. (2004). *The entry behavior of aggressive/rejected children: The contribution of temperament.* (Manuscript submitted for publication).

Wilson, B.J., & Gottman, J.M. (1996). Attention—the shuttle between emotion and cognition: Risk, resiliency, and physiological bases. In E.M. Hetherington & E.A. Blechman (Eds.), *Stress, coping, and resiliency in children and families* (pp. 189–228). Mahwah, NJ: Lawrence Erlbaum Associates.

Youngblade, L.M., & Belsky, J. (1992). Parent–child antecedents of 5-year-olds' close friendships: A longitudinal analysis. *Developmental Psychology, 28,* 700–713.

Zakriski, A.L., & Coie, J.D. (1996). A comparison of aggressive/rejected and nonaggressive-rejected children's interpretations of self-directed and other-directed rejection. *Child Development, 67,* 1048–1070.

Zahn-Waxler, C., Radke-Yarrow, M., & Kind, R.A. (1979). Child rearing and children's prosocial initiations toward victims of distress. *Child Development, 50,* 319–330.

13

Adjustment Disorders

Don MacDonald and Ginger MacDonald

● ●

Chapter Concepts

- Adjustment disorders in comparison with other mental health disorders
- Adjustment disorders in the context of developmental, daily, and situational stressors
- Intervention options
- Role of school personnel in working with students who have adjustment disorders

Adjustment disorders are common among children with psychiatric diagnoses; although usually diagnosed in adolescence, these disorders may occur at any age (Kaplan & Sadock, 1996). The ratio of adjustment disorder diagnoses for females and males is approximately two to one. Among children and adolescents of either gender, common precipitating stressors include school problems, parental rejection or divorce, and substance abuse problems (American Psychiatric Association [APA], 2000). The following vignette illustrates a possible adjustment disorder.

Carlo, age 10, is in fifth grade. At the end of fourth grade, he was reading at fourth-grade level and his math skills were at beginning fifth-grade level. His height and weight were normal. He was very sociable, and other children often interacted with him. Now, at the start of fifth grade, however, Carlo cannot seem to concentrate on his schoolwork. He daydreams and draws pictures, which often depict Carlo and his brother together. He frequently falls asleep in class.

Carlo's fifth-grade teacher found out that at the end of his fourth-grade year, Carlo's parents had an acrimonious divorce. His father disappeared and his mother started working two jobs. Despite his protests, Carlo went to live with his maternal grandmother while his 7-year-old brother, Michael, continued to live with their mother.

Over the summer between fourth and fifth grades, Carlo and his brother were enrolled in swimming lessons. Carlo always walked to his mother's house to pick up Michael; then, they walked to their lessons together. One day in August, however, Carlo spent the night at a friend's house. This friend lived on the other side of town, so Carlo and Michael walked to their swimming lessons separately. As Michael crossed the street by the recreation center, he was killed when a car hit him. Carlo arrived moments after the accident happened.

• •

Carlo's situation exemplifies something that often occurs in schools. A student's behavior changes, sometimes suddenly, and a teacher or some other staff member wonders how to help. It is possible the student is physically ill. If physical illness is unlikely or, better yet, ruled out by a medical examination, then the student is probably experiencing a mental health disorder. As other chapters in this book make clear, many different disorders are possible. Among the most common, however, are adjustment disorders. This chapter discusses adjustment disorders, illustrating them through Carlo's story.

The text revision of the *Diagnostic and Statistical Manual of Mental Disorders, Fourth Edition* (DSM-IV-TR), defines *adjustment disorders* as definite emotional and / or behavioral signs of distress in reaction to one or more identifiable stressful events in an individual's life (APA, 2000). Most people have immediate reactions to stressful events. It is also typical for people to have initial reactions (e.g., feeling frightened) or delayed, secondary reactions (e.g., having scary dreams). To meet the criteria for adjustment disorder, however, the reactions must occur within 3 months of the start of the stressful event. In addition, once the stressful events end, the reactions continue no longer than 6 months (APA, 2000). Furthermore, an adjustment disorder diagnosis is appropriate when the reactions are 1) more severe than those of most people in similar situations, 2) are more severe than how that person normally reacts, or 3) are accompanied by obvious complications in social relationships, employment, and/or school achievement.

Stressors may be single events (e.g., birth of a sibling), multiple events, chronic (e.g., best friend has cancer), or seasonal (e.g., a child moving during the summer to live with a noncustodial parent). In Carlo's case, the stressors were multiple and chronic: his brother's death, his parents' divorce, his father's absence, and separation from his mother.

DIFFERENTIAL DIAGNOSIS

The DSM-IV-TR definition of an adjustment disorder is broad enough to apply to daily life, yet this broadness makes it difficult to interpret. That is, the experience is recognizable but few can define it. In addition, educational literature (e.g., Kauffman, 2001; King, Randolph, McKay, & Bartell, 1995) tends to avoid DSM terms. Instead, terms such as *emotional disorder, behavioral disorder,* or *at risk* are common in educational circles. Neither nomenclature—educational nor psychiatric—is better. However, it is important to recognize that both use different terms to refer to similar phenomena.

Symptoms

The most challenging factor in differential diagnosis is that many symptoms of adjustment disorders are also symptoms of other disorders (Strain, 1995; Widiger & Clark, 2000). Other diagnoses that especially overlap are substance-related disorders (especially drug abuse), anxiety disorders, mood disorders (particularly regarding emotional swings), somatoform disorders (i.e., mental distress manifesting as physical symptoms), and sleep disorders. Such an overlap makes sense, given that humans consist of interrelated parts that continuously affect each other (Bee & Boyd, 2003; McGoldrick & Carter, 1999). For example, a child may show emotional distress over a pet being killed by a car. The distress might look like depression, with the symptoms of appetite loss, sleeping longer than usual, and frequent crying. Or the distress may look like anxiety, with the symptoms of engagement in incessant activities, insomnia, and drug use. Depending on the individual, either scenario (or other symptom combinations) could characterize an adjustment disorder. Untreated adjustment reactions in these scenarios could evolve into a diagnosable mood disorder (depression, in this case) or an anxiety disorder.

In addition to having overlapping symptoms, adjustment disorders can function, in effect, as gateways into and out of other disorders (Widiger & Clark, 2000). Thus, an accurate diagnosis of adjustment disorder might identify, for example, movement into what would later be diagnosed as depression or movement out of a diagnosable depressive episode. Chapters 8, 10, 11, and 12 describe disorders particularly relevant to the gateway function of adjustment disorders.

Another difficulty is determining what is meant by an identifiable symptom. An *identifiable symptom* is a symptom that appears in a pattern of observable behavior and is a notable change from an individual's usual behavior. Therefore, it is important for at least one educator (usually a teacher) to become familiar with particular students' typical behaviors. In some educational settings and with some students (e.g., those who are quiet and uninvolved in class activities), this can be a challenge. Carlo's teacher is likely more familiar with student behaviors because elementary school teachers and students have regular interactions and spend much of the school day together. Middle school/junior high and high school teachers face a greater challenge in this respect. Unless they have contact with students outside of the classroom (e.g., sports, student government, yearbook staff), teachers may only see a particular group of students during a few class periods per week. As difficult as it may be for secondary educators to observe typical actions of each student, they may nevertheless recognize departures from what is usual.

Timing

Timing can also present challenges for diagnosing an adjustment disorder. Initially, it may be difficult to tie behavioral changes to specific events because, by definition, it may take up to 3 months for symptoms to be expressed, and symptoms do not always subside as soon as the stressor ceases (Kaplan & Sadock, 1996). At the beginning of the school year, teachers typically do not know students well. Teachers also may be unaware of student stressors from the previous school year or summer vacation. Little to nothing may be known about a new student, so the educators have no baseline with which to compare behavior.

Determining when a problem exists is highly subjective. One person might see a problem when another sees positive development. Often, the person who has the most authority determines whether student actions are problematic (Ungar, 2001). School staff members and parents, of course, have more influence than other students. Thus, school officials or parents are most likely to determine when a problem exists and to define the nature of the problem. However, others— including students—may not agree with these decisions.

Culture

Adjustment disorders have been diagnosed in children and adolescents all over the world; it is truly a universal, multicultural issue. For example, there has been a dramatic increase in school refusal among elementary and middle school students in Japan, where there is extremely high pressure for school success. One study analyzed the underlying problems and found that adjustment disorders formed the most common diagnosis (Iwamoto & Yoshida, 1997). In 1999, children were affected by an earthquake in Turkey's Marmara region. Those who actually experienced the quake and those who experienced vicarious stress by being part of the community near the quake region had trauma reactions. Many of these children were diagnosed as having an adjustment disorder (Demir, Demir, Alkas, & Kayaalp, 2000).

Many cultures are represented within the United States, each of which has unwritten rules about how one should respond to stress (Carter & McGoldrick, 1999). Sometimes, these rules take counterproductive forms of helping, such as excessive doting or pampering the child, encouraging a stoic "don't cry" approach, ignoring emotions, or attempting to pacify problems with food or money (O'Hanlon & Weiner-Davis, 1989). Educators must try to become somewhat familiar with the family's normal coping mechanisms before asking anyone to respond in a manner that may be unfamiliar or contradictory.

DIAGNOSTIC SIGNS AND CLASSROOM SYMPTOMS

Diagnosing adjustment disorders is difficult. Teachers are on the front line for identifying changes that may indicate emotional or behavioral disorders. Although teachers are not responsible for making diagnoses, identification of symptoms may come through direct teacher observations. Table 13.1 lists symptoms that often appear in elementary and secondary school classrooms. The table shows that although some symptoms overlap, students frequently display distress differently according to developmental level.

In some cases, such information may come directly from the individual. That is, students such as Carlo may simply tell a custodian, teacher, or office staff member about the major life stressors that they are experiencing. Students also may be the primary source of information by alluding to stressors in their lives.

Table 13.1. Common symptoms of an adjustment disorder

Elementary school students	Secondary school students
Crying, tearfulness	Crying, tearfulness
Falling asleep in class	Falling asleep in class
Loss of bladder or bowel control	Voicing hopelessness, apathy
Arguments with teacher or peers	Arguments with teacher or peers
Refusal to follow directions	Drug use (legal or illegal)
Voicing sadness	Voicing sadness
Inattention to classroom activities	Inattention to classroom activities
Extreme activity	Physically fighting with teacher or peers
Physically fighting with teacher or peers	Skipping school or classes
Skipping school or classes	Decline in assignment completion
Decline in assignment completion	Decline in academic achievement
Decline in academic achievement	Refusal to follow directions
	Reckless driving
	Accruing debts

Source: American Psychiatric Association (2000).

For example, when asked why he had been falling asleep in class during the past week, one student commented, "You wouldn't understand—I wish I could just run away." This comment may connote significant stressors, and an observant educator would be wise to gently question the student about the comment's meaning.

Distress often surfaces in a student's academic work (Carlson & Lewis, 2002; Orton, 1997). Overall achievement usually drops somewhat and sometimes dramatically. Contents of academic work can also be revealing. Hence, class journal entries, stories, visual art, or other work that requires students to draw on their own lives may at times evidence distress. In Carlo's case, his achievement dropped and his drawings revealed distress.

Friends constitute a second key source regarding excessive stress in a student's life. A worried friend might tell a teacher or school counselor that a student is going through difficulties. The friend might seek the advice of a school nurse or coach about a friend who is experiencing a specific problem and ask what he or she should do about it. This truly could be one friend seeking advice about another. However, this "friend" could be the student him- or herself, trying to determine whether the adult is a safe person in whom he or she can confide.

A student's family may also volunteer information about stressors. This is more likely to occur at the elementary level than at the secondary level because parents tend to be more directly involved with elementary school staff. Such disclosures often happen at elementary school parent–teacher conferences. A school open house or extracurricular event is another occasion that brings educators and parents together, increasing the possibility that parents might share stressors that their children are experiencing.

Sometimes, an educator gets clues about distress from observing a student's interactions with the whole class or a particular group of students. Just as departures from typical individual behavior may indicate distress, alterations in group behavior can indicate distress. Sometimes teachers notice this change, as shown in the vignette that follows.

Alexia is a junior high student who usually converses and jokes with a particular group of students. During the past 2 weeks, however, a teacher notices that Alexia hardly speaks to anyone in the class, the group of students include her less in their interactions, and the other group members talk less in class. These changes signal different group dynamics, which, among other possibilities, might connote that Alexia is experiencing an adjustment disorder.

CAUSES OF ADJUSTMENT DISORDERS

Why does an adjustment disorder arise? A detailed review of this question is beyond this chapter's objectives, and the exact etiology of the diagnosis is unclear.

Nevertheless, the following section presents current thinking about the topic. This information is presented to highlight that an adjustment disorder is not a simplistic diagnosis that is attributable to one or even two factors. In addition, understanding its origins may help an educator respond to a distressed student with greater perspective.

One factor is genetics. Although there is still a lot to learn about genetics and human behavior, research suggests that much of the way individuals respond to the world—that quality commonly called *personality*—is genetically influenced. Temperament, resiliency (i.e., the ability to bounce back after a stressful event), and vulnerability to stress all have genetic components (Everett & Gallop, 2001). People are born with tendencies to act and react, and these tendencies seem to persist throughout life (Bee & Boyd, 2003; Kail & Cavanaugh, 1996). Thus, some people always have emotional and behavioral difficulty adapting to changes in their environment, some adapt very easily, and others adapt somewhere between the two extremes. Someone who has difficulty adapting generally is at higher risk for developing an adjustment disorder than an individual who adapts easily. These tendencies, of course, are modified by environmental factors, such as learned coping skills, family support, and the overall stressfulness of a person's living circumstances (Strain, 1995).

A second general factor involves brain–behavior connections (Bloom, Nelson, & Lazerson, 2001; Silver, 2001). That is, the nervous system, especially the brain, continually interacts with the individual's external environment in sensing, perceiving, interpreting, remembering, and acting on endless life events and decisions. This factor is related to genetics in that humans probably inherit most of the potential for such connections. Research is clear, however, that brain and behavior mutually influence each other. The nature or nurture argument is passé; both contribute to life developments, including adjustment disorders (Bee & Boyd, 2003; Ostrander, 2001).

A third general factor concerns the nature of stressors. Stressors emerge from daily life experiences. They also arise from issues that families and cultural groups address over many years (Carter & McGoldrick, 1999; McKenry & Price, 2000). Regarding daily stressors, a student who acquires a sexually transmitted disease, for instance, has a high chance of experiencing an adjustment disorder. Another student who has never engaged in sexual intercourse but is strongly considering the possibility may also be at risk for developing an adjustment disorder if he or she was raised in a family with strong prohibitions against about such behavior. This scenario is an instance of a historical stressor: The pressure of obedience to family rules that have perhaps existed for several generations can induce stress in the same manner as a definable external event (Carter & McGoldrick, 1999).

Related to this discussion is the nature of the trauma itself and the cultural context in which it occurs. The amount of control the student has over the situation and the qualitative and quantitative variability in the events influence the student's emotional reactions (Everett & Gallop, 2001). For example, the various types of sexual abuse, from touching to sadistic, violent aggression, may prompt a variety of responses in a child or teenager (Rind, Tromovitch, & Bauserman, 1998;

Schreiber & Lyddon, 1998). In such situations, perceptions held by parents and other significant people in a child's life can range from "child as victim" to "child as seducer of an adult." Hence, it is vital to discern the type of trauma and its perceptual context.

A fourth general factor is development. Certain times in life may predispose a student to react to stressors more severely than other times (Arnett, 1999; Ivey & Ivey, 1998; Walsh, Galassi, Murphy, & Park-Taylor, 2002). Reaction to a stressful event is often affected by the individual's developmental stage. If a student is entering a transition between developmental stages, the next stage of development may be delayed or signs of regression may appear. For example, consider a 7-year-old student who is just learning to read. A severe crisis occurs in her family. If she reacts by developing an adjustment disorder, her reading readiness is likely to regress and perhaps will be delayed. This may then contribute to delays in other learning processes for which reading skills lay a foundation (e.g., reading story problems in math).

Trauma during adolescent transitions can affect identity development. For instance, consider an adolescent who is in the process of moving away from her close identity with her mother and toward defining herself. If her mother suddenly dies, the adolescent might need to care for her younger siblings. Loss of her mother as a model plus her new child care responsibilities might foster a severe delay in her ability to establish her own identity (Murray, 2000). She may experience an adjustment disorder as a result.

As noted previously, an extreme reaction to events is one criterion for the diagnosis of an adjustment disorder. For example, Carlo reacted to multiple traumas. It is important to remember, however, that everyone reacts to stressors differently, especially those at different age levels. Children react differently than teenagers. Teenagers react differently than adults. So, it is not appropriate to compare a student to how an educator would respond; rather, it is necessary to compare the behavior to how that student typically reacts at difficult times. Although people react differently, comparing a student to how other same-age students typically respond is also a reasonable developmental measure when necessary (Bee & Boyd, 2003).

This discussion has addressed many of the major causes of adjustment disorders. None of the factors operate alone; some or all interact. Whereas making the diagnosis is complex, the good news is that identification of a potential adjustment disorder—along with intervention—is possible without knowing exactly why the disorder developed. It is still necessary to appreciate the complexity of the disorder because equally complex are interventions needed to address it.

SCHOOL-BASED INTERVENTIONS

Teachers are seldom the direct therapeutic agents for students with mental health disorders. Even so, they are often the first to recognize problems in students' daily lives and are often contacted for support and advice in the treatment process.

This section discusses direct helping services—both in and out of school—that need to occur for educators to maintain supportive relationships with these students and to help them succeed academically. Some students do recover from adjustment disorders without assistance; for others, however, the absence of help contributes to more serious mental health problems (Strain, 1995).

A key to recovering from an adjustment disorder is for the student to recognize his or her stressor(s) and begin working to cope intellectually, emotionally, and relationally (Strain, 1995). This may involve breaking through denial, whether it is about the death of a loved one, a runaway pet, or some other loss. This includes admitting that life will not be the same. Acknowledging the difficulty of a transition raises the odds of understanding that it can be handled and will eventually end (Bee & Boyd, 2003). It may be useful to help older children and adolescents understand how their current reaction is a barrier to getting life back to normal (Carlson & Lewis, 2002; Orton, 1997). Therapy or counseling can help students adapt to chronic stressors and can serve as preventive intervention should the stress recur (Kaplan & Sadock, 1996).

Crisis intervention may be necessary (Brammer & MacDonald, 2003). This direct and sometimes invasive intervention is aimed at helping a student resolve an immediate severe reaction so that he or she can eventually work through the issue. It can take various forms, including hospitalization or removal from school for a few days under the care of a helpful adult. By nature, it involves direct action, sometimes without the child's knowledge or consent. If this type of intervention is necessary, it should be done under the guidance of a mental health professional. In any event, if a crisis reaction (e.g., uncontrollable crying) occurs at school, a teacher should not attempt crisis intervention alone; immediate notification of and support from the principal, school counselor, and/or security personnel is required. Notification and consent of parents or guardians is necessary for treatment beyond the immediate crisis event.

In most situations, adjustment disorders that are evident at school may be treated by supportive interventions. The student typically needs three types of support: 1) a relationship in which the student feels accepted; 2) a degree of direct counseling or intervention by a trained mental health professional; and 3) a clear plan, developed with the student, by which he or she can work through the stressful time in a structured fashion. A support strategy that entails multiple sources of assistance is most helpful (Brammer & MacDonald, 2003).

Supportive, caring relationships are critical because a student with an adjustment disorder does not act like him- or herself. Adults and peers may not know how to react or may avoid the student. The student may be unaware of how his or her coping behaviors annoy or worry others. Although not the student's primary caregiver, the teacher needs to be a caring adult during this difficult time. An adult can demonstrate caring through acts such as spending extra time with a student after school, protecting the student from teasing, and showing additional patience with the student's mood swings. It is equally important for the teacher to help build a schoolwide system of adult relationships for this student so that the student does not become overly dependent on one adult. Whatever the teacher can do to develop supportive actions from other students is helpful as well (e.g., assigning the distressed student to a learning group whose members are likely to treat the student with understanding).

Another option is referring the student to group therapy with those who have similar experiences (Jacobs & Schimmel, 2005; Sullivan, 2002; Toth & Erwin, 1998). This can occur at school (e.g., an after-school group for children of divorce) or in another setting (e.g., a hospital-based group for children with cancer).

Teachers can support students by alerting other responsible adults to these students' needs. In addition, educators can offer support through various methods: basic helping skills, individual conversations with students (e.g., at a special time before or after school), and normal classroom activities. These methods are explored in the ensuing paragraphs.

Brammer and MacDonald (2003) noted various basic helping skills that can be used to support students. One skill is listening, which includes attending to verbal and nonverbal behaviors. Leading skills are important, too, especially for encouraging students to share and elaborate on their situations. Reflecting skills involve empathetic responding to core messages. Finally, informing skills are useful, particularly for providing basic information and making referrals. Educators are generally effective in these areas because the skills help constitute what is considered good teaching.

The primary advice for effective conversations with students is to listen more and talk less. Would-be helpers often accuse people with adjustment disorders of being in denial or trying to get attention. It is important for educators to realize that knowledge is not necessarily related to acceptance or deep understanding. Students may intellectually know that something stressful has happened but have emotional and/or social blocks to acceptance. Conversely, sometimes children are denied important information that could help them process a stressful event. For example, some families choose not to tell children about the illness or imminent death of a loved one. Children often sense that something is wrong. School personnel must respect family wishes in this regard but can still encourage students to talk about their feelings and concerns.

A real challenge for a teacher is finding the time needed to engage a student in such a significant discussion. Therefore, if the teacher decides to help the student in this manner, it is imperative that the educator does not rush the conversation or schedule it when outside interruptions are likely. Teachers who seek to provide such support must understand that it might become a significant time investment. This is a cogent reason for referral to a school counselor.

Teachers and other school staff also must be careful not to enter into a relationship that provides secondary gain for a student. *Secondary gain* means that the student likes the extra attention or release from responsibility, which can have the unintended effect of reinforcing the symptoms requiring help (O'Hanlon & Weiner-Davis, 1989). Students should not continually be excused from experiencing the consequences of their behaviors but, rather, be helped to understand them and to adjust. This is a reason that no educator in the school should be a student's sole compassionate caregiver.

Teachers should be aware that all students are telling their stories in their everyday interactions with the world. Thus, teachers may use normal classroom activities and regular assignments to help students work through issues, being aware that students who are facing difficult life issues often respond more extremely than others. These activities can be done with all students or for an individual student. For a student with an adjustment disorder or other serious mental health issue, these activities should only be done in consultation with the student's mental health provider, such as the school counselor. Table 13.2 gives examples of curricular ideas which allow students to process ideas in the classroom. Multidisciplinary units may be especially helpful.

Whichever venue or assignment is used, teachers should realize that a student's understanding or telling of a distressing story is his or her current perception of it. It may be exaggerated or minimized compared with how others see it. It may be a direct description, or it may be a metaphoric representation of the emotional experience. Chronology and the sense of time may be distorted. It is therefore important not to over- or underreact or make too many assumptions without putting the story in the context of the student's life.

At a certain point, an action plan for recovery is necessary for all people who have experienced a crisis or chronic stressors. This plan should be developed in conjunction with counselors, social workers, or others who work with the student. Furthermore, students make better progress if they participate in developing plans for their recovery (Carlson & Lewis, 2002; Orton, 1997). If a student has fallen behind academically, a plan that breaks the unfinished work into smaller steps is helpful. Whenever possible, parents or other caregivers should be included in this planning.

It is important to note that school districts have legal and financial responsibilities for providing interventions and accommodations for students with physical or emotional/behavioral disabilities. Outside services for treating adjustment disorders may be costly, so teachers should never recommend that parents seek outside services. School counselors, school psychologists, and principals are trained in making such recommendations in a manner that helps families without

Table 13.2. Curricular activities for helping students process personal issues

Journals or creative writing	The teacher can assign topics that allow the student to explore issues gently. This also allows the student to find a comfortable level of personal disclosure.
Books	The teacher can assign reading that explores experiences similar to those experienced by the student. Fiction or biographies can be helpful.
Social studies	The teacher can lead discussions of cultural issues that are similar to those experienced by the student or that mirror the student's background.
Music	Choral music in particular can be helpful when the student vicariously identifies with the message of certain songs.
Drama	Acting out stories or scenes with appropriate and personally meaningful themes can be helpful for the student.

making the school or district financially responsible for the services (unless the district chooses to become responsible) (Fischer & Sorensen, 1996).

Duties of Educational Personnel

Many people in a school system interact with a student who has an adjustment disorder. This section discusses some frequent responsibilities of school personnel in this regard as well as some unexpected ways in which school staff may be able to help. Regardless of exact responsibilities, communication and cooperation among educators, family, mental health professionals, and other community resources optimize the student's chance for improvement (Deveaux, 1997; Guishard, 1998; Rotter & Boveja, 1999).

Teachers   Although the role of the teacher has been discussed throughout this chapter, it is helpful to synthesize the topic here. The teacher's primary role is the academic development of his or her students. Of course, teachers know that the whole student is of value and to be nurtured, but the explicit task is academic achievement. The teacher is charged to teach each student, so when one student struggles or needs additional attention, the teacher must weigh how much time and energy should be devoted to that individual in light of the other students' needs. This is why the teacher must have networks with school and community resources and must communicate effectively with parents. As soon as a teacher senses barriers to a student's academic success, those networks and parent–teacher relationships may be explored.

Administrators   School administrators, such as the principal and vice principal, are responsible for a school's academic and social climate. They are also responsible for the school's fiscal and legal matters. Administrators often are the ones who notify relevant school staff members about a student's stressors. The principal may assemble a team for a meeting on how to handle announcements to students and parents regarding schoolwide stressors. If a stressor is a public event, administrators, perhaps even at the district level, need to address the media. This could include protecting the affected student(s) from reporters, instructing staff about talking to reporters, and keeping members of the media off school property.

Except in small schools, principals seldom provide direct services to students. Regardless of the setting, principals ensure that services are provided by others in the school, the school district, and/or the community.

School Counselors   Depending on the grade level, the size of the school and/or district, and the way that helping services are organized, the roles of the school counselor, school psychologist, and school social worker may overlap. A discussion of each includes typical functions for these professionals, but functions can vary from school to school.

The school counselor may play a significant role in working with a student who has an adjustment disorder. It may be the counselor's responsibility to talk to the education staff about the student's disorder and to explain the interactions of emotional, behavioral, and academic achievement issues. The counselor may be the first (or the only) school staff member to talk to the student's parents or guardians. If there has been a prolonged absence, the counselor may need to help the student return to his or her classes and design a workable schedule to catch up. It is generally the counselor's role to determine whether the student should receive in-school intervention services, such as individual or small group counseling sessions (Rotter & Boveja, 1999; Sink, 2005).

Another significant role for the counselor is the education of other students about the individual's situation. This must be considered very carefully, but it is frequently helpful to have a class meeting prior to a student's return to school. This type of meeting helps the students know how to act when their peer returns, as shown in the following vignette.

Leilani, age 11, has cancer and an adjustment disorder. Because her cancer treatment caused hair loss, she was afraid of being laughed at and refused to leave the house. Leilani's counselor and sixth-grade teacher held a class meeting to help the other students become sensitive to Leilani's situation. The counselor explained what cancer is and how Leilani might be afraid. She also normalized the classmates' potential irrational fears, such as the fear that cancer is contagious. As a result, some of the other students decided to shave their heads so that their friend would not feel so different, and the class welcomed Leilani back in a supportive manner.

• •

Many adjustment disorders are influenced by complications at home, such as parental conflict (Demo, Fine, & Ganong, 2000), abuse of alcohol or other drugs (Hudak, Krestan, & Bepko, 1999), family violence (Ford et al., 2000), loss or grief (Murray, 2000), chronic illness (Rolland, 1999), or a myriad of other stressors. School may be the only place where the student feels safety and structure. It is very important for the counselor to ask the student how much he or she wants to talk about personal issues at school. The student may not want changed expectations or behaviors because these would alter the comforts of structure. This request would not be seen as denial but as a positive coping mechanism. Thus, careful counselor–student exploration of the issues is necessary to reach appropriate intervention decisions.

A significant role of the school counselor is preventing emotional and behavioral problems through what Sears (2005) has called *large group guidance*. With this approach, counselors and teachers work together to meld positive mental health instruction and the general classroom curriculum. Large group guidance can teach students how to cope with stress in daily life and in difficult situations, thereby reducing the likelihood of overreaction to stress and the development of an adjustment disorder.

The job descriptions of most school counselors do not supply the time or permission to conduct intensive counseling with students (Sink, 2005). Frequently, a student is referred to a community mental health counselor or the family is referred to a marriage and family therapist to provide the ongoing counseling and support (Deveaux, 1997; Walsh et al., 2002). Schools seldom mandate such counseling but often strongly recommend it. It is desirable, then, for the community therapist and the school counselor to maintain contact to gauge the impact of therapy on the student's academic performance. The school counselor should facilitate a release of information from the student's parent(s) so that school and community counselors may talk with each other.

School Psychologists   The school psychologist is often the professional who first determines the diagnosis. A school psychologist may be consulted by a parent, teacher, or other staff member who observes the student behaving in ways that are unexpected or extreme for the situation. The school psychologist can then assess the student's academic, intellectual, social, and emotional functioning. Any developmental difficulties may be assessed. With these assessment results, the school psychologist can compare past and current behavior. If the student has been previously identified to receive special education services, an adjustment disorder may complicate or interfere with the progress expected by his or her individualized education program (IEP); modifications may have to be made with the entire special education team and noted in the IEP (Kauffman, 2001). Because school psychologists are also limited in the time that they can commit to any one individual student, they may be the point of referral to a licensed psychologist, mental health counselor, family therapist, social worker, or community agency.

A licensed psychologist in the community may work with the student to deal with the underlying stressor(s) that precipitated the adjustment disorder. The psychologist should have expertise in working with young people. It is also helpful if the psychologist has experience working with families, because many students' reactions are embedded in complex family dynamics, as illustrated by Carlo's situation (Johnson, Cowan, & Cowan, 1999; McGuire et al., 1999).

If medication is needed, a child psychiatrist may be involved as well. Although laws in some states are changing, most psychologists cannot write prescriptions. It is quite common for psychologists and psychiatrists to work together for a combined treatment approach (Strain, 1995).

A Note About Medication   Treatment of children and adolescents with medication dictates caution and should be undertaken by a child psychiatrist who is trained in childhood mental health disorders. Few, if any, adjustment disorders can be adequately treated by medication alone. In most cases, psychotherapy or other forms of person-to-person assistance are the most significant part of treatment (Kappan & Sadock, 1996; Strain, 1995). When medication is prescribed, it is typically the type used to treat depression or anxiety, depending on the presenting symptoms.

Medication for other disorders (e.g., attention-deficit/hyperactivity disorder) may need to be adjusted. As Preda, Madlener, and Hetherington (1998) noted, care should be taken in treating children with mental health issues because overlapping diagnoses sometimes yield overlapping drug treatments. They also suggested that managed care health care providers or parents frequently push the prescription of multiple medications to stabilize symptoms as rapidly as possible. In such cases, a new problem may then develop: medications masking symptoms that need to be addressed for recovery.

School Social Workers Although some school social workers have roles similar to those of school counselors, they traditionally work with students and families and act as liaisons to necessary outside services. It may be that the precipitating crisis for the student is a parent's unemployment or eviction from the family's home. The social worker can connect the family to social services such as emergency housing agencies, food banks, or emergency medical care providers. These services may not directly address the student's adjustment disorder or academic performance, but they relieve some stressors. In turn, this allows a greater likelihood of success for other mental health or academic interventions.

School social workers commonly refer students and families to community social service agencies for continued support. Furthermore, in cases of abuse or neglect, it is frequently the social worker who makes the mandatory contact and follow-through with child protective services.

School Nurses The school nurse is commonly involved with a student who has an adjustment disorder, especially if the student has multiple diagnoses with physical components. For example, a high school student who had an abortion has developed an adjustment disorder, which manifests in extreme ritualistic behaviors that serve as her "penance." Yet, the student is continuing to engage in sexual behavior that could result in another pregnancy. The school nurse could provide needed information and consultation that would benefit this student.

The school nurse is also responsible for dispensing any medications, including those used to treat adjustment disorders. It is unusual for schools to have full-time nurses, however, so this job often goes to an office staff member.

Other School Personnel Many schools have peer assistance organizations, by which students are available to help other students. This type of help might be appreciated by a student with an adjustment disorder, especially if the helper has experienced a similar stressor. A few caveats are in order, however. It is not appropriate to assign a helper to such a student without adequate adult supervision; doing so could make the helper feel overwhelmed or solely responsible for the student's welfare. Also, peer support can be one of many services offered to the student but should not be the only source of help (Brammer & MacDonald, 2003).

Other professionals at the school may be involved, such as occupational therapists, physical therapists, or speech-language pathologists. It is critical that all adults who work with the student are aware of the disorder because it is highly likely (at least temporarily) to affect other types of therapeutic progress. It is also essential that these professionals know which roles, if any, they have in assisting students with adjustment disorders.

Other school staff can be very helpful to students who need extra attention, support, and structure. A librarian, secretary, paraeducator, custodian, or grounds-keeper may be the first to identify a particular student's distress. It may be appropriate to allow time each week for the student to serve as this person's assistant. Serving as an assistant may offer some social and emotional distance from stressors, help build up a sense that an adult cares, give relief from the demands of the classroom, and provide a sense of purpose or accomplishment in the student.

The continuation of Carlo's story demonstrates the roles that school staff members can play in helping a student who may have an adjustment disorder.

Carlo's teacher estimates that his reading and math performances have further dropped—almost to a second-grade level. The teacher expressed concern to the principal about these significant changes.

The principal reviewed Carlo's case and called a staff meeting. She reminded the staff of the media coverage of Michael's accident the previous summer and of the effects that the accident might still have on Carlo and other students. Then, she asked the school counselor to talk with Carlo.

Over the course of a 20-minute meeting, Carlo told the school counselor his story of loss and grief. Furthermore, he related that after Michael's funeral, life for the family quickly got "back to normal." His mother, now living alone, went back to work. Carlo stayed with his grandmother, who told Carlo to be brave and get over it because, as she said, "People die—it's a fact." Carlo did not receive counseling or any other services for his grief. The school counselor referred Carlo to a school psychologist for a more complete evaluation.

The school psychologist discovered through testing and an interview that the decline in Carlo's achievement scores was attributable to more than obsessive thoughts about Michael and his family. That is, the tests and interview also evidenced a true regression in ability and an inability to finish tasks. Carlo's eating patterns had also become sporadic, and he had lost weight. Due to his obsessive thinking, for instance, he was not able to eat lunch during the time allotted at school. Lunch supervisory staff also noticed that Carlo ate alone and, during after-lunch recess, wandered around the playground talking to himself but not to other children. The school psychologist diagnosed Carlo as having an adjustment disorder with mixed disturbance of emotions and conduct.

When the school psychologist asked Carlo what he was telling himself, Carlo said that he was going over Michael's death and how it was all his fault for not being there to protect his brother. He believed that his parents were angry with him and that he would be punished by God for his brother's death, so he was telling God he was sorry. Carlo would tell Michael he was sorry, too. He told the psychologist that bad dreams about Michael and his parents' arguing made him afraid to go to sleep at night, so he tried to stay awake as long as he could.

Overall, Carlo was very open to talking about his situation. He was a bit worried that his grandmother might not approve of his talking about it, however, because they did not discuss such matters at home.

SCHOOL-BASED ASSESSMENTS FOR INTERVENTION PLANNING

School personnel use many types of assessments to determine a student's degree of academic, social, emotional, and behavioral problems. Some of the most helpful involve surveys or observations made by the student, the parent, the teacher, and/or the students' peers. It is common to employ tools such as the Child Behavior Checklist (Achenbach, 2001), the Revised Behavior Problem Checklist (Quay & Peterson, 1987), or the Behavior Rating Profile, Second Edition (Brown & Hammill, 1990), among others. These tools quantify the hunches or more qualitative observations that cause school staff to be concerned. As always, it is helpful to use actual data for decision making, so educators are encouraged to record and report findings from classroom-based assessment. Psychologists will likely also use other cognitive tests to help complete the picture.

Coordination of Services

This chapter has shown that many people may be involved in the diagnosis and treatment of an adjustment disorder. The situation could become confusing without effective coordination. Indeed, uncoordinated efforts might introduce more stressors into the student's life, compounding his or her existing distress.

One staff member should be designated as the student's care provision coordinator. Because the principal is responsible for staff duties, he or she should make this designation. The designated staff member monitors student progress, regularly checks with other relevant professionals (in the school district and in the community), and gives progress reports to the principal. Usually, the school counselor, psychologist, or social worker is best qualified to assume the coordinator role (Sink, 2005).

The coordinator's key job is communicating with the student's parents or legal guardians. In most instances, the parents or legal guardians have the personal interest, power of attorney, and financial means to secure necessary assistance for their child. Parents who learn that their children have adjustment disorders are naturally concerned and, unless they already suspected that something was amiss, may be shocked. Therefore, it is imperative that the coordinator demonstrates sensitivity to these concerns via basic communication skills already discussed under the "School-Based Interventions" heading.

Further developments in Carlo's story illustrate the coordination of services.

The school psychologist and school counselor met with the school nurse and Carlo's teacher to discuss the assessment findings. They then invited Carlo's grandmother and mother to a meeting, but only his grandmother came. His grandmother was reluctant to agree to a plan, but she did so because she was concerned about Carlo's schoolwork.

The school counselor found a child-centered grief counselor in the community and located social services funds to pay for several counseling sessions. These sessions focused on the guilt and blame that Carlo felt about his brother's death. In addition,

Carlo joined a small group of other children at school who had experienced divorce or death of a parent. He also met weekly with the school counselor for several months. Carlo was allowed to have lunch with one friend in the classroom for a 2-week period. If Carlo got tired at school, he could take a nap in the nurse's office. In class, his teacher frequently checked with him to ascertain his understanding of new concepts. The teacher also provided remedial instruction for concepts that Carlo did not acquire from the first lesson. Furthermore, a paraeducator was assigned to Carlo. The paraeducator tutored Carlo three times per week on homework completion and attention skills.

• •

Another vital task of the service coordinator is that of referral agent. Appropriate referral to other professionals in the school, in the district, or in the community is essential to provide continuity of services to students. It is especially easy to lose continuity when outside professionals are involved. For instance, the physician who prescribes temporary medication or the family therapist might not keep school staff informed about issues that have implications for the student's school experiences. Hence, the coordinator should occasionally contact such professionals to stay abreast of student developments. Table 13.3 provides recommended steps for processing effective referrals.

Intervention Effects

As mentioned previously, sometimes students move from having an adjustment disorder to having a more serious mental health disorder. With appropriate interventions, however, students typically recover from adjustment disorders within

Table 13.3. Making effective referrals

1. Make plans for a possible crisis referral, including a specific contact person at the referral site, **before** it is necessary to actually refer; trying to initiate a referral at a flash point is too late.

2. Discuss referral issues and what you have already tried with potential referral sources. In preliminary discussions, you must observe confidentiality of the student.

3. Check to see if your school or district has untapped resources. If they exist, investigate how helpful they might be for the particular student with whom you are working.

4. Find out who, if anyone, had prior health care contact (physical and/or mental) with the student and what the outcomes were.

5. If someone other than you is responsible for coordinating referrals, discuss the referral possibility with him or her well in advance of actually processing the referral.

6. Discuss referral possibilities with your student, including reasons for the referral, services available at other sources, and the student's options.

7. As much as possible, have the student make his or her own arrangements with the referral. Except for crises, for students who are mentally or physically unable to make their own arrangements, or for elementary level students, having them make the contacts will hopefully engage them more in the process and follow-through.

8. **Only** give specific information about the student to referrals with written release from the student or his or her legal representative, as required by the Family Educational Rights and Privacy Act of 1974 (see Fischer & Sorenson, 1996).

9. If you continue seeing the student in some helping capacity, you may be informed about the progress toward the referral, but the student and the referral are not required to share such information with you.

3–6 months. They gradually reduce their need for support services from educators. Signs of stress—such as periodic bouts of crying, anger, or withdrawal—may still appear but gradually lessen. Students usually resume academic and social behaviors similar to those demonstrated prior to the stressful event(s). In one study of school–home–community collaboration (Guishard 1998), for instance, 77% of the families of children and adolescents who displayed symptoms similar to those of adjustment disorders reported satisfactory outcomes after brief school counseling and family therapy. Among the remaining students, 13% sought further in-school help and 10% required referral to other services in the school district. Although this is only one study, its results provide data illustrating reasonable expectations for interventions with students with adjustment disorders.

The end of Carlo's vignette illustrates how intervention can help students with adjustment disorders.

Within 2 months of his intervention plan's initiation, Carlo continued to be more reserved around other students than he was before his brother's death. Yet, Carlo was showing a significant return to his former personality and behavior. He still daydreamed occasionally but was accomplishing more at school. The self-talk significantly diminished.

• •

CONCLUSION

This chapter has addressed the definition, identification, etiology, and treatment of adjustment disorders, particularly as they relate to school. Given that all educational personnel seek to enhance students' welfare and learning, all staff are potential observers, reporters, and helpers regarding possible distress in students' lives. It is crucial, therefore, that all staff maintain ongoing communication with each other and with students. Teachers are the most likely to observe daily student actions—and students are more likely to confide in teachers than in other staff members—but anyone may be a critical link in identifying student distress.

Adjustment disorders are like a severe case of the common cold in a number of ways. Many people experience them more than once. Adjustment disorders often run their course, with little or no intervention, although treatment of major symptoms makes life more pleasant for all involved. Yet, if ignored, they can also turn into something potentially dangerous. It is precisely because they are common that they might be underestimated as a mental health issue. It is the authors' hope, however, that the information presented in this chapter helps educators effectively recognize and address these disorders as they occur with their students.

REFERENCES

Achenbach, T.M. (2001). *Manual for the ASEBA school-age forms & profiles.* Burlington: University of Vermont, Department of Psychiatry.

American Psychiatric Association. (2000). *Diagnostic and statistical manual of mental disorders* (4th ed., text rev.). Washington, DC: Author.

Arnett, J.J. (1999). Adolescent storm and stress, reconsidered. *American Psychologist, 54,* 317–326.

Bee, H., & Boyd, D. (2003). *Lifespan development* (3rd ed.). Boston: Allyn & Bacon.

Bloom, F., Nelson, C.A., & Lazerson, A. (2001). *Brain, mind, and behavior* (3rd ed.). New York: Worth Publishers.

Brammer, L., & MacDonald, G. (2003). *The helping relationship* (8th ed.). Boston: Allyn & Bacon.

Brown, L.L., & Hammill, D.D. (1990). *Behavioral Rating Profile: An ecological approach to behavioral assessment* (2nd ed.). Austin, TX: PRO-ED.

Carlson, J., & Lewis, J. (Eds.). (2002). *Counseling the adolescent* (4th ed.). Denver, CO: Love Publishing Co.

Carter, B., & McGoldrick, M. (1999). Overview: The expanded family life cycle. In B. Carter & M. McGoldrick (Eds.), *The expanded family life cycle: Individual, family, and social perspectives* (3rd ed., pp. 1–26). Boston: Allyn & Bacon.

Demir, T., Demir, D.E., Alkas, L., & Kayaalp, L. (2000). Characteristics of children presenting with emotional-behavioral symptoms related to the Marmara earthquake and the distribution of their diagnoses. *Psikiyatri Psikoloji Psikofarmakoloji Dergisi, 8*(3), 206–214.

Demo, D.H., Fine, M.A., & Ganong, L.H. (2000). Divorce as a family stressor. In P.C. McKenry & S.J. Price (Eds.), *Families and change: Coping with stressful events* (2nd ed., pp. 279–302). Thousand Oaks, CA: Sage Publications.

Deveaux, F. (1997). The triadic partnership: School, home, and community. *Journal of Family Psychotherapy, 8,* 43–51.

Everett, B., & Gallop, R. (2001). *The link between childhood trauma and mental illness: Effective interventions for mental health professionals.* Thousand Oaks, CA: Sage Publications.

Fischer, L., & Sorenson, G.P. (1996). *School law for counselors, psychologists, and social workers* (3rd ed.). New York: Longman Publishing.

Ford, J.D., Racusin, R., Ellis, C.G., Davis, W.B., Reiser, J., Fleischer, A., & Thomas, J. (2000). Child maltreatment, other trauma exposure, and posttraumatic symptomatology among children with oppositional defiant and attention deficit hyperactivity disorders. *Child Maltreatment: Journal of the American Professional Society on the Abuse of Children, 5,* 205–217.

Guishard, J. (1998). The parents' support service: Brief family work in a school context. *Educational Psychology in Practice, 14,* 135–139.

Hudak, J., Krestan, J.A., & Bepko, C. (1999). Alcohol problems and the family life cycle. In B. Carter & M. McGoldrick (Eds.), *The expanded family life cycle: Individual, family, and social perspectives* (3rd ed., pp. 455–469). Boston: Allyn & Bacon.

Ivey, A.E., & Ivey, M.B. (1998). Reframing DSM-IV: Positive strategies from developmental counseling and therapy. *Journal of Counseling and Development, 76,* 334–350.

Iwamoto, S., & Yoshida, K. (1997). School refusal in Japan: The recent dramatic increase in incidence is a cause for concern. *Social Behavior and Personality, 25,* 315–319.

Jacobs, E., & Schimmel, C. (2005). Small-group counseling. In C.A. Sink (Ed.), *Contemporary school counseling: Theory, research, and practice.* Boston: Lahaska Press.

Johnson, V.K., Cowan, P.A., & Cowan, C.P. (1999). Children's classroom behavior: The unique contribution of family organization. *Journal of Family Psychology, 13,* 355–371.

Kail, R.V., & Cavanaugh, J.C. (1996). *Human development.* Belmont, CA: Brooks/Cole.

Kaplan, H.I., & Sadock, B.J. (1996). *Concise textbook of clinical psychiatry.* Philadelphia: Lippincott Williams & Wilkins.

Kauffman, J.M. (2001). *Characteristics of emotional and behavioral disorders of children and youth* (7th ed.). Upper Saddle River, NJ: Prentice Hall.

King, B., Randolph, L., McKay, W.A., & Bartell, M. (1995). Working with families in the schools. In L. Combrinck-Graham (Ed.), *Children in families at risk: Maintaining the connections.* New York: The Guilford Press.

McGoldrick, M., & Carter, B. (1999). Self in context. In B. Carter & M. McGoldrick (Eds.), *The expanded family life cycle: Individual, family, and social perspectives* (3rd ed., pp. 27–46). Boston: Allyn & Bacon.

McGuire, S., Manke, B., Saudino, K.J., Reiss, D., Hetherington, E.M., & Plomin, R. (1999). Perceived competence and self-worth during adolescence: A longuitudinal behavioral genetic study. *Child Development, 70,* 1283–1296.

McKenry, P.C., & Price, S.J. (2000). Families coping with problems and change: A conceptual overview. In P.C. McKenry & S.J. Price (Eds.), *Families and change: Coping with stressful events* (2nd ed., pp. 1–21). Thousand Oaks, CA: Sage Publications.

Murray, C.I. (2000). Coping with death, dying, and grief in families. In P.C. McKenry & S.J. Price (Eds.), *Families and change: Coping with stressful events* (2nd ed., 120–153). Thousand Oaks, CA: Sage Publications.

O'Hanlon, W.H., & Weiner-Davis, M. (1989). *In search of solutions: A new direction in psychotherapy.* New York: W.W. Norton.

Orton, G.L. (1997). *Strategies for counseling with children and their parents.* Belmont, CA: Brooks/Cole.

Ostrander, R. (2001). Emotional and behavioral disorders. In F.M. Kline, L.B. Silver, & S.C. Russell (Eds.), *The educator's guide to medical issues in the classroom* (pp. 123–142). Baltimore: Paul H. Brookes Publishing Co.

Preda, A., Madlener, A., & Hetherington, P. (1998). Premature polypsychophrmacology. *Journal of the American Academy of Child and Adolescent Psychiatry, 37,* 348–349.

Quay, H.C., & Peterson, D.R. (1987). *Revised Behavior Problem Checklist.* Coral Gables, FL: Author.

Rind, B., Tromovitch, P., & Bauserman, R. (1998). A meta-analytic examination of assumed properties of child sexual abusing using college samples. *Psychological Bulletin, 124,* 22–53.

Rolland, J.S. (1999). Chronic illness and the family life cycle. In B. Carter & M. McGoldrick (Eds.), *The expanded family life cycle: Individual, family, and social perspectives* (3rd ed., pp. 492–511). Boston: Allyn & Bacon.

Rotter, J.C., & Boveja, M.E. (1999). Family therapists and school counselors: A collaborative endeavor. *Family Journal: Counseling and Therapy for Couples and Families, 7,* 276–279.

Schreiber, R., & Lyddon, W.J. (1998). Parental bonding and current psychological functioning among childhood sexual abuse survivors. *Journal of Counseling Psychology, 45,* 358–362.

Sears, S. (2005). Large-group guidance: Curriculum development and instruction. In C.A. Sink (Ed.), *Contemporary school counseling: Theory, research, and practice.* Boston: Lahaska Press.

Silver, L.B. (2001). Brain–mind interactions. In F.M. Kline, L.B. Silver, & S.C. Russell (Eds.), *The educator's guide to medical issues in the classroom* (pp. 13–25). Baltimore: Paul H. Brookes Publishing Co.

Sink, C.A. (2005). The contemporary professional school counselor. In C.A. Sink (Ed.), *Contemporary school counseling: Theory, research, and practice.* Boston: Lahaska Press.

Strain, J.J. (1995). Adjustment disorders. In G.O. Gabbard (Ed.), *Treatments of psychiatric disorders: Vol. 2* (2nd ed., pp. 1656–1665). Washington, DC: American Psychiatric Publishing.

Sullivan, J.R. (2002). The collaborative group counseling referral process: Description and teacher evaluation. *Professional School Counseling, 5,* 366–368.

Toth, P.L., & Erwin, W.J. (1998). Applying skill-based curriculum to teach feedback in groups: An evaluation study. *Journal of Counseling and Development, 76,* 294–301.

Ungar, M.T. (2001). Constructing narratives of resilience with high-risk youth. *Journal of Systemic Therapies, 20*(2), 58–73.

Wagner, W.G. (1996). Optimal development in adolescence: What it is and how can it be encouraged? *The Counseling Psychologist, 24,* 360–399.

Walsh, M.E., Galassi, J.P., Murphy, J.A., & Park-Taylor, J. (2002). A conceptual framework for counseling psychologists in schools. *The Counseling Psychologist, 30,* 682–704.

Widiger, T.A., & Clark, L.A. (2000). Toward DSM-V and the classification of psychopathology. *Psychological Bulletin, 128,* 946–963.

14

Oppositional Defiant Disorder and Conduct Disorder

Rick Ostrander

• •

Chapter Concepts

- Description of oppositional defiant and conduct disorders
- Differences between oppositional defiant and conduct disorders
- Differences between normal oppositional behavior and pathological oppositional behavior
- Potential causes of oppositional defiant and conduct disorders
- Protective factors that mitigate the development of oppositional defiant and conduct disorders
- Role of educators in diagnosing and treating oppositional defiant and conduct disorders

During the "terrible twos," most children display oppositional behavior; indeed, it would be unusual if a 2-year-old did not ignore parental commands and have temper tantrums when denied having his or her way. During this time, a child attempts to assert greater independence and to establish him- or herself as an autonomous individual. The process of saying "no" to parental requests allows the child to determine the extent of his or her autonomy and to establish the limits that society imposes on the child's impulses. Ultimately, through consistent feedback from the environment, the child is able to internalize parental expectations and to reign in impulses that are deemed socially unacceptable. Thus, early oppositional behaviors may serve as an opportunity for the child to learn, in a concrete fashion, the rules for functioning effectively in the larger society.

Some children never seem to emerge from this stage in development. They continue to manifest a broad range of acting-out behaviors. During the preschool and early school-age years, these acting-out behaviors may be in the form of overt defiance, temper tantrums, yelling, and whining. During adolescence, more troubling behaviors may emerge, such as aggression, stealing, and vandalism (Moffitt, Caspi, Dickson, Silva, & Stanton, 1996). When these behaviors occur in isolation, they can be effectively addressed through rather conventional disciplinary actions from parents and teachers. Yet, when these behaviors are displayed in a cluster, they may represent a more serious psychiatric diagnosis. For example, an otherwise well-behaved student who has a shoving match on the playground is unlikely to require much further intervention than a meeting with his or her parents. A child who repeatedly fights, steals, and disobeys the rules at school, however, may have oppositional defiant disorder (ODD) or conduct disorder (CD). Children and adolescents may display a wide variety of oppositional behaviors; there can be wide variability in the nature, etiology, and developmental course of ODD and CD. The following vignette involves a disturbance in conduct during childhood.

Tom, an orphan, is being raised by his elderly Aunt Polly. Although Tom's aunt has considerable love and affection for him, she is troubled by his escalating misbehavior. She has repeatedly caught Tom lying, stealing, and fighting. In addition, although Tom loves to read, he frequently skips school. More disconcerting, Tom may have been instrumental in killing a friend's pet. Tom does not share much with his aunt, who, as Tom's sole caregiver, has difficulty in keeping track of him. She admits that she does not always discipline Tom consistently or effectively. As a result, even when she tries to teach him a lesson, her actions can inadvertently reward his misbehavior. Aunt Polly has become particularly disturbed by Tom's hanging around with one of the most troubled boys in the neighborhood. This new friend stays out all night, never seems to attend school, and lives with his alcoholic father.

• •

Some readers may recognize the boy depicted in the vignette. He is the title character from Mark Twain's novel *The Adventures of Tom Sawyer.* Given the lack of parental supervision and his undesirable social affiliations, some would maintain that Tom and his friend, Huckleberry Finn, do not suffer from a psychological disorder. Rather, they are normal boys living under abnormal circumstances. Some boys who behave as Tom and Huck do in fact outgrow their rebellious tendencies and eventually become productive citizens. However, many children like Tom Sawyer and Huckleberry Finn do not have someone like Mark Twain to ensure that everything turns out all right. For many such children, the story does not have a happy ending. Some may be expelled from school or even go to jail. Nonetheless, Tom and Huck's behavior may be seen largely as a product of their environment; in other cases, the causes of behavioral problems seem to originate from within. This point is shown in a description of Mafia boss John Gotti that is based on Cummings and Volkman (1992).

When teachers first encountered the young John Gotti, his apparently uncontrollable temper was regarded as a severe disability. He was clearly a very bright boy; in fact, his IQ score was once assessed to be 140. Yet, he had no interest in school. Even during his elementary school years, he seemed to be in a constant rage. His aggression was often unprovoked, unpredictable, and remorseless.

The nature and etiology of the behavior presented by Tom Sawyer and John Gotti are different, but the two cases share some common elements. Both individuals seemed to rebel against authority and were willing to defy the rules that most children accept without question. Ultimately, Tom Sawyer's and John Gotti's situations took them to court. In Tom Sawyer's case, the judge saw beyond Tom's disagreeable qualities and recognized his adaptive attributes. In fact, near the end of *The Adventures of Tom Sawyer,* the judge predicts that Tom will someday become a great soldier or lawyer. In John Gotti's case, however, the disruptive behavior displayed in elementary school escalated during high school and adulthood. His behavior resulted in a lifetime of crime and tragic consequences for those who crossed him. John Gotti's judge sentenced him to life in prison.

This chapter covers the topics of identifying, preventing, and treating ODD and CD. It also addresses factors that protect children from the biological and social risks associated with these disorders. Furthermore, it discusses the role of educators in this process. These issues are complex, yet an adequate understanding of them is critical for accomplishing the fundamental goal of education—helping children become productive citizens.

DIAGNOSTIC CRITERIA FOR OPPOSITIONAL
DEFIANT DISORDER AND CONDUCT DISORDER

Conduct problems are among the most concerning psychiatric issues confronting teachers and parents. Although the incidences of ODD (6%–10%) and CD (2%–9%) in the general population are comparable to other psychiatric disorders, these two disorders represent the largest source of referrals to mental health outpatient clinics (McMahon & Wells, 1998).

The essential feature of ODD is a defiant and hostile pattern of behavior that is directed toward authority figures. The text revision of the *Diagnostic and Statistical Manual of Mental Disorders, Fourth Edition* (DSM-IV-TR, American Psychiatric Association [APA], 2000) specifies that at least four of the following behaviors must be present: losing one's temper, arguing with adults, not complying with adults' rules, deliberately doing things that annoy other people, blaming others for one's own mistakes, being easily annoyed by others, exhibiting anger and resentment, and showing spite and vindictiveness. In addition, this cluster of behaviors must impair academic and social functioning, last for at least 6 months, and be manifested at a higher frequency than seen in other children at a similar developmental level.

Whereas ODD tends to be represented by negative behaviors directed at authority figures, the symptoms of CD tend to be broader and represent behaviors that oppose societal rules and/or may represent a violation of others' basic rights. The DSM-IV-TR describes two subtypes of CD, depending on the age of onset. The childhood onset type requires at least one symptom to be exhibited prior to 10 years of age, whereas adolescent onset type requires onset after 10 years of age. The subtype distinction reflects the different causes and prognoses, depending on the age of onset. Early onset is more frequently associated with males, a comorbid diagnosis of attention-deficit/hyperactivity disorder (ADHD), and higher levels of aggression. More detailed descriptions of the developmental courses for early and late onset of ODD and CD are discussed later in this chapter. See Appendix A at the end of the book for the specific DSM-IV-TR criteria for making a diagnosis of ODD or CD.

ASSOCIATED CHARACTERISTICS

Although the DSM-IV-TR represents the most common means of conceptualizing and describing children with conduct problems, other characteristics are particularly salient. All of the associated characteristics are seldom represented within one individual; however, when they occur, the characteristics may have specific implications for prognosis and treatment. Some of the more troubling characteristics frequently associated with children who have ODD or CD fall into the categories of 1) aggression and bullying and 2) covert behavior.

Aggression and Bullying

During the preschool years, it is not uncommon for children to strike other children. However, as children progress through school, episodes of aggression decline. Aggression that persists across developmental periods and during adolescence is uncommon. When it is manifested at these times, aggression is often associated with a number of other psychiatric problems, including depression, ADHD, and antisocial tendencies (Bloomquist & Schnell, 2002; Crick & Grotpetor, 1995).

Aggression can be manifested by severe oppositional displays, including high levels of verbal aggression (e.g., argumentativeness, temper tantrums). At extreme levels, children can display more overt displays of physical aggression. Sometimes the aggression is reactive in nature. Reactive aggression is manifested, for example, when a student who is jostled while lining up immediately responds by punching the offending student. Other aggressive outbursts are planned. Such proactive forms of aggression are used strategically to dominate others or to further self-serving goals. Although both forms of aggression are associated with negative outcomes, children who tend to be reactive in their aggression are more likely to be male, have ADHD, come from backgrounds of physical abuse, and exhibit poor social skills. In addition, children who are more reactive in their aggressive outbursts also tend to have more difficulty in self-regulating emotions (Bloomquist & Schnell, 2002).

Reactive and proactive forms of aggression are overt and typically involve some form of direct conflict with others. In contrast to more obvious displays of aggression, relational aggression is apt to be more covert. Children who display relational aggression intend to do harm through manipulation and damage to another's reputation (Crick, 1995). Rather than doing harm to others through direct physical or verbal aggression, relational aggression tends to do harm in a more indirect fashion. Whether through spreading rumors or constructing outright falsehoods about another, relational aggression attempts to disrupt the social affiliations of targeted children. Preschool and school-age girls are more likely to display relational aggression (Bloomquist & Schnell, 2002; Crick & Grotpetor, 1995).

Many children with ODD or CD also bully other children. Although bullying behavior is typically associated with boys who use physical intimidation, girls also are capable of bullying through verbal and psychological manipulation (Bloomquist & Schnell, 2002). Most bullies are capable of inflicting harm to fellow students because they have little empathy. Children who bully others are also at greater risk for being diagnosed with antisocial personality disorder as adults (Bloomquist & Schnell, 2002). In other instances, however, children who engage in this behavior are both bullies and victims of bullying. These children are particularly susceptible to a wide range of emotional, behavioral, and psychiatric problems, including depression and antisocial tendencies (Kumpulainen et al., 1998).

Covert Behavior

Elementary and middle school children who have ODD or CD may commit a range of covert acts, including lying, cheating, and truancy. However, stealing and fire setting represent the most serious covert manifestation of ODD and CD. Children who steal on a regular basis are likely to be involved with juvenile correction systems during their adolescent years. Therefore, addressing these issues early is particularly important and may help prevent long-term maladaptive outcomes.

Children who set fires are generally at risk for a range of social and emotional problems. Young people who set fires with the specific intent of destroying property and/or hurting others are apt to display many areas of maladjustment. They tend to have very impaired social interactions, display a number of psychological problems, and display other types of disruptive behaviors (e.g., aggression) (Kolko, 1996).

The families of children who engage in such covert behavior are typically unaware of the behavior. Indeed, poor parental monitoring is one of the more salient findings associated with the covert actions committed by individuals with ODD or CD (Patterson, 1982). Given this finding, it is not surprising that many efforts designed to prevent covert forms of ODD and CD aim to improve parental monitoring.

Some of the more troubling outcomes associated with ODD and CD are reflected by very high incidences of criminal behavior and substance abuse. Although these outcomes are rarely displayed prior to adolescence, the early warning signs appear early. Some of the more notable warning signs include onset of aggression at an early age, comorbid ADHD, and high rates of family adversity (e.g., poverty, parental psychopathology) (Bloomquist & Schnell, 2002). When these considerations are combined with ineffective parenting (e.g., poor parental monitoring), the risk for later substance abuse increases significantly. Again, this finding suggests that early preventive efforts are key to preventing substance abuse during adolescence and adulthood.

RISK FACTORS ASSOCIATED WITH OPPOSITIONAL DEFIANT DISORDER AND CONDUCT DISORDER

The risks associated with ODD and CD take many forms. This first section discusses the risk and protective factors regarding the development of the disorders. Then, it describes the associated academic risks and possibility of developing other psychiatric disorders.

Risks and Protective Factors

Research indicates that certain genetic, biological, parent, social/peer, and socioeconomic factors are associated with the development of ODD and CD. These factors, as well as protective factors, are detailed in the following subsections.

Genetic Considerations   Twin studies and other investigations of the genetic basis for ODD and CD have suggested that 50% of the variability in aggression and associated disruptive behavior can be attributed to genetics (Miles & Carey, 1997). However, genetic factors appear to play a more important role when combined with other environmental considerations. A paternal history of violence and aggression conveys clear genetic risks. Yet, the genetic risks for aggression are increased when combined with poverty, community violence, and inadequate schools. In particular, it is important to note that high drop-out rates, academic failure, and poor attendance can eventually lead to high levels of unemployment and negative psychosocial outcomes (e.g., aggression). Thus, genetic considerations can interact with school considerations and increase the risk of conduct problems. In contrast, the genetic risks may be muted if parents are skilled, neighborhoods are safe, and schools are effective.

Biological Markers A number of biological and neuropsychological deficits are associated with the diagnosis of ODD and CD. Researchers maintain that anomalies involving the central nervous system contribute to some of the behavioral manifestations of ODD and CD. One of the most common neuropsychological deficits associated with individuals who have ODD and CD involves executive functioning. Poor executive functioning primarily reflects anomalies in the frontal lobes that impair an individual's capacity to control other functions of the brain. Without effective executive control, an individual is less able to regulate attention and inhibit impulses. A number of studies have demonstrated that many children with the features of ODD and CD perform very poorly on tests of executive functioning (Moffit, 1993). Thus, some acting out behaviors of individuals with ODD or CD may be related to subtle neurological deficits, which are in turn reflected by the inability to control attention, inhibit impulses, or regulate emotions. Many of these same characteristics are found in children with ADHD, which may explain the high number of children who have both ODD or CD and ADHD.

Children with ODD or CD also display weaknesses in verbal comprehension and expression. There is frequently an indirect relationship between ODD or CD and deficits in language development. In some cases, children may resort to aggression because they cannot express their frustration through language. Language also allows individuals to efficiently learn and categorize broad classes of behavior. For instance, the child with good verbal abilities may be able to learn polite table manners through detailed conversations with a parent or guardian. Later, these details may be recalled faithfully and acted on when the parent tells the child to behave appropriately during supper. However, a child with less sophisticated verbal abilities may not profit from such verbal instructions and may require multiple concrete responses from the environment to fully understand the same material. Thus, poor verbal abilities may result in more noncompliance and a slow learning curve when acquiring rules of conduct (Moffit, 1993).

Verbal abilities are also essential in school. Children who understand and use verbal concepts effectively tend to receive positive reactions from teachers and are apt to be viewed positively by peers as well. In contrast, children who have verbal deficits are likely to experience school as stressful. They are unlikely to develop a strong connection with teachers or peers; as a result, they fail to form the close bonds that may prevent conduct problems (Moffit, 1993).

Parent Characteristics The mothers of children diagnosed with ODD or CD have relatively high rates of depression (Nigg & Hinshaw, 1998); in addition, the fathers of aggressive children frequently display aggression as well. These fathers are also apt to display other conduct problems, such as antisocial behavior and substance abuse (Frick, 1994). As noted previously, high rates of parental psychopathology (i.e., manifested mental health issues) suggest that genetics may increase the risk of developing ODD or CD. However, risk factors associated with parental characteristics also involve parent–child interactions. Aggressive parents are likely to model maladaptive behavior; over time, their children learn that aggression is an appropriate means for settling disagreements. Parents with depression are less likely to closely monitor their children or to reward their children's good behavior; instead, they tend to nag or use coercive behaviors when their children misbehave. These coercive parent–child interactions and their role in the etiology of ODD/CD are detailed in "Early Onset" part of the section titled "Developmental Progression."

Social and Peer Factors A combination of neuropsychological, biological, parental, and family considerations places children at increased risk for ODD or CD. However, children's early interactions with peers may further contribute to disruptive and aggressive behavior. Children who display early signs of ODD or CD tend to be aggressive with other children, and this leads to rejection by their prosocial peers. Once rejected by these peers, the children with characteristics of ODD and CD often affiliate with others who display similar characteristics. Affiliating with such peers limits exposure to adaptive role models; moreover, peers who present maladaptive behavior may actually reward antisocial behavior. These affiliations lead to increasing levels of oppositional behavior, antisocial tendencies, and aggression (Bloomquist & Schnell, 2002).

Socioeconomic Considerations There is a strong indirect relationship between poverty and rates of ODD and CD. Poverty alone does not place children at greater risk for developing ODD or CD. However, a number of other risk factors are embedded within neighborhoods with high rates of poverty. For example, single-parent homes, community violence, dilapidated housing, unsupportive families, and associated life stressors have been associated with poverty. Any of these considerations can have an adverse effect on parenting. Many of the risks associated with poverty can diminish parental resources.

The stress associated with living in poverty is further compounded by the added demands associated with raising children in poor neighborhoods. For example, Baldwin, Petersen, and Cole (1990) studied the parenting practices associated with academically competent children residing in neighborhoods that had high and low crime rates. Not surprisingly, the neighborhoods with the highest crime rates were more likely to have families that had higher rates of poverty, parents with less education, higher rates of single-parent households, and a higher minority representation. Parents that were able to successfully raise academically competent children in these high-risk environments differed considerably from the successful parents in low-risk environments. Specifically, Baldwin and colleagues noted that "successful high risk families were more restrictive and authoritarian in their policies and were more vigilant in monitoring their children's compliance than were successful low risk families" (p. 277). Thus, in order to foster competence in their children, the parents from high-risk environments needed to invest more time and effort than did parents residing in middle-class surroundings. In many cases, successful high-risk families were required to fight against the negative influences of their immediate environment; in fact, their laudable efforts were found to be deviant in relationship to the maladaptive standards that prevailed within some high-risk neighborhoods (Baldwin et al., 1990). The circumstances associated with these high-risk environments are in marked contrast to the situation that is found in low-risk, middle-class neighborhoods. In low-risk neighborhoods, the community is unified in supporting academic competence. Indeed, given the level of community support, it is easy to question whether the democratic parenting practices of successful middle-class families could be effective in the environment in which high-risk families reside. In any case, these findings have clear implications concerning intervention. Given the difficult challenge confronting the parents from high-risk environments, schools could serve as a welcomed ally in helping these families to cope with the threats associated with their environment. For example, community-based programs could include the schools in providing psychoeducational programs that would teach families how to protect their children. The focus of this training could be teaching the parent(s) to closely monitor the behavior of their child, limit their child's autonomy if necessary, and define rules very clearly.

Protective Factors Numerous factors appear to mitigate the risks associated with the previously described biological, neuropsychological, parental, and social considerations. These protective factors can involve child or family characteristics or larger contextual considerations. For example, children with strengths such as high cognitive functioning and appropriate social skills can frequently use these attributes to navigate the risks associated with poverty, parental psychopathology, and a harsh home environment. Similarly, a close relationship with a parent or other family member can protect children from the most severe and chronic forms of risk. For example, Masten and colleagues (1999) examined the long-term outcomes of children who lived in urban areas and experienced high levels of stress along with numerous associated traumas. The researchers found that children with high cognitive functioning and a warm, supportive family were protected against adversity. Contextual factors that seem to protect children from the risks associated with ODD and CD include intimate connections to community organizations (e.g., church) or connections with significant individuals outside the family (Bloomquist & Schnell, 2002). Of particular importance to school professionals, attending effective schools has been associated with protecting children against many of the psychological, family, or societal risk factors associated with ODD and CD. In some cases, the relationship between a teacher and a student can be instrumental in determining the outcomes of children who are risk for developing ODD or CD. For example, Hughes, Cavell, and Jackson (1999) found that aggressive children who had a negative relationship with their teacher in second- or third-grade were likely to persist in their aggression several years later. However, aggressive students who established good relationships with their primary school teachers were more likely to have positive outcomes several years later. Therefore, schools may not only play a role in identifying children at risk but also may actually protect children who have early risk factors for ODD and CD. This finding again emphasizes the possible therapeutic benefit of an effective and positive educational environment.

Academic Risks

Children with ODD or CD often experience considerable difficulty in school. These children tend to achieve at a level well below that of their same-age peers. Some academic underachievement results from neurological considerations associated with related learning disabilities and/or ADHD. As noted previously, individuals with ODD or CD often have relatively poor verbal abilities, impaired executive functioning, and associated reading difficulties. In some cases, the frustration caused by these learning problems may actually lead to conduct problems. For example, children with problems with verbal comprehension may have difficulty in effectively dealing with peers. Rather than verbally resolving disagreements, these children may resort to aggression as a means of solving disputes. Problems in executive functioning may compromise an individual's ability to accommodate the shifting demands of school, regulate behavior, and control impulses. These cognitive limitations limit the person's ability to reliably complete assignments while compromising their interactions with teachers and peers (Dishion, French, & Patterson, 1995; McMahon & Wells, 1998). Although neuropsychological considerations may cause some manifestations of ODD and CD, many researchers have noted that academic skill deficits are only partially explained by cognitive considerations. Because children with ODD and CD are generally noncompliant, they have difficulty in a range of skills necessary for successful academic functioning. Their frequent lack of compliance with teacher requests can lead to off-task behavior in the classroom and inconsistent completion of homework assignments (Dishion, French, & Patterson, 1995). In addition to problems in academic achievement, young people with ODD or CD also exhibit numerous disciplinary infractions at school. They display higher rates of aggression, tardiness, insubordination, and other minor rule violations. Whereas these behaviors are also displayed by other children, the high frequency with which children who have ODD or CD display these behaviors can lead to suspensions, expulsions, and out-of-school placements. These negative school behaviors contribute to ongoing negative interactions among the child, school, and family. Negative patterns of behavior can also lead to the child's dropping out of school, which further contributes to the risks associated with later maladjustment (McMahon & Wells, 1998).

Risks for Developing Other Psychiatric Disorders

Children with ODD and CD are at considerable risk for a variety of other psychiatric disorders. These include anxiety, depression, substance abuse, and somatic disorders (McMahon & Wells, 1998). However, ADHD is the comorbid disorder most commonly associated with ODD and CD. The relationship between these disorders is complex. Many researchers suggest that the hyperactivity and impulsivity associated with the combined subtype of ADHD typically precedes conduct problems and may serve to interact with psychosocial considerations to cause ODD or CD. Thus, ADHD places a child at greater risk for developing ODD or CD, particularly when combined with other environmental considerations.

DEVELOPMENTAL PROGRESSION

There are two types of ODD and CD: early onset and late onset. The progression of each is detailed in the following discussions.

Early Onset

As noted previously, various personal, environmental, and neuropsychological factors are associated with the development of ODD and CD. For example, some individuals have a sensation-seeking temperament or ADHD, causing them to need higher levels of arousal than other people; therefore, they tend to seek highly stimulating experiences. As a child develops, acting-out behavior may be one manifestation of this need to seek sensation (Dishion et al., 1995). As noted, young people with ODD or CD are more likely to interpret others' intentions in an overly negative manner (Dodge & Coie, 1987). The tendency to interpret hostile intent can contribute to negative exchanges with parents, peers, and teachers. Because these individuals tend to view others' intentions negatively, they are more likely to respond in a hostile manner to situations that others view as benign. For example, a child with ODD or CD is likely to consider an accidental push as an intentional shove. This may inspire further escalation and ultimately result in aggression.

Perhaps the most empirically supported cause of early onset ODD and CD is related to family interactional patterns. This is referred to as the *coercive model*, which was developed by Patterson and colleagues (Dishion et al., 1995; Patterson, 1982). In this model, ineffective parenting practices lead to an escalating cycle of conflict and opposition in the child. By inadequately rewarding adaptive behavior and inconsistently providing consequences for noncompliance, the parent or primary caregiver does not help the child internalize the rules of society. The negative interactions between parent and child escalate over time, and the interactions become increasingly aggressive. Several factors appear to increase the probability of these coercive exchanges. Parental psychopathology (e.g., maternal depression, parental antisocial behavior), marital distress, divorce, parental substance abuse, and family stress may increase the likelihood of ineffectual approaches to parenting (McMahon & Wells, 1998). For instance, a child diagnosed with ADHD tends to challenge his or her parents under the best circumstances. Parenting the child may be particularly difficult for a single mother who is depressed and confronting financial stress.

After entering school, the child's coercive interactional style is likely to extend to his or her interactions with teachers and peers. These negative interactions at school ultimately translate into confrontations with peers and teachers. The behaviors that emerge also become more extreme and often more covert (e.g., stealing). Rejected by the majority of his or her classroom peers, the child is increasingly apt to affiliate with peers who engage in deviant behavior during the middle school and high school years. Because of the potential for dropping out of school, these young people are at great risk for negative long-term outcomes, including a subsequent diagnosis of antisocial personality disorder, early problems with the law, and arrest as adults (Dishion et al., 1995).

Late Onset

Compared with individuals with early onset ODD and CD, less is known about young people who do not manifest symptoms until late childhood or early adolescence. Yet, most of the children who ultimately receive a diagnosis of ODD or CD do not manifest disruptive behavior until later in their development. The relatively few studies that have examined this group of children have indicated that these children have very few of the early risk factors that are associated with early onset. Unlike children who have early onset ODD or CD, children who have a later onset do not typically display significant cognitive impairments, academic problems, temperamental considerations, or psychosocial stress. In addition, the families of children who have late onset do not display the same ineffectual disciplinary practices, nor do these families have particularly high incidences of divorce, unemployment, poverty, or parental psychopathology. Children who have a later onset also tend to have a more benign long-term outcome. For example, the children with late onset have a much lower probability of being arrested as adults, and the problems they do have with the law tend to involve property offenses rather than violent infractions (Moffitt et al., 1996). Although relatively little is known concerning the causes of late onset, it has been suggested that these people probably develop effective social skills during early childhood and, therefore, are better equipped to conform to societal expectations (Moffitt, 1993). Some have speculated that affiliating with peers who engage in deviant behavior and mimicking their behaviors may be a way of asserting independence from the family (Moffitt, 1993). Once they assume a more autonomous adult role, individuals with late onset ODD or CD may be more capable of engaging in adaptive functioning. This tendency is more likely given their appropriate functioning early in their development (Moffitt, 1993).

DIAGNOSIS AND ASSESSMENT

If a school professional suspects that a child may be unusually aggressive, noncompliant, or disruptive, it is important to discuss these concerns with the school counselor or psychologist. There are a number of diagnostic and assessment techniques that will be included as part of evaluation conducted by a school-based clinician. The DSM-IV-TR provides the broad diagnostic criteria for diagnosing children with ODD and CD; however, it does not specify the methods that should be used to document the symptoms of ODD and CD. A wide variety of assessment methods may be needed to make a diagnosis. It is important to solicit the perspectives of the child and his or her parents and teachers. Each source of information provides unique information concerning a given child's characteristics. However, the respective reports are also influenced by other considerations including individual biases and variability in the contextual factors that might influence behavior. For example, the perceptions of a parent with depression might differ from those of the child's favorite teacher. Variability in reports across contexts (i.e., school versus home) and respondents (i.e., parent and teacher) are expected. Therefore, it is important to solicit information from multiple sources.

Sources of Information

In self-reports, children tend to underrepresent externalizing behaviors (e.g., aggression, temper tantrums) yet present important information for assessing a subjective distress (e.g., depression) or covert symptoms of ODD and CD. Parents tend to be particularly helpful when reporting on externalizing behaviors, such as aggression. Parental reports of internalizing conditions, such as anxiety and depression, tend to be influenced by parents' own psychological state. As such, parental depression, marital discord, and other similar psychological considerations can compromise reports on their child's internal state or covert behaviors.

Teachers are accurate reporters of academic functioning and overt behavioral problems at school. Teachers do not always differentiate very well among various disruptive or affective disorders; therefore, their perceptions sometimes take a broad and undifferentiated approach. As a result, teachers can assist in screening for overall behavioral problems. Typically, however, the reports of teachers lack specificity and are not particularly helpful for making differential diagnoses.

Numerous techniques are useful for obtaining information concerning children or adolescents. Behavioral checklists represent a systematic, objective means of soliciting parent, teacher, or self-reports. Two of the more common behavioral checklists used to evaluate childhood disorders are the Child Behavior Checklist (Achenbach, 2001) and the Behavioral Assessment System for Children (BASC; Reynolds & Kamphaus, 1992). These approaches require the respondent to indicate the degree which a child displays symptoms consistent with specific behavioral and emotional disorders. A given child's behavioral and emotional characteristics are then compared with national or clinic samples. Such objective techniques represent a very efficient, inexpensive, and comprehensive means of acquiring information. Objective techniques also allow behavior to be quantified. As a result, a given appraisal of childhood behavior can be compared with that of other children with similar demographic characteristics (e.g., gender, age).

Gleaning information from behavioral rating scales is a rather static approach to assessing children, so these approaches lack the flexibility necessary to address a variety of contextual considerations that may be critical in fully understanding a given child. As a result, it is important to supplement objective means of assessing a child's behavior with more subjective means, such as clinical interviews. Interviews are particularly helpful in determining the social, school, and family factors that may contribute to a child's behavior. Through clinical inquiries, a mental health worker may discover that a child's aggression coincided with the child's affiliating with a new group of friends. In other cases, these interviews may show that an escalation of disruptive behavior is related to the onset of a parent's depression. A well-trained clinician can integrate subjective and objective information and use this combined material to arrive at an accurate diagnosis.

Some ODD and CD behaviors may be linked to specific neuropsychological processes or be associated with a specific learning disability. To determine the role played by such considerations, a complete neuropsychological or psychoeducational evaluation may be necessary. At a minimum, such assessments can ascertain whether deficits involving verbal comprehension, executive functioning, or a specific learning disability contribute to a child's disruptive behaviors.

Beyond Diagnosis

It is not sufficient to merely diagnose children with ODD or CD. To fully appreciate a given child's various risk and protective factors, it is important to expand the assessment process and include an evaluation of the specific factors that may be contributing to a child's manifest symptoms. Research concerns the range of factors associated with ODD and CD, but it does not provide information concerning the specific factors that may be important for any given child. For example, Tom Sawyer exhibited behavior consistent with ODD and CD. Because of her advanced age and other factors, his aunt was unable to effectively monitor his behavior. Yet, he also had a number of academic (e.g., love of reading) and family (e.g., a loving and supportive grandmother) resources that might protect him from negative outcomes. John Gotti was also very bright; however, his explosive behavioral outbursts may have reflected poor impulse control and deficits in executive functioning. Moreover, his early onset of oppositional-defiant tendencies suggest that intensive interventions were probably needed at a very early age.

The treatment for any two individuals is likely to be very different. The specific treatment approach requires an assessment that encompasses more than mere identification of symptoms. For instance, its is necessary to ask questions such as the following:

- Is the child's aggression typically an impulsive reaction to perceived slights by others?

- Is the child's oppositional behavior linked to a specific learning disability or ADHD?

- Do other contextual factors play a role?

- Which resources or protective factors may help in treatment?

By understanding the complex interplay of these and other considerations, the specific treatment approach can be targeted more strategically.

TREATMENT

The treatment of ODD and CD centers on psychosocial and psychopharmacological interventions. The following sections briefly review these approaches.

Psychosocial Treatment

For the most part, psychosocial interventions for children with ODD and CD involve behavioral modification techniques to change the family, community, or classroom environment. This method assumes that the environment is a particularly important consideration in causing or maintaining the negative behaviors associated with ODD and CD. Family-based interventions for younger children involve the therapist's primarily working with the parents. The first stage of parent training includes direct instruction concerning the basics of learning theory. The parents are taught how to clearly define, monitor, and track both adaptive (e.g., compliance) and maladaptive (e.g., temper tantrums) behaviors. The early stages of intervention focus on using positive reinforcement to increase the rate of adaptive behavior. Rather than using physical means, such as corporal punishment, the parents are taught to provide consequences for maladaptive behavior through the appropriate use of ignoring the behavior (i.e., extinction), time-out, and response–cost (i.e., withdrawing rewards) (McMahon & Wells, 1998).

For adolescents, the basic intervention approaches remain the same; however, modifications are adopted. For example, there is a strong emphasis on parental monitoring, particularly as it relates to behaviors that place the child at increased risk for long-term difficulties. Thus, the parents will increasingly focus on rewarding and providing consequences for school attendance, homework completion, affiliations with peers who engage in deviant behavior, substance abuse, and curfew violations. In addition, the adolescent becomes more involved in the treatment (Patterson, 1975).

For the most part, these intervention techniques are directed toward changing aspects of the family environment; however, the same basic principles have also been incorporated in community-based programs. These community-based programs have included residential treatment and day treatment facilities. The best of these programs have been able to make significant changes in the problematic behavior of adolescents, but these improvements appear limited to the time when their participants are actively engaged in the program (McMahon & Wells, 1998). Improvements do not apparently generalize to other settings. Because residential and day treatment approaches often put together a number of adolescents who engage in deviant behavior, there is the distinct probability that the treatment goals may be compromised by the ongoing negative peer affiliations. Some approaches have attempted to separate the youth from such peers through the use of therapeutic foster care placements. A number of studies have suggested that using a multimodal component for treating youth with serious delinquency problems through this type of placement is effective and more likely to generalize to long-term improvement (McMahon & Wells, 1998).

School-Based Treatment Programs

School-based treatment programs take two forms: schoolwide prevention and intervention programs and individualized school-based intervention. Each approach is describe next.

Schoowide Prevention and Intervention Programs Many of the risk factors associated with ODD and CD have implications for schools. School staff frequently find themselves reacting to the most extreme negative behavior displayed by students with ODD or CD. Often, these efforts are unsuccessful, largely because the behaviors are so entrenched. As noted, the path to entrenched oppositional and conduct disorders is commonly associated with negative and coercive parent–child interactions. Unfortunately, the same types of interactions are frequently displayed within the school environment. A school that only reacts to negative behaviors is unlikely to change the long-term outcomes of children at risk for these disorders. Preventing ODD and CD at the earliest stages requires broad interventions that are specifically aimed at rewarding behaviors that are incompatible with the oppositional, aggressive, and disruptive behaviors associated with ODD and CD.

In far too many cases, children enter school having learned maladaptive ways of interacting with adults and other children. Given their negative behavior, it is not surprising that they have negative exchanges with others. To increase more adaptive ways of interacting, it is important for children to know not only what not to do (e.g., avoid aggression and noncompliance) but also how to behave more appropriately. A positive environment is needed to cultivate these appropriate behaviors in school. This requires schools to promote a sense of community, which fosters a sense of belonging among all children. Doing so has particular implications for students who have or are at risk for developing ODD or CD because these children are frequently insulated from the larger social context. As a result, they are unaware of the appropriate rules of behavior that operate outside their maladaptive social milieu. If younger children become more invested in school, they have improved chances to learn new, more adaptive behaviors. Furthermore, they must view the school as a place where they belong. To increase the likelihood of this, an increased number of positive comments should be directed toward children who are at risk for ODD or CD. In the process, school personnel may need to make a concerted effort to demonstrate an active interest in the child's ideas, interests, and activities. In addition to setting clear behavioral expectations within the school and making positive comments, school personnel should reward positive behavior and teach children how to use appropriate social skills. Bloomquist and Schnell (2002) reviewed the key elements of schoolwide intervention/prevention programs; Table 14.1 presents a summary of their findings.

Peer mediation is often incorporated into schoolwide prevention programs and is one of the most effective approaches to enhancing prosocial skills. Bloomquist and Schnell (2002) defined *peer mediation* as a process in which a peer functions as a facilitator to assist and resolve disputes and conflicts. Thus, peer assistance aids prevention efforts. Typically, a limited number of peer mediators are trained in using conflict-resolution techniques to help resolve disputes involving name calling, arguing, and fighting. The basic conflict-resolution skills include having the student mediator set ground rules and, in the process, assist his or her fellow students in identifying the sources of their conflict, developing solutions, and implementing or following through with these solutions.

Individualized School-Based Intervention Even the best prevention programs may prove unsuccessful for some children, for whom individualized

Table 14.1. Summary of best practices for schoolwide interventions: Program content

General area	Best practices
Creating a positive school climate	Plan activities that promote a sense of community; actively work on positive relationships with children with ACP by decreasing negative comments, increasing positive comments, and demonstrating interest in children's interests and activities.
Defining behavioral expectations	Develop a small set of general expectations and specific expectations for different school locations.
Supporting positive behavior	Closely monitor behavior, especially during common problem times; acknowledge and reward positive behavior; use reminders and reviews of behavioral expectations; train children in needed social skills.
Utilizing a consistent and *effective* response to problem behavior	Define categories of problem behaviors; use consistent procedures for responding to minor and serious problem behaviors; institute procedures for problem-solving meetings.

From Bloomquist, M.L., & Schnell, S.V. (2002). *Helping children with aggression and conduct problems* (p. 251). New York: The Guilford Press; reprinted by permission.
Key: ACP = aggressive/conduct problem

approaches may be required. Such school-based programs use some of the behavioral principles that are used within families. The best of these programs (e.g., Walker, Hops, & Greenwood, 1993) involve direct teaching of appropriate social behavior, rewards provided by school personnel for these behaviors in class and on the playground, and a response–cost procedure in which points (or tokens) are lost for inappropriate behavior (e.g., aggression, rule breaking). This approach also allows the targeted child to earn points that can be exchanged for group rewards provided at school, along with individual rewards provided at home.

The main drawback of school-based programs is the time investment required by school personnel. This is particularly true when the intervention involves targeting a single child in a general education classroom. These model programs are easier to implement within a special education classroom.

For children with less severe forms of oppositional behavior, a less comprehensive approach often proves effective. One intervention involves a behavioral monitoring program implemented at school, followed by reinforcement provided at home. Figure 14.1 is an example of a home–school note for behavioral monitoring. A number of studies have supported the positive benefits of using this type of home-based reinforcement. In addition, when compared with other behavioral techniques (e.g., token economies, time-out, ignoring the child's behavior), this type of intervention is more acceptable to teachers and students (McMahon & Wells, 1998).

Psychopharmacological Treatment

As of 2004, no specific drug has been used to target the aggression and conduct problems associated with ODD and CD. However, the following medications have been used to treat some of the symptoms often associated with ODD or CD.

Psychostimulants Because of the high comorbidity rate of ADHD and ODD or CD, it is not surprising that medication designed to treat ADHD can have a positive effect on the problems associated with ODD and CD. Research has found

---

Student's name: _____ Date: _____

Morning Report

Task   **Behavioral rating by teacher (circle one)**

Completed assignments   Needs improvement   Fair   Excellent

Gave compliments   Needs improvement   Fair   Excellent

Shared with others   Needs improvement   Fair   Excellent

Homework Assignments

Class   **Assignment (completed by student)**   **Teacher's Initials**

Math   _____   _____

Reading   _____   _____

Language arts   _____   _____

Teacher's signature: _____

Parent's signature: _____

Figure 14.1. Home–school note for behavioral monitoring. (From Ostrander, R. [2001]. Emotional and behavioral disorders [p. 129]. In F.M. Kline, L.B. Silver, & S.C. Russell [Eds.], *The educator's guide to medical issues in the classroom.* Baltimore: Paul H. Brookes Publishing Co.; reprinted by permission.)

that typically, psychostimulants (e.g., methylphenidate [Ritalin], dexedrine [Dexedrine, DextroStat], and pemoline [Cylert]) not only are successful at treating the inattention and hyperactivity associated with ADHD, but also result in decreased aggression and conduct problems (McMahon & Wells, 1998; Swanson, 1993).

Other Drugs Various other medications have also been used to treat children with ODD or CD. However, other treatments have typically been used with children and adolescents who exhibit a more extreme presentation, do not respond to alternate treatments, and/or have a mood disturbance associated with their presentation. Of these alternate medications, lithium (Eskalith) and antipsychotics (e.g., haloperidol [Haldol], thioridazine [Mellaril]) have the greatest empirical support (McMahon & Wells, 1998).

CONCLUSION

The causes of conduct problems and oppositional behaviors in children are often complex. It is rare that any single risk causes a child to be extremely disruptive, disobedient, and/or aggressive; rather, the cause often is a complex interplay among various societal, biological, family, and interpersonal factors. This chapter has provided a brief review of many of the risks associated with young people who have oppositional or conduct problems. Although understanding the specific risks associated with these behaviors is important, it is likewise important to recognize that many children are resilient and will go on to live productive lives. In many cases, schools can play an important part in changing the lives of children at risk for ODD or CD; in other cases, the path to a better outcome requires the concerted efforts of mental health and school professionals. The good news is that it is possible to help these children channel their behaviors more effectively. Armed with this knowledge, there is every reason to believe that effective treatment and prevention of ODD and CD can be fully realized.

REFERENCES

Achenbach, T.M. (2001). *Manual for the ASEBA School-Age Forms & Profiles.* Burlington: University of Vermont, Department of Psychiatry.

American Psychiatric Association. (2000). *Diagnostic and statistical manual of mental disorders* (4th ed., text rev.). Washington, DC: Author.

Baldwin, A.T., Petersen, A.C., & Cole, R.E. (1990). Stress-resistant families and stress-resistant children. In J. Rolf, A.S. Masten, D. Cicchetti, K.H. Nuechterlein, & S. Weintraub (Eds.), *Risk and protective factors in developmental psychopathology* (pp. 257–280). New York: Cambridge University Press.

Bloomquist, M.L., & Schnell, S.V. (2002). *Helping children with aggression and conduct problems.* New York: The Guilford Press.

Crick, N.R. (1995). Relational aggression: The role of intent attributions, feelings of distress, and provocation type. *Development and Psychopathology, 7,* 313–322.

Crick, N.R., & Grotpetor, J.K. (1995). Relational aggression, gender, and social-psychological adjustment. *Child Development, 66,* 710–722.

Cummings, J., & Volkman, E. (1992). *Goombalia: The improbable rise and fall of John Gotti and his gang.* New York: Avon Books.

Dishion, T.J., French, D.C., & Patterson, G.R. (1995). The development and ecology of antisocial behavior. In D. Cicchetti & D.J. Cohen (Eds.), *Developmental psychopathology: Vol. 2. Risk, disorder, and adaptation* (pp. 421–471). New York: John Wiley & Sons.

Dodge, K.A., & Coie, J.D. (1987). Social-information-processing factors in reactive and proactive aggression in children's peer groups. *Journal of Personality and Social Psychology, 53,* 1146–1158.

Frick, P.J. (1994). Family dysfunction and the disruptive behavior disorders: A review of recent empirical findings. In T.H. Ollendick & R.J. Printz (Eds.), *Advances in clinical child psychology: Vol. 16* (pp. 203–226). New York: Kluwer Academic/Plenum Publishers.

Hughes, J.N., Cavell, T.A., & Jackson, T. (1999). Influence of the teacher-student relationship on childhood conduct problems: A prospective study. *Journal of Clinical Child Psychology, 28,* 173–184.

Kolko, D.J. (1996). Education and counseling for child fire setters: A comparison of skills training programs with standard practice. In E.D. Hibbs & P.S. Jensen (Eds.), *Psychosocial treatment for child and adolescent disorders* (pp. 409–433). Washington, DC: American Psychological Association.

Kumpulainen, K., Rasanen, E., Henttonen, I., Almquist, F., Kresanor, K., Lina, S., Moilanen, I., Piha, J., Puura, K., & Tamminen, T. (1998). Bullying and psychiatric symptoms among elementary school-age children. *Child Abuse and Neglect, 22,* 705–717.

Masten, A.S., Hubbard, J.J., Gest, S.D., Tellegen, A., Garmezy, N., & Ramirez, M.L. (1999). Competence in the context of adversity: Pathways to resilience and maladaptation from childhood to late adolescence. *Development and Psychopathology, 11,* 143–169.

McMahon, R.J., & Wells, K.C. (1998). Conduct problems. In E.J. Mash & R.A. Barkley (Eds.), *Treatment of childhood disorders* (pp. 111–210). New York: The Guilford Press.

Miles, D.R., & Carey, G. (1997). Genetic and environmental architecture of human aggression. *Journal of Personality and Social Psychology, 72,* 207–217.

Moffitt, T.E. (1993). "Adolescence-limited" and "Life-course-persistent" antisocial behavior: A developmental taxonomy. *Psychological Review, 100,* 674–701.

Moffitt, T.E., Caspi, A., Dickson, N., Silva, P., & Stanton, W. (1996). Childhood-onset versus adolescent-onset antisocial conduct problems in males: Natural history from ages 3 to 18 years. *Development and Psychopathology, 8,* 399–424.

Nigg, J.T., & Hinshaw, S.P. (1998). Parent personality traits and psychopathology associated with antisocial behaviors in childhood attention-deficit hyperactivity disorder. *Journal of Child Psychology and Psychiatry, 39,* 145–159.

Patterson, G.R. (1975). *Families: Applications of social learning to family life* (Rev. ed.). Champaign, IL: Research Press.

Patterson, G.R. (1982). *Coercive family process.* Eugene, OR: Castalia.

Reynolds, C.R., & Kamphaus, R.W. (1992). *Behavioral Assessment System for Children.* Circle Pines, MN: American Guidance Service.

Swanson, J. (1993). Effect of stimulant medication on hyperactive children: A review of reviews. *Exceptional Children, 60,* 154–162.

Walker, H.M., Hops, H., & Greenwood, C.R. (1993). *RECESS: A Program for Reducing Negative-Aggressive Behavior.* Portland, OR: Educational Achievement Systems.

Webster-Stratton, C. (1984). Randomized trial of two parent-training programs for families with conduct-disordered children. *Journal of Consulting and Clinical Psychology, 52,* 666–678.

SECTION V

Tools and Techniques for Collaboration

Frank M. Kline

Being informed is important, but having all of the information available about mental health issues will not serve children. In addition to the information, it is necessary to have collaborative teamwork between educators and mental health professionals to develop and implement the best treatment plans. Educators and mental health professionals can and should work together to benefit the individuals whom they serve. Section V provides practical tips, techniques, and examples for successful collaboration.

The tasks and work schedules of mental health professionals and educators differ. Their communication patterns vary not only in content but also in style and logic. Chapter 15 explores ways to bridge the difference between the two fields.

Even when collaborative efforts are made, families are in a mediating position between professionals in the two fields. Understanding the pressures that families face is key to obtaining their cooperation in brokering communication across all service providers, as well as their active participation in treatment plans. Chapter 16 describes the various dynamics in families of children with mental health problems, including the families' challenges and strengths.

Families also play a role in Chapter 17. This chapter provides detailed examples of interactions among mental health workers, families, and educators, all working together to serve children.

Section V takes the information given throughout the book and applies it to ways that educators and mental health professionals can work together. Through such collaborative efforts, the needs of the children they serve will be identified more quickly and accurately and treated more successfully. In turn, students will be assisted in reaching their full potential.

15

Collaborating with Mental Health Professionals

Frank M. Kline

Chapter Concepts

- General observations on collaboration
- A theory of collaboration
- The implication of collaborative theory on collaboration between educators and mental health professionals
- Conditions necessary for effective collaboration between educators and mental health professionals

Collaboration deserves consideration because the ability to work together continues to shape and direct many of society's efforts. In turn, collaboration in schools has become increasingly important. The rise in student diversity makes it less likely that any one educator will have the background and understanding necessary to work with all students. Thus, to serve all students well, educators must work together.

Furthermore, it is obvious that fewer educators have sufficient information and skills necessary to serve the increasing numbers of students with special needs. That means that the education community must learn to work with other professional communities. Earlier work (Kline, Silver, & Russell, 2001) described the knowledge and skills necessary for educators to collaborate effectively with members of the medical community. This book focuses on the knowledge and skills necessary for collaboration with members of the mental health community. Whereas Chapter 3 has described the structure of the mental health field, this chapter covers general collaboration theory as applied to the mental health professions.

THEORY OF COLLABORATION

Collaboration can be defined as two or more people working together to complete a task. For the purposes of this book, collaboration between educators and mental health professionals is considered. How do differences between these groups affect collaborative efforts? Imagine that two people have the same genetic makeup and the same history. More than identical twins, these two people would have had exactly the same set of experiences (see Figure 15.1). If these two people are

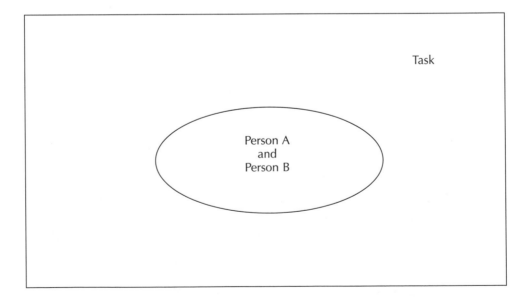

Figure 15.1. People with identical backgrounds who are facing a task.

indeed identical, it is reasonable to assume that they would approach any task in exactly the same fashion. If they use only the same kinds of problem-solving strategies when approaching any task, then they can do more work. That is, they can be more powerful, but they cannot do qualitatively different work. Therefore, they cannot learn from each other's differing approaches. The nature of collaboration on these tasks is captured in the adage "Many hands make light work." *Quantitative collaboration* is another term that describes this work. In some ways, this approach is similar to members of one profession working together. Whereas the differences between individual professionals can be profound, there are still basic similarities in their philosophical and theoretical orientations as well as in their definitions of and general approaches to a problem.

The next example more closely resembles the realm of human experience. Imagine two people who are completely different. They have nothing in common. They eat different food, dress in different kinds of clothing, listen to different types of music, communicate with different people, have learned from different thinkers, relate to their families in different ways—they may even speak different languages (see Figure 15.2). Given that pattern of difference, how successful can their collaborative efforts be? It is easy to see that they cannot work together at all. Only through sharing experiences and knowledge, as their lives develop some elements in common, can they begin to work together. This example can illustrate the experience of educators trying to collaborate with members of other professions. Approaches to the individuals served, theoretical orientations, and basic philosophical assumptions are very different. The very way that problems are defined—and even what constitutes a problem—may be different. Furthermore, the logistics of doing work differ. Different schedules, different reward systems, different social status, and many other differences work to create a situation in

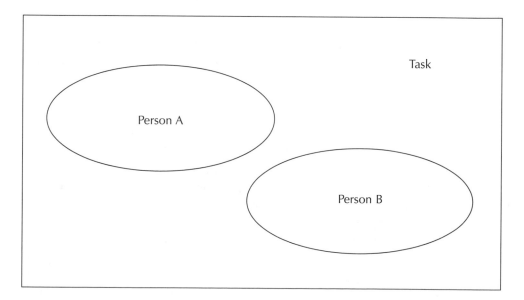

Figure 15.2. People with completely different backgrounds who are facing a task.

which there is minimal overlap between the two professions. In some ways, it is as if educators and members of other professional groups speak different languages.

Between the two extremes, it is possible to conceive of experiences overlapping enough to allow collaboration without restricting the quality of collaboration. Some overlap in experience must exist before potential collaborators can communicate well enough to work together. The aim of this book is to increase the overlap between the conceptual worlds of educators and mental health professionals. If the overlap is too great, however, a higher quantity of work can be completed, but there is little chance for qualitative differences in the work being completed. Thus, as long as such differences are not too great, they allow improvements to occur. This type of collaboration can be encapsulated in the adage "Two heads are better than one." *Qualitative collaboration* is another way to label this type of relationship. One task for schools that want to increase collaboration is helping people learn to profit from the differences between groups and individuals. The case studies presented by Silver and Kline (2001), as well as those detailed in this book, evidence the positive benefits of collaboration across professional groups.

With these considerations of the requirements for collaboration in mind, the discussion turns to the nature of the task. To a great degree, this defines what opportunities for collaboration exist. Again, a simple task with a straightforward, clearly specified definition of success is more conducive to quantitative collaboration than to qualitative collaboration. That is, the differences in background are not as important for tasks that are clearly defined. One example is grading a multiple-choice test, where the correct answers are concrete and objective. Although minor variations of this particular task may occur, there is essentially one way to do it. Two people can grade more papers than one person can, but they cannot necessarily grade "better" than one person. The clear definition of such tasks also makes them easier to automate. In this example, two educators—or, for that matter, two people with minimal training—can collaborate effectively in a quantitative fashion to grade the tests.

Other tasks are less clearly defined, allow for qualitative differences in approach or strategy, and result in higher quality task completion. One example of this may involve working with a child who has social problems. Whereas educators and mental health professionals may define the problems differently, approach intervention differently, and expect slightly different results, these variations can actually produce a more positive result for the child. These qualitative differences between the professionals will almost certainly result in a more comprehensive and more effective intervention for the child.

Motivation also plays a key role in collaboration. Some tasks are more motivating than others, and motivation varies by the unique set of interests brought to the task by the individuals involved. Again, the level of motivation influences the kind and amount of collaborative efforts expended by the individuals involved. The differences between people almost ensure differences in commitment to and motivation for doing any given task. If the differences in motivation are too extreme, collaboration can be a frustrating experience for the more motivated person, decreasing the likelihood of his or her engagement in further collaborative efforts.

Differences in motivation may also occur across professions. An enormous problem for an educator may be a minor inconvenience for another professional. For example, the culture of school settings means that educators are less tolerant of impulsive behavior than society in general. An acceptable level of impulsivity in many social settings would not be conducive to academic success in a classroom.

In summary, collaboration involves two or more people working together. The amount of overlap in the collaborators' experiences and backgrounds determines, in part, the kind of collaboration that can occur. Collaborative efforts capitalizing on the power of people working together emphasize the additional quantity of work that can be accomplished. Collaborative efforts that capitalize on different ways of working emphasize the qualitatively better work. Finally, motivation to work depends largely on the task and on the interests or needs of each person interacting with the task. With these thoughts in mind, several learning theories are examined regarding collaboration.

Sociocultural Theory

Sociocultural theory (e.g., Vygotsky, 1978) focuses on the relationship between two or more people in terms of learning. One premise of sociocultural theory is that the meaning of cultural symbols is co-constructed and negotiated through social interaction (Emerson, 1996). These cultural symbols, which include most forms of communication, are the tools of collaboration. Sociocultural theory relates to collaboration in two ways. First, those potential collaborators must share some co-constructed meanings to be able to collaborate. Co-construction of cultural symbols is a similar concept to the historical and experiential overlap described in the previous examples and figures. Without shared meaning, new meanings cannot be developed because their development depends on communication. If the base of meaning is entirely shared, then new meanings cannot be developed, either, because their development depends on differences in the communicators' experience. In terms of educators and mental health professionals working together, this co-construction of meaning comes from developing a shared understanding of language—including both vocabulary and related constructs. This book is designed to assist educators in developing an understanding of the mental health professional's perspective on certain problems that children face.

Second, a new type of relationship is formed on basis of each collaborator's relative expertise. The diagram in Figure 15.3 represents the larger amount of skill or knowledge that one collaborator may bring to a specific task or part of a task. Collaboration depends on differences in knowledge or skill among the people involved. Peer collaboration is a constantly shifting situation in which one person with particular expertise takes the lead, and then, as the task demands or motivation shifts (bringing different expertise into demand), the other person may take the lead. Figure 15.3 illustrates this concept by the relative size of the ovals, which shift in relation to some differences in background.

In educational terms, the larger oval is the teacher and the smaller oval is the student. In professional collaboration terms, one of the ovals is the educator and the other is the mental health professional. The task at hand—that is, the

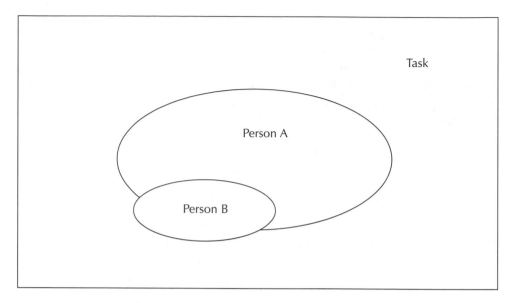

Figure 15.3. Collaboration between people of different skill levels who are facing a task.

type of expertise it requires—dictates which individual is represented by the larger oval. It is critical for both parties to realize that expertise is shared in both professions. There will be times when the educator takes the lead and times when the mental health professional takes the lead. Lead position depends on the task, the motivation to perform the task, and the particulars of the human relationships involved. For true collaboration to work, however, both parties must be willing to be the leader as well as the follower, recognizing the value that both professions bring to the discussion.

Sociocultural theory can help explain the importance of co-constructions and give-and-take between collaborators. In peer collaboration (e.g., collaboration between two professionals), that give-and-take is frequent and dynamic. In collaboration between an educator and a mental health worker, both parties will contribute depending on the student's circumstances, the particular problems being addressed, and the environment where the problem is located. Sociocultural theory clarifies how both parties contribute to collaborative work.

Cognitive Development Theory

For purposes of this chapter, the work of Piaget (1926) is used to represent cognitive development theory. In particular, his work on the process of knowledge construction is helpful because it focuses on the learner's interior life. Through the concepts of *assimilation* and *accommodation*, Piaget explained the cognitive dissonance and subsequent resolution that occurs within a person who is involved in the personal and corporate construction of knowledge. Piaget always recognized the environment's role in generating the cognitive conflict that is necessary for moving through the various stages of development. Later, some researchers and theorists (e.g., Almasi, 1995) recognized the importance of social elements in the environment. They have even noted peer collaboration as an environment that facilitates sociocognitive conflicts resulting in the individual's cognitive development.

In terms of collaboration and collaborative settings, Piaget's work provided premises that assist in the understanding of the personal and internal development within individuals. As one of the collaborative partners assumes the lead role, the other begins to assimilate and, possibly through the differences between the two people, is forced to accommodate. The assimilation and accommodation of ideas presented and processed through collaborative efforts can influence an individual's cognitive development as well as his or her knowledge and skills.

Regarding collaborative efforts between different professional groups, such as educators and mental health professionals, both groups must be ready to accommodate and to assimilate information. As points of view and philosophical orientations become more explicit, the groups need to recognize that accommodation—even a radical reshifting of orientation—may be necessary. Although analogies can be helpful tools in building understanding between groups, they inevitably break down at some point and do not further the process of assimilation. Cognitive development theory shows that individuals need to listen carefully and with a willingness to change—or at least add to—their assumptions.

Sociocognitive Theory

Key elements of sociocognitive theory (Bandura, 1978) situate learning within an interactive triangle of the individual's behavior, the individual's personal factors, and characteristics of the environment. Especially helpful is the theory's emphasis on the reciprocal nature of the relationship between an individual and the environment. That is, although the environment can and does influence an individual, the individual also influences the environment. This kind of reciprocity is one way of representing the give-and-take between members of a collaborative group as they assume various group tasks (e.g., leadership, summary, facilitation) as well as the give-and-take in various kinds of knowledge and skill presentation and representation within collaborative settings.

The strength of sociocognitive theory as it relates to collaborative settings is that it accounts for the various ways that 1) different individuals affect groups and group processes and 2) group work affects individuals. Concepts such as self-efficacy, self-regulation, goal setting, and related behaviors can both influence and be influenced by group processes in collaborative settings (Bandura, 1986). For example, a person with a highly developed sense of goal direction might come to a collaborative project with strong motivation. In addition to the increased capacity to accomplish work that such motivation may bring to a group, goal-directed behavior also serves as a model for other group members to use and generalize to other collaborative settings. In turn, the success or failure of the group relative to the task and to the individual's reception by various group members can increase or decrease the likelihood that the person with highly developed goal direction will continue to exhibit that behavior.

Thus, educators and mental health professionals will both shape and be shaped by each other through collaboration. This is a desirable outcome because it will inevitably lead to a broader understanding of human behavior by members of both professions. Sociocognitive theory explains the impact that an individual has on others as well as the impact that others have on the individual.

Information-Processing Models

Information processing is not understood as a singular theory but, rather, as a general model of human learning. This model is based on a variety of specific theories that emphasize human learning and use of information. Van Meter and Stevens stated that the model posits a "system with limited capacity in working memory and knowledge representations stored as interconnected networks" (2000, p. 121). The generally accepted tenets of this model are that information enters a person's mind through the senses and goes into a limited working memory system. From there, it may or may not be moved into a long-term storage as a memory. How the information is handled in the short-term memory system has profound implications for long-term storage and later use of the information. These models relate directly to the cognitive models of assimilation and accommodation that were pioneered by Piaget. That is, linking new information with prior knowledge can result in the new knowledge fitting well with the existing information (assimilation) or in the new information not fitting well (eventually leading to accommodation). The human tendency is to select or shape the new information to make it better fit current understanding, but when enough new information that does not fit is collected, cognitive dissonance builds to a point at which an individual must accommodate by creating new cognitive structures of information.

A second way in which information-processing models can provide understanding for collaboration is through the concepts of working memory and long-term storage. The group has a working memory that is collectively larger than any individual. By using language as a mediator, the group can effectively pool its working memory. That allows quantitative collaboration in the sense of "many hands make light work." Each collaborator can remember key parts of the issue being examined. In addition, the group has a collective long-term memory that is larger and more diverse than that of any individual within the group. This is the mechanism through which the group can work differently. That is, when the individuals' different collective histories and memories are accessible to the group as a whole, qualitative collaboration occurs. This is the mechanism that allows for qualitative collaboration in that "two heads are better than one."

Information-processing theory helps shows how assimilation and accommodation work as well as how groups can be more effective than individuals. As mentioned previously, educators working with mental health professionals must be willing to accommodate new frames of thought. Furthermore, educators and mental health professionals should look for ways to contribute to the collective work and long-term demands of the task.

BENEFITS OF COLLABORATION

Collaboration yields several benefits. The benefits of power and quality have already been discussed. In addition, motivation has been mentioned as a benefit. This section recapitulates the benefits of power and quality, expands the benefits of motivation, and describes the added benefit of accountability.

Power and Quality

Collaboration allows not only a multiplied effort (power) but also better work (quality). Although educators and mental health professionals have very different backgrounds, certain tasks are well defined, readily understood, and easily done by both groups. This allows for quantitative collaboration. More important, the differences between the groups allow for qualitative collaboration. That is, if both parties are open to accommodation, are willing to listen, and exhibit an attitude of respect, then tremendous power can be generated by these very differences in training and expertise.

Motivation

As stated previously, in the sociocognitive model of learning, motivation is a result of reciprocal interaction between the environment and the individual. The environment most likely includes other people and even working groups. Within the context of groups, a variety of motivations exist for doing the task at hand. Each person brings to the task his or her own interests, strengths, dislikes, and weaknesses. The interplay of these factors form a variety of motivations. Those motivations do not exist in a vacuum but, rather, in relationship with each other. That is, the reciprocal nature of group work posited by the sociocognitive model suggests that motivations are reciprocally shared among group members and that they affect each other. For example, even if not particularly motivated by the intrinsic nature of a task, one can be motivated to work with certain people and, through them, gain an appreciation of and motivation to do the task.

This fact is particularly important in working across professions. That is, educators must be willing to be motivated by mental health workers to examine and work with certain problems, even if educators do not consider these issues critical. Similarly, mental health professionals must be willing to accept the motivations of educators. This mutual acceptance of the other's perspective on what is important is critical to effective collaboration.

In summary, the motivation to accomplish a task within a group is often greater than that of any individual within the group. The individuals' various motivations are affected across the group in a reciprocal manner, with each individual within the group being influenced by the motivations of the others in the group. This motivation may be related in part to the group rather than to the task, which leads to accountability as a benefit of collaboration.

Accountability

Accountability comes out of the social expectations that individuals place on each other. Although they take different forms, such expectations exist regardless of culture. These expectations, within the context of a task-focused group, can increase the likelihood that the task will be completed. Accountability is nearly always a function of motivation. Sometimes, the most motivated person in the group can hold the rest of the group accountable for their parts of the task. However, in the best groups (i.e., in which all members attribute some level of importance to tasks), members can motivate each other to stay task oriented. Humans tend to meet the expectations that are placed on them. Furthermore, the social status differences between groups (e.g., between educators and mental health professionals) can influence accountability. That is, the group that is considered less important generally strives to meet the expectations of the group that is perceived as more important. Occasionally, the opposite effect occurs, with the lower-status group refusing to meet the other group's expectations because of some sort of principle. Collaboration works best when the groups perceive each other as valuable and capable of making positive contributions.

CONDITIONS REQUIRED FOR COLLABORATION

There are at least four generalizations that can be drawn about collaboration. They center on the background of the collaborators, the communication skills required to collaborate, the motivation for working together, and a common understanding of the task.

Overlap in Background

As noted, potential collaborators need some background in common. They must have sufficient shared history to allow for understanding and intelligent discussion. It is through the mediation of language that collaboration occurs. This book seeks to augment the language of educators so they can collaborate more effectively with mental health professionals. By learning the basic professional skills and knowledge associated with mental health work, educators will have a basis for communication.

Communication Skills

The specific communication skills that promote and enhance collaborative efforts are beyond the scope of this chapter. Unless group members are skilled and committed communicators, however, the diversity among group members that can produce the strongest qualitative collaboration also can make communication difficult. Differences in group social status can complicate this scenario as well. Yet, the education and mental health professions are both based, at least in part, in careful listening. It is this listening, combined with an attitude of appreciation, that will allow educators and mental health professionals to contribute to the work at hand.

Motivation for Working Together

Commitment can be expressed as motivation. Johnson and Johnson (1974, 1982, 1991) noted that specific goal structures enhance the satisfaction of members and the performance of cooperative groups. Whereas the goals of instructional groups can be artificially structured in a cooperative fashion, it cannot be assumed that collegial groups of educational and mental health professionals have cooperative goal structures. As educators and mental health professionals increasingly understand what the other group values, the goals and rewards of the group are more likely to be structured in a way that is meaningful to all participants.

Common Understanding of the Task

Goal structure relates directly to the understanding of the task. Educators profess the success of their students as the ultimate task. Even among educators, however, there is great controversy about what *success* actually means and how it is best achieved. It follows that educators and mental health workers may have profound differences in the definition of and approach to success. The more clearly the task is structured and the structure is communicated, the more likely it is that cross-professional collaborative efforts will be considered a success by all parties.

CONCLUSION

When collaboration is required between educators and mental health professionals, both groups need to develop common background and history by actively seeking to understand the other's professional background and the contexts in which it works. For collaboration to run smoothly, the groups need to learn each other's basic vocabulary and concepts and must have effective communication skills. In addition, goal structures must be developed that stipulate the success of all members as a requirement for any one member's reward. Finally, educators and mental health professionals need to agree on the definition of the task. To the degree that these conditions are met, educators and mental health professionals can collaborate so that many hands make work light and two heads are better than one.

REFERENCES

Almasi, J.F. (1995). The nature of fourth graders' sociocognitive conflicts in peer-led and teacher-led discussions of literature. *Reading Research Quarterly, 30,* 314–351.

Bandura, A. (1978). The self-system in reciprocal determinism. *American Psychologist, 33,* 344–358.

Bandura, A. (1986). *Social foundations of thought and action: A social-cognitive theory.* Upper Saddle River, NJ: Prentice-Hall.

Emerson, C. (1996). The outer word and inner speech: Bakhtin, Vygotsky, and the internalization of language. In H. Daniels (Ed.), *An introduction to Vygotsky* (pp. 123–142). New York: Routledge.

Johnson, D.W., & Johnson, R.T. (1974). Instructional goal structure: Cooperative, competitive or individualistic. *Review of Educational Research, 44,* 213–240.

Johnson, D.W., & Johnson, R.T. (1982). What research says about student-student interaction in science classrooms. In M. Rowe (Ed.), *Education in the 80's: Science* (pp. 98–125). Washington, DC: National Education Association.

Johnson, D.W., & Johnson, R.T. (1991). What cooperative learning has to offer the gifted. *Cooperative Learning, 11*(3), 24–27.

Kline, F.M., Silver, L.B., & Russell, S.C. (Eds.). (2001). *The educator's guide to medical issues in the classroom.* Baltimore: Paul H. Brookes Publishing Co.

Piaget, J. (1926). *Judgment and reasoning in the child.* New York: Harcourt.

Silver, L.B., & Kline, F.M. (2001). Examples of collaboration. In L.B. Silver, F.M. Kline, & S.C. Russell (Eds.), *The educator's guide to medical issues in the classroom* (pp. 181–188). Baltimore: Paul H. Brookes Publishing Co.

Van Meter, P., & Stevens, R.J. (2000). The role of theory in the study of peer collaboration. *Journal of Experimental Education 69*(1), 113–128.

Vygotsky, L.S. (1978). *Mind in society: The development of higher psychological processes.* Cambridge, MA: Harvard University Press.

16

Families of Children with Mental Health Issues

**Connie Kundahl Craig,
Scott Shiebler, Frank M. Kline, and Beverly J. Wilson**

Chapter Concepts

- Parental relationships in families that have a child with learning problems
- Sibling relationships in families that have a child with learning problems
- Methods for working with families that have a child with mental health issues

Children with mental health issues live in the context of their families. When a child has a mental health problem, it is the family that lives with the problem. The family is also the most common advocate for the child. As a result, the ability to work effectively with families is critical to the success of children who have mental health issues.

All families are unique. However, families with children who have mental health issues share certain characteristics with all families. This chapter seeks to describe these shared characteristics of families with children who have mental health issues. Even while examining characteristics that are potentially shared, it is important to honor the uniqueness of each family. Although this chapter may provide a useful guide, untested generalizations to particular families are not appropriate.

Because schools and educators focus primarily on learning, this chapter's focus is narrowed by considering families whose children have mental health issues that result in problems with learning. Each of the mental health issues discussed in Sections II, III, and IV of this book may result in significant learning problems. The treatment for some of them, such as autism and Asperger syndrome, includes significant educational components. In fact, treatments of these conditions are primarily educational. The treatment of others, such as substance abuse and mood disorders, may not have significant educational components. Regardless of the size of the role that education and educators play in the treatment of the mental health issue, the family always plays a critical role. Notwithstanding its structure, strength, and resilience, the family is the primary locus of responsibility for the child. As such, understanding the familial context will help educators make wise decisions about individual students.

Families are configured in a myriad of ways; no longer can one assume that a family consists of two parents with children. As mentioned previously, each family is unique and must be considered in the inimitable composition of its members, strengths, resources, and so forth. Yet, although it is dangerous to generalize, there are commonalities among families who have children with learning problems. This chapter considers commonalities in two key aspects of family life: the relationship of the adults in the family and the relationships of the children (i.e., marital satisfaction and sibling relationships). This focus is not used to suggest that educators will not encounter other family structures. After all, each family is unique. Certainly, some children with mental health issues live in single-parent families and do not have siblings. General trends and patterns are provided in these key areas not with the idea of exhaustively describing what families with children who have learning problems are like but, rather, with the hope that educators will be able to generalize an understanding of some of the problems and stresses in these families, regardless of their unique groupings.

This chapter begins by describing the factors related to marital relationships (specifically marital satisfaction) and family functioning. It also examines stressors that are specific to families whose children have disabilities. The chapter also considers the differences in relationships between siblings when one has a disability. Finally, the chapter examines the development of coping skills. It discusses the influence of family models, observation, and family members' stress management strategies.

MARITAL SATISFACTION

Marital satisfaction and factors that support and detract from it have been the subject of much research. One major factor that changes marital function—both positively and negatively—is the birth of a couple's first child (Belsky & Hsieh, 1998; Cowan & Cowan, 1992). This event places additional physical and emotional demands on each spouse and their relationship. Having a child with a disability places additional demands on the marital unit and the family (Beckman, 1991). Although some research has been conducted on marital satisfaction and stress in families of children with learning disabilities and families whose children have developmental delays, very few longitudinal studies are available (Dyson, 1993). The research that does exist suggests the presence of additional stressors. These stressors, as well as overall factors for marital satisfaction, are reviewed next.

Factors that Influence Marital Functioning

Many factors affect marital satisfaction at the time of marriage, styles of marital interactions, length of marriage, the amount of social support available to the couple, the amount of satisfaction with one's partner, and the couple's transition to parenthood.

Satisfaction at the Time of Marriage Karney and Bradbury (1997) discovered that couples who experienced higher levels of initial marital satisfaction had a lower risk for divorce over time. Further research by Kurdek (1999) revealed that over time, all marriages show some loss of marital satisfaction and increase in distress. This pattern can be understood as a linear curve representing the course of a couple's marital satisfaction. The authors noted that at the onset of marriage, levels of satisfaction are at their highest point. Although the initial level of marital satisfaction varies widely among couples, change in satisfaction can be expected at certain times during marriage; specific times of diminished satisfaction are years 4 and 8 (Kurdek, 1999). Marriages that have a higher level of initial marital satisfaction may be able to weather developmental marital stressors more effectively than those that begin with a lower level of satisfaction (Noller, Freeney, & Ward, 1997).

Styles of Marital Interaction Ridley, Wilhelm, and Surra (2001) found that couples who were able to engage in positive problem solving reported higher levels of marital satisfaction than couples whose style of interactions were negative and distancing. Belsky and Hsieh (1998) suggested that marital dissatisfaction was linked to poor communication between partners and noted that this impaired communication pattern between partners often included low levels of hostility in interpersonal exchanges. Fincham (1998) stated that such negative exchanges are the best single predictor of marital distress.

Length of Marriage   Several studies indicate higher satisfaction early and later in marriage, whereas the lowest marital satisfaction occurs during couples' middle-age years (Carstensen, Gottman, & Levenson, 1995; Noller et al., 1997). "Middle-age marriages" also show decreased overall marital quality, increased negativity in exchanges, and increased defensive responses by husbands when compared with "older marriages" (Carstensen et al., 1995). If marriages can survive this difficult period, couples report improvements in satisfaction and communication over time. It is also the case that during this time, factors within and outside marriage, such as social support, can affect marital satisfaction (Pasch & Bradbury, 1998).

Social Support   Bryant and Conger (1999) noted that during the early years of marriage, strong social support networks positively influence marital functioning. The researchers found that marriages with strong social support networks experience less distress than marriages without this protective factor. Bryant and Conger's findings are supported by other research showing that close, interdependent relationships positively influence individual functioning, which in turn may enhance marital satisfaction (Cook, 1998).

Satisfaction with Partner   Karney and Bradbury (1997) developed several theories of how individuals determine satisfaction in their relationships. In their social exchange theories, individuals evaluate the costs of staying in or leaving a relationship. According to this perspective, individuals tend to stay in relationships that are rewarding emotionally, sexually, and socially. Only when the attractions are weak and an alternative is viable do individuals choose to leave the relationship.

Transition to Parenthood   Although some authors suggest that having children can increase marital stability, the addition of children also results in additional stress on the marital relationship (Belsky & Hsieh, 1998; Devine & Forehand, 1996). In fact, childless couples show the highest levels of marital satisfaction (Noller et al., 1997). Not only is the presence of children a stressor, but the changing roles required of marital partners also put strains on the marital relationship. Although both partners in marriages with children are less satisfied, women seem to express dissatisfaction within such marriages sooner than their partners.

In a study describing marital satisfaction among parents, Rogers and White (1998) found that men's satisfaction with parenting depends on their satisfaction with the marriage in general; if the marriage is satisfying, they are happier in their parental role. Furthermore, men's satisfaction with parenting and marriage is greater if there is a male child in the family. In contrast, women respond separately to the roles of partner and parent and can express dissatisfaction with their marriage and still be satisfied and feel competent in their parenting role. However, Kitzmann (2000) found that if women are satisfied in their marriage, the overall level of satisfaction in family relationships is generally higher for all family members. In fact, in a study of families that have children with disabilities, marital satisfaction accounted for 79% of the variance in the mother's level of satisfaction regarding her ability to cope with a child's disability (Friedrich, 1979).

Stress affects marital relationships depending on how it is viewed. For example, a crisis, such as the birth of a child with a disability, can be interpreted negatively or positively. A spouse's inability to deal with this stress in an adaptive manner leads to less satisfaction with his or her partner, which may result in marital distress or dissolution (Beckman, 1991; Boyd & Mullins, 2001; Bristol, Gallagher, & Schopler, 1988; Dyson, 1993; Holroyd & McArthur, 1976; Kazak, 1987; Seligman & Darling, 1989). Yet, the birth could also be considered an event that draws parents closer and improves family functioning.

One important question is whether high levels of marital satisfaction are more important for families who have children with special needs than for other families. Marital satisfaction has been found to have a direct influence on the functioning of the marriage, the family unit, and each individual within the family (Sloper, Knussen, Turner, & Cunningham, 1991; Wikler, 1986). Whereas marital satisfaction buffers the family members from stressors, marital dissatisfaction makes them more vulnerable (Bristol et al., 1988; Kazak, 1987). Furthermore, marital dissatisfaction has a detrimental influence on children and family functioning.

Effects of Marital Discord on Children and Family Functioning

As noted previously, it is well documented that marital conflict affects all members of a household (Bickham & Fiese, 1997; El-Sheikh, 1997; Goodman, Barfoot, Frye, & Belli, 1999; Grych, 1998; Harold, Osborne, & Conger, 1997; Stocker & Youngblade, 1999). Whereas most research indicates that marital conflict influences relationships between parents and children in the home, not all researchers agree that such conflict is damaging (e.g., Goodman et al., 1999).

There are also differing views of how marital conflict affects children. Some researchers have suggested that a conflict's intensity and the level of implied threat influence children (e.g., Harold et al., 1997; Stocker & Youngblade, 1999); other researchers have examined the response and resolution of conflict by parents as they seek to understand the impact of marital conflict on children (e.g., El-Sheikh, 1997). Kitzmann (2000) suggested that marital conflict adversely affects children by weakening the interpersonal relationships within families. This idea is supported by evidence that marital discord may create a hostile environment that impairs children's relationships with siblings and peers (Bussell et al., 1999; Neiderhiser, Reiss, Hetherington, & Plomin, 1999; Rose & Asher, 1999; Stocker & Youngblade, 1999).

Children's Responses to Marital Conflict A number of research studies (Harold et al., 1997; Leadbeater, Kuperminc, Blatt, & Hertzog, 1999) have focused on child adjustment and distress as a function of marital conflict. Various factors influence how children experience their parents' marital stress differently. For instance, gender plays a role. Girls seem to internalize feelings of anxiety and have higher incidences of depression. Boys seem more likely to externalize their responses, become reactive, show distress, and show greater difficulty dealing with such conflicts (Harold et al., 1997; Leadbeater et al., 1999).

Age is another major factor in determining children's responses to marital conflict. Younger children are more likely to blame themselves for the conflict and see the conflict as a direct threat to their personal security (Stocker & Youngblade, 1999). Bickman and Fiese (1997) found that when exposed to marital conflict, younger children experience increased depression and anxiety and lower self-esteem. Adolescents are better able to attribute marital conflict to sources outside themselves, but they are still negatively affected by marital conflict (Bickman & Fiese, 1997; Grych, 1998). For example, McHale, Freitag, Crouter, and Bartko (1991) found that middle school boys who were exposed to marital stress had increased impulsivity and lower self-esteem compared with their counterparts.

Effect of Marital Conflict on the Family Structure Although most parents try to limit the negative effects of marital dysfunction on their children, research reveals that they often are not successful (Bickman & Fiese, 1997; Davies & Cummings, 1994; El-Sheikh, 1997; Goodman et al., 1999). Yamamoto and Mahlios (2001) found that although parents rated the impact of marital conflict as being low, their children rated it as major stressor in their lives. Kitzmann, for example, found "lower family warmth, and less democratic parenting in the triadic exchange" between parents and child after observing parents separately in conflicting interactions (2000, p. 9). Even though the children did not see the conflict, it spilled over into other family relationships.

Increased marital distress distracts parents from focusing on parenting, which then results in increased parent–child conflicts and poorer child adjustment outcomes (Bussell et al., 1999; Davies & Cummings, 1994; Gest, Neemann, Hubbard, Masten, & Tellegen, 1993; Katz & Gottman, 1993; Neiderhiser et al., 1999; Webster-Stratton & Hammond, 1999). Davies and Cummings (1994) noted that increased marital conflict causes both spouses to withdraw from each other and to be less available for their children. Gest et al. (1993) found that such parental withdrawal is associated with behavioral and emotional adjustment problems in boys. Furthermore, despite parents' attempts to maintain positive relationships with their children, research indicates that marital dissatisfaction negatively influences children's conduct and problem-solving skills (Webster-Stratton & Hammond, 1999).

As noted previously, the hostile family environment created by marital conflict affects relationships between siblings (Bussell et al., 1999; Stocker & Youngblade, 1999). Often, one sibling is more reactive than the others to the hostile environment or parental withdrawal. Reactive children are likely to have negative interactions in the home with parents and other siblings. These hostile and disruptive exchanges increase family stress and reinforce the negative family atmosphere (Bussell et al., 1999).

Effects of Marital Conflict on Children's Peer Interactions Impaired family interactions may also influence peer relationships outside the family system (Levine, Stein, & Liwag, 1999; MacKinnon-Lewis, Rabiner, & Starnes, 1999; Pope &

Bierman, 1999; Rose & Asher, 1999). Exposure to marital discord increases children's feelings of self-blame, results in poor social skill development, and impairs interactions with others (Goodman et al., 1999; Stocker & Youngblade, 1999). These impaired relationships occur because the children and adolescents model the aggressive or impaired interactions of their parents in their sibling and peer relationships.

STRESS AND COPING FACTORS
IN FAMILIES OF CHILDREN WITH DISABILITIES

Predictable life changes and daily stressful events are directly related to increased stress levels (Pianta & Egeland, 1994). Even positive changes (e.g., getting married, starting a new job) can be associated with increased stress. Overall, stress can burden the individual and the family system.

Some ongoing research on stress has focused on families of children and adolescents with significant developmental delays and chronic health problems (Dyson, 1993; Kazak, 1987; Seltzer, Greenberg, Floyd, Pettee, & Hong, 2001). This research has centered on how families interpret and adapt to the stress of having a child with serious developmental or health problems as well as how they respond to this challenge over time, both as individuals and as family units. Dyson (1982); Friedrich, Wilturner, and Cohen (1985); Weinhouse, Weinhouse, and Nelson (1992); and Wilton and Renaut (1986) looked at stress in families of children with disabilities using Holroyd's Questionnaire on Resources and Stress (QRS-F). Although these studies had a number of limitations, they did find that family stress and coping were linked to four factors: child characteristics, pessimism, parent and family problems, and physical incapacitation. Of those four characteristics, the one most closely related to this discussion is child characteristics.

Child Characteristics

Research indicates that families raising children with disabilities or chronic illnesses face different challenges depending on the age and gender of their children (Beckman, 1991; Boyd & Mullins, 2001; Bristol et al., 1988; Gallagher, Beckman, & Cross, 1983; Kazak, 1987). For example, the child's gender influences the father's ability to cope with the stress. Generally, fathers are better able to cope with having a daughter with disability than a son with a disability (Sloper et al., 1991).

The age of a child with a disability also appears to influence parents' stress levels. Waisbren (1980) noted that parents of children with disabilities younger than age 2 were less able to cope with the stress and expressed more negative feelings toward their child than parents of children without disabilities. These results are somewhat surprising because Waisbren's study took place in Denmark, where significant social support (formal and informal) is available at no cost to parents.

Some studies suggest that raising younger children with disabilities may be more stressful for parents than raising adolescents with disabilities. For example, Costigan, Floyd, Harter, and McClintock (1997) found that interactions in the homes of children and adolescents with mild to moderate mental retardation were much less stressful than those in homes of adolescents without disabilities. One possible explanation for this phenomenon is that typically functioning adolescents seek to differentiate themselves from their families, potentially causing a great deal of stress to themselves and other family members (Eccles et al., 1993, Minuchin, 1995). It is possible that some adolescents with disabilities do not feel the need to separate from their families, thereby reducing potential conflict and stress in family interactions. Furthermore, children and adolescents with disabilities often lag behind their peers developmentally, so they may not present their parents with behavioral challenges at the ages when children and adolescents without disabilities present challenges.

Other studies suggests that over all, stress increases in families of children with disabilities as the children move into adolescence. In a study of parents of children with Down syndrome from the children's infancy through adolescence, researchers found that as the children aged, maternal sense of competency with parenting skills diminished (Gallagher et al., 1983). It is possible that these results differ from those of Costigan et al. (1997) because the developmental changes associated with adolescence are stressful not only for an adolescent but also for the family in general. Raising adolescents with disabilities may be more stressful than raising typically developing adolescents because adolescents with disabilities require additional time, attention, and money, further reducing already limited resources for other family members (Nixon & Cummings, 1999).

Developmental Milestones

Floyd and Gallagher (1997) found that the biggest worry reported by parents of children with disabilities was how their child would function in adulthood. Dyson (1993) suggested that it is during periods of transition, when children reach significant developmental milestones, that parents experience increased stress. During these periods, parents must address the fact that their child or adolescent may not be progressing at the same rate as his or her counterparts and, in some cases, may never achieve certain adaptive skills that adults typically attain (Lin, 2000).

Studies have shown that family responses to these stressful periods are marked by feelings of sorrow. Shapiro (1988) found that fathers seemed to grieve deeply when their child was 3–4 years of age, because at that time it became most apparent that the relationship that they had anticipated would not be forthcoming. As time went on, however, both parents grieved; normative transitional periods were especially difficult (Wikler, Wasow, & Hatfield, 1981). Lin (2000) noted that grief and sorrow are normal responses to the stress that may accompany having a child with a disability.

Parent Gender

Research by Sloper et al. (1991) suggested that in general, fathers experienced less stress than mothers in coping with a child's disability. Yet, fathers did report that the child's disability and behavior problems increased the level of stress that they experienced. Fathers indicated increased feelings of anger when dealing with their child, lower levels of self-esteem, and less satisfaction in their interpersonal interactions (Sloper et al., 1991).

In Beckman's (1991) study, mothers of children with disabilities viewed themselves as less competent parents than mothers whose children did not have disabilities. This study also found that mothers of children with disabilities (ages 6 months to 5 years) experienced higher levels of depression. A study by Friedreich et al. (1985) yielded similar findings about maternal depression among mothers of young children with disabilities. Mothers of children and adolescents with disabilities may be especially vulnerable to depression because maternal depression appears to be directly related to the level of caregiving demands at home (Gowen et al., 1989). Maternal depression also compounds the level of family stress, making it less likely that all children in the family will receive sensitive and responsible parenting (Beckman, 1991; Stocker & Youngblade, 1999).

Marital Dissatisfaction

As this chapter has already established, the level of marital satisfaction plays a large role in family functioning. Friedrich et al. (1985) found that mothers of older children with disabilities had lower levels of marital satisfaction than mothers of younger children with disabilities. Although a mother's satisfaction and security in her marital relationship was the most important predictor of her ability to cope with the additional stress that a child's disability brings to a family (Friedrich, 1979), mothers of children with disabilities specifically expressed less satisfaction in their marriage and felt less supported in their marital relationship. Fathers felt less satisfied in their marital relationships, as well as with their interpersonal relationships within the family setting. This research indicates that marriages are clearly influenced by the stress of a child's disability. Furthermore, as women's marital satisfaction increases, family functioning improves (Pasch & Bradbury, 1998).

Stress and Resiliency in Families of Children with Disabilities

Some inconsistencies exist in the research on stress and resiliency among families of children with disabilities. For example, Van Riper, Ryff, and Pridham (1992) found no significant differences in family functioning between families of children with Down syndrome and families of children without disabilities. These results were unexpected because other research suggests that these families are under greater stress than families without children with disabilities (Dyson, 1991; Friedrich et al., 1985). Costigan et al. (1997) studied similar-age children (ages 6–18 years) and found that families of children with disabilities showed increased stress but also increased resiliency. Thus, although children with disabilities may add additional stress to families during childhood and early adolescence, such stress is not always maladaptive.

Dyson (1993) followed families of children (5–11 years) with disabilities across a 2-year period to see whether adjustments in functioning actually supported adaptation in the family system over time. Results suggest that families may be able to adapt to the needs of children with disabilities and cope with higher levels of stress without the stress becoming maladaptive over time. Whereas earlier research indicated increased levels of stress associated with raising children with special needs, little research has followed these families into adolescence. This lack of data on families with adolescents makes it difficult to predict how these families may adapt over time.

It may be that as children with special needs mature, parents are less likely to suffer from stress. Over time families are able to adapt and cope with these stressors and develop a greater level of competency. It is also likely that older children with special needs may require less direct care from parents. This may positively influence parents' ability to cope with family needs, which may in turn improve marital functioning (Costigan et al., 1997; Dyson, 1993).

ADOLESCENCE AND SIBLING RELATIONSHIPS

The previous section detailed how the marriage relationship affects family adjustment to a child's disability. It also examined the reciprocal question of how children with disabilities influence marital relationships. This section focuses on the part that sibling relationships play in the development of families who have children with disabilities. The specific focus is on how siblings help each other develop coping skills.

The families of children with mental health issues may contribute positively to their social and emotional development (Costigan, Floyd, Harter, & McClintock, 1997). Although the presence of a child with mental health issues can be a stressful event for families, family members are often able to adjust to this situation successfully and provide a support system allowing the children to practice and increase their social skills (Gardner, 1998; Patterson & McCubbin, 1987). Another way that families assist adolescents with learning problems is in the area of coping skills. As children with mental health issues move into adolescence, the coping mechanisms of other family members may serve as models for youth with learning problems. Many of the difficulties that youth with learning problems face may be ameliorated by this coping assistance (Thoits, 1986). Siblings in particular may provide a proximate model of adaptive coping methods that the youth with learning problems can imitate (Compas, Malcarne, & Banez, 1992; Folkman, 1991). Siblings also may use coping strategies when assisting youth with learning problems. Thus, this stress-buffering process on the part of the typically functioning sibling may provide coping assistance to youth with learning problems (Thoits, 1986).

Adolescents in General

Adolescence marks a transition from the less complex, task-centered latency age period to a more complex period of increased questioning of identity, decreased reliance on adults, and a heightened emphasis on peer relationships. This transition can be stressful because the need for independence may conflict with a developing youth's continued need for social support from family and others. It is important to consider what adolescents need as they move from childhood into this potentially stressful time of life. Roth and Brooks-Gunn (2000) suggested that successful adolescents need to promote positive and prevent negative actions, feelings, and thoughts. They also highlighted the role of family connectedness, including parental responsiveness. A positive family environment (Bronstein, Fitzgerald, Briones, Pieniadz, & D'Ari, 1993), and a web of peer relationships are important resources for adolescents.

The negotiating and sharing involved in typical peer relationships can increase a young person's social skills (Hartup, 1989; Youniss & Smollar, 1985, 1990). As adolescents acquire these skills, they are better prepared to handle the complicated demands of the school environment and may be protected from feeling isolated (Pavri, 2001). Unfortunately, youth without these experiences may encounter challenges in meeting age-appropriate demands (Woodward & Fergusson, 2000). Adolescents benefit from social support involving both family and friends, and these supports enable adolescents to succeed at school and home.

Adolescents with Learning Problems

Several aspects of problems faced by adolescents with learning problems have been noted by research. Critical problems include peer problems and behavioral difficulties, loneliness and isolation, the impact of temperament, and the impact of attention problems.

Peer Problems and Behavioral Difficulties   Adolescents with learning problems are more likely to be rejected by peers, have fewer peers in their social networks, and are less likely to turn to others as a means of coping (Siperstein, Leffert, & Wenz-Gross, 1997). Youth with learning problems differ from their typically functioning peers in that they report their closest friends to be among those in their special education classes, those not attending their school (neighborhood and community), or those who are 2 or more years younger than them. In contrast, typically functioning peers reported more friendships in general education classrooms (Wiener, 1995).

Adolescents with learning problems perceive their friendships with peers as less positive and supportive than typical youth do (Geisthardt & Munsch, 1996; Morrsion, Laughlin, Smith, Ollansky, & Moore, 1992; Wenz-Gross & Siperstein, 1998). The peer connections made by these youth with students who do not have learning problems appear to be comprised primarily of superficial contact and lack the mutual reciprocity of more typical friendships (Guralnick, 1997). Many of these social relationships more closely resemble acquaintances than close friendships; they tend to be more individualistic, involve less sharing and cooperation, and have more rigid roles (Siperstein, Brownley, & Scott, 1989). These findings are particularly striking when one considers Sullivan's assertion that the greatest single predictor of subsequent mental health is a close "chum" during middle childhood (cited in Chapman, 1980).

Such social isolation from peers places adolescents with learning problems at risk for externalizing problems (Deater-Deckard, 2001; Foster, 1997). Lardieri (1996) found that youth with learning problems had higher levels of externalizing behaviors than typically functioning youth but that these problems fell within a nonpathological range. However, even nonpathological levels of externalizing problems may lead to problems with peers and, thus, feelings of rejection.

Socioemotional Problems: Loneliness and Isolation When adolescents experience restricted peer interactions such as those noted previously, they are more likely to feel lonely and show features of depression (Heiman & Margalit, 1998; Huntington & Bender, 1993; Olsson, 1999; Williams & Asher, 1992). Heiman and Margalit suggested one reason why adolescents with learning problems are at particular risk for loneliness and depression is that as they mature, the gap between them and their typically developing peers increases, as does their sensitivity to feeling lonely.

The presence of a learning problem also affects social and academic self-concepts and confidence. Dykens (2000) found that adolescents with learning problems report the following: They do not believe in themselves, do not reach out to others for help, and do not know what to do when problems overwhelm them. Dykens further suggested that psychological factors, including a less individualized self-concept, lack of self-trust, feelings of helplessness and despondency, extreme dependency, withdrawal tendencies, and impulse control problems affect their problem-solving abilities.

Temperament Drever defined *temperament* as "the general nature of an individual, determined by an organic, physical or constitutional condition or process" (1952, p. 290). Compas (1998) suggested that temperamental differences may influence children's ability to acquire certain coping strategies. For example, strategies such as seeking information from others and instrumental problem-solving skills may be more difficult for children who are inhibited (Kagan, Snidman, & Arcus, 1995). In contrast, children who are impulsive may find it more difficult to master coping strategies requiring behavioral delay or distraction.

Lengua and Sandler (1996) found that certain aspects of temperament moderated the relationship between coping responses and psychological symptoms in children of divorce. For children with high levels of approach behaviors and flexibility, active coping efforts (e.g., cognitive decision making, seeking understanding) were easier to accept and learn. Conversely, avoidant actions were more closely associated with children who were low in approach behaviors and flexibility. Inadequate coping strategies are associated with depression in adolescents (Velazquez Colomba, Saez Santiago, & Rossello, 1999).

Attention Problems Substantial research indicates a relationship between problems in attention processes and children's socioemotional problems (Eisenberg et al., 1995; Eisenberg, Fabes, Nyman, Bernzweig, & Pinnelas, 1994). For example, Wilson (1999) found that children with learning problems who had better control over their attention had fewer social problems when they were 6 years old and also 3 years later. Positive associations also have been found in children's social competence and coping responses and their ability to manage attention effectively.

Attention problems may adversely influence children's social relationships by decreasing their ability to detect and benefit from social cues in their environment (Nabuzoka & Smith, 1999). The ability to use attention processes to detect subtle cues in the social environment becomes increasingly important in adolescence because peer communication increases in complexity (Deater-Deckard, 2001). Attention problems may also influence the socioemotional problems of adolescents with learning problems by decreasing their ability to regulate negative emotions and cognitions (Eisenberg et al., 1994; Eisenberg et al., 1995; Rothbart & Derryberry, 1981; Wilson, 2003; Wilson & Gottman, 1996).

Coping: Strategies for Dealing with Stress

Lazarus and Folkman defined *coping* as "constantly changing cognitive and behavioral efforts to manage specific external and/or internal demands that are appraised as taxing or exceeding the resources of the person" (1984, p. 141). The ability to implement effective coping strategies when stressed is a major predictor of current and future adjustment and psychopathology in young people (Compas et al., 2001). Dykens (2000) suggested that the link between mental health issues and cognitive disabilities can be understood as diminished problem-solving abilities followed by stressful behaviors, which lead to poor coping skills (Ziegler & Holden, 1988).

Adolescents with learning problems tend to cope with peer-related stress by using inactive and avoidant problem-solving strategies, such as denial of the existence of problems, or a tendency to delay handling complicated and sometimes painful interactions. Such inactive coping strategies may prevent the development of sophisticated social skills needed to improve peer relationships (Geisthart & Munsch, 1996).

Geisthart and Munsch (1996) also found that adolescents with learning problems use similar inactive coping strategies when dealing with academic problems. Although such strategies allow people to cope in the short-term, the strategies compound problems in the future and deprive the individuals of critical learning opportunities. Most research suggests that inactive coping responses are associated with more negative outcomes and active coping strategies are associated with more positive outcomes (Compas, 1998; Ebata & Moos, 1991; Maddi, 1999).

Family Modeling of Coping Families can offer adolescents with learning problems support in developing effective social and coping skills. If families provide a cohesive home environment, there may be more opportunities for a child with a disability to engage in active coping strategies (Kliewer & Lewis, 1995). Family members also may serve as a buffer against the negative impact of stressful events for youth with learning problems (Velazquez Colomba et al., 1999).

Active behavioral responses to social stressors have been labeled *social problem solving* (Compas, Malcarne, et al., 1992). Individuals are likely to observe others identify problems, generate solutions, consider the results of certain courses of action, and adjust plans when necessary. As a result of this observation, children begin to generate alternatives to stressors by middle childhood and are able to consider the most effective way to attain a desired goal by adolescence. Such an active, means–end approach to problem-solving is thought to be the strongest indicator of social adjustment (Compas, Malcarne, et al., 1992). Modeling is most powerful when the model is important to the child.

Social Learning　Many people still consider social learning, first proposed by Bandura (1977), to be the primary mechanism by which individuals learn new behaviors. Bandura proposed several necessary components to the modeling process: sufficient attention, an attractive model, memorable actions by the model, opportunities to practice the new behavior, and a perception that the result of the new behavior will be of greater value than the effort applied to the learned action. Family members play an important role in social learning because of the frequency of contact and the variety of settings where modeling is observed. Observing and practicing new social behaviors in the family context allows the youth with learning problems to apply these skills in new environments in an incremental, step-by-step fashion (Bandura, 1977).

Observing Coping Behavior　Members of the family system are believed to provide the most important source of modeling for youth in learning how to cope with stress (Bandura, 1977; Compas, Malcarne, et al., 1992; Compas, Worsham, & Ey, 1992; Kliewer, Sandler, & Wolchik, 1994). Supportive adults outside the family, both professional and personal, also may serve as potential resources for adolescents with learning problems.

Families also aid adolescents' coping by serving as a bridge to social settings outside the home—for example, the school and community. Epstein's (1984) model of overlapping spheres of influence between home and school illustrates how families can reinforce adaptive bonds between youth with learning problems and individuals in the school setting (Coots, 1998). Family members also may serve as a primary resource by assisting youth who have disabilities with learning effective problem-solving skills. Family factors that affect adolescents' development of problem-solving skills also include parental coping and adjustment to stress (Dykens, 2000).

Parent Stress and Coping　Families handle the stress associated with caring for children with significant mental health issues in varied ways. The stresses these families encounter include a sense of incompetence, marital strife, and conflict between siblings (Crnic, Friedrich, & Greenberg, 1983). The stress that these families experience may also negatively affect parental health status (Feldman, Hancock, Rielly, Minnes, & Cairns, 2000).

Due to the high level of stress experienced by families caring for a child with mental health issues, one might assume that such families would show increased levels of frustration. It is interesting to note, however, that some families of youth with learning problems demonstrate resilience in handling difficulties. These families show adaptive strengths such as a greater sensitivity to the needs of others and an increased use of unique coping strategies (Costigan et al., 1997). Floyd,

Costigan, and Phillippe (1997) found that families of children with learning problems were not more likely than other families to express negativity or coercion in their parenting. In fact, these families were appropriately responsive to their child's developmental behaviors and stated needs.

Much of the early research on families of children with disabilities focused on the weaknesses within these families. For example, the general tendency was to attribute most of the problems associated with youth with disabilities to the mother's functioning (Dykens & Hodapp, 2001). Crnic et al. (1983) were among the first to dispute the notion that families that have a member with a disability are necessarily pathological. They introduced the hypothesis that these families merely experience more stress than families who do not have a child with a disability, thereby recognizing the potential strengths of these families.

A dynamic approach taking into account many interacting variables—such as socioeconomic status, family size, and support from outside the family (Feldman et al., 2000)—fosters understanding of the coping strategies of families whose children have disabilities. Hill (1949) initially conceptualized the processes involved when a family reacts to a stressful event or crisis through a "Double ABCX" model of family reaction to crisis (Hill, 1949; McCubbin & McCubbin, 1993; McCubbin & Patterson, 1983; Minnes, 1988). Among the model's components, X is the crisis of raising a child with disabilities. A stands for the child's personal characteristics, B denotes family resources (internal and external), and C is the family's perception of the child. *Double* demonstrates the dynamic, interactive nature of this pattern. This model has also been expanded to include a longitudinal model of families (McCubbin & McCubbin, 1993; McCubbin & Patterson, 1983; Wikler, 1986). In this model, family resources may include marital satisfaction, positive parental affect, a sense of cohesion within the family, and a warm sibling relationship. These resources have been shown to serve as protective factors for children (Fisman et al., 1996). Weinger (1999) found that in families with positive attitudes, children with mental retardation demonstrated increased successful communication and coping skills. Increased levels of optimism from both mothers and siblings were associated with higher levels of family functioning.

Sibling Influence and Coping Siblings play a particularly important role in each other's lives. They serve critical modeling roles, especially for younger children and children with disabilities. The following subsection reviews research related to siblings of children with disabilities and adolescents.

Stress and Coping in Siblings of Youth with Disabilities Siblings make unique contributions to their brothers' and sisters' social and emotional competence (Patterson & McCubbin, 1987; Rowitz, 1989). Siblings of youth with disabilities experience a complex set of demands and opportunities within their families. Nixon and Cummings (1999) found that compared with children without siblings who have disabilities, children with siblings who have disabilities experienced more emotional stress and had greater responsibility for helping their siblings. Although these siblings showed a decreased ability to handle conflict and had greater problems adjusting to the demands of their environment, they used more active coping strategies (Nixon & Cummings, 1999; Reed, 1996–1997). This mixed picture of siblings of youth with disabilities points to the complexity of having a family member with a disability.

It is interesting to note that other researchers have identified few psychological or adjustment problems in siblings of children who have cognitive disabilities compared with siblings of children who do not have cognitive disabilities (Hara & Nishimura, 1998). Cuskelly, Chant, and Hayes (1998) found no differences between siblings of children with Down syndrome and siblings of typically functioning children in the areas of behavioral problems and their contribution to family tasks, as reported by parents. For brothers of children with Down syndrome, however, there was a significant negative correlation between involvement in household tasks and behavioral problems, as reported by fathers. The less often brothers of children with Down syndrome helped with household tasks, the greater the reported behavioral problems.

Siblings of youth with disabilities also may be influenced by the strategies that they observe their parents using (Holden, Brown, & Mott, 1988). Research indicates that sibling reactions can be related to parental reactions and ability to cope (Graliker, Fishler, & Koch, 1962). As families of youth with disabilities encounter significant challenges, siblings may draw lessons from their parents about how to best interact with the family member who has a disability (Dunn & Kendrick, 1982).

Although siblings of youth with learning problems face specific challenges, these difficulties are minimized by parental modeling of positive reactions to the child with disabilities and effective parental coping with the family's unique needs (Grossman, 1972). These findings suggest that despite obstacles to healthy socioemotional functioning for siblings of youth with learning problems, the situation is not hopeless (Dyson, 1993; Ellis, 1995; Lardieri, Blacher, & Swanson, 2000).

CONCLUSION

This chapter has provided information about the functioning of families who have children with disabilities. The specific focus has been the impact of children with disabilities on marital and sibling relationships. Considering these critical family variables can provide important information to educators.

In terms of marital satisfaction, the level of initial marital satisfaction seems to influence later satisfaction. In addition, couples with healthy communication styles that focus on positive problem solving are happier with each other. The length of marriage also has an impact on marital satisfaction. Marriages in the middle years are usually less happy than either initial marriages or longer-lasting marriages. Along with the length of marriage, the amount of social support has an impact on marital satisfaction. Especially in the early years of marriage, a strong community of support provides a protective factor against marital dissatisfaction.

Although moving to parenthood can increase marriage stability, it also increases marriage stresses. These stresses are different for men and women. Men tend to relate marital satisfaction to the satisfaction with parenting. Although women's marital satisfaction has an impact on their parenting, women seem more able to separate the two functions.

When there is marital conflict, children are affected. The amount and quality of impact varies with a child's age. Younger children tend to internalize the impact, thinking that they are the cause of the marital conflict. Older children do not internalize the impact as much but may react in other ways, including increased impulsivity and decreased self-esteem. These effects occur despite parents' attempts to shelter children from marital conflicts. There is also evidence that marital conflict influences a child's peer relationships negatively.

How these general patterns of marital satisfaction vary among families of children with disabilities depends at least in part on the nature of the disability, the age of the child, parent gender, the level of maternal depression, and the level of marital stress from other factors. Parenting a child with a disability is not entirely negative. Studies show not only additional stress but also additional coping mechanisms that develop in families of children with disabilities.

The chapter's section on sibling relationships focused on developing peer relationships in adolescents because it is at this stage that peer relationships become more critical to a person's development. It is also apparent that if an adolescent has siblings, they significantly affect peer relationships. Sibling relationships become more critical for children with disabilities because their peer relationships are fewer, less reciprocal in nature, and less positive than those of typically developing adolescents. Acquaintances, rather than friendships, may be the best way to characterize peer relationships of adolescents with disabilities. These relationships can result in feelings of loneliness and isolation. Specific child characteristics related to these feelings are an individual's temperament and ability to attend. Sibling relationships, along with marital relationships, seem especially critical in the development of coping skills. Both parents and siblings act as models of particular coping skills. Children with disabilities tend to model their coping skills from those around them.

Understanding the family relationships and dynamics of the children they serve can assist educators in providing a quality service to their students. In particular, marital satisfaction and sibling relationships are key factors to understanding the family dynamics of children with mental health issues.

REFERENCES

Bandura, A. (1977). *Social learning theory.* Upper Saddle River, NJ: Prentice Hall.

Beckman, P.J. (1991). Comparison of mothers' and fathers' perceptions of the effect of young children with and without disabilities. *American Journal of Mental Retardation, 95*(5), 585–595.

Belsky, J., & Hsieh, K. (1998). Patterns of marital change during the early childhood years parent personality, coparenting, and division-of-labor correlates. *Journal of Family Psychology, 12*(4), 511–528.

Bickham, N.L., & Fiese, B.H. (1997). Extension of the children's perceptions of interparental conflict scale for use with late adolescents. *Journal of Family Psychology, 11*(2), 246–250.

Boyd, M.L., & Mullins, L.L. (2001, August). *Parents of children with developmental disabilities: Influence of family functioning.* Paper presented at the conference of the American Psychological Association, Washington, DC.

Bristol, M.M., Gallagher, J.J., & Schopler, E. (1988). Mothers and fathers of young developmentally disabled and nondisabled boys adaptation and spousal support. *Developmental Psychology, 24*(3), 441–451.

Bryant, C.M., & Conger, R.D. (1999). Marital success and domains of social support in long-term relationships: Does the influence of network members ever end? *Journal of Marriage and the Family, 61*(2), 437–521.

Bronstein, P., Fitzgerald, M., Briones, M., Pieniadz, J., & D'Ari, A. (1993). Family emotional expressiveness as a predictor of early adolescent and psychological adjustment. *Journal of Early Adolescence, 13,* 448–471.

Bussell, D.A., Neiderhiser, J.M., Pike, A., Plomin, R., Simmens, S., Howe, G.W., Hetherington, Carroll, E., & Reiss, D. (1999). Adolescents' relationships to siblings and mothers: A multivariate genetic analysis. *Developmental Psychology, 35*(5), 1248–1259.

Carstensen, L.L., Gottman, J.M., & Levenson, R.W. (1995). Emotional behavior in long-term marriage. *Psychology and Aging, 10*(1), 140–149.

Chapman, A.H. (1980). *Harry Stack Sullivan's concepts of personality development and psychiatric illness.* Philadelphia: Brunner/Routledge.

Compas, B.E. (1998). An agenda for coping research and theory: Basic and applied developmental issues. *International Journal of Behavioral Development, 22,* 231–237.

Compas, B.E., Howell, D.C., Phares, V., Williams, R.A., & Ledoux, N. (1989). Parent and child stress and symptoms: An integrative analysis. *Developmental Psychology, 25*(4), 550–559.

Compas, B.E., Malcarne, V.L., & Banez, G.A. (1992). Coping with psychosocial stress: A developmental perspective. In B.N. Carpenter (Ed.), *Personal coping: Theory, research, and application* (pp. 47–63). Westport, CT: Praeger Publishers.

Compas, B.E., Malcarne, V.L., & Fondacaro, K.M. (1998). Coping with stress in older children and young adolescents. *Journal of Consulting and Clinical Psychology, 56,* 405–411.

Compas, B.E., Connor-Smith, J.K., Saltzman, H., Harding Thomsen, A., & Wadsworth, M.E. (2001). Coping with stress during childhood and adolescence problems: Progress, and potential in theory and research. *Psychological Bulletin, 127*(1), 87–127.

Compas, B.E., Worsham, N.L., & Ey, S. (1992). Conceptual and developmental issues in children's coping with stress. In A.M. La Greca, L.J. Siegel, J.L. Wallander, & C.E. Walker (Eds.), *Stress and coping in child health* (pp. 7–24). New York: The Guilford Press.

Cook, W.L. (1998). Integrating models of interdependence with treatment evaluations in marital therapy research. *Journal of Family Psychology, 12*(4), 529–542.

Coots, J.J. (1998). Family resources and parent participation in schooling activities for their children with developmental delays. *The Journal of Special Education, 31*(4), 498–520.

Costigan, C., Floyd, F.J., Harter, K.S., & McClintock, J.C. (1997). Family process and adaptation to children with mental retardation: Disruption and resilience in family problem-solving interactions. *Journal of Family Psychology, 11*(4), 515–529.

Cowan, C., & Cowan, P. (1992). *When partners become parents: The big life change for couples.* New York: Basic Books.

Crnic, K., Friedrich, W., & Greenberg, M. (1983). Adaptation of families with mentally handicapped children: A model of stress, coping, and family ecology. *American Journal of Mental Deficiency, 88,* 125–138.

Crouter, A.C., McHale, S.M., & Tucker, C.J. (1999). Does stress exacerbate parental differential treatment of siblings? A pattern-analytic approach. *Journal of Family Psychology, 13*(2), 286–299.

Cuskelly, M., Chant, D., & Hayes, A. (1998). Behaviour problems in the siblings of children with Down syndrome: Associations with family responsibilities and parental stress. *International Journal of Disability, Development, and Education, 45*(3), 295–311.

Davies, P.T., & Cummings, E.M. (1994). Marital conflict and child adjustment: An emotional security hypothesis. *Psychological Bulletin, 116*(3), 387–411.

Deater-Deckard, K. (2001). Annotation: Recent research examining the role of peer relationships in the development of psychopathology. *Journal of Child Psychology and Psychiatry, 42*(3), 565–579.

Devine, D., & Forehand, R. (1996). Cascading toward divorce: The roles of marital and child factors. *Journal of Consulting and Clinical Psychology, 64*(2), 424–427.

Donovan, A.M. (1988). Family stress and ways of coping with adolescents who have handicaps: Maternal perceptions. *American Journal on Mental Retardation, 92*(6), 502–509.

Drever, J. (1952). *The Penguin dictionary of psychology.* New York: Penguin Books.

Dunn, J., & Kendrick, C. (1982). *Siblings: Love, envy, and understanding.* Cambridge, MA: Harvard University Press.

Dykens, E.M. (2000). Annotation: Psychopathology in children with intellectual disability. *Journal of Child Psychology and Psychiatry, 41,* 407–417.

Dykens, E.M., & Hodapp, R.M. (2001). Research in mental retardation: Toward an etiologic approach. *Journal of Child Psychology and Psychiatry, 42*(1), 49–71.

Dyson, L. (1982). Stress and adaptation in parents of young handicapped and nonhandicapped children: A comparative study. *Journal of the Division for Early Childhood, 10*(1), 25–35.

Dyson, L.L. (1991). Families of young children with handicaps: Parental stress and family functioning. *American Journal on Mental Retardation, 95*(6), 623–629.

Dyson, L.L. (1993). Response to the presence of a child with disabilities: Parental stress and family functioning over time. *American Journal on Mental Retardation, 98*(2), 207–218.

Dyson, L.L. (1997). Fathers and mothers of school-age children with developmental disabilities: Parental stress, family functioning, and social support. *American Journal on Mental Retardation, 102*(3), 267–279.

Ebata, A.T., & Moos, R.H. (1991). Coping and adjustment in distressed and healthy adolescents. *Journal of Applied Developmental Psychology, 12,* 33–54.

Eccles, J.S., Midgley, C., Wigfield, A., Buchanan, C.M., Reuman, D., Flanagan, C., & MacIver, D. (1993). Development during adolescence the impact of stage-environment fit on young adolescents' experiences in schools and in families. *American Psychologist, 48*(2), 90–101.

Eisenberg, N., Fabes, R.A., Murphy, B., Maszk, P., Smith, M., & Karbon, M. (1995). The role of emotionality and regulation in children's social functioning: A longitudinal study. *Child Development, 66,* 1360–1384.

Eisenberg, N., Fabes, R.A., Nyman, M., Bernzweig, J., & Pinuelas, A. (1994). The relations of emotionality and regulation to children's anger-related reactions. *Child Development, 65,* 109–128.

Ellis, W. (Ed.). (1995). *Their world.* New York: National Center for Learning Disabilities.

El-Sheikh, M. (1997). Children's responses to adult–adult and mother–child arguments: The role of parental marital conflict and distress. *Journal of Family Psychology, 11*(2), 165–175.

Erickson, M., & Upshur, C.C. (1989). Caretaking burden and social support: Comparison of mothers of infants with and without disabilities. *American Journal on Mental Retardation, 94*(3), 250–258.

Feldman, M.A., Hancock, C.L., Rielly, N., Minnes, P., & Cairns, C. (2000). Behavior problems in young children with or at risk for developmental delay. *Journal of Child and Family Studies, 9*(2), 247–261.

Fincham, F.D. (1998). Child development and marital relations. *Child Development, 69*(2), 543–574.

Fisman, S., Wolf, L., Ellison, D., Gillis, B., Freeman, T., & Szatmari, P. (1996). Risk and protective factors affecting the adjustment of siblings of children with chronic disabilities. *Journal of the American Academy of Child and Adolescent Psychiatry, 35*(11), 1532–1541.

Floyd, F., Costigan, C., & Phillippe, K.A. (1997). Developmental change and consistency in parental interactions with school-age children who have mental retardation. *American Journal on Mental Retardation, 101*(6), 579–594.

Floyd, F., & Gallagher, E. (1997). Parental stress, care demands, and use of support services for school-age children with disabilities and behavior problems. *Family Relations, 46*(4), 359–371.

Folkman, S. (1991). Coping across the life span: Theoretical issues. In E.M. Cummings, A.L. Greene, & K.H. Karraker (Eds.), *Life-span developmental psychology: Perspectives on stress and coping* (pp. 3–19). Mahwah, NJ: Lawrence Erlbaum Associates.

Foster, P.L. (1997). The impact on siblings of having a brother or sister with learning disabilities. *Dissertation Abstracts International: Section A. Humanities and Social Sciences, 58*(6-A), 2069.

Friedrich, W.N. (1979). Predictors of the coping behavior of mothers of handicapped children. *Journal of Consulting and Clinical Psychology, 47*(6), 1140–1141.

Friedrich, W.N., Greenberg, M.T., & Crnic, K.A. (1983). A short-form of the Questionnaire on Resources and Stress. *American Journal of Mental Deficiency, 88,* 41–48.

Friedrich, W.N., Wilturner, L.T., & Cohen, D.S. (1985). Coping resources and parenting mentally retarded children. *American Journal of Mental Deficiency, 90*(2), 130–139.

Gallagher, J.J., Beckman, P., & Cross, A.H. (1983). Families of handicapped children: Sources of stress and its amelioration. *Exceptional Children, 50*(1), 10–18.

Gardner, E. (1998). Siblings of chronically ill children: Towards an understanding of process. *Clinical Child Psychology and Psychiatry, 3*(2), 213–227.

Geisthart, C., & Munsch, J. (1996). Coping with school stress: A comparison of adolescents with and without learning disabilities. *Journal of Learning Disabilities, 29*(3), 287–297.

Gest, S.D., Neemann, J., Hubbard, J.J., Masten, A.S., & Tellegen, A. (1993). Parenting quality, adversity, and conduct problems in adolescence: Testing process-oriented models of resilience. *Development and Psychopathology, 5*, 663–682.

Goodman, S.H., Barfoot, B., Frye, A.A., & Belli, A.M. (1999). Dimensions of marital conflict and children's social problem-solving skills. *Journal of Family Psychology, 13*(1), 33–45.

Graliker, B.V., Fishler, K., & Koch, R. (1962). Teenage reactions to a mentally retarded sibling. *American Journal of Mental Deficiency, 66*, 838–843.

Grossman, F.K. (1972). *Brothers and sisters of retarded children: An exploratory study.* Syracuse, NY: Syracuse University Press.

Grych, J.H. (1998). Children's appraisals of interparental conflict situational and contextual influences. *Journal of Family Psychology, 12*(3), 437–453.

Guralnick, M.J. (1997). Peer social networks of young boys with developmental delays. *American Journal on Mental Retardation, 101*(6), 595–612.

Hara, K., & Nishimura, B. (1998). Psychological adjustment of children with disabilities. *Japanese Journal of Special Education, 36*(1), 1–11.

Harold, G.T., Osborne, L.N., & Conger, R.D. (1997). Mom and Dad are at it again: Adolescent perceptions of marital conflict and adolescent psychological distress. *Developmental Psychology, 33*(2), 333–350.

Hartup, W.W. (1989). Social relationships and their developmental significance. *American Psychologist, 44*(2), 120–126.

Heiman, T., & Margalit, M. (1998). Loneliness, depression, and social skills among students with mild mental retardation in different educational settings. *The Journal of Special Education, 32*(3), 154–163.

Hill, R. (1949). *Families under stress.* New York: Harper & Row.

Holden, M.G., Brown, S.A., & Mott, M.A. (1988). Social support network of adolescents: Relation to family alcohol abuse. *American Journal of Drug and Alcohol Abuse, 14*(4), 487–498.

Holroyd, J., & McArthur, D. (1976). Mental retardation and stress on the parents a contrast between Down's syndrome and childhood autism. *American Journal of Mental Deficiency, 80*(4), 431–436.

Kagan, J., Snidman, N., & Arcus, D.M. (1995). The role of temperament. In G.P. Chrousos et al. (Eds.), *Stress: Basic mechanisms and clinical implications (Annals of the New York Academy of Science: Vol. 771)* (pp. 485–490). New York: New York Academy of Science.

Karney, B.R., & Bradbury, T.N. (1997). Neuroticism, marital interaction, and the trajectory of marital satisfaction. *Journal of Personality and Social Psychology, 72*(5), 1075–1092.

Katz, F.L., & Gottman, J.M. (1993). Patterns of marital conflict predict children's internalizing and externalizing behaviors. *Developmental Psychology, 29*(6), 940–950.

Kazak, A.E. (1987). Families with disabled children: Stress and social networks in three samples. *Journal of Abnormal Child Psychology, 15*(1), 137–146.

Kitzmann, K.M. (2000). Effects of marital conflict on subsequent triadic family interactions and parenting. *Developmental Psychology, 36*(1), 3–13.

Kliewer, W., & Lewis, H. (1995). Family influences on coping processes in children and adolescents with sickle cell disease. *Journal of Pediatric Psychology, 20*(4), 511–525.

Kliewer, W., Sandler, I.N., & Wolchik, S. (1994). Family socialization of threat appraisal and coping: Coaching, modeling, and family context. In K. Hurrelmann & F. Festmann (Eds.), *Social networks and social support in childhood and adolescence* (pp. 271–291). Berlin: Walter de Gruyter.

Kolter, T., & Hammond, S.B. (1981). Marital quality and disturbed child behavior. *British Journal of Clinical Psychology, 20*, 187–198.

Kurdek, L.A. (1999). The nature and predictors of the trajectory of change in marital quality for husbands and wives over the first 10 years of marriage. *Developmental Psychology, 35*(5), 1283–1296.

Lardieri, L.A. (1996) Sibling relationships in families of children with and without learning disabilities. *Dissertation Abstracts International Section A: Humanities and Social Sciences, 57*(11-A), 4648.

Lardieri, L.A., Blacher, J., & Swanson, H.L. (2000). Sibling relationships and parent stress in families of children with and without learning disabilities. *Learning Disability Quarterly, 23*(2), 105–116.

Larson, R., & Ham, M. (1993). Stress and "storm and stress" in early adolescence: The relationship of negative events with dysphoric affect. *Developmental Psychology, 29*(1), 130–140.

Lazarus, R.S., & Folkman, S. (1984). *Stress, appraisal, and coping.* New York: Springer-Verlag.

Leadbeater, B.J., Kuperminc, G.P., Blatt, S.J., & Hertzog, C. (1999). A multivariate model of gender differences in adolescents' internalizing and externalizing problems. *Developmental Psychology, 35*(5), 1268–1282.

Lengua, L.J., & Sandler, I.N. (1996). Self-regulation as a moderator of the relationship between coping and symptomatology in children of divorce. *Journal of Abnormal Child Psychology, 24,* 681–701.

Levine, L.J., Stein, N.L., & Liwag, M.D. (1999). Remembering children's emotions: Sources of concordant and discordant accounts between parents and children. *Developmental Psychology, 35*(3), 790–801.

Liddle, H.A., Rowe, C., Diamond, G.M., Sessa, F.M., Schmidt, S., & Ettinger, D. (2000). Toward a developmental family therapy: The clinical utility of research on adolescence. *Journal of Marital and Family Therapy, 26*(4), 485–500.

Lin, S. (2000). Coping and adaptation in families of children with cerebral palsy. *Exceptional Children, 66*(2), 201–218.

Maddi, S.R. (1999). The personality construct of hardiness, I: Effect on experiencing coping and strain. *Consulting Psychology Journal, 51,* 83–94.

MacKinnon-Lewis, C., Rabiner, D., & Starnes, R. (1999). Predicting boys' social acceptance and aggression: The role of the mother-child interactions and boys' beliefs about peers. *Developmental Psychology, 35*(3), 632–639.

McCubbin, H., & Patterson, J. (1983). Family stress adaptation to crises: A Double ABCX model of family behavior. In H. McCubbin, M. Sussman, & J. Patterson (Eds.), *Social stresses and the family: Advances and development in family stress theory and research* (pp. 7–37). Binghamton, NY: The Haworth Press.

McCubbin, M.H., & McCubbin, I.H. (1993). Families coping with illness: The resiliency model of family stress adjustment and adaptation. In C. Danielson, B. Hamel-Bissel, & P. Winstead-Fry (Eds.), *Families, health, and illness* (pp. 21–61). St. Louis: Mosby.

McHale, S.M., Freitag, M.K., Crouter, A.C., & Bartko, W.T. (1991). Connections between dimensions of marital quality and school-age children's adjustment. *Journal of Applied Developmental Psychology, 12,* 1–17.

Minnes, P. (1988). Family stress associated with a developmentally handicapped child. *International Review of Research on Mental Retardation, 15,* 195–226.

Minuchin, P. (1995). Children and family therapy: Mainstream approaches and the special case of the multicrisis poor. In R.H. Miskesell, D.D. Lusterman, & S.H. McDaniel (Eds.), *Integrating family therapy* (pp. 113–124). Washington, DC: American Psychological Association.

Nabuzoka, D., & Smith, P.K. (1999). Distinguishing serious and playful fighting by children with learning disabilities and non-disabled children. *Journal of Child Psychology and Psychiatry, 40*(6), 883–890.

Neiderhiser, J.M., Reiss, D., Hetherington, E.M., & Plomin, R. (1999). Relationships between parenting and adolescent adjustment over time: Genetic and environmental contributions. *Developmental Psychology, 35*(3), 680–692.

Nixon, C.L., & Cummings, E.M. (1999). Sibling disability and children's reactivity to conflicts involving family members. *Journal of Family Psychology, 13*(2), 274–285.

Noller, P., Feeney, J.A., & Ward, C.M. (1997). Determinants of marital quality: A partial test of Lewis and Spanier's model. *Journal of Family Studies, 3*(2), 226–251.

Pasch, L.A., & Bradbury, T.N. (1988). Social support, conflict, and the development of marital dysfunction. *Journal of Consulting and Clinical Psychology, 66*(2), 219–230.

Patterson, J.M., & McCubbin, H.I. (1987). Adolescent coping style and behaviors: Conceptualization and measurement. *Journal of Adolescence, 10,* 163–186.

Pavri, S. (2001). Loneliness in children with disabilities: How teachers can help. *Teaching Exceptional Children, 33*(6), 52–58.

Pianta, R.C., & Egeland, B. (1994). Relation between depressive symptoms and stressful life events in a sample of disadvantaged mothers. *Journal of Consulting and Clinical Psychology, 62*(6), 1229–1234.

Pope, A.W., & Bierman, K.L. (1999). Predicting adolescent peer problems and antisocial activities: The relative roles of aggression and dysregulation. *Developmental Psychology, 35*(2), 335–346.

Reed, J.A. (1996–1997). Fostering children and young people with learning disabilities: The perspectives of birth children and carers. *Adoption & Fostering, 20*(4), 36–41.

Reimer, M.S., Overton, W.F., Steidl, J.H., Rosenstein, D.S., & Horowitz, H. (1996). Familial responsiveness and behavioral control: Influences on adolescent psychopathology, attachment and cognition. *Journal of Research on Adolescence, 6,* 87–112.

Ridley, C.A., Wilhelm, M.S., & Surra, C.A. (2001). Married couples' conflict responses and marital quality. *Journal of Social and Personal Relationships, 18*(4), 517–534.

Rogers, S.J., & White, L.K. (1998). Satisfaction with parenting: The role of marital happiness, family structure, and parents' gender. *Journal of Marriage and the Family, 60*(2), 293–309.

Rose, A.J., & Asher, S.R. (1999). Children's goals and strategies in response to conflicts within a friendship. *Developmental Psychology, 35*(1), 69–79.

Roth, J., & Brooks-Gunn, J. (2000). What do adolescents need for healthy development? Implications for youth policy. *Society for Research in Child Development Social Policy Report, 14*(1), 3–19.

Rothbart, M.K., & Derryberry, D. (1981). Development of individual differences in temperament. In M.E. Lamb & A.L. Brown (Eds.), *Advances in Developmental Psychology: Vol. 1* (pp. 37–86). Mahwah, NJ: Lawrence Erlbaum Associates.

Rowitz, L. (1989). Editorial: Trends in mental retardation in the 1990s. *Mental Retardation, 27*(1), iii–vi.

Seligman, M., & Darling, R.B. (1989). *Ordinary families special children: A systems approach to childhood disability.* New York: The Guilford Press.

Seltzer, M.M., Greenberg, J.S., Floyd, F.J., Pettee, Y., & Hong, J. (2001). Life course impacts of parenting a child with a disability. *American Journal on Mental Retardation, 106*(3), 265–286.

Shapiro, J. (1988). Stresses in the lives of parents of children with disabilities: Providing effective caregiving. *Stress Medicine, 4,* 77–93.

Siperstein, G.N., Brownley, M.V., & Scott, C.K. (1989, April). *Social interchanges between mentally retarded and nonretarded friends.* Paper presented at a meeting of the Society for Research in Child Development, Kansas City, MO.

Siperstein, G.N., Leffert, J., & Wenz-Gross, M. (1997). The quality of friendships between children with and without learning problems. *American Journal of Mental Retardation, 102,* 111–125.

Sloper, P., Knussen, C., Turner, S., & Cunningham, C. (1991). Factors related to stress and satisfaction with life in families of children with Down's syndrome. *Journal of Child Psychological Psychiatry, 32*(4), 655–676.

Stocker, C.M., & Youngblade, L. (1999). Marital conflict and parental hostility: Links with children's sibling and peer relationships. *Journal of Family Psychology, 13*(4), 598–609.

Thoits, P.A. (1986). Social support as coping assistance. *Journal of Consulting and Clinical Psychology, 54*(4), 416–423.

Van Riper, M., Ryff, C., & Pridham, K. (1992). Parental and family well-being in families of children with Down syndrome: A comparative study. *Research in Nursing & Health, 15,* 227–235.

Velazquez Colomba, M., Saez Santiago, E., & Rossello, J. (1999). Coping strategies and depression in Puerto Rican adolescents: An exploratory study. *Cultural Diversity and Ethnic Minority Psychology, 5*(1), 65–75.

Waisbren, S.E. (1980). Parents' reaction after the birth of a developmentally disabled child. *American Journal of Mental Deficiency, 84*(4), 345–351.

Webster-Stratton, C., & Hammond, M. (1999). Marital conflict management skills, parenting style, early-onset conduct problems: Processes and pathways. *Journal of Child Psychology and Psychiatry, 40*(6), 917–929.

Weinger, S. (1999). Views of the child with retardation: Relationship to family functioning. *Family Therapy, 26*(2), 63–79.

Weinhouse, D., Weinhouse, M., & Nelson, G. (1992). Stress factors in families of young children with exceptional educational needs. *School Psychology International, 13*, 51–59.

Wenz-Gross, M., & Siperstein, G.N. (1998). Students with learning problems at risk in middle school: Stress, social support, and adjustment. *Exceptional Children, 65*, 91–100.

Wiener, J. (1995, April). *Friendship selection and quality in children with and without learning disabilities.* Paper presented at the meeting of the Society for Research in Child Development, Indianapolis.

Wikler, L.M. (1986). Family stress theory and research on families of children with mental retardation. In J.J. Gallagher & P.M. Vietze (Eds.), *Families of handicapped persons: Research, programs, and policy issues* (pp. 167–195). Baltimore: Paul H. Brookes Publishing Co.

Wikler, L., Wasow, M., & Hatfield, E. (1981). Chronic sorrow revisited: Parent versus professional depiction of the adjustment of parents of mentally retarded children. *American Journal of Orthopsychiatry, 51*, 63–70.

Williams, G.A., & Asher, S.R. (1992). Assessment of loneliness at school among children with mild mental retardation. *American Journal of Mental Retardation, 96*(4), 373–385.

Wilson, B.J. (1999). Entry behavior and emotional regulation abilities of developmentally delayed boys. *Developmental Psychology, 35*(1), 214–222.

Wilson, B.J. (2003). The role of attentional process in children's behavior with peers: Attention shifting and emotions. *Development and Psychopathology, 15*, 313–329.

Wilson, B.J., & Gottman, J.M. (1996). Attention—The shuttle between cognition and emotion: Risk, resiliency, and physiological bases. In E.M. Hetherington & E.A. Blechman (Eds.), *Stress, coping, and resiliency in children and families* (pp. 189–228). Mahwah, NJ: Lawrence Erlbaum Associates.

Wilton, K., & Renaut, J. (1986). Stress levels in families with intellectually handicapped preschool children and families with nonhandicapped preschool children. *Journal of Mental Deficiency, 30*, 163–169.

Woodward, L.J., & Fergusson, D.M. (2000). Childhood peer-relationship problems and later risks of educational under-achievement and unemployment. *Journal of Child Psychology and Psychiatry, 41*, 191–201.

Yamamoto, K., & Mahlios, M.C. (2001). Home is where it begins: Parents, children, and stressful events. *Journal of Psychology and Psychiatry, 42*(4), 533–537.

Youniss, J., & Smollar, J. (1985). *Adolescent relations with mothers, fathers, and friends.* Chicago: University of Chicago Press.

Youniss, J., & Smollar, J. (1990). Self through relationship development. In B. Harke & S. Jackson (Eds.), *Coping and self-concept in adolescence* (pp. 48–72). New York: Springer-Verlag.

Ziegler, R., & Holden, L. (1988). Family therapy for learning disabled and attention-deficit disordered children. *American Journal of Orthopsychiatry, 58*(2), 196–210.

17

Examples of Collaboration

Larry B. Silver

• •

Chapter Concepts

- The potential benefits of collaboration between educators and health or mental health professionals
- The problems that may occur even in successful collaborative relationships
- Illustrations of positive collaboration between educators and health or mental health professionals

The intent of this book is to prepare educators to collaborate more effectively and efficiently with mental health professionals for the benefit of students. The specific professionals with whom a teacher might interact are discussed in Chapter 3. The examples in this chapter illustrate how such collaborative relationships might actually work. These examples present real-life circumstances and, therefore, techniques that can be applied to any collaboration between teachers and mental health professionals, as well as to their communications with other outside health professionals (e.g., family physicians). Critical in each example is the mutual respect between mental health professionals and teachers and the awareness that everyone involved in a student's life must be involved in any treatment plan.

EXAMPLE 1: ATTENTION-DEFICIT/HYPERACTIVITY DISORDER

Mr. and Mrs. Gordon were concerned about their 8-year old son, Bret. His second- and third-grade teachers complained about his difficulty with sitting still and paying attention in class. The parents told their pediatrician, Dr. Samuels, about the teachers' comments and added that Bret acted the same way at home. In addition, Bret was disruptive, getting in fights with his sister and being oppositional with his parents. Dr. Samuels referred Bret to a psychologist for consultation. The psychologist asked Mr. and Mrs. Gordon and Bret's current teacher, Ms. Anders, to complete the revised Conners' Rating Scales. The psychologist also did a computerized test for attentional problems. All of the data supported a probable diagnosis of attention-deficit/hyperactivity disorder (ADHD) because Bret showed a chronic and pervasive history of hyperactivity, inattention (auditory and visual distractibility), and impulsivity.

Because the psychologist could not prescribe medication for Bret, Dr. Samuels prescribed 5 milligrams (mg) of methylphenidate (Ritalin), to be taken at 8:00 A.M. and 12:00 P.M. After 1 week, however, Ms. Anders reported to Mrs. Gordon that Bret's problems did not appear to be improving. Thus, the dose was raised to 10 mg at 8:00 A.M. and 12:00 P.M. Neither his teacher nor Bret's parents noted improvement after a month. Thus, Bret was referred to Dr. Gold, a child and adolescent psychiatrist.

Dr. Gold met with Mr. and Mrs. Gordon and Bret. He reviewed previous comments by Bret's second-grade teacher and the psychologist's report. He believed that it was important to get more details from Ms. Anders. School started at 8:15 A.M., so Dr. Gold tried to reach Ms. Anders at 8:00 A.M. This was a good time for Dr. Gold, and he anticipated that the teacher would have some free time before her students arrived. Ms. Anders was not free, however, so the psychiatrist left a message for her to return his call and say when she would be available for an extended discussion. Ms. Anders returned the call, and an extended discussion took place at 3:15 P.M.

Dr. Gold explained who he was and why he was calling. He asked Ms. Anders for her comments about and observations of Bret in the classroom. She described his high activity level and fidgety behavior, noting that he seemed to pay attention to everything but his schoolwork. Her examples reflected that any noise, talking, or activity distracted Bret. When Dr. Gold asked if Bret ever called out in class or blurted out comments to other students, Ms. Anders said yes.

Ms. Anders also expressed her concern that the medication was not helping. Dr. Gold mentioned that he would begin to increase the dose and that he would like Ms. Anders to take note of Bret's behavior. He asked Ms. Anders to share her observations with Mrs. Gordon, who would then contact him. Dr. Gold also described the side effects of a dosage that was too high and asked that Ms. Anders watch for them.

At a dose of 15 mg three times per day, both Bret's teacher and his parents noted a significant improvement within 2 days. To clarify whether this was the best therapeutic dose for Bret, Dr. Gold increased the dose to 20 mg three times per day. Within 2 days, Ms. Anders reported to Mrs. Gordon that Bret was very irritable and tearful in class. His mother noted the same behavior at home. This information helped Dr. Gold determine that 15 mg was the best dose for each 4-hour period. On this medication regimen, Bret improved at home, with his peers, and in school. Dr. Gold sent Ms. Anders a note, thanking her for her help.

EXAMPLE 2: CLINICAL DEPRESSION

Mrs. Sullivan, a middle school counselor, met often with the team of teachers for her assigned group of eighth-grade students. Each teacher expressed concern about a particular student, Allison. Mrs. Sullivan called Dr. Trent, a clinical psychologist. Dr. Trent had treated Mrs. Sullivan's daughter for difficulties in relating to peers, so Mrs. Sullivan felt comfortable asking Dr. Trent for her advice about what she was hearing from the teachers. Mrs. Sullivan described how this 13-year-old student was progressively completing fewer school assignments. The student's grades were dropping during each marking period. In addition, the student seemed more irritable and unpleasant with her friends. Dr. Trent agreed that the student may have a mental health issue and encouraged Mrs. Sullivan to share her observations and concerns with Allison's parents. The doctor and the teacher discussed how best to meet with the parents and what might be discussed.

Mrs. Sullivan requested a meeting with Allison's parents, but only Allison's mother could attend. When Mrs. Sullivan described her concerns, Allison's mother began to cry and said that there was much stress at home. Her husband lost his job 6 months ago, and the family was facing major financial problems. Their health insurance was no longer in effect. She believed that her husband was depressed and angry at all of the children, especially Allison. Allison's mother agreed that her daughter needed help, as did the other family members; however, there was no money to pay for such treatment.

The next day, Mrs. Sullivan contacted the family services agency for their county. She spoke to the person who handles new intakes. By sharing the information that she obtained from Allison's mother, plus the observations of Allison's teachers and herself, it was possible to facilitate obtaining help for this family on a sliding-fee scale based on ability to pay. Mrs. Sullivan then called Allison's mother and gave her the case worker's name and telephone number so that Allison and the family could get help.

With permission from Allison's mother, Mrs. Sullivan shared her information with Allison's teachers. Each teacher was distressed but relieved to understand Allison's problems. The team collaboration among teachers, the school counselor, and the mental health professionals from the family services agency opened up a level of understanding that helped each teacher be more supportive of Allison.

EXAMPLE 3: SUBSTANCE ABUSE

James, a tenth-grade student, repeatedly got into trouble in school. He no longer did his homework and was always unprepared for class. Teachers noted that he cut classes and hung out with students who were considered troublemakers. Several teachers tried to talk with James, but he was annoyed and said that everything was fine.

One morning, two of James's former friends asked Mr. Patrick, their English teacher, if they could speak with him. They shared that James was drinking a lot and sometimes came to school drunk. They also recently saw him drinking in the bathroom. They asked Mr. Patrick to help, and he agreed to do so. At lunch on the next day, he mentioned the situation to another teacher. This teacher reminded Mr. Patrick that if he went to the school administration for help, James would be suspended. Their school system had a zero tolerance policy for alcohol use, especially on school property.

Mr. Patrick wanted to help James and was concerned that suspending him would only add to his problems and leave him with more unsupervised time. Mr. Patrick was torn. In addition to wanting to help James and not make James's situation worse, he did not want to let down the friends who took the risk of sharing their concerns. He decided to speak with the school psychologist about the problem without mentioning names. Perhaps James's parents could be called in for a conference about his falling grades. During this conference, they could look for an opening to share their concerns.

During the conference, James's parents were concerned but quiet. As they left the meeting, Mr. Patrick decided to take a chance. He needed to respect the students' request not to tell, yet he needed to help James. He walked into the hallway with the parents and asked if they were worried that James's problems might be because of his new group of friends. James's parents were relieved to hear this and agreed, sharing their worries about him. "Do you think this group might be into alcohol or drugs?" the teacher asked. (Mr. Patrick wanted to respect the request of James's friends not to tell anyone what they had said, so he decided not to ask James's parents whether they thought James was using.) Their "yes" reply opened the door for Mr. Patrick to urge the parents to speak with James's family doctor, alerting the physician in advance of the appointment about their concerns. The parents agreed.

When James went to his family doctor for an examination, the urine sample confirmed the presence of alcohol and marijuana. The doctor knew that the first step in treatment would be to help James stop using alcohol and drugs, so he arranged for James to enter an inpatient program and initiated a treatment plan. James was angry but seemed almost relieved. He remained in this program for 2 weeks and then moved to a day program, through which he attended individual and group therapy. His parents felt that there was progress because James was less combative and more interested in school, and he spoke of finding new friends.

Prior to James's discharge from the day program, Mr. Patrick received a call from James's mother. James would attend a group program and be monitored carefully. The treatment team believed it was critical for James not to associate with his old group of friends. Mr. Patrick replied by suggesting that the clinician treating James contact the school psychologist. Thus, the psychiatrist from the treatment program worked with the school psychologist to find ways of minimizing James's contact with the peer group that facilitated his previous behaviors.

If the school administration had learned what Mr. Patrick knew without reporting it—that James was using alcohol on school property—the teacher might have been in serious trouble. Yet, had Mr. Patrick told the school administration, James might still be using, especially because he would have so much free time on his hands if suspended. Mr. Patrick took a risk. His ability to collaborate with the school psychologist and James's parents as well as his ability to facilitate collaboration between the school psychologist and the treating psychiatrist were critical to James's recovery.

EXAMPLE 4: CONTINUUM OF NEUROLOGICALLY BASED DISORDERS

Elliot was in the fourth grade and receiving special education services for his learning disabilities and speech-language services for his language disability. In addition, his pediatrician had him on medication to treat ADHD.

The services and medication helped Elliot improve his school performance. However, Elliot's parents were concerned that he seemed overly anxious and fearful of being alone at night. Elliot also appeared sad and often said that he hated his life. Although he did not exhibit behavioral problems at school, he frequently had extended angry outbursts at home, lasting 15–20 minutes. As a result, his parents decided to attend family therapy sessions. The social worker helping the family was concerned with Elliot's level of anxiety, depression, and anger and referred him to a child and adolescent psychiatrist.

The psychiatrist, Dr. Green, agreed with these clinical impressions. She was able to confirm a long history of anxiety, depression, and anger control. She also found out that Elliot's mother, maternal grandmother, and uncle struggled with depression and anxiety. In addition, Elliot's father had a long history of problems with controlling his anger. Dr. Green explained to Elliot's parents the concept of a continuum of neurologically based disorders that are often found together. She pointed out that Elliot's learning disabilities, language disability, ADHD, anxiety disorder, depression, and anger control problems could be related. Therefore, she recommended using a specific medication that treats regulatory problems such as anxiety, depression, and anger control. This medication would be used along with the medication that Elliot took for ADHD. Elliot's parents agreed to this treatment approach.

With the permission of Elliot's parents, Dr. Green decided to speak with Elliot's teacher. The teacher was very busy during the day but gave Dr. Green her home telephone number. Dr. Green was able to discuss the possible side effects for Elliot's two medications. Dr. Green asked the teacher to contact her or Elliot's mother if side effects were noticed.

Elliot responded positively to the medication plan, and there were no side effects. Nonetheless, both his mother and Dr. Green felt more comfortable knowing that had there been side effects, his teacher would have noted them and shared this essential information.

EXAMPLE 5: ADJUSTMENT DISORDER

Mr. Thomas, a fourth-grade teacher, was concerned about one of his students. Jonathan had no academic problems; however, several times per month, Jonathan became negative and oppositional with him and aggressive with the other students. These behaviors usually lasted for a day or less.

Mr. Thomas could not understand this behavior, so he met with the school counselor to discuss it. They decided to keep a diary of Jonathan's behaviors in class. Within a month, it became clear that this student's negative behaviors occurred only on specific Mondays. The school counselor knew that Jonathan's parents were divorced. He lived with his mother and spent every other weekend with father. By talking to Jonathan in a general way, the school counselor confirmed that these behaviors occurred on the Mondays following weekends spent with his father.

The school counselor set up a meeting with Jonathan's mother. She shared the teacher's observations and confirmed that her ex-husband was still very angry about the divorce. When Jonathan and his sister spend time with their father, he is angry and critical of their mother. The school counselor also learned that Jonathan was receiving therapy from a clinical psychologist regarding his conflicts with his father. With permission from Jonathan's mother, the school counselor contacted this psychologist and shared the teacher's observations and mother's comments.

The psychologist was not surprised and agreed to work on the problems with Jonathan and with each parent. He asked the counselor to help by getting to know Jonathan. He asked if it would be possible for the counselor to meet with Jonathan on those alternating Monday mornings. Maybe knowing that someone in the school understood and having an opportunity to talk about his experiences before entering the classroom would reduce Jonathan's need to vent his frustration and anger with his teacher and peers.

The school counselor arranged to carry out this suggestion. With the mother's permission, the counselor also shared what she had learned with Jonathan's teacher. As a result, Jonathan's teacher could pull Jonathan aside on these mornings and say, "Guess you're having a rough morning. Would you like to talk about it? Can I help?" Seeing the counselor on these Mondays and having an understanding teacher greatly decreased Jonathan's problems almost immediately.

CONCLUSION

These examples reflect good attempts at collaboration, through which educators and mental health professionals respect each other and understand the need to communicate. Each person understood that the other's schedule may not always match theirs and, by remaining flexible, facilitated communication. Each respected the other's professional skills and shared his or her own professional expertise. Each professional had one focus: *helping the student.*

These examples show how critical it is for a health or mental health professional to learn what goes on in the classroom and, thus, to respect an educator's feedback. They also show that a mental health professional can provide the teacher with necessary information. It is important to note that the health or mental health professional need not be expected to have an educator's knowledge and expertise. In turn, the educator should not feel intimidated because he or she does not have a mental health professional's knowledge and expertise. Readers should share their perspectives as educators. Educators know how their students behave in school, and mental health professionals need this information.

Together, educators and mental health professionals can make a significant difference in the lives of children and adolescents. It is hoped that this book will be a source of help in reaching that goal.

Diagnostic
Categories and Criteria

The official categories and criteria for making a diagnosis are developed by the World Health Organization. Representatives from each member country participate in this process. Through such efforts, there is consistency around the world on the names and criteria for diagnosis of all medical disorders.

Approximately every 10 years, the World Health Organization publishes an updated manual covering all medical disorders, *The International Classification of Diseases*. Each member country may modify this manual to meet the special issues within that country as long as the basic concepts and criteria remain the same. In the United States, the American Medical Association has this job. Different parts of the manual are assigned to different U.S. professional organizations to work on any needed modifications. The American Psychiatric Association is given the task of addressing all disorders considered mental health disorders. The modified list of official diagnostic categories and the required criteria for establishing these diagnoses is published as the *Diagnostic and Statistical Manual of Mental Disorders*. The text revision of the fourth edition, published in 2000, is referred to as the DSM-IV-TR.

The mental health disorders mentioned in this book are listed next, noting the DSM-IV-TR criteria needed to establish each diagnosis. The reader might wonder why attention-deficit/hyperactivity disorder (ADHD), for example, is listed in a manual on mental health disorders. The reason is that in *The International Classification of Diseases*, ADHD falls under the broader category of mental health disorders.

ADJUSTMENT DISORDERS

Diagnostic criteria for Adjustment Disorders

A. The development of emotional or behavioral symptoms in response to an identifiable stressor(s) occurring within 3 months of the onset of the stressor(s).

B. These symptoms or behaviors are clinically significant as evidenced by either of the following:

    (1) marked distress that is in excess of what would be expected from exposure to the stressor

    (2) significant impairment in social or occupational (academic) functioning

C. The stress-related disturbance does not meet the criteria for another specific Axis I disorder and is not merely an exacerbation of a preexisting Axis I or Axis II disorder.

D. The symptoms do not represent Bereavement.

E. Once the stressor (or its consequences) has terminated, the symptoms do not persist for more than an additional 6 months.

Specify if:

Acute: if the disturbance lasts less than 6 months

Chronic: if the disturbance lasts for 6 months or longer

Adjustment Disorders are coded based on the subtype, which is selected according to the predominant symptoms. The specific stressor(s) can be specified on Axis IV.

309.0 With Depressed Mood

309.24 With Anxiety

309.28 With Mixed Anxiety and Depressed Mood

309.3 With Disturbance of Conduct

309.4 With Mixed Disturbance of Emotions and Conduct

309.9 Unspecified

ANXIETY DISORDERS

Criteria for Panic Attack

Note: A Panic Attack is not a codable disorder. Code the specific diagnosis in which the Panic Attack occurs (e.g., 300.21 Panic Disorder With Agoraphobia [p. 441]).

A discrete period of intense fear or discomfort, in which four (or more) of the following symptoms developed abruptly and reached a peak within 10 minutes:

(1) palpitations, pounding heart, or accelerated heart rate

(2) sweating

(3) trembling or shaking

(4) sensations of shortness of breath or smothering

(5) feeling of choking

(6) chest pain or discomfort

(7) nausea or abdominal distress

(8) feeling dizzy, unsteady, lightheaded, or faint

(9) derealization (feelings of unreality) or depersonalization (being detached from oneself)

(10) fear of losing control or going crazy

(11) fear of dying

(12) paresthesias (numbness of tingling sensations)

(13) chills or hot flushes

Reprinted with permission from the *Diagnostic and Statistical Manual of Mental Disorders* (4th ed., text rev., p. 432). Copyright © 2000 American Psychiatric Association.

Diagnostic criteria for 300.02 Generalized Anxiety Disorder

A. Excessive anxiety and worry (apprehensive expectation), occurring more days than not for at least 6 months, about a number of events or activities (such as work or school performance).

B. The person finds it difficult to control the worry.

C. The anxiety and worry are associated with three (or more) of the following symptoms (with at least some symptoms present for more days than not for the past 6 months). **Note:** Only one item is required in children.

   (1) restlessness or feeling keyed up or on edge

   (2) being easily fatigued

   (3) difficulty concentrating or mind going blank

   (4) irritability

   (5) muscle tension

   (6) sleep disturbance (difficulty falling or staying asleep, or restless unsatisfying sleep)

(continued on next page)

D. The focus of the anxiety and worry is not confined to features of an Axis I disorder, e.g., the anxiety or worry is not about having a Panic Attack (as in Panic Disorder), being embarrassed in public (as in Social Phobia), being contaminated (as in Obsessive-Compulsive Disorder), being away from home or close relatives (as in Separation Anxiety Disorder), gaining weight (as in Anorexia Nervosa), having multiple physical complaints (as in Somatization Disorder), or having a serious illness (as in Hypochondriasis), and the anxiety and worry do not occur exclusively during Posttraumatic Stress Disorder.

E. The anxiety, worry, or physical symptoms cause clinically significant distress or impairment in social, occupational, or other important areas of functioning.

F. The disturbance is not due to the direct physiological effects of a substance (e.g., a drug of abuse, a medication) or a general medical condition (e.g., hyperthyroidism) and does not occur exclusively during a Mood Disorder, a Psychotic Disorder, or a Pervasive Developmental Disorder.

Diagnostic criteria for 300.3 Obsessive-Compulsive Disorder

A. Either obsession or compulsion:
Obsessions as defined by (1), (2), (3), and (4):

   (1) recurrent and persistent thoughts, impulses, or images that are experienced, at some time during the disturbance, as intrusive and inappropriate and that cause marked anxiety or distress

   (2) the thoughts, impulses, or images are not simply excessive worries about real-life problems

   (3) the person attempts to ignore or suppress such thoughts, impulses, or images, or to neutralize them with some other thought or action

   (4) the person recognizes that the obsessional thoughts, impulses, or images are a product of his or her own mind (not imposed from without as in thought insertion)

Compulsions as defined by (1) and (2):

   (1) repetitive behaviors (e.g., hand washing, ordering, checking) or mental acts (e.g., praying, counting, repeating words silently) that the person feels driven to perform in response to an obsession, or according to rules that must be applied rigidly

   (2) the behaviors or mental acts are aimed at preventing or reducing distress or preventing some dreaded event or situation; however, these behaviors or mental acts either are not connected in a realistic way with what they are designed to neutralize or prevent or are clearly excessive

B. At some point during the course of the disorder, the person has recognized that the obsessions or compulsions are excessive or unreasonable. **Note:** This does not apply to children.

C. The obsession or compulsions cause marked distress, are time consuming (take more than 1 hour a day), or significantly interfere with the person's normal routine, occupational (or academic) functioning, or usual social activities or relationships.

D. If another Axis I disorder is present, the content of the obsessions or compulsions is not restricted to it (e.g., preoccupation with food in the presence of an Eating Disorder; hair pulling in the presence of Trichotillomania; concern with appearance in the presence of Body Dysmorphic Disorder; preoccupation with drugs in the presence of a Substance Use Disorder; preoccupation with having a serious illness in the presence of Hypochondriasis; preoccupation with sexual urges or fantasies in the presence of a Paraphilia; or guilty ruminations in the presence of a Major Depressive Disorder).

E. The disturbance is not due to the direct physiological effects of a substance (e.g., a drug of abuse, a medication) or a general medical condition.

Specify if:

With Poor Insight: if, for most of the time during the current episode, the person does not recognize that the obsessions and compulsions are excessive or unreasonable.

Diagnostic criteria for 309.81 Posttraumatic Stress Disorder

A. The person has been exposed to a traumatic event in which both of the following were present:

(1) the person experienced, witnessed, or was confronted with an event or events that involved actual or threatened death or serious injury, or a threat to the physical integrity of self or others

(2) the person's response involved intense fear, helplessness, or horror. **Note:** In children, this may be expressed instead by disorganized or agitated behavior.

B. The traumatic event is persistently reexperienced in one (or more) of the following ways:

(1) recurrent and intrusive distressing recollections of the event, including images, thoughts, or perceptions. **Note:** In young children, repetitive play may occur in which themes or aspects of the trauma are expressed.

(2) recurrent distressing dreams of the event. **Note:** In children, there may be frightening dreams without recognizable content.

(3) acting or feeling as if the traumatic event were recurring (includes a sense of reliving the experience, illusions, hallucinations, and dissociative flashback episodes, including those that occur on awakening or when intoxicated). **Note:** In young children, trauma-specific reenactment may occur.

(continued on next page)

(4) intense psychological distress at exposure to internal or external cues that symbolize or resemble an aspect of the traumatic event

(5) physiological reactivity on exposure to internal or external cues that symbolize or resemble an aspect of the traumatic event

C. Persistent avoidance of stimuli associated with the trauma and numbing of general responsiveness (not present before the trauma), as indicated by three (or more) of the following:

(1) efforts to avoid thoughts, feelings, or conversations associated with the trauma

(2) efforts to avoid activities, places, or people that arouse recollections of the trauma

(3) inability to recall an important aspect of the trauma

(4) markedly diminished interest or participation in significant activities

(5) feeling of detachment or estrangement from others

(6) restricted range of affect (e.g., unable to have loving feelings)

(7) sense of foreshortened future (e.g., does not expect to have a career, marriage, children, or a normal life span)

D. Persistent symptoms of increased arousal (not present before the trauma), as indicated by two (or more) of the following:

(1) difficulty falling or staying asleep

(2) irritability or outbursts of anger

(3) difficulty concentrating

(4) hypervigilance

(5) exaggerated startle response

E. Duration of the disturbance (symptoms in Criteria B, C, and D) is more than 1 month.

F. The disturbance causes clinically significant distress or impairment in social, occupational, or other important areas of functioning.

Specify if:

Acute: if duration of symptoms is less than 3 months

Chronic: if duration of symptoms is 3 months or more

Specify if:

With Delayed Onset: if onset of symptoms is at least 6 months after the stressor

Diagnostic criteria for 309.21 Separation Anxiety Disorder

A. Developmentally inappropriate and excessive anxiety concerning separation from home or from those to whom the individual is attached, as evidenced by three (or more) of the following:

    (1) recurrent excessive distress when separation from home or major attachment figures occurs or is anticipated

    (2) persistent and excessive worry about losing, or about possible harm befalling, major attachment figures

    (3) persistent and excessive worry that an untoward event will lead to separation from a major attachment figure (e.g., getting lost or being kidnapped)

    (4) persistent reluctance or refusal to go to school or elsewhere because of fear of separation

    (5) persistently and excessively fearful or reluctant to be alone or without major attachment figures at home or without significant adults in other settings

    (6) persistent reluctance or refusal to go to sleep without being near a major attachment figure or to sleep away from home

    (7) repeated nightmares involving the theme of separation

    (8) repeated complaints of physical symptoms (such as headaches, stomachaches, nausea, or vomiting) when separation from major attachment figures occurs or is anticipated

B.   The duration of the disturbance is at least 4 weeks.

C.   The onset is before age 18 years.

D.   The disturbance causes clinically significant distress or impairment in social, academic (occupational), or other important areas of functioning.

E.   The disturbance does not occur exclusively during the course of a Pervasive Developmental Disorder, Schizophrenia, or other Psychotic Disorder and, in adolescents and adults, is not better accounted for by Panic Disorder With Agoraphobia.

Specify if:

Early Onset: if onset occurs before age 6 years

Diagnostic criteria for 300.23 Social Phobia

A.   A marked and persistent fear of one or more social or performance situations in which the person is exposed to unfamiliar people or to possible scrutiny by others. The individual fears that he or she will act in a way (or show anxiety symptoms) that will be humiliating or embarrassing. **Note:** In children, there must be evidence of the capacity for age-appropriate social relationships with familiar people and the anxiety must occur in peer settings, not just in interactions with adults.

B.   Exposure to the feared social situation almost invariably provokes anxiety, which may take the form of a situationally bound or situationally predisposed

(continued on next page)

Panic Attack. **Note:** In children, the anxiety may be expressed by crying, tantrums, freezing, or shrinking from social situations with unfamiliar people.

C. The person recognizes that the fear is excessive or unreasonable. **Note:** In children, this feature may be absent.

D. The feared social or performance situations are avoided or else are endured with intense anxiety or distress.

E. The avoidance, anxious anticipation, or distress in the feared social or performance situation(s) interferes significantly with the person's normal routine, occupational (academic) functioning, or social activities or relationships, or there is marked distress about having the phobia.

F. In individuals under age 18 years, the duration is at least 6 months.

G. The fear or avoidance is not due to the direct physiological effects of a substance (e.g., a drug of abuse, a medication) or a general medical condition and is not better accounted for by another mental disorder (e.g., Panic Disorder With or Without Agoraphobia, Separation Anxiety Disorder, Body Dysmorphic Disorder, a Pervasive Developmental Disorder, or Schizoid Personality Disorder.

H. If a general medical condition or another mental disorder is present, the fear in Criterion A is unrelated to it, e.g., the fear is not of Stuttering, trembling in Parkinson's disease, or exhibiting abnormal eating behavior in Anorexia Nervosa or Bulimia Nervosa.

Specify if

Generalized: if the fears include most social situations (also consider the additional diagnosis of Avoidant Personality Disorder)

Reprinted with permission from the *Diagnostic and Statistical Manual of Mental Disorders* (4th ed., text rev., p. 456). Copyright © 2000 American Psychiatric Association.

Diagnostic criteria for 300.29 Specific Phobia

A. Marked and persistent fear that is excessive or unreasonable, cued by the presence or anticipation of a specific object or situation (e.g., flying, heights, animals, receiving an injection, seeing blood).

B. Exposure to the phobic stimulus almost invariably provokes an immediate anxiety response, which may take the form of a situationally bound or situationally predisposed Panic Attack. **Note:** In children, the anxiety may be expressed by crying, tantrums, freezing, or clinging.

C. The person recognizes that the fear is excessive or unreasonable. **Note:** In children, this feature may be absent.

D. The phobic situation(s) is avoided or else is endured with intense anxiety or distress.

E. The avoidance, anxious anticipation, or distress in the feared situation(s) interferes significantly with the person's normal routine, occupational (or academic) functioning, or social activities or relationships, or there is marked distress about having the phobia.

F. In individuals under age 18 years, the duration is at least 6 months.

G. The anxiety, Panic Attacks, or phobic avoidance associated with the specific object or situation are not better accounted for by another mental disorder, such as Obsessive-Compulsive Disorder (e.g., fear of dirt in someone with an obsession about contamination), Posttraumatic Stress Disorder (e.g., avoidance of stimuli associated with a severe stressor), Separation Anxiety Disorder (e.g., avoidance of school), Social Phobia (e.g., avoidance of social situations because of fear of embarrassment), Panic Disorder with Agoraphobia, or Agoraphobia Without History of Panic Disorder.

Specify type:

Animal Type

Natural Environment Type (e.g., heights, storms, water)

Blood-Injection-Injury Type

Situational Type (e.g., airplanes, elevators, enclosed places)

Other Type (e.g., fear of choking, vomiting, or contracting an illness; in children, avoidance of loud sounds or costumed characters)

ATTENTION-DEFICIT/HYPERACTIVITY DISORDER

Diagnostic criteria for Attention-Deficit/Hyperactivity Disorder

A. Either (1) or (2):

(1) six (or more) of the following symptoms of **inattention** have persisted for at least 6 months to a degree that is maladaptive and inconsistent with developmental level:

Inattention

(a) often fails to give close attention to details or makes careless mistakes in schoolwork, work, or other activities

(b) often has difficulty sustaining attention in tasks or play activities

(c) often does not seem to listen when spoken to directly

(d) often does not follow through on instructions and fails to finish schoolwork, chores, or duties in the workplace (not due to oppositional behavior or failure to understand instructions)

(e) often has difficulty organizing tasks and activities

(f) often avoids, dislikes, or is reluctant to engage in tasks that require sustained mental effort (such as schoolwork or homework)

(g) often loses things necessary for tasks or activities (e.g., toys, school assignments, pencils, books, or tools)

(h) is often easily distracted by extraneous stimuli

(i) is often forgetful in daily activities

(2) six (or more) of the following symptoms of **hyperactivity-impulsivity** have persisted for at least 6 months to a degree that is maladaptive and inconsistent with developmental level:

Hyperactivity

(a) often fidgets with hands or feet or squirms in seat

(b) often leaves seat in classroom or in other situations in which remaining seated is expected

(c) often runs about or climbs excessively in situations in which it is inappropriate (in adolescents or adults, may be limited to subjective feelings of restlessness)

(d) often has difficulty playing or engaging in leisure activities quietly

(e) is often "on the go" or often acts as if "driven by a motor"

(f) often talks excessively

Impulsivity

(g) often blurts out answers before questions have been completed

(h) often has difficulty awaiting turn

(i) often interrupts or intrudes on others (e.g., butts into conversations or games)

B.   Some hyperactive-impulsive or inattentive symptoms that caused impairment were present before age 7 years.

C.   Some impairment from the symptoms is present in two or more settings (e.g., at school [or work] and at home).

D.   There must be clear evidence of clinically significant impairment in social, academic, or occupational functioning.

E.   The symptoms do no occur exclusively during the course of a Pervasive Developmental Disorder, Schizophrenia, or other Psychotic Disorder and are not better accounted for by another mental disorder (e.g., Mood Disorder, Anxiety Disorder, Dissociative Disorder, or a Personality Disorder).

Code based on type:

314.01 Attention-Deficit/Hyperactivity Disorder, Combined Type: if both Criteria A1 and A2 are met for the past 6 months

314.00 Attention-Deficit/Hyperactivity Disorder, Predominantly Inattentive Type: if Criterion A1 is met but Criterion A2 is not met for the past 6 months

314.01 Attention-Deficit/Hyperactivity Disorder, Predominantly Hyperactive-Impulsive Type: if Criterion A2 is met but Criterion A1 is not met for the past 6 months

Coding note: For individuals (especially adolescents and adults) who currently have symptoms that no longer meet full criteria, "In Partial Remission" should be specified.

BEHAVIORAL DISORDERS

Diagnostic criteria for Conduct Disorder

A. A repetitive and persistent pattern of behavior in which the basic rights of others or major age-appropriate societal norms or rules are violated, as manifested by the presence of three (or more) of the following criteria in the past 12 months, with at least one criterion present in the past 6 months:

Aggression to people and animals

(1) often bullies, threatens, or intimidates others

(2) often initiates physical fights

(3) has used a weapon that can cause serious physical harm to others (e.g., a bat, brick, broken bottle, knife, gun)

(4) has been physically cruel to people

(5) has been physically cruel to animals

(6) has stolen while confronting a victim (e.g., mugging, purse snatching, extortion, armed robbery)

(7) has forced someone into sexual activity

Destruction of property

(8) has deliberately engaged in fire setting with the intention of causing serious damage

(9) has deliberately destroyed others' property (other than by fire setting)

Deceitfulness or theft

(10) has broken into someone else's house, building, or car

(11) often lies to obtain goods or favors or to avoid obligations (i.e., "cons" others)

(12) has stolen items of nontrivial value without confronting a victim (e.g., shoplifting, but without breaking and entering; forgery)

Serious violations of rules

(13) often stays out at night despite parental prohibitions, beginning before age 13 years

(14) has run away from home overnight at least twice while living in parental or parental surrogate home (or once without returning for a lengthy period)

(15) is often truant from school, beginning before age 13 years

B. The disturbance in behavior causes clinically significant impairment in social, academic, or occupational functioning.

C. If the individual is age 18 years or older, criteria are not met for Antisocial Personality Disorder.

Code based on age at onset:

312.81 Conduct Disorder, Childhood-Onset Type: onset of at least one criterion characteristic of Conduct Disorder prior to age 10 years

312.82 Conduct Disorder, Adolescent-Onset Type: absence of any criteria characteristic of Conduct Disorder prior to age 10 years

312.89 Conduct Disorder, Unspecified Onset: age at onset is not known

Specify severity:

Mild: few if any conduct problems in excess of those required to make the diagnosis **and** conduct problems cause only minor harm to others

Moderate: number of conduct problems and effect on others intermediate between "mild" and "severe"

Severe: many conduct problems in excess of those required to make the diagnosis **or** conduct problems cause considerable harm to others

Diagnostic criteria for 313.81 Oppositional Defiant Disorder

A. A pattern of negativistic, hostile, and defiant behavior lasting at least 6 months, during which four (or more) of the following are present:

(1) often loses temper

(2) often argues with adults

(3) often actively defies or refuses to comply with adults' requests or rules

(4) often deliberately annoys people

(5) often blames others for his or her mistakes or behavior

(6) is often touchy or easily annoyed by others

(7) is often angry and resentful

(8) is often spiteful or vindictive

Note: Consider a criterion met only if the behavior occurs more frequently than is typically observed in individuals of comparable age and developmental level.

B. The disturbance in behavior causes clinically significant impairment in social, academic, or occupational function.

C. The behaviors do not occur exclusively during the course of a Psychotic or Mood Disorder.

D. Criteria are not met for Conduct Disorder, and, if the individual is age 18 years or older, criteria are not met for Antisocial Personality Disorder.

Diagnostic criteria for 312.34 Intermittent Explosive Disorder

A. Several discrete episodes of failure to resist aggressive impulses that result in serious assaultive acts or destruction of property.

B. The degree of aggressiveness expressed during the episode is grossly out of proportion to any precipitating psychosocial stressors.

C. The aggressive episodes are not better accounted for by another mental disorder (e.g., Antisocial Personality Disorder, Borderline Personality Disorder, a Psychotic Disorder, a Manic Episode, Conduct Disorder, or Attention-Deficit/Hyperactivity Disorder) and are not due to the direct physiological effects of a substance (e.g., a drug of abuse, a medication) or a general medical condition (e.g., head trauma, Alzheimer's disease).

EATING DISORDERS

Diagnostic criteria for 307.1 Anorexia Nervosa

A. Refusal to maintain body weight at or above a minimally normal weight for age and height (e.g., weight loss leading to maintenance of body weight less than 85% of that expected; or failure to make expected weight gain during period of growth, leading to body weight less than 85% of that expected).

B. Intense fear of gaining weight or becoming fat, even though underweight.

C. Disturbance in the way in which one's body weight or shape is experienced, undue influence of body weight or shape on self-evaluation, or denial of the seriousness of the current low body weight.

D. In postmenarcheal females, amenorrhea, i.e., the absence of at least three consecutive menstrual cycles. (A woman is considered to have amenorrhea if her periods occur only following hormone, e.g., estrogen, administration.)

Specify type:

Restricting Type: during the current episode of Anorexia Nervosa, the person has not regularly engaged in binge-eating or purging behavior (i.e., self-induced vomiting or the misuse of laxatives, diuretics, or enemas)

Binge-Eating/Purging Type: during the current episode of Anorexia Nervosa, the person has regularly engaged in binge-eating or purging behavior (i.e., self-induced vomiting or the misuse of laxatives, diuretics, or enemas)

Reprinted with permission from the *Diagnostic and Statistical Manual of Mental Disorders* (4th ed., text rev., p. 589). Copyright © 2000 American Psychiatric Association.

Diagnostic criteria for 307.51 Bulimia Nervosa

A. Recurrent episodes of binge eating. An episode of binge eating is characterized by both of the following:

   (1) eating, in a discrete period of time (e.g., within any 2-hour period), an amount of food that is definitely larger than most people would eat during a similar period of time and under similar circumstances

   (2) a sense of lack of control over eating during the episode (e.g., a feeling that one cannot stop eating or control what or how much one is eating)

B. Recurrent inappropriate compensatory behavior in order to prevent weight gain, such as self-induced vomiting; misuse of laxatives, diuretics, enemas, or other medications; fasting; or excessive exercise.

C. The binge eating and compensatory behaviors both occur, on average, at least twice a week for 3 months.

D. Self-evaluation is unduly influenced by body shape and weight.

(continued on next page)

E. The disturbance does not occur exclusively during episodes of Anorexia Nervosa.

Specify type:

Purging Type: during the current episode of Bulimia Nervosa, the person has regularly engaged in self-induced vomiting or the misuse of laxatives, diuretics, or enemas

Nonpurging Type: during the current episode of Bulimia Nervosa, the person has used other inappropriate compensatory behaviors, such as fasting or excessive exercise, but has not regularly engaged in self-induced vomiting or the misuse of laxatives, diuretics, or enemas

Diagnostic criteria for 307.50 Eating Disorder Not Otherwise Specified

1. For females, all of the criteria for Anorexia Nervosa are met except that the individual has regular menses.

2. All of the criteria for Anorexia Nervosa are met except that, despite significant weight loss, the individual's current weight is in the normal range.

3. All of the criteria for Bulimia Nervosa are met except that the binge eating and inappropriate compensatory mechanisms occur at a frequency of less than twice a week or for a duration of less than 3 months.

4. The regular use of inappropriate compensatory behavior by an individual of normal body weight after eating small amounts of food (e.g., self-induced vomiting after the consumption of two cookies).

5. Repeatedly chewing and spitting out, but not swallowing, large amounts of food.

6. Binge-eating disorder: recurrent episodes of binge eating in the absence of regular use of inappropriate compensatory behaviors characteristics of Bulimia Nervosa (see p. 785 for suggested research criteria).

MOOD DISORDERS

Criteria for Major Depressive Episode

A. Five (or more) of the following symptoms have been present during the same 2-week period and represent a change from previous functioning; at least one of the symptoms is either (1) depressed mood or (2) loss of interest or pleasure. **Note:** Do not include symptoms that are clearly due to a general medical condition, or mood-incongruent delusions or hallucinations.

  (1) depressed mood most of the day, nearly every day, as indicated by either subjective report (e.g., feels sad or empty) or observation made by others (e.g., appears tearful). **Note:** In children and adolescents, can be irritable mood.

  (2) markedly diminished interest or pleasure in all, or almost all, activities most of the day, nearly every day (as indicated by either subjective account or observation made by others)

  (3) significant weight loss when not dieting or weight gain (e.g., a change of more than 5% of body weight in a month), or decrease or increase in appetite nearly every day. **Note:** In children, consider failure to make expected weight gains.

  (4) insomnia or hypersomnia nearly every day

  (5) psychomotor agitation or retardation nearly every day (observable by others, not merely subjective feelings of restlessness or being slowed down)

  (6) fatigue or loss of energy nearly every day

  (7) feelings of worthlessness or excessive or inappropriate guilt (which may be delusional) nearly everyday (not merely self-reproach or guilt about being sick)

  (8) diminished ability to think or concentrate, or indecisiveness, nearly every day (either by subjective account or as observed by others)

  (9) recurrent thoughts of death (not just a fear of dying), recurrent suicidal ideation without a specific plan, or a suicide attempt or a specific plan for committing suicide

B. The symptoms do not meet criteria for a Mixed Episode (see p. 365). 350

C. The symptoms cause clinically significant distress or impairment in social, occupational, or other important areas of functioning.

D. The symptoms are not due to the direct physiological effects of a substance (e.g., a drug of abuse, a medication) or a general medical condition (e.g., hypothyroidism).

E. The symptoms are not better accounted for by Bereavement, i.e., after the loss of a loved one, the symptoms persist for longer than 2 months or are characterized by marked functional impairment, morbid preoccupation with worthlessness, suicidal ideation, psychotic symptoms, or psychomotor retardation.

Criteria for Manic Episode

A. A distinct period of abnormally and persistently elevated, expansive, or irritable mood, lasting for at least 1 week (or any duration if hospitalization is necessary).

B. During the period of mood disturbance, three (or more) of the following symptoms have persisted (four if the mood is only irritable) and have been present to a significant degree:

    (1) inflated self-esteem or grandiosity

    (2) decreased need for sleep (e.g., feels rested after only 3 hours of sleep)

    (3) more talkative than usual or pressure to keep talking

    (4) flight of ideas or subjective experience that thoughts are racing

    (5) distractibility (i.e., attention too easily drawn to unimportant or irrelevant external stimuli)

    (6) increase in goal-directed activity (either socially, at work or school, or sexually) or psychomotor agitation

    (7) excessive involvement in pleasurable activities that have a high potential for painful consequences (e.g., engaging in unrestrained buying sprees, sexual indiscretions, or foolish business investments)

C. The symptoms do not meet criteria for a Mixed Episode (see p. 365).

D. The mood disturbance is sufficiently severe to cause marked impairment in occupational functioning or in unusual social activities or relationships with others, or to necessitate hospitalization to prevent harm to self or others, or there are psychotic features.

E. The symptoms are not due to the direct physiological effects of a substance (e.g., a drug of abuse, a medication, or other treatment) or a general medical condition (e.g., hyperthyroidism).

Note: Manic-like episodes that are clearly caused by somatic antidepressant treatment (e.g., medication, electroconvulsive therapy, light therapy) should not count toward a diagnosis of Bipolar I Disorder.

Criteria for Mixed Episode

A. The criteria are met both for a Manic Episode (see p. 362) and for a Major Depressive Episode (see p. 356) (except for duration) nearly every day during at least a 1-week period.

B. The mood disturbance is sufficiently severe to cause marked impairment in occupational functioning or in usual social activities or relationships with others, or to necessitate hospitalization to prevent harm to self or others, or there are psychotic features.

C. The symptoms are not due to the direct physiological effects of a substance (e.g., a drug of abuse, a medication, or other treatment) or a general medical condition (e.g., hyperthyroidism).

Note: Mixed-like episodes that are clearly caused by somatic antidepressant treatment (e.g., medication, electroconvulsive therapy, light therapy) should not count toward a diagnosis of Bipolar I Disorder.

Criteria for Hypomanic Episode

A. A distinct period of persistently elevated, expansive, or irritable mood, lasting throughout at least 4 days, that is clearly different from the usual nondepressed mood.

B. During the period of mood disturbance, three (or more) of the following symptoms have persisted (four if the mood is only irritable) and have been present to a significant degree:

   (1) inflated self-esteem or grandiosity

   (2) decreased need for sleep (e.g., feels rested after only 3 hours of sleep)

   (3) more talkative than usual or pressure to keep talking

   (4) flight of ideas or subjective experience that thoughts are racing

   (5) distractibility (i.e., attention too easily drawn to unimportant or irrelevant external stimuli)

   (6) increase in goal-directed activity (either socially, at work or school, or sexually) or psychomotor agitation

   (7) excessive involvement in pleasurable activities that have a high potential for painful consequences (e.g., the person engages in unrestrained buying sprees, sexual indiscretions, or foolish business investments)

C. The episode is associated with an unequivocal change in functioning that is uncharacteristic of the person when not symptomatic.

D. The disturbance in mood and the change in functioning are observable by others.

E. The episode is not severe enough to cause marked impairment in social or occupational functioning, or to necessitate hospitalization, and there are no psychotic features.

F. The symptoms are not due to the direct physiological effects of a substance (e.g., a drug of abuse, a medication, or other treatment) or a general medical condition (e.g., hyperthyroidism).

Note: Hypomanic-like episodes that are clearly caused by somatic antidepressant treatment (e.g., medication, electroconvulsive therapy, light therapy) should not count toward a diagnosis of Bipolar II Disorder.

Diagnostic criteria for 296.0x Bipolar I Disorder, Single Manic Episode

A. Presence of only one Manic Episode (see p. 362) and no past Major Depressive Episodes.

Note: Recurrence is defined as either a change in polarity from depression or an interval of at least 2 months without manic symptoms.

B. The Manic Episode is not better accounted for by Schizoaffective Disorder and is not superimposed on Schizophrenia, Schizophreniform Disorder, Delusional Disorder or Psychotic Disorder Not Otherwise Specified.

Diagnostic criteria for 296.40
Bipolar I Disorder, Most Recent Episode Hypomanic

A. Currently (or most recently) in a Hypomanic Episode (see p. 368).

B. There has previously been at least one Manic Episode (see p. 362) or Mixed Episode (see p. 365).

C. The mood symptoms cause clinically significant distress or impairment in social, occupational, or other important areas of functioning.

D. The mood episodes in Criteria A and B are not better accounted for by Schizoaffective Disorder and are not superimposed on Schizophrenia, Schizophreniform Disorder, Delusional Disorder, or Psychotic Disorder Not Otherwise Specified.

Diagnostic criteria for 296.4x Bipolar I Disorder, Most Recent Episode Manic

A. Currently (or most recently) in a Manic Episode (see p. 362).

B. There has previously been at least one Major Depressive Episode (see p. 356), Manic Episode (see p. 362), or Mixed Episode (see p. 365).

C. The mood episodes in Criteria A and B are not better accounted for by Schizoaffective Disorder and are not superimposed on Schizophrenia, Schizophreniform Disorder, Delusional Disorder, or Psychotic Disorder Not Otherwise Specified.

Diagnostic criteria for 296.6x Bipolar I Disorder, Most Recent Episode Mixed

A. Currently (or most recently) in a Mixed Episode (see p. 365).

B. There has previously been at least one Major Depressive Episode (see p. 356), Manic Episode (see p. 362), or Mixed Episode (see p. 365).

C. The mood episodes in Criteria A and B are not better accounted for by Schizoaffective Disorder and are not superimposed on Schizophrenia, Schizophreniform Disorder, Delusional Disorder, or Psychotic Disorder Not Otherwise Specified.

Diagnostic criteria for 296.5x Bipolar I Disorder, Most Recent Episode Depressed

A. Currently (or most recently) in a Major Depressive Episode (see p. 356).

B. There has previously been at least one Manic Episode (see p. 362) or Mixed Episode (see p. 365).

C. The mood episodes in Criteria A and B are not better accounted for by Schizoaffective Disorder and are not superimposed on Schizophrenia, Schizophreniform Disorder, Delusional Disorder, or Psychotic Disorder Not Otherwise Specified.

Diagnostic criteria for 296.7
Bipolar I Disorder, Most Recent Episode Unspecified

A. Criteria, except for duration, are currently (or most recently) met for a Manic (see p. 362), a Hypomanic (see p. 368), a Mixed (see p. 365), or a Major Depressive Episode (see p. 356).

B. There has previously been at least one Manic Episode (see p. 362) or Mixed Episode (see p. 365).

C. The mood symptoms cause clinically significant distress or impairment in social, occupational, or other important areas of functioning.

D. The mood symptoms in Criteria A and B are not better accounted for by Schizoaffective Disorder and are not superimposed on Schizophrenia, Schizophreniform Disorder, Delusional Disorder, or Psychotic Disorder Not Otherwise Specified.

E. The mood symptoms in Criteria A and B are not due to the direct physiological effects of a substance (e.g., a drug of abuse, a medication, or other treatment) or a general medical condition (e.g., hyperthyroidism).

Diagnostic criteria for 296.89 Bipolar II Disorder

A. Presence (or history) of one or more Major Depressive Episodes (see p. 356).

B. Presence (or history) of at least one Hypomanic Episode (see p. 368).

C. There has never been a Manic Episode (see p. 362) or a Mixed Episode (see p. 365).

D. The mood symptoms in Criteria A and B are not better accounted for by Schizoaffective Disorder and are not superimposed on Schizophrenia, Schizophreniform Disorder, Delusional Disorder, or Psychotic Disorder Not Otherwise Specified.

E. The symptoms cause clinically significant distress or impairment in social, occupational, or other important areas of functioning.

Diagnostic criteria for 301.13 Cyclothymic Disorder

A. For at least 2 years, the presence of numerous periods with hypomanic symptoms (see p. 368) and numerous periods with depressive symptoms that do not meet criteria for a Major Depressive Episode. **Note:** In children and adolescents, the duration must be at least 1 year.

B. During the above 2-year period (1 year in children and adolescents), the person has not been without the symptoms in Criterion A for more than 2 months at a time.

C. No Major Depressive Episode (p. 356), Manic Episode (p. 362), or Mixed Episode (see p. 365) has been present during the first 2 years of the disturbance.

    Note: After the initial 2 years (1 year in children and adolescents) of Cyclothymic Disorder, there may be superimposed Manic or Mixed Episodes (in which case both Bipolar I Disorder and Cyclothymic Disorder may be diagnosed) or Major Depressive Episodes (in which case both Bipolar II Disorder and Cyclothymic Disorder may be diagnosed).

D. The symptoms in Criterion A are not better accounted for by Schizoaffective Disorder and are not superimposed on Schizophrenia, Schizophreniform Disorder, Delusional Disorder, or Psychotic Disorder Not Otherwise Specified.

E. The symptoms are not due to the direct physiological effects of a substance (e.g., a drug of abuse, a medication) or a general medical condition (e.g., hyperthyroidism).

F. The symptoms cause clinically significant distress or impairment in social, occupational, or other important areas of functioning.

Diagnostic Criteria for 300.4 Dysthymic Disorder

A. Depressed mood for most of the day, for more days than not, as indicated either by subjective account or observation by others, for at least 2 years.

Note: In children and adolescents, mood can be irritable and duration must be at least 1 year.

B. Presence, while depressed, of two (or more) of the following:

    (1) poor appetite or overeating

    (2) insomnia or hypersomnia

    (3) low energy or fatigue

    (4) low self-esteem

    (5) poor concentration or difficulty making decisions

    (6) feelings of hopelessness

C. During the 2-year period (1 year for children and adolescents) of the disturbance, the person has never been without the symptoms in Criteria A and B for more than 2 months at a time.

D. No Major Depressive Episode (see p. 356) has been present during the first 2 years of the disturbance (1 year for children and adolescents), i.e., the disturbance is not better accounted for by chronic Major Depressive Disorder, or Major Depressive Disorder, In Partial Remission.

Note: There may have been a previous Major Depressive Episode provided there was a full remission (no significant signs or symptoms for 2 months) before development of Dysthymic Disorder. In addition, after the initial 2 years (1 year for children and adolescents) of Dysthymic Disorder, there may be superimposed episodes of Major Depressive Disorder, in which case both diagnoses may be given when the criteria are met for a Major Depressive Episode.

E. There has never been a Manic Episode (see p. 362), a Mixed Episode (see p. 365), or a Hypomanic Episode (see p. 368), and criteria have never been met for Cyclothymic Disorder.

F. The disturbance does not occur exclusively during the course of a chronic Psychotic Disorder, such as Schizophrenia or Delusional Disorder.

G. The symptoms are not due to the direct physiological effects of a substance (e.g., a drug of abuse, a medication) or a general medical condition (e.g., hypothyroidism).

H. The symptoms cause clinically significant distress or impairment in social, occupational, or other important areas of functioning.

Specify if:

Early Onset: if onset is before age 21 years

Late Onset: if onset is age 21 years or older

Specify (for most recent 2 years of Dysthymic Disorder):

With Atypical Features (see p. 420)

PERVASIVE DEVELOPMENTAL DISORDERS

Diagnostic criteria for 299.00 Autistic Disorder

A. A total of six (or more) items from (1), (2), and (3), with at least two from (1), and one each from (2) and (3):

(1) qualitative impairment in social interaction, as manifested by at least two of the following:

(a) marked impairment in the used of multiple nonverbal behaviors such as eye-to-eye gaze, facial expression, body postures, and gestures to regulate social interaction

(b) failure to develop peer relationships appropriate to developmental level

(c) a lack of spontaneous seeking to share enjoyment, interests, or achievements with other people (e.g., by a lack of showing, bringing, or pointing out objects of interest)

(d) lack of social or emotional reciprocity

(2) qualitative impairments in communication as manifested by at least one of the following:

(a) delay in, or total lack of, the development of spoken language (not accompanied by an attempt to compensate through alternative modes of communication such as gesture or mime)

(b) in individuals with adequate speech, marked impairment in the ability to initiate or sustain conversation with others

(c) stereotyped and repetitive use of language or idiosyncratic language

(d) lack of varied, spontaneous make-believe play or social initiative play appropriate to developmental level

(3) restricted repetitive and stereotyped patterns of behavior, interests, and activities, as manifested by at least one of the following:

(a) encompassing preoccupation with one or more stereotyped and restricted patterns of interest that is abnormal either in intensity or focus

(b) apparently inflexible adherence to specific, nonfunctional routines or rituals

(c) stereotyped and repetitive motor mannerisms (e.g., hand or finger flapping or twisting, or complex whole-body movements)

(d) persistent preoccupation with parts of objects

B. Delays or abnormal functioning in at least one of the following areas, with onset prior to age 3 years: (1) social interaction, (2) language as used in social communication, or (3) symbolic or imaginative play.

C. The disturbance is not better accounted for by Rett's Disorder or Childhood Disintegrative Disorder.

Diagnostic criteria for 299.80 Rett's Disorder

A. All of the following:

(1) apparently normal prenatal and perinatal development

(2) apparently normal psychomotor development through the first 5 months after birth

(3) normal head circumference at birth

B. Onset of all of the following after the period of normal development:

(1) deceleration of head growth between ages 5 and 48 months

(2) loss of previously acquired purposeful hand skills between ages 5 and 30 months with the subsequent development of stereotyped hand movements (e.g., hand-wringing or hand washing)

(3) loss of social engagement early in the course (although often social interaction develops later)

(4) appearance of poorly coordinated gait or trunk movements

(5) severely impaired expressive and receptive language development with severe psychomotor retardation

Diagnostic criteria for 299.10 Childhood Disintegrative Disorder

A. Apparently normal development for at least the first 2 years after birth as manifested by the presence of age-appropriate verbal and nonverbal communication, social relationships, play, and adaptive behavior.

B. Clinically significant loss of previously acquired skills (before age 10 years) in at least two of the following areas:

(1) expressive or receptive language

(2) social skills or adaptive behavior

(3) bowel or bladder control

(4) play

(5) motor skills

C. Abnormalities of functioning in at least two of the following areas:

(1) qualitative impairment in social interaction (e.g., impairment in nonverbal behaviors, failure to develop peer relationships, lack of social or emotional reciprocity)

(2) qualitative impairments in communication (e.g., delay or lack of spoken language, inability to initiate or sustain a conversation, stereotyped and repetitive use of language, lack of varied make-believe play)

(3) restricted, repetitive, and stereotyped patterns of behavior, interests, and activities, including motor stereotypies and mannerisms

(continued on next page)

D. The disturbance is not better accounted for by another specific Pervasive Developmental Disorder or by Schizophrenia.

Diagnostic criteria for 299.80 Asperger's Disorder

A. Qualitative impairment in social interaction, as manifested by at least two of the following:

(1) marked impairment in the use of multiple nonverbal behaviors such as eye-to-eye gaze, facial expression, body postures, and gestures to regulate social interaction

(2) failure to develop peer relationships appropriate to developmental level

(3) a lack of spontaneous seeking to share enjoyment, interests, or achievements with other people (e.g., by a lack of showing, bringing, or pointing out objects of interest to other people)

(4) lack of social or emotional reciprocity

B. Restricted repetitive and stereotyped patterns of behavior, interests, and activities, as manifested by at least one of the following:

(1) encompassing preoccupation with one or more stereotyped and restricted patterns of interest that is abnormal either in intensity or focus

(2) apparently inflexible adherence to specific, nonfunctional routines or rituals

(3) stereotyped and repetitive motor mannerisms (e.g., hand or finger flapping or twisting, or complex whole-body movements)

(4) persistent preoccupation with parts of objects

C. The disturbance causes clinically significant impairment in social, occupational, or other important areas of functioning.

D. There is no clinically significant general delay in language (e.g., single words used by age 2 years, communicative phrases used by age 3 years).

E. There is no clinically significant delay in cognitive development or in the development of age-appropriate self-help skills, adaptive behavior (other than social interaction), and curiosity about the environment in childhood.

F. Criteria are not met for another specific Pervasive Developmental Disorder or Schizophrenia.

PSYCHOTIC DISORDERS

Diagnostic criteria for Schizophrenia

A. *Characteristic symptoms:* Two (or more) of the following, each present for a significant portion of time during a 1-month period (or less if successfully treated):

    (1) delusions

    (2) hallucinations

    (3) disorganized speech (e.g., frequent derailment or incoherence)

    (4) grossly disorganized or catatonic behavior

    (5) negative symptoms, i.e., affective flattening, alogia, or avolition

    Note: Only one Criterion A symptom is required if delusions are bizarre or hallucinations consist of a voice keeping up a running commentary on the person's behavior or thoughts, or two or more voices conversing with each other.

B. *Social/occupational dysfunction:* For a significant portion of the time since the onset of the disturbance, one or more major areas of functioning such as work, interpersonal relations, or self-care are markedly below the level achieved prior to the onset (or when the onset is in childhood or adolescence, failure to achieve expected level of interpersonal, academic, or occupational achievement).

C. *Duration:* Continuous signs of the disturbance persist for at least 6 months. This 6-month period must include at least 1 month of symptoms (or less if successfully treated) that meet Criterion A (i.e., active-phase symptoms) and may include periods of prodromal or residual symptoms. During these prodromal or residual periods, the signs of the disturbance may be manifested by only negative symptoms or two or more symptoms listed in Criterion A present an attenuated form (e.g., odd beliefs, unusual perceptual experiences).

D. *Schizoaffective and Mood Disorder exclusion:* Schizoaffective Disorder and Mood Disorder With Psychotic Features have been ruled out because either (1) no Major Depressive, Manic, or Mixed Episodes have occurred concurrently with the active-phase symptoms; or (2) if mood episodes have occurred during active-phase symptoms, their total duration has been brief relative to the duration of the active and residual periods.

E. *Substance/general medical condition exclusion:* The disturbance is not due to the direct physiological effects of a substance (e.g., a drug of abuse, a medication) or a general medical condition.

F. *Relationship to a Pervasive Developmental Disorder:* If there is a history of Autistic Disorder or another Pervasive Developmental Disorder, the diagnosis of Schizophrenia is made only if prominent delusions or hallucinations are also present for at least a month (or less if successfully treated).

Classification of longitudinal course (can be applied only after at least 1 year has elapsed since the initial onset of active-phase symptoms):

(continued on next page)

Episodic With Interepisode Residual Symptoms (episodes are defined by the reemergence of prominent psychotic symptoms); *also specify if:* **With Prominent Negative Symptoms**

Episodic With No Interepisode Residual Symptoms

Continuous (prominent psychotic symptoms are present throughout the period of observation); *also specify if:* **With Prominent Negative Symptoms**

Single Episode In Partial Remission; *also specify if:* **With Prominent Negative Symptoms**

Single Episode With In Full Remission

Other or Unspecified Pattern

Reprinted with permission from the *Diagnostic and Statistical Manual of Mental Disorders* (4th ed., text rev., pp. 312–313). Copyright © 2000 American Psychiatric Association.

Diagnostic criteria for 295.70 Schizoaffective Disorder

A. An uninterrupted period of illness during which, at some time, there is either a Major Depressive Episode, a Manic Episode, or a Mixed Episode concurrent with symptoms that met Criterion A for Schizophrenia.

    Note: The Major Depressive Episode must include Criterion A1: depressed mood.

B. During the same period of illness, there have been delusions or hallucinations for at least 2 weeks in the absence of prominent mood symptoms.

C. Symptoms that meet criteria for a mood episode are present for a substantial portion of the total duration of the active and residual periods of the illness.

D. The disturbance is not due to the direct physiological effects of a substance (e.g., a drug of abuse, a medication) or a general medical condition.

Specify type:

Bipolar Type: if the disturbance includes a Manic or a Mixed Episode (or a Manic or a Mixed Episode and Major Depressive Episodes)

Depressive Type: if the disturbance only includes Major Depressive Episodes

Reprinted with permission from the *Diagnostic and Statistical Manual of Mental Disorders* (4th ed., text rev., p. 323). Copyright © 2000 American Psychiatric Association.

SUBSTANCE-RELATED DISORDERS

Criteria for Substance Abuse

A. A maladaptive pattern of substance use leading to clinically significant impairment or distress, as manifested by one (or more) of the following, occurring within a 12-month period:

   (1) recurrent substance use resulting in a failure to fulfill major role obligations at work, school, or home (e.g., repeated absences or poor work performance related to substance use; substance-related absences, suspensions, or expulsions from school; neglect of children or household)

   (2) recurrent substance use in situations in which it is physically hazardous (e.g., driving an automobile or operating a machine when impaired by substance use)

   (3) recurrent substance-related legal problems (e.g., arrests for substance-related disorderly conduct)

   (4) continued substance use despite having persistent or recurrent social or interpersonal problems caused or exacerbated by the effects of the substance (e.g., arguments with spouse about consequences of intoxication, physical fights)

B. The symptoms have never met the criteria for Substance Dependence for this class of substance.

Reprinted with permission from the *Diagnostic and Statistical Manual of Mental Disorders* (4th ed., text rev., p. 199). Copyright © 2000 American Psychiatric Association.

Criteria for Substance Dependence

A maladaptive pattern of substance use, leading to clinically significant impairment or distress, as manifested by three (or more) of the following, occurring at any time in the same 12-month period:

(1) tolerance, as defined by either of the following:

   (a) a need for markedly increased amounts of the substance to achieve intoxication or desired effect

   (b) markedly diminished effect with continued use of the same amount of the substance

(2) withdrawal, as manifested by either of the following:

   (a) the characteristic withdrawal syndrome for the substance (refer to Criteria A and B of the criteria sets for Withdrawal from the specific substances)

   (b) the same (or a closely related) substance is taken to relieve or avoid withdrawal symptoms

(3) the substance is often taken in larger amounts or over a longer period than was intended

(continued on next page)

(4) there is a persistent desire or unsuccessful efforts to cut down or control substance use

(5) a great deal of time is spent in activities necessary to obtain the substance (e.g., visiting multiple doctors or driving long distances), use the substance (e.g., chain-smoking), or recover from its effects

(6) important social, occupational, or recreational activities are given up or reduced because of substance use

(7) The substance use is continued despite knowledge of having a persistent or recurrent physical or psychological problem that is likely to have been caused or exacerbated by the substance (e.g., current cocaine use despite recognition of cocaine-induced depression, or continued drinking despite recognition that an ulcer was made worse by alcohol consumption)

Specify if:

With Physiological Dependence: evidence of tolerance or withdrawal (i.e., either Item 1 or 2 is present)

Without Physiological Dependence: no evidence of tolerance or withdrawal (i.e., neither Item 1 or 2 is present)

Course specifiers (see text for definitions):

Early Full Remission

Early Partial Remission

Sustained Full Remission

Sustained Partial Remission

On Agonist Therapy

In a Controlled Environment

Diagnostic criteria for 303.00 Alcohol Intoxication

A. Recent ingestion of alcohol.

B. Clinically significant maladaptive behavioral or psychological changes (e.g., inappropriate sexual or aggressive behavior, mood lability, impaired judgment, impaired social or occupational functioning) that developed during, or shortly after, alcohol ingestion.

C. One (or more) of the following signs, developing during, or shortly after, alcohol use:

(1) slurred speech

(2) incoordination

(3) unsteady gait

(4) nystagmus

(5) impairment in attention or memory

(6) stupor or coma

D. The symptoms are not due to a general medical condition and are not better accounted for by another mental disorder.

Diagnostic criteria for 292.89 Amphetamine Intoxication

A. Recent use of amphetamine or a related substance (e.g., methylphenidate).

B. Clinically significant maladaptive behavioral or psychological changes (e.g., euphoria or affective blunting; changes in sociability; hypervigilance; interpersonal sensitivity; anxiety, tension, or anger; stereotyped behaviors; impaired judgment; or impaired social or occupational functioning) that developed during, or shortly after, use of amphetamine or a related substance.

C. Two (or more) of the following, developing during, or shortly after, use of amphetamine or a related substance:

　(1) tachycardia or bradycardia

　(2) pupillary dilation

　(3) elevated or lowered blood pressure

　(4) perspiration or chills

　(5) nausea or vomiting

　(6) evidence of weight loss

　(7) psychomotor agitation or retardation

　(8) muscular weakness, respiratory depression, chest pain, or cardiac arrhythmias

　(9) confusion, seizures, dyskinesias, dystonias, or coma

D. The symptoms are not due to a general medical condition and are not better accounted for by another mental disorder.

Specify if

With Perceptual Disturbances

Diagnostic criteria for 292.89 Cannabis Intoxication

A. Recent use of cannabis.

B. Clinically significant maladaptive behavioral or psychological changes (e.g., impaired motor coordination, euphoria, anxiety, sensation of slowed time, impaired judgment, social withdrawal) that developed during, or shortly after, cannabis use.

C. Two (or more) of the following signs, developing within 2 hours of cannabis use:

  (1) conjunctival injection

  (2) increased appetite

  (3) dry mouth

  (4) tachycardia

D. The symptoms are not due to a general medical condition and are not better accounted for by another mental disorder.

Specify if

With Perceptual Disturbances

Reprinted with permission from the *Diagnostic and Statistical Manual of Mental Disorders* (4th ed., text rev., p. 238). Copyright © 2000 American Psychiatric Association.

Diagnostic criteria for 292.89 Cocaine Intoxication

A. Recent use of cocaine.

B. Clinically significant maladaptive behavioral or psychological changes (e.g., euphoria or affective blunting; changes in sociability; hypervigilance; interpersonal sensitivity; anxiety, tension, or anger; stereotyped behaviors; impaired judgment; or impaired social or occupational functioning) that developed during, or shortly after, use of cocaine.

C. Two (or more) of the following, developing during, or shortly after, use of cocaine:

  (1) tachycardia or bradycardia

  (2) pupillary dilation

  (3) elevated or lowered blood pressure

  (4) perspiration or chills

  (5) nausea or vomiting

  (6) evidence of weight loss

  (7) psychomotor agitation or retardation

  (8) muscular weakness, respiratory depression, chest pain, or cardiac arrhythmias

  (9) confusion, seizures, dyskinesias, dystonias, or coma

D. The symptoms are not due to a general medical condition and are not better accounted for by another mental disorder.

Specify if

With Perceptual Disturbances

Diagnostic Criteria for 292.89 Hallucinogen Intoxication

A. Recent use of a hallucinogen.

B. Clinically significant maladaptive behavioral or psychological changes (e.g., marked anxiety or depression, ideas of reference, fear of losing one's mind, paranoid ideation, impaired judgment, or impaired social or occupational functioning) that developed during, or shortly after, hallucinogen use.

C. Perceptual changes occurring in a state of full wakefulness and alertness (e.g., subjective intensification of perceptions, depersonalizaion, derealization, illusions, hallucinations, synestheisas) that developed during, or shortly after, hallucinogen use.

D. Two (or more) of the following signs, developing during, or shortly after, hallucinogen use:

    (1) pupillary dilation

    (2) tachycardia

    (3) sweating

    (4) palpitations

    (5) blurring of vision

    (6) tremors

    (7) incoordination

E. The symptoms are not due to a general medical condition and are not better accounted for by another mental disorder.

Diagnostic Criteria for 292.89 Inhalant Intoxication

A. Recent intentional use or short-term, high-dose exposure to volatile inhalants (excluding anesthetic gases and short-acting vasodilators).

B. Clinically significant maladaptive behavioral or psychological changes (e.g., belligerence, assultiveness, apathy, impaired judgment, impaired social or occupational functioning) that developed during, or shortly after, use of or exposure to volatile inhalants.

(continued on next page)

C. Two (or more) of the following signs, developing during, or shortly after, inhalant use or exposure:

(1) dizziness

(2) nystagmus

(3) incoordination

(4) slurred speech

(5) unsteady gait

(6) lethargy

(7) depressed reflexes

(8) psychomotor retardation

(9) tremor

(10) generalized muscle weakness

(11) blurred vision or diplopia

(12) stupor or coma

(13) euphoria

D. The symptoms are not due to a general medical condition and are not better accounted for by another mental disorder.

Reprinted with permission from the *Diagnostic and Statistical Manual of Mental Disorders* (4th ed., text rev., p. 260). Copyright © 2000 American Psychiatric Association.

Diagnostic Criteria for 292.89 Opioid Intoxication

A. Recent use of an opioid.

B. Clinically significant maladaptive behavioral or psychological changes (e.g., initial euphoria followed by apathy, dysphoria, psychomotor agitation or retardation, impaired judgment, or impaired social or occupational functioning) that developed during, or shortly after, opioid use.

C. Pupillary constriction (or pupillary dilation due to anoxia from severe overdose) and one (or more) of the following signs, developing during, or shortly after, opioid use:

(1) drowsiness or coma

(2) slurred speech

(3) impairment in attention or memory

D. The symptoms are not due to a general medical condition and are not better accounted for by another mental disorder.

Specify if:

With Perceptual Disturbances

Reprinted with permission from the *Diagnostic and Statistical Manual of Mental Disorders* (4th ed., text rev., p. 272). Copyright © 2000 American Psychiatric Association.

Diagnostic Criteria for 292.89 Phencyclidine Intoxication

A. Recent use of phencyclidine (or a related substance).

B. Clinically significant maladaptive behavioral changes (e.g., belligerence, assultiveness, unpredictability, psychomotor agitation, impaired judgment, or impaired social or occupational functioning) that developed during, or shortly after, phencyclidine use.

C. Within an hour (less when smoked, "snorted," or used intravenously), two (or more) of the following signs:

   (1) vertical or horizontal nystagmus

   (2) hypertension or tachycardia

   (3) numbness or diminished responsiveness to pain

   (4) ataxia

   (5) dysarthria

   (6) muscle rigidity

   (7) seizures or coma

   (8) hyperacusis

D. The symptoms are not due to a general medical condition and are not better accounted for by another mental disorder.

Specify if:

With Perceptual Disturbances

TICS

Diagnostic criteria for 307.21 Transient Tic Disorder

A. Single or multiple motor and/or vocal tics (i.e., sudden, rapid, recurrent, nonrhythmic, stereotyped motor movements or vocalizations)

B. The tics occur many times a day, nearly every day for at least 4 weeks, but for no longer than 12 consecutive months.

C. The disturbance causes marked distress or significant impairment in social, occupational, or other important areas of functioning.

D. The onset is before age 18 years.

E. The disturbance is not due to the direct physiological effects of a substance (e.g., stimulants) or a general medical condition (e.g., Huntington's disease or postviral encephalitis).

F. Criteria have never been met for Tourette's Disorder or Chronic Motor or Vocal Tic Disorder.

Specify if:

Single Episode or **Recurrent**

APPENDIX B

Medications

Information about existing medications increases almost daily. New medications are always being developed to become available for physician use. Thus, newer medications or findings may not be listed in this appendix. If a student is on medication, request parent permission to contact the child's physician regarding the prescribed medication. Ask the physician to explain the purpose of the medication and its side effects. Establish a way of communicating with the physician or someone in her or his office in case of future questions.

Another informative source for medications is the *Physicians' Desk Reference* (published by Medical Economics, Montvale, New Jersey). This book is updated each year. It can be found in libraries and on the Internet (http://www.pdr.net). The school nurse might have one. If not, it would be an appropriate reference addition for the library, health room, or principal's office. This book details all medications approved for use in the United States, including their purposes, dosages, effects, and possible side effects.

This appendix lists *psychotropic medications,* which are used to treat emotional and behavior disorders. Two basic principles apply to the use of psychotrophic medications with children and adolescents. First, medication is never used in isolation. Appropriate psychological, social, and educational intervention may also be needed. Second, the appropriate medication for treating adults with emotional and/or behavior disorders is usually based on an established diagnosis. If an adult has an anxiety disorder, depression, or a psychotic disorder, his or her physician knows which medications are appropriate for the diagnosis. At the beginning of the 21st century, medications to treat children and adolescents are often prescribed based on presenting behavior rather than a diagnosis. No specific medications exist for a learning disability, autism, mental retardation, and certain other diagnostic categories. If a child or adolescent with one of these disorders also demonstrates anxiety, depression, anger-control problems, or aggressive behaviors, medications are used to address these behaviors. If a child has multiple diagnoses, for example, attention-deficit/hyperactivity disorder, an anxiety disorder, and tics, it may be necessary to use two or more medications to address each disorder.

Please note that this appendix is not comprehensive; it should be used for general information only. It is beyond the scope of the appendix to cover medications or medication groups for all disorders mentioned in this book. If a student has one of the diagnoses discussed in this book and receives medication, his or her teacher should discuss the medication(s) with the student's parents. If the parents are unable to provide adequate information, the teacher should request permission to speak with or to receive information from the physician who prescribes the medication. Ideally, specific information on any student should be obtained from his or her prescribing physician.

ANXIETY DISORDERS

(Chapters 10 and 13)

Selective serotonin reuptake inhibitors (SSRIs)

Generic name:	Fluoxetine
Brand name:	**Prozac**
How supplied:	10 and 20 milligram (mg) capsules
	Liquid form
Usual dose:	10 to 20 mg per day (possibly less for children)
Side effects:	Nausea, weight loss, anxiety, nervousness, insomnia, excessive sweating, sedation

Generic name:	Sertraline
Brand name:	**Zoloft**
How supplied:	50 and 100 mg tablets
Usual dose:	25 to 50 mg per day (possibly less for children)
Side effects:	Same as fluoxetine

Generic name:	Fluvoxamine
Brand name:	**Luvox**
How supplied:	50 and 100 mg tablets
Usual dose:	25 to 50 mg per day (possibly less for children)
Side effects:	Same as fluoxetine

Generic name:	Paroxetine
Brand name:	**Paxil**
How supplied:	10, 20, and 30 mg tablets
Usual dose:	10 to 20 mg per day (possibly less for children)
Side effects:	Same as fluoxetine

Generic name:	Citalopram
Brand name:	**Celexa**
How supplied:	20 mg tablets
Usual dose:	20 mg per day (possibly less for children)
Side effects:	Same as fluoxetine

Other

The usage of the next medications is so individualized for children and adolescents that the reader is referred to the prescribing physician for specific details.

Generic name: Diazepam
Brand name: **Valium**

Generic name: Alprazolam
Brand name: **Xanax**

Generic name: Clonazepam
Brand name: **Klonopin**

Generic name: Buspirone
Brand name: **BuSpar**

See also the following Appendix B entries: "Obsessive-Compulsive Disorder" and "Panic Disorder."

ATTENTION-DEFICIT/HYPERACTIVITY DISORDER

(Chapter 4)

Generic name: Methylphenidate
Brand name: **Concerta, Metadate, Ritalin**
How supplied: 4-hour tablets (Ritalin): 5, 10, and 20 mg
                 8-hour tablets (Metadate ER): 10 and 20 mg
                 8-hour capsules (Metadate CD): 20 mg
                 8-hour capsules (Ritalin LA): 20, 30, and 40 mg
                 12-hour capsules (Concerta): 18, 27, 36, and 54 mg
Usual dose: Must be individually determined
Side effects: Typical side effects include loss of appetite, difficulty going to sleep at night, headaches, stomachaches, and motor tics. Other less frequent side effects include a "rebound" when the last dose wears off (with increased hyperactivity) and the onset of anxiety or depression. Two side effects suggest that the dose is too high for the individual: 1) emotional lability (e.g., more irritable or tearful) and 2) overfocusing, with a resulting "spacey" appearance.

Generic name: Dextroamphetamine
Brand name: **Dexedrine, DextroStat**
How supplied: 4-hour tablets (Dexedrine): 5 mg
                 4-hour tablets (DextroStat): 5 and 10 mg
                 8-hour capsules (Dexedrine): 5, 10, and 15 mg
Usual dose: Must be individually determined
Side effects: Same as methylphenidate

Generic name:　　Dextroamphetamine and levoamphetamine
Brand name:　　**Adderall**
How supplied:　　4-hour tablets: 5, 7.5, 10, 12.5, 15, 20, and 30 mg
　　　　　　　　8-hour capsules (Adderall XR): 5, 10, 15, 20, 25, and 30 mg
Usual dose:　　　Must be individually determined
Side effects:　　Same as methylphenidate

Generic name:　　Dexmethylphenidate
Brand name:　　**Focalin**
How supplied:　　4-hour tablets: 2.5, 5, and 10 mg
Usual dosage:　　Must be individually determined
Side effects:　　Same as methylphenidate

Generic name:　　Atomoxetine
Brand name:　　**Strattera**
How supplied:　　10, 18, 25, 40, 60 mg tablets
Usual dosage:　　Must be individually determined
Side effects:　　Same as methylphenidate

Generic name:　　Imipramine
Brand name:　　**Tofranil**
How supplied:　　10, 25, and 50 mg tablets; 75, 100, 125, and 150 mg capsules
Usual dose:　　　Must be individually determined
Side effects:　　Fatigue, constipation, dry mouth, and blurred vision are common. Waking up very early and not being able to go back to sleep occurs less frequently. It is important to monitor liver functioning and the electrical pattern of the heart while an individual is taking this medication.

Generic name:　　Nortriptyline
Brand name:　　**Pamelor**
How supplied:　　10, 25, 50, and 75 mg tablets
　　　　　　　　Oral solution
Usual dose:　　　Must be individually determined
Side effects:　　Same as imipramine

Generic name:　　Desipramine
Brand name:　　**Norpramin**
How supplied:　　10, 25, 50, 75, 100, and 150 mg tablets
Usual dose:　　　Must be individually determined
Side effects:　　Same as imipramine

Generic name: Amitriptyline
Brand name: **Elavil**
How supplied: 10, 25, 50, 75, and 100 mg tablets
Usual dose: Must be individually determined
Side effects: Same as imipramine

Generic name: Bupropion
Brand name: **Wellbutrin**
How supplied: 75 and 100 mg tablets
Usual dose: Must be individually determined
Side effects: Same as imipramine

Generic name: Clonidine
Brand name: **Catapres**
How supplied: 0.1, 0.2, and 0.3 mg tablets
                   Transdermal patch at 0.1, 0.2, and 0.3 mg
Usual dose: Must be individually determined
Side effects: Fatigue, sedation, reduction of blood pressure

Generic name: Guanfacine
Brand name: **Tenex**
How supplied: 1 and 2 mg tablets
Usual dose: Must be individually determined
Side effects: Same as clonidine

INTERMITTENT EXPLOSIVE DISORDER—AGGRESSIVE BEHAVIORS

(Chapters 2 and 14)

SSRIs (see "Anxiety Disorders")

Atypical anitpsychotics (see "Mood Disorders")

Other

Generic name: Propranolol
Brand name: **Inderal**
How supplied: 10, 20, 40, 60, and 80 mg tablets
Usual dose: Must be individualized
Side effects: Insomnia, lethargy, weakness, fatigue, nightmares; cardiac
                   functioning must be monitored

MOOD DISORDERS

(Chapters 11 and 13)

SSRIs (see "Anxiety Disorders")

Tricyclic Antidepressants

Tricyclic antidepressants were discussed under "Attention-Deficit/Hyperactivity Disorder" and include imipramine, nortriptyline, desipramine, and amitriptyline. When used as antidepressants, the dose is significantly higher. Ask the prescribing physician for specific details.

Other

Generic name:	Bupropion
Brand name:	**Wellbutrin**

This medication was discussed under "Attention-Deficit/Hyperactivity Disorder." When used for depression, the dose is higher than when used for attention-deficit/hyperactivity disorder. Ask the prescribing physician for specific details.

Special Notes on Bipolar Disorder (Chapter 11)

Children and adolescents with bipolar disorder might have two types of mood swings. They might cycle from being depressed to being happy, euphoric, and hypomanic. Or, they might cycle from being calm to being agitated, angry, and full of rage. Some individuals frequently cycle up and down within each pattern. Medication is based on the pattern of cycling. It is often difficult to discern which medication or group of medication can help control the mood swings. Often, a combination of medications is used. Thus, this subsection describes the "families" of medications considered for treating bipolar disorder. Because dosages and side effects are so individualized, the reader is referred to the prescribing physician for specific details.

For upswings (euphoria to hypomania and anger to rage)

Two families of medications might be considered. The first family is anticonvulsants, which are also used to treat seizure disorders; the second is atypical psychotics, which are a new generation of medications that can also be used to treat psychotic disorders. Sometimes, it is necessary to use one or two medications from each family.

Anticonvulsants

Generic name:	Lithium carbonate
Brand name:	**Eskalith**
Generic name:	Valproic acid
Brand name:	**Depakote**
Generic name:	Carbamazepine
Brand name:	**Tegretol**
Generic name:	Gabapentin
Brand name:	**Neurontin**

Generic name: Lamotrigine
Brand name: **Lamictal**

Generic name: Oxcarbazepine
Brand name: **Trileptal**

Generic name: Tiagabine
Brand name: **Gabitril**

Atypical Antipsychotics

Generic name: Risperidone
Brand name: **Risperdal**

Generic name: Olanzapine
Brand name: **Zyprexa**

Generic name: Quetiapine
Brand name: **Seroquel**

Generic name: Ziprasidone
Brand name: **Geodon**

For the down swings (depression)
SSRIs should not be used to treat depression associated with bipolar disorder, as these medications might exacerbate a manic or rage reaction. Other medications listed under "Mood Disorders" might be used; bupropion (Wellbutrin) is considered most frequently.

OBSESSIVE-COMPULSIVE DISORDER

(Chapter 10)

SSRIs (see "Anxiety Disorders")

Other

Generic name: Clomipramine
Brand name: **Anafranil**
How supplied: 25, 50, and 75 mg capsules
Usual dose: 25 to 100 mg per day
Side effects: Fatigue, dizziness, tremors, headache, sleep disturbance, increased sweating, possible seizures at higher doses

PANIC DISORDER

(Chapters 10)

SSRIs (see "Anxiety Disorders")

Other

Generic name:	Alprazolam
Brand name:	**Xanax**
How supplied:	0.25, 0.50, 1, and 2 mg tablets
Usual dose:	Must be individualized
Side effects:	Drowsiness, lightheadedness

Generic name:	Hydroxyzine
Brand name:	**Atarax**
How supplied:	10, 25, 50, and 100 mg tablets
Usual dose:	Must be individualized
Side effects:	Sedation, dry mouth

Generic name:	Clonazepam
Brand name:	**Klonopin**
How supplied:	0.5, 1, and 2 mg tablets
Usual dose:	Must be individualized
Side effects:	Sleepiness, depression, dizziness, anxiety, reduced cognitive functioning

Generic name:	Buspirone
Brand name:	**BuSpar**
How supplied:	5 and 10 mg tablets
Usual dose:	Must be individualized
Side effects:	Dizziness, drowsiness, nausea, headache, insomnia, light-headedness

PERVASIVE DEVELOPMENTAL DISORDERS

(Chapters 5 and 6)

Atypical antipsychotics (see "Mood Disorders")

Other

Generic name:	Thioridazine
Brand name:	**Mellaril**
How supplied:	10, 15, 25, 50, 100, 150, and 200 mg tablets
	Concentrate, suspension
Usual dose:	Must be individualized

Side effects:	Sedation and dulled thinking are common. Careful monitoring of liver functioning and blood cells is necessary. Neurological disorders might occur: dystonia (i.e., an increase in muscular tone, with spasms of muscles of the neck, mouth, and tongue) and oculogyric crisis (i.e., eyes rolling upward and remaining in that position). Tardive dyskinesia (i.e., involuntary movements in one or more body areas: face, lips, jaw, tongue, upper or lower extremities, trunk) occurs much less frequently but is possible after prolonged treatment.

Generic name:	Chlorpromazine
Brand name:	**Thorazine**
How supplied:	10, 25, 50, 100, and 200 mg tablets
	Syrup, concentrate
Usual dose:	Must be individualized
Side effects:	Same as thioridazine

Generic name:	Haloperidol
Brand name:	**Haldol**
How supplied:	0.5, 1, 2, 5, 10, and 20 mg tablets
	Concentrate
Usual dose:	Must be individualized
Side effects:	Same as thioridazine

Generic name:	Trifluoperazine
Brand name:	**Stelazine**
How supplied:	1, 2, 5, and 10 mg tablets
	Concentrate
Usual dose:	Must be individualized
Side effects:	Same as thioridazine

Generic name:	Fluphenazine
Brand name:	**Prolixin**
How supplied:	1, 2.5, 5, and 10 mg tablets
	Elixir, concentrate
Usual dose:	Must be individualized
Side effects:	Same as thioridazine

Generic name:	Pimozide
Brand name:	**Orap**
How supplied:	2 mg tablets
Usual dose:	Must be individualized
Side effects:	Same as thioridazine

TIC DISORDERS

(Chapter 2)

Haloperidol (**Haldol**) (see "Pervasive Developmental Disorders")

Pimozide (**Orap**) (see "Pervasive Developmental Disorders")

Clonidine (**Catapres**) (see "Attention-Deficit/Hyperactivity Disorder")

Guanfacine (**Tenex**) (see "Attention-Deficit/Hyperactivity Disorder")

Resources

GENERAL MENTAL HEALTH ISSUES AND ORGANIZATIONS

**American Academy of
Child and Adolescent Psychiatry**
3615 Wisconsin Avenue, NW
Washington, DC 20016
202-966-7300 (telephone)
202-966-2891 (fax)
http://www.aacap.org

National professional medical association dedicated to treating and improving the quality of life for children, adolescents, and families affected by mental health issues. Provides fact sheets about mental health issues that affect children, adolescents, and families.

American Psychiatric Association
1000 Wilson Boulevard, Suite 1825
Arlington, VA 22209
703-907-7300 (telephone)
http://www.psych.org

Medical specialty society that is recognized world wide. Member physicians work together to ensure humane care and effective treatment for all people with mental health issues.

American Psychological Association
750 First Street, NE
Washington, DC 20002
202-336-5510 (telephone)
800-374-2721 (toll free)
202-336-6123 (TDD/TTY)
http://www.apa.org

Scientific and professional organization that represents psychology in the United States.

**Justice In Mental
Health Organization (JIMHO)**
421 Seymour Street
Lansing, MI 48933
517-371-5770 (fax)
http://hometown.aol.com/jimhofw/jimho.htm

Nonprofit, self-help organization and advocacy group that offers a network of support. It advocates for the rights of people with mental health issues.

**National Alliance
for the Mentally Ill (NAMI)**
Colonial Place Three
2107 Wilson Boulevard, Suite 300
Arlington, VA 22201
703-524-7600 (telephone)
800-950-NAMI (toll free)
703-516-7227 (TDD)
703-524-9094 (fax)

Nonprofit grass roots organization of consumers, families, and friends of people with severe mental health issues. Provides self-help, support, and advocacy.

**National Association
of School Psychologists**
4340 East West Highway, Suite 402
Bethesda, MD 20814
301-657-0270 (telephone)

301-657-0275 (fax)
http://www.nasponline.org

Member organization that represents and supports school psychology through leadership to enhance the mental health and educational competence of all children.

National Institute of Mental Health

Office of Communications
6001 Executive Boulevard, Room 8184
MSC 9663
Bethesda, MD 20892
301-443-4513 (telephone)
866-615-NIMH (toll free)
301-443-8431 (TTY)
301-443-4279 (fax)
http://www.nimh.nih.gov

Component of the National Institutes of Health that funds research and disseminates information on the causes, occurrence, and treatment of mental illness.

National Mental Health Association (NMHA)

2001 North Beauregard Street, 12th Floor
Alexandria, VA 22311
703-684-7722 (telephone)
800-969-NMHA (Mental Health Resource Center)
800-433-5959 (TTY)
703-684-5968 (fax)
http://www.nmha.org

Nonprofit organization that addresses all aspects of mental health and mental illness and works to improve the mental health of all Americans.

SPECIFIC MENTAL HEALTH ISSUES

Anxiety

Anxieties.com
http://www.anxieties.com

Free self-help site regarding various types of anxiety disorders.

Anxiety Disorders Association of America (ADAA)

8730 Georgia Avenue, Suite 600
Silver Spring, MD 20910
240-485-1001 (telephone)
240-485-1035 (fax)
http://www.adaa.org

National nonprofit organization that promotes the early diagnosis, treatment, and cure of anxiety disorders and is committed to improving the lives of the people who have them.

The Anxiety Panic Internet Resource (tAPir)

http://www.algy.com/anxiety/index.html

Grass roots web site dedicated to providing information, relief, and support for those recovering from anxiety.

Canadian Network for Mood and Anxiety Treatments

http://www.canmat.org

Extensive, cohesive network linking health care professionals across Canada who have a special interest in mood and anxiety disorders.

National Anxiety Foundation (NAF)

3135 Custer Drive
Lexington, KY 40517
http://www.lexington-on-line.com/naf.html

An organization whose web site offers educational information about anxiety disorders.

Social Phobia/Social Anxiety Association (SP/SSA)

2058 E. Topeka Drive
Phoenix, AZ 85024
http://www.socialphobia.org

Nonprofit organization that meets the growing needs of people who have social phobia/social anxiety.

Virtual Hospital
http://www.vh.org/pediatric
/patient/pediatrics/cqqa
/schoolanxiety.html

Addresses some of the most common questions about school anxiety.

Asperger Syndrome

Asperger's Connection
The Shriver Center
200 Trapelo Road
Waltham, MA 02452
781-642-0229 (telephone)
http://www.ddleadership.org
/aspergers

An interactive web site that allows individuals with Asperger syndrome, their families, and others to interact and support one another as well as to share ideas and problem-solving strategies and suggestions.

**MAAP Services for
the Autism Spectrum**
Post Office Box 524
Crown Point, IN 46307
219-662-1311 (telephone)
219-662-0638 (fax)
http://www.maapservices.org

A nonprofit organization dedicated to providing information and advice to families of individuals with autism, Asperger syndrome, and pervasive developmental disorder (PDD).

Attention-Deficit/ Hyperactivity Disorder

ADHD News
Post Office Box 1596
Pleasanton, CA 94566
http://www.adhdnews.com

A community for families dealing with attention-deficit/hyperactivity disorder (ADHD) and attention deficit disorder (ADD) that offering tips, testimonials and information.

**Attention Deficit
Disorder Association (ADDA)**
Post Office Box 543
Pottstown, PA 19464
484-945-2101 (telephone)
610-970-7520 (fax)
http://www.add.org

National nonprofit organization that focuses on individuals and families and provides referrals to local support groups, holds national conferences and symposiums, and offers materials on ADD and related issues.

**The Attention Deficit
Information Network (AD-IN)**
58 Prince Street
Needham, MA 02492
781-455-9895 (telephone)
http://www.addinfonetwork.com

Nonprofit volunteer organization with a network of affiliated support groups that provides information and support to families, children, adults, and professionals. Involved in an annual conference.

**Children and Adults with
Attention Deficit Disorder (CHADD)**
8181 Professional Place, Suite 150
Landover, MD 20785
800-233-4050 (toll free)
301-306-7090 (fax)
http://www.chadd.org

National nonprofit membership organization that provides information, sponsors conferences, and holds meetings and support groups.

Autism

Autism Research Institute (ARI)
4182 Adams Avenue
San Diego, CA 92116
619-563-6840 (fax)
http://www.autism.com/ari
/contents.html

Nonprofit organization that conducts and disseminates research concerning the causes of autism and methods for preventing, diagnosing, and treating autism and other severe behavioral disorders of childhood.

The Autism Society of America
7910 Woodmont Avenue, Suite 300
Bethesda, MD 20814
301-657-0881 (telephone)
800-3AUTISM (toll free)
http://www.autism-society.org

Provides information and referral regarding autism, with a working network of local chapters in nearly every state.

Autism-PDD Resource Net
http://www.autism-pdd.net

Web site that addresses the key issues associated with autism spectrum disorders

Cure Autism Now (CAN) Foundation
5455 Wilshire Boulevard, Suite 715
Los Angeles, CA 90036
323-549-0500 (telephone)
888-8-AUTISM (toll free)
323-549-0547 (fax)
http://www.canfoundation.org

Organization of parents, clinicians, and leading scientists committed to accelerating the pace of biomedical research in autism through present research, education, and outreach.

MAAP Services for the Autism Spectrum
Post Office Box 524
Crown Point, IN 46307
219-662-1311 (telephone)
219-662-0638 (fax)
www.maapservices.org

Nonprofit organization dedicated to providing information and advice to families of individuals with autism, Asperger syndrome, and pervasive developmental disorder (PDD).

Eating Disorders

Academy for Eating Disorders (AED)
6728 Old McLean Village Drive
McLean, VA 22101
703-556-9222 (telephone)
556-8729 (fax)
http://www.aedweb.org

Promotes effective treatments and prevention initiatives, stimulates research, and sponsors international conferences.

Anorexia Nervosa and Related Eating Disorders (ANRED)
http://www.anred.com

Nonprofit organization whose web site provides information about the following eating disorders topics: definitions, statistics, warning signs, etiology, and complications.

Harvard Eating Disorders Center (HEDC)
WACC 725
15 Parkman Street
Boston, MA. 02114
617-236-7766 (telephone)
http://www.hedc.org

A dynamic, interdisciplinary community dedicated to cutting-edge research, education, and public discourse in the field of eating disorders.

**National Association
of Anorexia Nervosa and
Associated Disorders (ANAD)**
847-831-3438 (telephone)
847-433-4632 (fax)
http://www.anad.org

National nonprofit organization dedicated to alleviating the problems of eating disorders and promoting healthy lifestyles. Distributes listings of therapists, hospitals, and informative materials; also sponsors support groups, conferences, advocacy, campaigns, research, and a crisis hotline.

**National Eating
Disorders Association (NEDA)**
603 Stewart St., Suite 803
Seattle, WA 98101
206-382-3587 (telephone)
http://www.edap.org

Not-for-profit organization that works to prevent eating disorders, provides treatment referrals, and provides general information on eating disorders and body image and weight issues.

**National Eating Disorders
Screening Program (NEDSP)**
One Washington St. Suite 304
Wellesley Hills, MA 02181
781-239-0071 (telephone)
http://www.nmisp.org/eat.htm

Free and anonymous public outreach and education program that offers the opportunity to get information, take a written self-test, meet with a health professional, and get a referral for further evaluation.

*Mood Disorders
and Psychotic Disorders*

**Depression and Bipolar
Support Alliance (DBSA)**
730 North Franklin Street, Suite 501

Chicago, IL 60610
312-642-0049 (telephone)
800-826-3632 (toll free)
312-642-7243 (fax)
http://www.dbsalliance.org

Provides information on mood disorders, suicide prevention, and support groups.

**National Alliance for
Research on Schizophrenia
and Depression (NARSAD)**
60 Cutter Mill Road, Suite 404
Great Neck, NY 11021
800-829-8289 (toll free)
516-487-6930 (fax)
http://www.narsad.org

Supports research into the causes, cures, treatments, and prevention of severe psychiatric disorders and provides information on mental health issues such as schizophrenia and depression.

Schizophrenia.com
http://schizophrenia.com

Web community dedicated to providing high-quality information, support, and education to family members, caregivers, and individuals whose lives have been affected by schizophrenia.

**Suicide Awareness
Voices of Education (SAVE)**
7317 Cahill Road, Suite 207
Minneapolis, MN 55439
952-946-7998 (telephone)
800-SUICIDE (toll free)
http://www.save.org

Provides education about suicide prevention and supports those touched by suicide. Committed to the education of the general public about mental health issues that can result in suicide if left untreated.

Peer Problems

Adolescent Transition Program (ATP)
http://www.uoregon.edu/~exper
/honors/2003/Cost%20Analysis%
20of%20Adolescent%20Transition
%20Program_files/frame
.htm#slide0001.htm

Intervention program that promotes self-regulation.

Anger Coping Program
http://www.prevention.psu.edu
/ACP.htm

Intervention program that addresses anger management.

Big Brothers Big Sisters of America
230 North 13th Street
Philadelphia, PA 19107
215-567-7000 (telephone)
215-567-0394 (fax)
http://www.bbbsa.org

Organization that develops mentoring relationships.

Bullying Prevention Program (BPP)
Institute on Family and
Neighborhood Life
Clemson University
158 Poole Agricultural Center
Clemson, SC 29634
http://www.colorado.edu/cspv
/blueprints/model/programs/BPP
.html

Intervention program that builds socioemotional and cognitive skills.

Child Development Project (CDP)
Developmental Studies Center
2000 Embarcadero, Suite 305
Oakland, CA 94606-5300
510-533-0213 (telephone)
510-464-3670 (fax)

http://www.devstu.org/cdp
Intervention program that builds socioemotional and cognitive skills.

**Consortium on Child
and Adolescent Research**
http://www.nimh.nih.gov/childhp
/prfan.cfm

Web site sponsored by the National Institute of Mental Health regarding the importance of social and emotional competence early in the school years.

**Earlscourt
School-Based Program (ESP)**
http://www.hamfish.org/programs
/id/48

Intervention program that addresses aggressive and disruptive behaviors.

**Effects of Domestic
Violence on Children's
Social and Emotional Development**
http://www.acf.hhs.gov/programs
/cb/publications/compendium/nichd
/nichda3.htm

Article regarding the effects of domestic violence and children's social and emotional competence.

Fast Track
http://www.fasttrackproject.org

Intervention program that promotes skills for children at risk of developing peer problems.

First Steps
Family and Social Services
Administration
Division of Family and Children
Bureau of Child Development
402 West Washington Street,
Room W 386

Indianapolis, IN 46204
317-232-1144 (telephone)
http://www.state.in.us/fssa
/first_step

Intervention program that promotes adaptive behavior.

I Can Problem Solve (ICPS)
NCO Youth and Family Services
1305 W Oswego Rd
Naperville, IL 60540
630-961-2992 (telephone)
http://www.ncoyouth.org/icps.htm

Intervention program that builds socioemotional and cognitive skills.

The Incredible Years
1411 8th Avenue West
Seattle, WA 98119
206-285-7565 (telephone)
(888) 506-3562 (toll free)
http://www.incredibleyears.com

Intervention for increasing social and emotional competence and reducing conduct problems.

**Linking the Interests of
Families and Teachers (LIFT)**
Oregon Social Learning Center
160 East 4th Avenue
Eugene, OR 97401
541-485-2711 (telephone)
541-485-7087 (fax)
http://www.oslc.org/dproj.html#lift

Intervention program that develops social and problem-solving skills for children and addresses discipline and supervision issues.

**Peer Rejection and
Aggression and Early Starter
Models of Conduct Disorder**
http://www.findarticles.com/cf_0
/m0902/3_30/86874929/p1/article
.jhtml?term=%2BPeer+%2BMediation

Article on peer relationship and conduct problems in children.

**Responding in Peaceful
and Positive Ways (RIPP)**
http://www.prevention.psu.edu
/RIPP.htm
http://vinst.umdnj.edu/sdfs
/Abstract.asp?Code=RIPP

Intervention program that promotes nonviolence in adolescents.

**School Transitional
Environment Project (STEP)**
http://www.prevention.psu.edu
/STEP.htm
http://www.colorado.edu/cspv
/blueprints/promising/programs/BP
P12.html

Intervention program that focuses on successful transitions from elementary to middle schools or middle to high schools.

Seattle Social Development Project
http://depts.washington.edu/ssdp

Intervention program that develops children's social skills and fosters bonding.

Second Step
Committee for Children
568 First Avenue South, Suite 600
Seattle, WA 98104
800-634-4449 (toll free)
206-343-1445 (fax)
http://www.cfchildren.org
/program_ss.shtml

Intervention program that teaches anger management, empathy, and impulse control.

**Social Competence
Promotion Program for**

Young Adolescents (SCPP-YA)
http://www.dsgonline.com
/WebEffects/dhtml_slide_tree/Title
V_MPG_Table_Ind_Rec.asp?ID=206

Intervention program that builds socioemotional and cognitive skills.

**Social Decision Making/
Problem Solving (SDM/PS) Program**
University of Medicine and Dentistry
of New Jersey
University Behavioral Health Care
Behavioral Research and Training
Institute
151 Centennial Avenue, Suite 1140
Piscataway, NJ 08854
732-235-9280 (telephone)
732-235-9277 (fax)
http://www2.umdnj.edu/spsweb

Intervention program that teaches skill
building to bolster resilience.

Substance Abuse

Alcoholics Anonymous (AA)
Grand Central Station
Post Office Box 459
New York, NY 10163
http://www.alcoholics-
anonymous.org

Fellowship of individuals who share
their experiences with each other to
solve their common problem and help
others to recover from alcoholism.

**Center for Substance
Abuse Research (CESAR)**
4321 Hartwick Road, Suite 501
College Park, MD 20740
301-405-9770 (telephone)
301-403-8342 (fax)
http://www.cesar.umd.edu

Center that addresses the problems that
substance abuse creates for individuals,
families, and communities.

**Center on Addiction
and Substance Abuse (CASA)**
633 Third Avenue, 19th Floor
New York, NY 10017
212-841-5200 (telephone)
http://www.casacolumbia.org

National organization that brings
together all of the professional disciplines needed to study and combat
abuse of all substances in all sectors
of society.

Narcotics Anonymous (NA)
World Service Office
Post Office Box 9999
Van Nuys, CA 91409
818-773-9999 (telephone)
818-700-0700 (fax)
http://www.na.org

An international community-based
association of individuals recovering
from drug addiction.

**National Council on Alcoholism
and Drug Dependence (NCADD)**
20 Exchange Place, Suite 2902
New York, NY 10005
212-269-7797 (telephone)
800-NCA-CALL (24-hour affiliate
referral)
212-269-7510 (fax)
http://www.ncadd.org

Organization that provides education
and information to the public and advocates prevention, intervention, and
treatment.

**National Substance
Abuse Web Index (NSAWI)**
http://ncadi.samhsa.gov/dbases
/nsawi.aspx

Clearinghouse for information about
substance abuse prevention and addiction treatment.

Substance Abuse and Mental Health Services Administration (SAMHSA)
Room 12-105 Parklawn Building
5600 Fishers Lane
Rockville, MD 20857
Center for Mental Health Services:
301-443-0001 (telephone)
Center for Substance Abuse Prevention:
301-443-0365 (telephone)
Center for Substance Abuse Treatment:
301-443-5700 (telephone)
http://www.samhsa.gov/index.html

U.S. federal agency charged with improving the quality and availability of prevention, treatment, and rehabilitative services to reduce illness, death, disability, and cost to society resulting from substance abuse and mental illness.

OTHER DISABILITIES AND SPECIAL EDUCATION SERVICES

American Speech-Language-Hearing Association (ASHA)
10801 Rockville Pike
Rockville, MD 20852
800-638-8255 (voice/TTY)
http://www.asha.org

Membership organization comprised of speech-language pathologists and audiologists that provides information and referrals to the public on speech, language, communication, and hearing disorders.

Association of Educational Therapists (AET)
1804 West Burbank Boulevard
Burbank, CA 91506
800-286-4267 (toll free)
818-843-7423 (fax)
http://www.aetonline.org

National professional organization that maintains standards for professional educational therapists.

The Council for Exceptional Children (CEC)
1110 North Glebe Road, Suite 300
Arlington, VA 22201
703-620-3660 (telephone)
888-CEC-SPED (toll free)
703-264-9494 (fax)
http://www.cec.sped.org

Nonprofit membership organization that has 17 specialized divisions. CEC and its divisions hold conferences and publish newsletters and journals.

Council for Learning Disabilities (CLD)
Post Office Box 4014
Leesburg, VA 20177
571-258-1010 (telephone)
571-258-1011 (fax)
http://www.cldinternational.org

International organization dedicated to assisting professionals who work in the field of learning disabilities. *Learning Disabilities Quarterly*, a professional publication, is available through CLD.

The International Dyslexia Association
8600 La Salle Road
Chester Building, Suite 382
Baltimore, MD 21286
410-296-0232 (telephone)
800-ABCD-123 (toll free)
410-321-5069 (fax)
http://www.interdys.org

International nonprofit membership organization that offers training in language programs and provides publications relating to dyslexia. Chapters are located in most states.

Learning Disabilities Association of America (LDA)
4156 Library Road
Pittsburgh, PA 15234
412-341-1515 (telephone)
412-344-0224 (fax)
http://www.ldanatl.org

A nonprofit, volunteer organization made of parents, individuals with learning disabilities, and professionals. There is a national office, and there are chapters in each state and in most major cities. LDA advocates for individuals with learning disabilities and their families, provides direct help to individuals and families, provides literature and other resources, and encourages research on learning disabilities.

Learning Disabilities Association of Canada (LDAC)
323 Chapel Street
Ottawa, Ontario K1N 7Z2
Canada
613-238-5721 (telephone)
613-235-5391 (fax)
http://educ.queensu.ca/~lda

Nonprofit membership organization with provincial and territorial offices that conducts programs and provides information for children and adults with learning disabilities. Resources include books and pamphlets that may also be useful to U.S. residents.

National Association for the Education of Young Children (NAEYC)
1509 16th Street, NW
Washington, DC 20036
800-424-2460 (toll free)
http://www.naeyc.org

National membership organization that focuses on children from birth to age 8. Sponsors an annual conference; publishes a bimonthly journal; and has a catalog of books, brochures, videos, and posters.

National Association of State Directors of Special Education (NASDSE)
1800 Diagonal Road, Suite 320
Alexandria, VA 22314
703-519-3800 (telephone)
703 519-7008 (TDD)
703-519-3808 (fax)
http://www.nasdse.org

Not-for-profit corporation that promotes and supports educational programs for students with disabilities and holds annual meetings.

National Center for Law and Learning Disabilities (NCLLD)
Post Office Box 368
Cabin John, MD 20818
301-469-8308 (telephone)
http://www.his.com/~plath3/nclld.htm

Nonprofit organization that provides education, advocacy, analysis of legal issues, policy recommendations, and resources materials.

National Center for Learning Disabilities (NCLD)
381 Park Avenue South, Suite 1401
New York, NY 10016
212-545-7510 (telephone)
888-575-7373 (toll free)
212-545-9665 (fax)
http://www.ncld.org

National nonprofit membership organization that offers a free information and referral service, conducts educational programs, raises public awareness of learning disabilities, and advocates for improved legislation and services for those with learning disabilities.

National Center to Improve the Tools of Educators (NCITE)

805 Lincoln Street
Eugene, OR 97401
http://idea.uoregon.edu/~ncite

Organization that is funded by the U.S. Department of Education. Dedicated to the improvement of instructional methods and materials. Publishes articles on educational practices.

National Dissemination Center for Children with Disabilities
P.O. Box 1492
Washington, DC 20013
800-695-0285 (telephone/TTY)
202-884-8441 (fax)
http://www.nichcy.org

Clearinghouse that provides information on disabilities and disability-related issues. Formerly called the National Information Center for Children and Youth with Disabilities (NICHCY).

National Institute of Child Health and Human Development (NICHD)
NICHD Information Resource Center
Post Office Box 3006
Rockville, MD 20847
800-370-2943 (toll free)
301-496-7101 (fax)
http://www.nichd.nih.gov

Organization that provides reviews of literature and information related to NICHD research.

Office of Special Education and Rehabilitative Services (OSERS)
U.S. Department of Education
400 Maryland Avenue, SW
Washington, DC 20202
202-205-5465 (telephone)
http://www.ed.gov/about/offices/list/osers/index.html

Federal office providing information about special education programs, vocational rehabilitation programs, and information about national and international research regarding disabilities and rehabilitation.

Schwab Foundation for Learning
1650 South Amphlett Road, Suite 300
San Mateo, CA 94402
650-655-2410 (telephone)
800-230-0988 (toll free)
650-655-2411 (fax)
http://www.schwablearning.org

Membership organization that provides information and referral to national and local resources as well as research and guidance for parents, teachers, clinicians, and others who work with children who have learning differences.

State Departments of Education

State Departments of Education can provide information about Individuals with Disabilities Education Act (IDEA) implementation requirements and regulations. Educators should contact directory assistance in their state capitol for further information.

PARENT AND FAMILY RESOURCES

Families and Advocates Partnership for Education (FAPE)
8161 Normandale Boulevard
Minneapolis, MN 55437
952-838-9000 (telephone)
952-838-0190 (TTY)
952-838-0199 (fax)
http://www.fape.org

Partnership that aims to improve the educational outcomes for children with disabilities. Links families, advocates, and self-advocates to communicate the new focus of the Individuals with Disabilities Education Act (IDEA).

**Federation of Families
for Children's Mental Health**
1101 King Street, Suite 420
Alexandria, VA 22314
703-684-7710 (telephone)
703-836-1040 (fax)
http://www.ffcmh.org

National parent-run nonprofit organization focused on the needs of children and youth with emotional, behavioral, or mental health disorders and their families.

**KidsPeace: National
Center for Overcoming Crisis**
5300 KidsPeace Drive
Orefield, PA 18069
800-334-4KID (toll free)
http://www.kidspeace.org

A private not-for-profit charity dedicated to serving the critical behavioral and mental health needs of children, preadolescents, and teenagers.

**National Parent
Network on Disabilities (NPND)**
1727 King Street, Suite 305
Alexandria, VA 22314
703-684-6763 (telephone/TDD)
703-836-1232 (fax)
http://web.syr.edu/~thechp/
npnd.htm

Membership organization open to all agencies, organizations, parent centers, parent groups, professionals, and individuals concerned with the quality of life for people with disabilities.

**National Parent to Parent
Support and Information System**
Post Office Box 907
Blue Ridge, GA 30513
706-632-8822 (telephone/TDD)
800-651-1151 (toll free)

706-632-8830 (fax)
http://www.nppsis.org

Networking program matching parents with other parents based on the disabilities of their children.

Not My Kid
333 West Indian School Road
Phoenix, AZ 85013
602-652-0163 (telephone)
602-266-1958 (fax)
http://www.notmykid.org

Dedicated to facilitating improved understanding about youth behavioral health issues, including suicide, drug abuse, eating disorders, and depression.

**Parents Engaged
in Education Reform (PEER)**
Federation for Children with Special Needs
1135 Tremont Street, Suite 420
Boston, MA 02120
617-236-7210 (telephone)
617-572-2094 (fax)
http://www.fcsn.org/peer

A national technical assistance project with the purpose of increasing the participation of parents of children with disabilities and their organizations in school reform efforts.

**Parent Training and
Information Project (PTI)**
Federation for Children with Special Needs
1135 Tremont Street, Suite 420
Boston, MA 02120
617-236-7210 (telephone)
617-572-2094 (fax)
http://www.fcsn.org/pti/home.htm

Federally funded program that provides local resources and advocacy training for disability and special education issues.

Sibling Support Project
The Arc of the United States
6512 23rd Avenue, NW, Suite 213
Seattle, WA 98117
206-297-6368 (telephone)
http://www.thearc.org/
siblingsupport

Organization for families that publishes a newsletter and holds support group meetings. Provides regional and state-wide training and makes international referrals for sibling support groups.

TOUGHLOVE International
Post Office Box 1069
Doylestown, PA 18901
215-348-7090 (telephone)
215-348-9874 (fax)
http://www.toughlove.org

Nonprofit self-help organization that provides education and ongoing support to families through parent support groups to empower parents and encourage young people to accept responsibility for their actions and stop destructive behaviors.

Index

Page references followed by *t* or *f* indicate tables or figures, respectively.